Derek Wilson read Italian at Oxford, and took up his first foreign
assignment in Rome as a junior correspondent for Reuter's news
agency in 1960. He taught at Italy's Naval Academy in Livorno for a
time, then became a war correspondent for the BBC, *The Times* and
Agence France Presse, reporting from Africa, the Middle East,
Cyprus, Aden, India and Vietnam. From 1975 he served as BBC
correspondent in Latin America and the West Mediterranean, based
in Madrid. He is at present a correspondent for the BBC in Rome,
where he has lived since 1980.

**Other Collins Independent
Travellers Guides include:**

Greek Islands by Victor Walker
Mainland Greece by Victor Walker
Morocco by Christine Osborne
Provence, Languedoc & Côte d'Azur by John Ardagh
Portugal by Martha de la Cal
Spain by Harry Debelius
Southern Italy by Ian Thomson
South-west France by Rex Grizell
Soviet Union by Martin Walker
Turkey by Daniel Farson

COLLINS
INDEPENDENT TRAVELLERS
GUIDE

ROME, UMBRIA & TUSCANY

DEREK WILSON

Series Editor Robin Dewhurst

Collins
8 Grafton Street, London
1990

Note

Whilst every effort has been made to ensure that prices, hotel and restaurant recommendations, opening hours and similar factual information in this book are accurate at the time of going to press, the Publishers cannot be held responsible for any changes found by readers using this guide.

For Contessa Silvia Salerni

William Collins Sons & Co Ltd
London · Glasgow · Sydney
Auckland · Toronto · Johannesburg

First published in 1990
© Derek Wilson 1990

Series Commissioning Editor: Louise Haines
Editor: Jane Havell

Maps by Cartograph

Cover photographs: front: *Barga, Tuscany (Landscape Only/Waite)*
back: *Massa Marittima (Landscape Only/Waite)*

A CIP catalogue record for this book is available from the British Library.

ISBN 000 410979 1

Typeset by Ace Filmsetting Ltd, Frome, Somerset
Printed and bound in Great Britain by
William Collins Sons & Co. Ltd, Glasgow

Contents

Introduction	7
History	9
Central Italy Today	17
The Weather and When to Go	36
Travelling Around	37
Where to Stay	45
Eating and Drinking	49
Entertainment	54
Shopping	56
General Basics	57
Glossary	68

GAZETTEER

Introduction	71
Beaches	74
Tuscany	80
Florence	97
Umbria	156
The Marches	190
Lazio	208
Rome	210
Abruzzo and Molise	266

Further Reading	274
Index	276

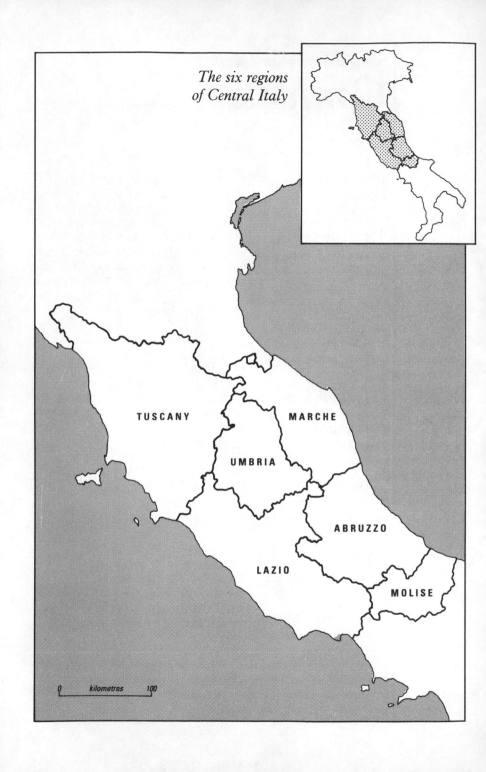

The six regions
of Central Italy

TUSCANY

MARCHE

UMBRIA

ABRUZZO

LAZIO

MOLISE

0   kilometres   100

Introduction

In Central Italy, people are enjoying a boom without precedent. It is psychological as well as economic. They are still getting used to it, dazed at their good fortune, and not sure where it came from. After centuries of drudgery and poverty, their disorientation is understandable. But the old attitudes of mind, including a certain subservience towards foreigners, are fading fast; among the young, they have vanished. Anyone who has not been to Italy for, say, fifteen years would be astonished at the change. Italians *look* different: younger people are actually physically taller. There's a new confidence about. As a visitor, you will no longer be quite as privileged as you once were.

Sandwiched between the industrialised North and the ever underdeveloped South, Central Italy is best placed to benefit from the country's sudden recovery. Northern Italy has smoke and cold; the South has Mafia murders and continuing misery. The Centre – Tuscany, Umbria, the Marches and Abruzzo along the Adriatic, Rome and the surrounding region of Lazio – has sun, beautiful countryside, the proud cities of the Middle Ages and, of course, the glory of the Renaissance.

According to a startling Unesco survey based on rather abstruse mathematics, half of the cultural heritage of the entire world derives from Italy. If that is true, most of that half was created in the Centre. There can be no area of the same small size on earth so weighed down with treasure and delight. From delicate Etruscan vases to the hulks of ancient Rome, from Byzantine mosaics to the Sistine Chapel of Michelangelo, from Giotto to Caravaggio, from small early Christian churches to the massiveness of St Peter's . . . the Centre of Italy is virtually the history of Western man. Visiting it is like checking out a collective memory, or like calling on a rich grandmother in exotic parts to be reminded of your family history. Much of what she has to show is surprisingly intact. Entire towns are as they were four or five centuries ago. Much of Central Italy is frozen time. Even in an area as contemporary as volatile Italian politics, there is evidence of this ice: the brittleness of pacts made in Rome today in the turnstile governments simply carries forward the eternal fractiousness between and within the city-states down the centuries.

Many Italians, boom or not, are impatient with these leftovers from the past. They may be richer, but they feel that they and Italy would be richer still were it not for the chronic paralysis at the top and a crushing bureaucracy. They live life shuffling in queues, stranded by strikes. Italians are good, genuine Europeans – all of them – but they fear that because of the ineptness of their masters they will come off worst in 1992, with the single European market. They fear an invasion of British banks, French cars, German washing-machines. They also feel a little hurt that other EC countries don't take them more seriously; for this, again, they blame their quarrelling leaders who are unable to stay any course.

'I don't understand these tourists,' says an Italian angry young man. 'They don't come for the Italy I know. They come to glare at the past. My Italy's right in front of them, and they don't see it. They see what they want to see. If they saw mine, they wouldn't come. My God!'

They don't sing in the streets as they once did.

This book can put in only a few punctuation marks to the speech of Central Italy, leaving most unsaid. But I have attempted to put what is past into the present.

History

The Etruscans

One of the most fascinating sensations of Central Italy is to step quietly out of the sun, away from motorbikes and blaring stereos, into the chilling, underground world of its former masters, the Etruscans. Their presence is palpable: you will discover it in their eerie tombs, in the oblique glances of their portraits. A new Etruscan tomb is found every month (usually by grave-robbers), but the Etruscans remain as puzzling as their language which can now be transliterated, though the key to it is still not understood.

Etruria, their homeland, stretched over Tuscany, eastern Umbria and northern Lazio. They touched the zenith of their power in the sixth century BC, and tradition has it that an Etruscan family, the Tarquins, were kings of Rome. The Etruscans were warriors and farmers, who also mined Tuscan soil for precious metals. Recently, they have been found to be enterprising, seafaring traders as well, whose routes criss-crossed the Mediterranean. They built their cities usually atop pugnacious bluffs, solitary places commanding horizons. Hefty traces of their great civilisation remain, but their homes were built of wood and have not survived. They entrusted the record of their life and art only to their tombs.

Sometimes, the tombs seem from a distance to be extra-terrestrial domes that have landed in the middle of nowhere; sometimes they resemble toolsheds. Or they can be cut into cliff faces, or laid out in streets, as if in a town, complete with squares. The tombs themselves are homes for the departed, laid out and equipped in the same way as their earthly homes. Some are decorated with stunning scenes of Etruscan life. You'll enjoy their painters' gifts of the light touch and an eye for detail, sometimes comic; they excelled at faces. Etruscan society certainly lived it up.

By the first century BC, they had given in to Rome, either through alliance or conquest. They received the kiss of death in 91 BC when, awarded Roman citizenship, they were swallowed up.

The most obviously Etruscan towns to visit are Volterra in Tuscany, and Perugia, Orvieto and Todi in Umbria. The most accessible burial sites are at Tarquinia and Cerveteri near the coast of Lazio. Some twenty Etruscan museums dot Central Italy; the best are at Tarquinia and in Rome.

The Romans

If you are travelling by train and happen to stop in a station *inside* a town, it is almost certain you are in a former Roman settlement, or *municipium*. The Romans always built at the bottoms of valleys, on natural lines of communication. They had Lazio under their iron wing by the fourth century BC, and the whole of peninsular Italy was paying tribute to them by 270 BC.

Their instruments of colonisation were their roads which, until the motorways came, remained the main axes of post-war Italy. The longest is the *Aurelia*, today the SS 1, which hugs the Western coastline. Today, just south of Livorno, people peer down from the cliffs into murderous blue inlets with surely just the same fascination as dry-throated centurions must have felt on their way home from keeping woad-stained Brits in order.

You can still take the *Cassia*, the SS 2, from Florence to Rome via Siena and Viterbo. The *Flaminia*, the SS 3, is the dramatic road linking Rome to Umbria and the upper Adriatic. The *Salaria* or Salt Road, the SS 4, could be your route for the Southern Marches.

At the far end of a pompous avenue built by Mussolini linking central Rome to the Colosseum, four stone relief maps show vividly how Rome exploded from a dot into a world in nine centuries. Today's Rome is headily redolent of that imperial clout, but the feel of everyday ancient life comes across more forcibly in the capital's rambling old port town of Ostia Antica, a wonderful place strangely ignored by most tourists.

One of the most telling insights into ancient Rome will be gained when you look at the coins welded into a marble floor in the Forum by the heat of the fire during the ferocious sack of Rome by Alaric's Visigoths in AD 410. Tales of how his barbarians behaved sent a shudder through the entire Romanised world. The Emperor Constantine had already founded a safer new Imperial capital further east, in Constantinople. He had proclaimed Christianity as the state religion, partly in the belief that it would be a factor for unity. But sixty-six years after Alaric, with visitations by Attila the Hun and the Vandals, the last line of Roman emperors fizzled out, bringing the Western part of the divided Empire to an end.

Goths, Byzantines and Longobards

In the sixth century, the Eastern Emperor Justinian sent armies from Constantinople to Italy to drive out the invading Goths and to reunite the Empire under Byzantine command. The so-called 'Gothic War' lasted twenty years, and was the most devastating of all the barbaric conflicts. Hundreds of thousands were killed by combat, famine and disease, and the countryside was laid to waste. In the Marches solitary hills still tower over rippling valleys where the Goths held out against the Byzantines; to reach the top of them, it can still take ten grinding minutes in second gear. At one point, the Gothic King Totila ('The Immortal One') held all of Italy except Ravenna, Byzantine's Italian headquarters.

'The Immortal' was slain in Umbria; the Byzantines prevailed and, for a time, Rome became a backyard of Constantinople. But the 'Greek' liberators soon showed themselves to be harsh masters. The Italians couldn't wait for them to be gone – but they had to wait, for 160 years. The next invaders were the Germanic Longobards hailing from the Elbe delta, whose presence in Italy bred a momentous sequel – the creation of the Christian Church's earthly kingdom.

Unlike the Goths, they left a firm imprint on Italy: you still come upon Longobard churches and, in some areas, people still use Longobard words. They swarmed down upon Italy with wives and children; they intermarried, and blended in. The towns of Lucca and Spoleto still stand out as somehow 'different', because the Longobards made them seats of duchies from which they ruled for nearly two centuries.

But the Longobards displeased the Papacy, and a Roman Pontiff crossed the Alps in person to enlist the aid of King Pippin of the Franks to put them down. Pippin obliged, and handed over the parts of the Marches and Umbria they had occupied to the Papacy. His famous son, Charlemagne, confirmed this so-called 'donation' with a second victory. Until modern times, this served as the judicial basis for the temporal power of the Papacy.

The emergence of the city-state

Beneath St Peter's in Rome, you can see the foundations of the original church built by Constantine. It was there, on Christmas Day in the year 800, that Charlemagne knelt before the Pope and received the crown of Emperor – of what was virtually a new Roman Empire,

BACKGROUND INFORMATION

under the dual authority of the Papacy and its powerful Teutonic protectors. Intended to usher in a new order, it was a formula for disaster.

Beginning in the twelfth century, modern Italy began to take shape, because of a power vacuum. On the one hand, the Germanic princes, the successors of Charlemagne, were distracted from Italy by domestic squabbles. On the other, depravity had enfeebled the once authoritative Papacy: at one point, the Pope was manipulated by a Roman matron. Church titles were auctioned.

Seeing their chance, the towns of Italy began a quiet insurrection, slowly stripping power from their bishops, who had become virtual sheriffs by Imperial decree. It was Europe's first liberation movement. Trade and wealth began to circulate for the first time since the fall of the Roman Empire; emboldened, the better-off citizenry asserted themselves further. Feudal rivets flew. Nowhere else in Europe was feudalism dismantled so thoroughly. Nowhere else did towns develop so splendidly; they became, to remain, the fulcrum of Italian life. When the smoke cleared, Italy appeared as a constellation of hilltop mini-republics, each fiercely independent. The so-called *Comune* was born.

This is the Italy you will still see today, astonishingly petrified, more or less just as it was at the end of the thirteenth century. This is when the great Romanesque cathedrals appeared, together with the magnificent civic *palazzi* of flamboyant severity, symbols of the cities' status and pride. The merchants and bankers of Central Italy travelled across Europe. Their products were the finest; their coin the safest; their fleets the busiest. The first Italian sculptors emerged, and Dante, their greatest poet. But behind the superb façades in the main squares, there was turmoil.

Every *Comune* lived through an almost identical pattern of disillusion. Each city-state:

● Began with an elected body, often known as the 'consuls'.
● Eventually removed the nobles from power.
● At one point came under the leaders of guilds, the 'Priors'.
● Called in an outsider to be the temporary chief magistrate after attempts at self-discipline failed.
● Witnessed a class struggle between the 'small' and 'fat', as the classes were sometimes called.
● Was dragged into protracted gang warfare as rival families fought for supremacy, often with blood-curdling ruthlessness.
● Sought protection, usually from soldiers of fortune.
● Was at last subjugated by an outside force.

The inner-city fighting coincided with inter-city warfare. The smaller places ganged up with the bigger ones in major league conflicts; one pitted Florence against Pisa, with attendant satellites (Florence won, of course).

Empire versus Pope

The conflict between cities was further whipped up by the epic struggle between the Empire and the Church, which raged for nearly two centuries, fiercely splitting Central Italy. Luigi Pirandello's play, *Enrico IV*, tells of the occasion when the struggle flared into crisis. At the castle of Canossa, in Reggio Emilia, the great reforming Pope Gregory VII made the German Emperor Henry IV wait in the snow for three days before rescinding his excommunication. The apparent issue was over who had the right to appoint top churchmen; the real issue was over who ran the Empire.

The Emperor Frederick I, Barbarossa, invaded Italy six times to demonstrate who did. He saw himself as a medieval Caesar on a mission to restore the Roman Empire. He is still very popular in the deep south-east, where they make German specialists on Frederick honorary citizens. His son, Frederick II, Italian-born, gifted and cultured, nearly brought off the vision, and Central Italy was split into pro-Empire Ghibellines and pro-Papal Guelfs. If these epithets strike you as a bit un-Italian, that is not surprising: they are Italian mimickings of German war-cries. Waiblingen was the name of a castle owned by Frederick; Welf that of a rival one.

The Italians sided with whomever would serve them best. Ghibelline Siena wangled valuable trading privileges in Europe from the Teutons; Guelf Viterbo hoped to become a desirable Papal residence. Other than that, the yells were simply new labels for old hatreds, and fresh pretexts for aggression.

The armies of Pope and Emperor rarely clashed head-on, but tried to take, or woo, each other's towns. Frederick II could be quite violent when a targeted flirtee refused to smile; at Ascoli Piceno, for example, there was considerable destruction.

In the end, the Empire lost. Frederick II's illegitimate son Manfred, after galvanising the whole of Ghibelline Italy, was killed in battle by Charles d'Anjou, called into Italy by a French Pope. In Abruzzo, the French then defeated Frederick's 15-year-old grandson Conradin, who had ridden down into Italy with a final trumpet call. It was 1268.

The Imperial dream was over but, ironically, for the entire fourteenth century and beyond the Papacy disappeared as well. Arguing that Rome was unsafe, a French Pope shifted the Papal court to Avignon. The Grand Schism discredited the Papacy further; at one point, three men lay claim to the throne of St Peter.

The Renaissance

Left to themselves, Italian cities were almost as free of government as they are today. They struck a pact and, at the end of the fifteenth century, Italy enjoyed forty years of quite unprecedented peace. Giotto had revolutionised painting in Assisi, and Duccio di Buoninsegna had created a new style in Siena. The peace brought to flower the full, dazzling bloom of the Renaissance in Florence. Botticelli painted *The Birth of Venus*; Michelangelo astonished all as an insolent apprentice.

As you travel through Central Italy, you will notice vividly how the cities thrived and created while they enjoyed might, money and peace, and how they slumped and dried up when handcuffed to masters. When the politics were right, they lit up, but as you travel south, you will see how they went out one by one as they lost their independence. Eventually the whole area, except Rome, lay in darkness, its spirit dead.

The warning bell of that fate sounded through Central Italy when King Charles VIII of France, at the behest of Milan, swept south to Naples in search of *gloire* in 1494. Nothing came of his adventure, but it was a precedent for a showdown in Italy between France and Emperor Charles V of Austria, ruler of the Netherlands, heir to Spain, Sicily and Naples. Both were out for supremacy in the peninsula.

The Sack of Rome

The Sack of Rome in 1527 marked the end of the Renaissance. A turncoat Pope had switched his support to France; aware of the treachery, Charles turned his attention to Rome and 30,000 Spanish and German troops, mutinous and out of control, laid the city to waste in an orgy of murder and plunder.

For almost two centuries Italy was under the Spanish boot, its soil the pitch for other peoples' battles. In the fully retrieved Papal States, the repressive control of the Church was total, all creativity stifled. Central Italy slowly rotted.

The Risorgimento

The recurrent street names you will notice in Central Italy all tell the story of its recovery. There is hardly a town, for instance, without a Piazza **Risorgimento**, recalling Italy's struggle for unification (resurgence) in the nineteenth century. It was partly inspired by the French Revolution, although today Napoleon is chiefly remembered as an art thief.

Mazzini was the name of the first visionary champion of unity who incited revolt and played the key role in a short-lived 'Roman Republic', which was suppressed by the French in 1849. The Piazza **Garibaldi** everywhere honours the commander of the small army of the Roman Republic who held the French at bay for weeks. A sailor's son, a guerilla leader in South America, Garibaldi was the dashing hero of the Risorgimento. In 1860, at the head of his famous thousand redshirts, he seized Sicily and then Naples. He then handed over to King Victor Emmanuel of Savoy, whose army had seized Papal Umbria and part of the Marches.

Every town and village has a Via **Cavour**, the political giant who engineered unification under the House of Savoy. As Prime Minister of the kingdom of Piedmont and Sardinia, he secretly won the much-needed support of France; in return he handed over Savoy and Garibaldi's birthplace, Nice. In 1861, Italy became a united kingdom – except for Papal Rome.

The Pope, supported by the French, held out for nine more years. The controversial British Embassy building in Rome is only yards from the point where royal troops breached the walls of Rome and compelled the Papal forces to surrender. The Embassy's address commemorates the date: Via **XX Settembre**.

The World Wars

In the First World War, Italy withdrew from an alliance with Germany and Austria to side with Britain and France. She lost 600,000 men in heavy fighting in the North of Italy where, despite one heavy defeat, her unprepared army managed to hold the line. The city of Trieste was one of her rewards.

Benito Mussolini, a socialist blacksmith's son, founded his Fascist army in 1919. The back-drop to his rise was formed of post-war depression, unemployment, strikes and chronic political instability. With the complicity of the army, the police and industrialists, his gangs of black-shirted thugs, dedicated to the eradication of socialism and trades unions, attacked and pillaged labour exchanges, co-operatives and workers' clubs. Nobody stopped them.

Mussolini, with thirty-five other Blackshirts, was elected to Parliament in 1921 declaring himself 'anti-parliamentarian, anti-democratic, anti-socialist'. The next year, his cohorts threatened a march on Rome. Powerless, King Victor Emmanuel III called off plans to prevent it, and asked Mussolini instead to form a government. The march became a triumphal entry.

With 300,000 armed Fascists behind him, Mussolini was now in complete control; through rigged elections he took over Parliament. The assassination of a Socialist deputy, which was blamed on the Fascists, and the alleged threat of unrest, led to a reign of terror and the destruction of all opposition. The press was muzzled; the fear of secret police ruled people's lives; human rights ceased to exist.

In 1935, 100,000 Italian troops brutally conquered Ethiopia. Next year the 'Rome–Berlin Axis' was proclaimed, and Mussolini was dragged in to the Second World War. For Italy, this was a catastrophe. Ill-equipped, badly led Italian troops lost every battle, and surrendered in their thousands . . .

As the Allies landed in Sicily in 1943, the King, together with the *Duce*'s former henchmen, had Mussolini arrested, but he was rescued by the Germans from a mountain-top prison. Italy announced an armistice, but it was not until May 1945 that the last Germans in Italy surrendered. The slogging fighting as they were slowly driven north was overshadowed on the world stage by the Second Front, and the extent of the damage wreaked could come as a surprise to you.

As the war ended, Mussolini was caught fleeing to Switzerland by partisans and, in circumstances which are still disputed, executed. His body and that of his mistress, Claretta Petacci, were hung upside down from a petrol station in Milan. The following year, 54 per cent of Italians voted to abolish the monarchy, which was irrevocably tarred by its acquiescence to Fascism.

Central Italy Today

The miracle that has taken place in Central Italy is no credit to a creaking political system whose reform would take a second miracle. Almost overnight, the Centre, like the North, has become rich. The Italy of the early 1970s has vanished. The builder in his newspaper boat-hat and doubtful singlet has gone (he now probably flies to Cuba for winter holidays). The shoe-shine men have also disappeared; so have most of the humble wine shops, and the white oxen from the fields. In 1951, 8 million Italians worked in agriculture. Today, only 2 million do.

Many Italians now take holidays abroad, and 9 per cent can afford three holidays a year. They spend only 25 per cent of their earnings on food, against 40 per cent a decade ago. They lavish the rest on their homes and on jewellery, especially gold. The best status symbol is to wonder aloud what kind of car to buy for your 18-year-old daughter.

Some have dubbed it the Second Renaissance. Great artists have not yet appeared but craftsmen are just as numerous, active and gifted as they always were. They have spread the word Italian across the world, as a password for quality and beauty. Another point in common with the 'real' Renaissance is the prosperity being enjoyed by modern Italy. The comparison, in fact, is not so far-fetched. Italians lived through the harshest times of all in the aftermaths of the two World Wars, when 'Italian' signified 'emigrant', and lordly outsiders dismissed them with that contemptuous nickname derived from the stamp used by US Customs Officers, 'With Out Papers'. Today, they are high on the list of the West's wealthy nations.

Meat was once a rarity for the average Italian family; now a butcher's with a fillet steak left is a rarity. The *average* income of a family of three in the Centre is estimated at 34.5 million lire (£15,000) a year, a spectacular jump over 1980. In the Marches, families hit the national record, having 2.8 million lire (£1,200) a month to spend, more than in the UK or the USA. They spend far less on heating and transport, and they usually dodge the taxman.

As many as 62 per cent of Italians in the Centre own their own homes, and 80 per cent have a bank account. Many now have a second home and two cars. It is not unusual for a woman to possess five or six furs; in winter, teenagers can spend about 70,000 lire (£30) a month in sun-tan parlours. Finally, incredible as it may sound, Italy is the biggest importer of Scotch whisky in the world. And the traditional sense of inferiority has evaporated, except perhaps from the minds of the old. Little of all this, of course, applies to that other Italy – anywhere south of Rome.

How it happened

No one reason exists for the change, but the most cogent is domestic peace following the defeat of the Red Brigade terrorists, the worst nightmare of post-war Italy. The Brigate Rosse, the BR, threatened modern Italy's survival. Those dark years in the 1970s are known as the *anni di piombo*, the years of lead, because of the amount of it that flew around. It killed 506 people and injured 2,454.

The most prominent corpse was that of Italy's Christian Democrat Prime Minister, Aldo Moro. Ambushed in a residential suburb of Rome in 1978, he was held captive for fifty-five days before his body was found in the boot of a red Renault, parked between the headquarters of the Christian Democrats and the Communists.

With the murder of Moro, the BR played their highest card. The politicians had refused to bargain, and it was the start of the terrorists' end. In those days, the streets of Rome were empty at night, and restaurants deserted for fear of hold-ups. Ladies kept their jewels locked up, and newspapers took anonymous calls as routinely as they reported the plunging stock prices.

Now all the BR leaders are behind bars. Most have repudiated their former revolutionary principles and have acknowledged a mistaken strategy. Every so often, cells of inexperienced young rebels plot a minor comeback, but the police usually trap them in time. Italians believe that their defeat of the BR by democratic means – without recourse even to a state of emergency – did them great honour, and their realisation of what they had pulled off did much to repair their battered confidence. That victory was the most important single event in Italy since the Second World War.

Surf-boards

With the recovery came a return to normal life, with a resumed demand for goods, services and ideas. A favourite explanation of the boom is that peace re-opened the field to Italian inventiveness – to the imagination and initiative of thousands of small firms working on their own, untrammelled by an absent State. They saw potential profit in design and quality, and knew how to promote their ideas.

They captured the sweater market by anticipating favourite styles through instant computer analysis of each transaction, re-setting machinery overnight. They somehow got into blankets for the Iraqi army during the Gulf War. They designed bathroom tiles that New York hostesses swooned over. One Umbrian firm produces two-storey houses that can withstand violent earthquakes, and sells them to Japan.

Top artists shape new forms of pasta; fashion designers besiege the big houses in Paris and New York, ready to produce any fabric, of any design, at any price, at once. They have been quick to corner big engineering contracts in the developing world, and were swift into factory automatisation, because the unions agreed.

They even sold surf-boards to California.

Laissez-faire

Italian ingenuity is proverbial. One big market-gardener in the Marches who had won a juicy contract to supply a London department store with fresh produce found a dock strike threatening to ruin him. All ports were closed and a hired plane would have ruined him too. But he discovered that cross-channel passenger-trains were not on strike, and somehow managed to arrange to have railway wagons full of his vegetables hitched to the back of them.

A significant aspect of this anecdote is the freedom of operation such men can enjoy in Italy. The State does not get in the way. What Italians, and many foreigners, appreciate about Italy is this sense of liberty. It is partly due to highly advanced legislation protecting the individual. But it is partly because so little legislation is actually enforced. Businessmen prefer it when Italy is without a government, which is often. As they say in Rome: 'When the police are on strike, the traffic's all right.'

Crime and corruption

Other explanations of Italy's well-being are not flattering. Apart from massive tax evasion, mainly by those best able to pay, crime keeps money swilling around. It is calculated that in Italy as a whole the Mafia yearly launders 'dirty money' from drug-trafficking to the tune of some 280 billion lire (£13,000 million), about 10 per cent of the national revenue.

Further, official figures disclose, 20–40,000 State employees regularly pocket bribes – the 'little envelope', as it's called, being still the quickest cure for inaction. Parking fines will melt away; a permit for a fast-food outlet in a town's historic centre will come through. Some 14 billion lire (£6,000 million) a year are spent on 'making things happen'.

Bribery is a symptom of 'The Italy that doesn't work', as the headlines dub State inefficiency. Today, with the European deadline of 1992 looming, the problem of how to fight it has suddenly become Italy's most urgent problem.

● The Health Service is the sickest of the State services, for ever on the verge of collapse, with spending out of control. New hospitals are built which become graveyards for lack of patients while elsewhere the sick are left to groan in corridors. Waiting lists are long, wards wanting in hygiene, nurses few and disputes frequent. The situation is far less critical than in the South of Italy, but Italians still eschew State ministrations if they can.

● The transport sector breathes sporadically between paralytic fits. Strikes break out because of unending four-sided conflicts between the State, the weakening unions, their obedient members and wildcatters.

● The Post Office is called 'The Snail'. A scholar has discovered that a letter from Rome to Bologna was delivered more quickly during the Roman Empire than it is today. With every omen right, a missive from Rome to Florence needs six days. Small packets from abroad can take six weeks.

● The judiciary is engulfed, with too many cases, too few judges and archaic procedures. An average criminal case, including appeal, will take thirty months; jails are packed by those awaiting trial. To speed it up, the British and American-style courtroom trial is being introduced.

● Bureaucracy is the greatest cause of anger among Italians. Despite gross over-staffing, it wallows in an ocean of rules, among cardboard files bound in ribbon, with little effort and much rudeness. The monthly agony for most Italians, especially in the summer heat, is the payment of their utilities bills. This involves standing in motionless queues at the Post Office, while the cross woman at the window does her accounts, goes absent, or stops work because the pensioner in front of her has no change. Or else, without warning, the window will be snapped shut. Or you are told, having reached the unnumbered window, that it is the wrong one.

The bureaucratic monster has a ravenous appetite for certificates, which must be renewed every three months. They attest to changes of address or of spouse, but the most humiliating simply certify that the bearer is alive.

The staff, mostly employed as a reward for political loyalty or through personal recommendation (they are known as *raccomandati*), believe they have life tenure. They greet all ideas of market management with a knowing little smile. They know that the System, based on the status quo, is – contrary to the impression abroad – the most stable, and stagnant, in the West.

Politics

Outsiders tend to smirk because since the Second World War Rome has overthrown some fifty governments. The fact appears to fit the image of a volatile and chaotic country, gesticulating and incapable. The opposite is true. *Cabinets* may have fallen fifty times, but not parliaments. Nor do ministers really fall; they often pop up in the next government on a different chair. The same handful of politicians have held sway for generations. Some never seem to go; they simply move from table to table, as if at a buffet supper. Italy is a kind of political square-dance. (Some of the dancers are civilians. The most *soave* is Gianni Agnelli, the urbane *Signore* of the vast Fiat company. Some hail him 'uncrowned King of Italy'. He would not object, and his opinion weighs.)

Furthermore, the Italian electorate is the most consistent in Europe. It sticks to habit, and fluctuations in votes are measured in terms of only a few percentage points. There are no landslides. The relative strengths of the parties has remained more or less constant for decades.

The influential Christian Democrat Party (DC) always comes first, with over 30 per cent of the vote (there has been just one exception). The Communist Party (PCI), the biggest in Western Europe, is always second past the finish, sometimes only a few points behind. And, far back in third place, comes the Socialist Party (PSI), with around 10 per cent of the vote. Half a dozen other parties follow.

Although it is the second-biggest party in Italy, the Communists have never been in government partly because they could never muster an overall majority, and partly because of an unspoken pact by the so-called democratic parties to ostracise them on the grounds of vassalage to Moscow, despite their proclaimed autonomy.

Since none of the democrats ever win an overall majority either, their governments are usually jumpy coalitions. They are held to ransom by the ambivalent Socialists, so that each time a Socialist leader girds himself to speak, Italy trembles for fear of the endless boredom of yet another crisis. The Socialists are not past winking at the Communists now and again, either.

So far, big swings of the pendulum have been inconceivable. The pundits call it 'blocked democracy'; most call it 'partyocracy'. The parties have exploited this fossilisation by creating a more permanent, solid basis of power, within the fabric of the State. They have each taken possession of a slice of the State cake, its thickness proportionate to the latest election figures. In this share-out, the Communists do take part.

The system applies to many spheres. The receptionist at the tourist office you visit, for instance, will almost certainly be a party nominee, and the 'political' make-up of her office will doubtless reflect the colouring of the local junta. If you barged into a meeting of a ten-man Hospital Management Committee, possibly three would be DC and three PC, whether they were acquainted with medicine or not.

It's the old boy network, Italian-style. If you spot an Italian photographer at the airport, he may be there rather than in front of a reporter's screen in Head Office because, as a member of the small Republican Party, he has had his promotion blocked by a Socialist editor.

This rigorous partition extends even to a sphere where a pretence at hands-off may have been expected. State television's main channel, RAI Uno, is in DC hands. RAI Due is a joint PSI–PCI domain, and RAI Tre is a rag-bag of the also-rans. The same pattern applies to radio, except that the main network there is a PSI fief. It is certainly no secret. A well-known newsreader may appear in a news item himself, chairing some party seminar.

This system of government, it is acknowledged, is fragile and cumbersome. The Prime Minister, for instance, can take no decision without the say-so of the parties, who thus virtually control him. Parliament is a faceless assembly of party candidates, silenced by leaden procedure and usually absent. Debate, Anglo-Saxon style, is unknown.

The parties themselves now concede the need for reform if Italy is to face up to the year 2000. But with the memory of Mussolini's rise to power, they will be careful about tampering with safeguards against dictatorship. And before they agree to begin to dismantle their empires, time will pass. No wonder the civil servants smile.

Where partyocracy most affects Italians is, of course, on the very local level. Town councils are expected to be genetic mirrors of the mother-government in Rome. If Rome suddenly suffers paralysis, they therefore can/may/will/refuse to/become muscle-bound, too. It is far graver if the local image kicks against the format: for instance, if Christian Democrats do a wicked local deal with outlawed Communists; in such cases, immediate concern ripples through the Rome of the share-out, of such intensity that it inhibits the rebels from even a nerve-movement. As a result, plans for an improved water-supply (an eternal problem), for a ring-road around the village, or even for the local saint's day, climb on to the ample shelf.

Partyocracy largely explains the Italians' heavy involvement in politics, and their massive turn-outs at elections, unequalled anywhere in the West. It is not unusual to find 85–90 per cent of the electorate trooping to the polls. In many cases, they will be defending a job or ensuring a present sponsor remains in power, so as not to be left out of the next share-out. The position defended could be theirs or that of a helpful family member. But they vote as inveterate political animals, too, always ready for a fight, as they have been down all the centuries. Voting brings out their historic yen for fierce loyalties. It is also 'done' to vote.

The Centre of Italy is where the dominant Christian Democrats are weakest, and the Communists strongest – especially in Tuscany and Umbria where they usually pick up well over 40 per cent of the vote. In Siena, they cap 50 per cent. The Socialists in these super-red areas, however, come only a poor third, trailing the DC. In the Marches, too, the Communists usually pip the DC, whereas in Rome and Lazio it is usually the reverse. In isolated Abruzzo, the odd region out, the Christian Democrat majority is always overwhelming.

Italians always have a stake in politics, but few follow the game – its terms are impossibly abstruse. The politicians hide behind a linguistic smokescreen of changing codes, elided references and ambiguous inference. Few see through it except other politicians and specialist journalists who, to defend their preserve, fail to dispel the fog. To most Italians, the nightly political report on television is meaningless. If you can understand some Italian but find newspaper headlines incomprehensible, it is almost certain that the Italian next to you is just as perplexed.

The stuff of Italian politics is not debate on issues of public interest, but eternal rethinking of party relationships, and of the 'true' identity of each party – a process of oriental complexity. It causes non-stop political guerilla warfare. Alliances are made and dissolved. Agreements are reached and reneged upon. Solidarity for the sake of peace does not exist; Italy is like Lebanon, without the guns. You see the fight raging in every medieval township, through the tradition of virulent wall-posters which has never changed.

The only belief shared by all parties is that of a united Europe. As they see it, it is the only sure protection against war and dictatorship, of which they have had their fill.

Pollution

The Italians discovered pollution late; Italy's Green Party was founded only in 1984. But overnight it became The Big Issue, overshadowed only by State misrule, and they invented a new name for noise: 'acoustic pollution'. Pollution came home to them when they realised that the river Po had become a gigantic sewer, pouring phosphates and waste into the shallow Adriatic which killed all the fish and fouled the beaches. A scandal followed with the discovery that Italian industry was hiring ghost ships to dump its toxic waste in Third World countries.

Environmentalists won their first big victory when, in a referendum, Italy voted against nuclear energy. As a result, a controversial nuclear plant at Montalto di Castro, north of Civitavecchia in Lazio, began re-conversion.

Pollution in Central Italy is most apparent in the few traffic-clogged towns still hesitating over whether to ban the car. But it has mainly hit the monuments; you will find many in splints and bandages as patient restorers in white smocks try to arrest a malady that in a few years can undo an existence that has lasted for centuries. Fumes from diesel engines and heating fuels cause marble to crumble quickly into carbonate of calcium. Restorers try to hold the fabric together with injections of ethyl silicate and/or resin. But definitive restoration does not exist; these measures are stop-gap and the salvage attempts will have to be repeated. In the meantime, monuments should be washed down twice a year – funds willing.

It is wise to travel stoutly girded against shock. Restoration of buildings, sculptures and paintings is an unending, if essential, process, and it would be a sheer miracle if everything listed for seeing is there waiting to be seen. Something vital is bound to be wrapped in scaffolding which, once it has begun its embrace, can maintain it for years.

The family

The Italian family remains the basic cell of life. If in northern countries of Europe it is breaking up, in Italy it is undergoing consolidation. Surveys show that Italians see 'the family' – from the latest newborn to the oldest grandad – as 'the most important thing in life'. It is still the point of reference for them; they have few others. Nationality isn't one, and neither is the State. They can rely upon the family, but on little else. Above all, the family is what confers on an Italian his or her difference from other Italians. This is vital (see National characteristics, page 30).

Although Italian life still revolves around the great family occasions – Easter, Christmas, baptism, confirmation, marriage, death – the myth of the family as swarming with *bambini* has exploded. Italian couples now have fewer children (1.3 on average) than any others in the world, except West Germany. Even the Swedes have more.

Experts are ringing the alarm: if the trend continues, they warn, the birthrate in thirty years will be 38 per cent below replacement rate.

Central Italy's present population of about 11.5 million will shrink by 15 per cent.

By a hair's breadth, more families now live in the countryside than in the towns. The rural exodus of the 1950s and 1960s has been reversed. In the late 1980s, many began deserting the big towns, escaping high rents, pollution and anonymity. Between 1971 and 1986, for instance, Florence 'lost' 30,000 inhabitants; they went off in search of clean air and the easy familiarity of village life. Many former emigrants to the US are among those returning to their places of birth.

In Italy, sons and daughters have always lived with their parents for much longer than in northern Europe, but now they are staying at home longer still. As many as 33 per cent of Italians between the ages of 25 and 34 now will not budge. A television farce called *But They Just Won't Go!* made them a national joke.

Boys stay put longer than girls, and most have degrees. They find home convenient; they contribute no money and they take over. When their friends come, ma and pa shut themselves up in the bedroom or go to the cinema. Now it is the parents who dream of leaving home. Less well educated than their children, they are bossed around and they resent it. They are landed with their 'adult babies' partly because of the length of study courses, partly because the young find it hard to get a job or a flat but, above all, sociologists explain, because of the sexual freedom they now enjoy at home.

The modern-day level of parental tolerance would have been inconceivable in the 1970s. A boy and his *fidanzata* now quite often live together under the parental roof. More casual sex is also admitted; the kids slip into the bedroom while the parents settle down to television. The consequence has been a waning of the old longing for freedom. For those who knew Italy two decades ago, with its rigid rules of behaviour, the odd slap in the face and the dread of 'scandal', this is the most striking revolution of all. Some experts, in fact, describe Italy today as an 'adolescent society', in that grown-ups as well as the young now learn to roll with the changes.

Grandpa and grandma still, on the whole, live with the family. They die later – he aged 72 and she 79. They are treated as amiable nuisances but often in a cavalier way; one family went on holiday leaving granny in the back of a car parked in a side street.

One thing has not changed: if it's a male child, they bring out the champagne.

The Church

Catholicism ceased to be the official religion of Italy in 1984. Under a new Concordat with the Vatican, achieved after eight years of gentlemanly tussling between the Christian Democrats and the Church, Rome is no longer a Holy City and Italy is a secular state. But in Central Italy, the Church is still by far the wealthiest single agent in the region – in terms of land, landmarks and treasure. Since most of it once belonged to the Papal States that is hardly surprising. Up to a short time ago, the Church spoke with an authority to match. On the eve of elections even in 1960, priests pinned notices to their church doors threatening excommunication for any of their flock who dared to vote Socialist. (They took for granted the realisation that any truck with the Communists led straight to hell fire.)

Today their power is less and the Centre has almost reverted to evangelical frontier territory. Through a kind of nemesis, the descendants of the former, neglected, subjects of the Papacy have now embraced the causes of the devilish Left.

In hill villages, however, the power of the Church remains strong. The priest is still the lord of the manor or tower, often quite literally, as well as the central performer in the year's biggest event. He will head the procession to celebrate the local saint's day amid fireworks and exploding rustic mortar tubes. If he's savvy, he will have invited the nearest Communist mayor to walk beside him.

But elsewhere, especially down in the towns, the Church's influence has dramatically weakened, except among the old. Vocations are falling off and, by Italian standards, congregations have thinned. The Church bowed down to its diminished status in the 1984 Concordat. It recognises, for the first time, that Church and State are each 'sovereign and independent', and it subjects Church property not used for religious purposes to taxation. The State has ceased to pay priests a regular stipend, and findings of ecclesiastical courts in matrimonial cases must now be endorsed by civil courts. Under provision fiercely resisted by the Church, religious education is no longer compulsory. State schools do provide an hour of religious instruction a week, but pupils can opt out.

The Polish Pontificate of John Paul II, which began in 1978, is unlikely to go down among Italians as one of the most popular. They prefer Italian Popes, of course; they can understand them. They find the present Pontiff distant; he speaks above their heads, in academic terms heavy with theology. The Pope they loved most this century was John XXIII, with his paternal bonhomie, lack of 'side', and reforming vision. They were also charmed by the winning ways of John Paul I, who died in muddy circumstances after ruling for only 33 days.

His successor invented the itinerant Papacy, dedicated to first-person re-evangelisation of the world. This spectacle tends to disturb Italians. Whatever their politics, they have an unspoken proprietary attitude towards the Papacy, and they have watched its continuing de-Italianisation under John Paul II without enthusiasm. Furthermore, by being so often away on business, the Pope demonstrates, in Italian eyes, that his attachment to Rome is less than fervent. Then when they see the mighty Roman Pontiff prostrate himself on the ground of some of the smallest, and non-Catholic, states on earth, their sense of what is fitting is sometimes ruffled.

But their most troubled misgivings are over the present Pope's teachings. A disciplinarian and a conservative, he has set out to reimpose the authority of the Papacy as the fount of a unified, unquestionable doctrine. Deviants are brought to Rome and scolded. He is at his most adamant on sexual matters. He has made taboos the pillars of his Pontificate, and expounds them with unappealable clarity: marriage is indissoluble; abortion a crime against life; coitus is a 'grave disorder' unless within the context of marriage, aimed at procreation; artificial contraception is abhorrent. He rules that 'insistent advertising of contraceptives must be resisted'.

Between married couples, guessing the moment is permitted, as well as *coitus interruptus*. Petting is banned, and masturbation 'contradicts the will of God'. The Church can in no way grant homosexuals a 'moral justification'; their condition derives from 'personal difficulties' and prevents them reaching 'sexual maturity' (from a keynote document issued by the Sacred Congregation for Catholic Education, December 1983). The spread of Aids has not modified the ban on contraception.

As the falling birthrate shows, Italians in Central Italy quietly ignore this Papal vade-mecum. Commercial television runs condom spots, and Rome's buses advertise them too . . . But within Italy, unlike in the USA, Latin America and northern Europe, there is no overt, organised protest within the Church. The senior Italian prelates are all 'the Pope's men'.

A fashionable lay movement called 'Communion and Liberation', virtually the youth wing of the Christian Democrat Party, has had some success in appealing to the bright young. The Pope himself tends to have less interest in the Italian adult lay body, 'Catholic Action', than in its powerful Spanish counterpart, 'Opus Dei', whose senior members, pledged to celibacy, are sworn to obedience and secrecy.

In May 1984, the Vatican officially acknowledged that its bank had become 'involuntarily involved' in one of the biggest frauds in postwar Italy. It argued that it had been duped and had had recognised 'dealings' with a bank that had gone flamboyantly bankrupt. The body of its president, Roberto Calvi, was found hanging beneath Blackfriars Bridge in London on 18 June 1982.

In perhaps the murkiest affair of post-war Italy, still unclarified, Calvi is alleged to have had dealings with Licio Gelli, Grand Master of the illegally secret Masonic Lodge known as P2, whose members, according to some Italian prosecutors, included key figures in the Establishment, the Armed Forces and high finance. One charge adumbrated that P2 was contemplating a virtual *coup d'état*. Licio Gelli is now back in Italy at home, partly because an extradition order issued by Switzerland, where he ended up in jail a second time after escape and a jaunt to South America, precluded prosecution in Italy on main charges, reported by the Italian press to include fraud and subversion.

Crime

An unmarked white van speeds into a small square and slews round with a squeal of brakes. Sirens wailing, police cars ring it on all sides, disgorging plain-clothes men, who push back the nosing traffic with aimed pistols. Women scream, people scatter, and police in bullet-proof jackets crouch in the doorways pointing stubby machine-guns at an entrance. Silence has descended upon the square. A whistle blows. Two figures run out of the entrance, a man holding a small packet above his head with one hand, his other handcuffed to a police-man who is balancing a cocked rifle in the crook of his free arm. They jump into the revving van. In a second, the entire scene has dissolved.

You may well witness such a sequence any day in Rome. It is enacted every time valuables are transferred from one Post Office to another.

The police take the opposition very seriously. Italy is a crime haven. Its hills and mountains make ideal hide-outs. Collusion between the under and upper worlds often ensures the element of surprise. Experience also proves that it is a way of life that pays dividends. At any one time, an estimated one million Italians are gainfully employed in crime, each earning about 120 million lire (£50,000) a year.

Naturally, the Mafia (Cosa Nostra) has the tightest grip. Its coinage is the hugely lucrative drug traffic, although police say that the Sicilian Mafia at one point sub-contracted much of the actual pushing in mainland Italy to its Neapolitan counterpart, the Camorra. The Mafia proper now again concentrates on Sicily, a huge clearing-house for traffic between South-East Asia and the USA. In Central Italy, Cosa Nostra concentrates on dirty dollar rinsing behind legitimate façades which are often hard to scrutinise, but are thought to be actually on the ground in parts of Lazio and Tuscany.

It is unlikely that you will become acquainted with, but sadly likely that you *will* see the consequences of, another brand of Italian crime. On the hotel television, only too often, there is the harrowing interview with a family waiting for a phone call from the kidnappers of a daughter, father or other relative.

'Kidnappers Anonymous' operate throughout the mainland, and in Sardinia. Their usually well-off victims are ambushed somewhere near their homes, and then bundled down to the wild, inaccessible Aspromonte mountains, where they are held for months in caves or shacks, chained and blindfolded. Victims may be 8-year-old girls or men in their eighties with heart complaints. Many never see light again, even though their families may have sold everything to pay the ransom.

Normally, the families do pay, because the police, despite their massive beats and helicopter assaults, do not unearth the hide-outs often enough to warrant hope. Families can come under official pressure to hold out, but suffer no social stigma for dealing with the sub-humans.

Despite the massive ransoms, kidnapping is far less of an affair than the much more typically Italian crimes of extortion, swindle and fraud. The victims of extortion are reckoned to sing to the tune of 14 billion lire (£6,000 million) a year. On the whole, Italians see force as the refuge of the uninventive, and prefer to use their wits. They did in Dante's time too, and he lodged them deep in hell for abusing intelligence.

Overall, Central Italy is peaceful and the after-dinner stroll is a glide. The Marches have the lowest crime rate in Italy; Florence is worry-less too, and in Rome, the muggers work in the dark of the distant suburbs. But in Rome, be forever on guard against bag- and watch-snatchers.

Drugs

Italy's young are obviously the Mafia's softest target. The first youth died of an overdose in 1973. In the late 1980s, 'poison-dependents', as they are known, were thought to number some 300,000, and the deaths multiply monthly.

The majority of those who die are 18–25 years old, male, and heroin addicts. Most started at 15. The problem is worst in North Italy. In the Centre, most dependents are in Lazio, the fewest in the Marches. Surveys show that they are generally young, unemployed, and from restricted backgrounds.

Government policy – challenged by some parent groups – was to prosecute the pushers, not their clients, who were considered to be sick. If found with only a so-called 'modicum' of any drug, an addict was usually let off, although what a 'modicum' means was left to individual police officers to decide.

National characteristics

'Who are you?' Be rash enough to ask an Italian to define an Italian and he would be extremely hurt. Your question would imply that you thought he was like the others. It would show that you hadn't noticed his *difference*. Every Italian is an Italy to himself. Each would find being likened to others thoroughly indecent, and would totally deny that any similarities existed at all. But seen from the outside, they have far, far more in common than they ever fancied.

Firstly, what binds them together like glue is precisely their adamant conviction that nothing does, their utter dedication to being loners. They are the biggest individualists of Europe, and the idea of a collective society is something they find rather sickly. Another Italian characteristic, in fact, is their total lack of civic sense: they scorn this 'foreign' concept as a constraint on freedom. You will see it in their carefree driving, in where they park, in their contempt for queues, their glee in *confusione*, their refusal to fill in forms or pay taxes.

Their rejection of togetherness extends even to their nationality. They share an inability to feel 'Italian'. They find the word irrelevant. Few Italians believe it belongs to them, the exceptions being only those who have lived or travelled abroad. Nationhood is as abstract to an Italian as a trade union is to a child.

Their loyalty goes instead to their family and to the place where they were born. This is the most binding common denominator of all – the fierce, very local patriotism of the Italians – especially those from Central Italy, where most of the townships are just as they were thirty grandfathers ago, with the memory of what happened then as sharp as goats' cheese.

Fourteenth-century battles happened only yesterday, and the sight of somebody from the opposing camp – a village ten kilometres down the motorway, perhaps – still quickens the pulse. They call it *campanilismo*, an 'excessive, even narrow-minded, love for one's own town and its traditions'. It means, literally, 'bell-towerism', attachment to the parish, and it goes far towards explaining every Italian's sense of difference.

Some condemn it as a poisonous worm, eating into the timbers needed for nation-building. Others thank the Italian Almighty for it, since with nothing else to love, certainly not the State, they would be adrift with no identity. And without this partisanship, what would happen to vitality, so crucial to the wellbeing of Italy?

Campanilismo is more virulent and serious than many foreigners think, and is linked to yet another common trait, which is the Italians' passion for fractiousness. One of their assets – since it is the source of all their gusto – is a total disinterest in agreement. It bores everybody, from two motorists after a crash to two ministers at a press conference. This love of disagreement paralyses governments and town councils throughout Central Italy, especially Rome and Florence. It ensures that all meetings of flat-dwellers break up in full-throated discord, so the *palazzi* never get painted.

But it is through disagreement that the Italians perpetuate their creative past. Since the fall of the Roman Empire, dissension has often cut Italy into shreds. Their inability to perceive or submit to a common good deprived their country of unity and power for 1,200 years. But, on the other hand, it produced the Italian genius, which thrives in the brilliance of diversity, uncramped or distracted by deadening overall schemes.

In Central Italy especially, Italians are also similar in their strong attachment to the past, perhaps not surprising because most of them live amid it; most of their towns and villages have emerged from the centuries relatively unscathed. A medieval banker or tradesman probably slept in the same bedroom and woke up to the same walls. The past was usually also a time of glory unmatched since, so Italians tend to dwell on it with nostalgia and pride.

Part of the mind simply lives off the past. The Florentines would be, as Italians say, compassless without their Renaissance. The sleepy Pisans dream of the era when they held sway over the Mediterranean. And the Milanese in Rome for the first time always exclaim, astonished: 'But these Romans! They're still with their Caesars!'

The Italians are, above all, alike because of the unashamed importance they place on appearance. Their lives are ruled by the imperious dictates of the *bella figura*, the need to make 'a good impression', physically and socially. They will respect the blackest soul if it is in a nice suit.

They consider it an obligation to appear as striking and attractive as nature allows. The soul is a private affair, but appearance a public one. The few who do not comply are outlawed as 'strange', which is largely why punk, for instance, never caught on in Italy. How could it in a country where the policewomen insisted on uniforms designed by Fendi and shoes from Gucci?

Any suggestion that appearance may be a minor affair to some is greeted with a blank stare, compounded of incomprehension and a suspicion of mockery. Males as well as females pay narcissistic attention to dress. A few years ago it was common to hear the comment, 'He hasn't got a lira to his name but have you *seen* that jacket!' – the ultimate accolade to somebody with his priorities right.

You can see *bella figura* in action every evening before dinner in all provincial towns. This is the time for the time-honoured *passeggiata*. In English, this merely means 'the walk', but in Italy its connotations are rich: it figures in the greatest satirical epic of eighteenth-century Italy by Giuseppe Parini. It is the peacock parade, the peak of the day when people, mainly young, swarm into the centre looking their best, preening and peering, noting and being noted.

Basically, it is a mating ritual, masquerading as polite intercourse. In some towns, you will find them packed into the main square, suddenly a beehive of gossip; in others, they use the main street, up one side and down the other, going through their daily reappraisals.

To outsiders, Italians may seem to overdress, even to be faintly ridiculous, and the impression strengthens the further you travel south. They are formal, too. Television reporters doing 'to camera' pieces from shell-gutted Beirut or starving Cambodia usually sport a pocket handkerchief to set off something casual by Valentino.

The opposite of *bella figura* is naturally *brutta figura*. This, for instance, would be to cuff your son in public. The very worst example would be to be drunk in public, especially in the street. That the Italians utterly scorn. They seem constantly torn between their need to be individuals and to be totally conformist. Their sense of the proprieties is rigid. On the whole, the buoyant first need wins – the love of being striking. It is enshrined in their art, especially architecture, which freezes their priorities in stone. Perhaps the most perfect, outrageous, image of *bella figura* is the façade of the Church of San Michele in Lucca. Nothing could be more theatrical, more astounding. It is a screen, in its own right. Behind it is nothing but gloom.

Still other shared traits are:

● A below-zero esteem for politicians, above all MPs, who are viewed as democracy's parasites, elected to represent bank accounts and to field bribes.

● An absence of class consciousness. Ability matters; accent doesn't.

● A tendency towards racism. Domestic racism isn't new: the people of the Centre, for instance, regard Southerners, especially Sicilians, with a shudder. Italy's new foreigners, particularly those from black Africa, now receive similar treatment, as well as gypsies and other minorities.

● Unremittingly chauvinistic men, who treat women as pleasant objects of convenience.

● A shared pride in the beauty of their country, the triumph of their artists, and their role in civilising others.

● A realisation that eating well is one of the higher aims of existence.

● And, of course, football mania.

Italians and tourists

Italians have been used to tourists since Hannibal. Transients are their stock-in-trade. When the pilgrims began hobbling down to Rome

– via Lucca, Siena and Viterbo – thousands of early Italians began to live off their needs. They were Europe's first tourist operators.

Italy is Europe's most trampled-over country, so the foreign imprint is now indelible; foreigners are part of the fabric. If Italians one day found Florence empty of long-legged northern youths striding down its stern streets, or no longer saw the Irish seminarist bent over his soup in a cheap Roman *trattoria*, they would feel lost.

This is why most Western tourists quickly feel at ease in Italy. They come as no surprise and they merit no stares. It is why, wise from centuries of experience, Italians usually greet their guests today with friendly efficiency and little fuss. They may lay on the cheerfulness a little but, toned down, it is the preferred *lingua franca* among themselves. And, of course, niceness talks. Tourism is still Italy's biggest spinner of foreign income, bringing in 8 per cent of the GNP.

Not long ago, when Italy was still *sole, pane e pasta*, a foreigner was a privileged person, treated with deference and envy accompanied by bows. With affluence, nearly all traces of this servility have gone. Now they will stand for no airs. If they can, they will overcharge, though that usually requires the connivance of their victim. In hotels, it would mean ignoring the official tariffs behind the door, and in restaurants ordering without seeing the menu – a hoary con.

No one knows how Italian tourist officials acquire this sort of knowledge, but they report growing 'disappointment' among north European girls who, apparently, descend upon Italy in search of a 'Latin lover'. The Italians, they explain, are beginning to turn to their own girls, now that more relaxed sexual mores allow them to do so. After all, Italian girls dress better.

Women travelling alone

Regardless of age or shape, the foreign lady will be whistled at, shouted at, stopped, pestered and, if possible, pinched. It is dangerous to dismiss such attention as a harmless nuisance or Latin playfulness. It often is, but sometimes is not, and unless a single woman seeks diversion, she may well find life in Italy a misery.

This applies less to Florence and more to Rome, but a single woman, merely by being alone, is assumed at once to be odd and 'available', and no remonstrances will persuade the suitors otherwise. They see something inherently wanton in a lone female. Even middle-aged foreign women who have lived in Rome for years often feel uncomfortable if they lose their husband or lover. They are made to feel vaguely freakish, and get served last.

A foreign woman alone on the streets after dinner is viewed as blatantly free and courts real peril. In 1988, a lone *Italian* woman was gang-raped yards from the most crowded square in Rome. The defence was that she must have been 'asking for it' to be there at all. Even *two* women travelling together need to be tough, since the males troll in twos and fours, and like pairing. They fish by car and coast along kerbstones after quarries who have to be sharp to escape. This is not exaggerated. Take a taxi.

Homosexuality and unmarried couples

That emperors, generals, great painters and famous cardinals dreamt of Adonis instead of Venus is part of the legend, but the norm is still discretion. Italians are tolerant towards homosexuality as long as they do not see it. They happily deal with homosexuals as long as no 'i's are dotted. Any explanation but the right one will do. If two gay men travelling together are 'brothers', so be it. Definition brings down a barrier because it calls for a stance.

The homosexual minority in Italy is large, as usual in Mediterranean countries, but it accommodates society's behest and it lies low, especially in small towns where discovery would still spell ostracism. A result is that Rome *appears* to be the least gay capital of Europe, with only five gay bars. The Vatican is categorical: homosexuality is 'intrinsically disordered'. Bishops must disown gay Catholics and ban them from all Church premises (from a 'Letter to Bishops from the former Holy Office, 30 October 1986).

Except in some circles of the 'Black Aristocracy' (those titled by the Church), few care whether couples are married or not nowadays. On the Rome party circuit, guests arrive with the partner of their choice and, 'Sorry, I didn't quite get the name!' is not heard. Little attempt is made at secrecy. In restaurants, the older man engaged in earnest conversation with a shy young friend in the corner is a stock cameo. It is supposed of every man of moderate success that he can afford infidelity, and it is almost expected of him. Not even a prime minister would be damaged on such a score. The Italians find Anglo-Saxon sex-and-politics scandals utterly incomprehensible.

The police

The police are efficient but, in a country given to show and colour, they naturally operate under a bewildering array of garbs and cloaks that would serve the most intricate opera plot. The cast is as follows:

● **The Municipal Police.** Uniforms differ, but they are the
flashiest, often in white and cream, with epaulettes, braid and ties.
They often look like a cross between town band-leaders and ice-cream
sellers. They regulate local traffic with much semaphore, and will look
the other way if you commit murder, that not being their sphere.
● **The State Police.** In blue shirts, white cross-belts and berets,
they police the towns nationwide, screeching through the streets in
blue-and-white patrol cars driven with mind-boggling skill. They
come under the Interior Ministry and deal in serious crime only; they
are far too busy to notice mere traffic offences.
● **The Riot Police.** You will find them patrolling airports in olive-
green battledress. They are part of the State Police.
● **The Road Police.** The most feared, all leather and huge goggles
on big bikes, or in cars marked *Polizia Stradale.* They set traps for
unsuspecting motorists and wave you down in mid-countryside when
you have done no wrong. Be meek.
● **The Judiciary Police.** You will notice these the least; they
stand guard at the unmarked doors of anonymous big buildings, in
sober blue jackets and light blue trousers. They are the detectives, and
are usually in plain clothes.
● **The Carabinieri.** Italy's para-military police, in dark blue with
a leather chest-bandolier and red-striped trousers, they are the most
respected of the country's law-enforcers, although favourite figures of
fun in numerous film farces. They are much more of a 'presence' than
the State Police, manning outposts in the remotest hamlets, but the
two forces overlap and complement each other. Run by the Ministry
of Defence, headed by an Army general, their parish is the gamut of
crime and they *can* book you for speeding. They specialise, as the other
police do not, in protecting Italy's artistic treasures and in hunting
down art-thieves.
● **The Cavalry Carabinieri.** These are the extras, who pose in
languid pairs, wearing long black capes and spurs. They lean on polished swords.
● **The Financial Police.** The *Finanzieri* wear grey uniforms and
their emblem is a yellow flame. They are the customs and excise men,
whose domain is smuggling, swindling, evasion and fraud.

The young people milling around in rough-spun chocolate brown
are doing their national service in the fire brigade; others under arms
are merely cropped. Their stint lasts a year from the age of 18.

The Weather and When to Go

Central Italy has no one way about it. At any time of the year, it offers different climates. In January, they could be wedging logs into the fire-places of snowbound villages in the Abruzzo while ninety minutes away down in Rome, tourists lunch in the sun. In summer, they could be suffocating in Florence while up in the Alban hills, sudden shivers come on as the sun disappears behind the curtain-rail of the horizon like an orange wafer. Along the narrow coasts, the climate is classic Mediterranean: endless scorching summers, brief autumns and springs, and generally mild winters. December, February and March usually compose the *brutta stagione*, with rain, damp and wind. January is often magnificent, with blue skies and balmy temperatures.

The balmiest place of all is Rome: in the ugly season, Rome and Palermo are usually the two warmest places in Italy. In summer, a breeze often ruffles hair on the hottest days, when it is 34–36°C. This breeze is called *il ponentino*, 'the little one from the west'. It has an ugly little brother from the south-east, called the *scirocco*. This is like a blast from a pizza kiln, and the 'rain' it deposits on Rome spatters cars with mud – from the Sahara. Ever since a North African country tried, and failed, to strike an Italian island with a rocket, it has been known as 'the Colonel's revenge'.

In the Apennine foothills, cold evenings set in early in October; higher up, even earlier. In L'Aquila, *al fresco* diners retire inside when August has hardly finished.

August is the month to avoid. You will find only fellow-tourists, the Italians having fled to the hills, coastal umbrellas, or beds. Italy in August is Italy with the sound-track killed and, with it, Italy itself. The better restaurants are closed, the better hotels empty, and the reflexes are sluggish. The city to be given the widest berth in August is Florence. It sits there in its basin and sizzles. You might hate it.

The second half of August usually brings on storms. So the time to see the Centre most comfortably is from late May to the start of July, and then from September until the end of October. Beaches and swimming are on the cards at least until mid-September and, though it may be coolish in Perugia, October in Florence and Rome is perhaps the most evocative month. It is particularly popular with Germans.

Travelling Around

Central Italy can play hard to get unless courted by car. She often hides her jewels on the tops of hills which trains cannot get at. Buses can, but their timetables may not be yours. Some of her possessions she keeps even from them – Etruscan palaces, remote monasteries.

Even so, if you plan simply to look at cities – Pisa, Florence, Siena, Perugia, Rome – a car is a thorough nuisance, hard to park and of no use. The answer would be a combination of train and bus.

By car

A car involves coming to terms with Italian drivers, a breed apart. On the whole, Italians prefer accommodation to confrontation, but with the flick of an ignition key they are suddenly unrecognisable – mini-monsters, aggressive, bad tempered, impatient and full of bravado. The concept of road courtesy simply does not exist, because there is no parent file. Italy as a state is too young for civic sense. 'Everyone for himself and all for God,' they say. The point of driving in Italy is to find adversaries and put them down. It is brinkmanship; the essence is provocation.

A good Italian planning to debouch from a country track on to a highway waits until his speeding opponent is 100 metres away before skidding out on to the tarmac, forcing him to brake the tread off his tyres or swerve right into the oncoming lane. He will not wait.

Italians also enjoy overtaking on the inside, and then swerving left across your bows. They delight in attacking you with their headlamps from behind when you are in the outside lane, held up by cars in front. When they do zoom past, an obscene gesture is to be expected. Or they will follow you quietly until you signal that you are about to overtake. At that instant, they will lunge forward with blaring horn and try to force you back in behind that slow lorry, with a jolt of brakes.

In the towns, they treat red lights as mere suggestions; they never stop at zebra crossings but execute arabesques around pedestrians. They have a mad vision of so swamping towns with their machines that pedestrians as a race will one day go under.

In their relations with other motorists, the art of the nudge comes into play. It consists of trying it on inch-by-inch. In a crossroads crush,

Distance Chart
(in kilometres)

	Volterra	Viterbo	Urbino	Spoleto	Siena	Rome	Pistoia	Pisa	Pesaro	Perugia	Orvieto	Lucca	Loreto	Livorno	L'Aquila	Gubbio	Grosseto	Florence	Assisi
Ancona	303	277	99	166	253	291	310	364	63	149	232	300	27	315	200	126	310	274	125
Assisi	185	131	104	45	135	177	219	267	265	25	96	237	152	215	294	66	170	183	
Florence	75	214	184	258	68	277	36	96	197	157	169	73	281	115	327	198	161		
Grosseto	120	136	250	205	79	187	207	140	286	170	130	190	338	135	297	198			
Gubbio	191	170	65	105	141	210	234	294	101	41	124	271	148	313	221				
L'Aquila	197	107	300	116	275	117	363	395	263	180	178	378	238	413					
Livorno	73	271	299	280	115	391	78	20	312	216	256	41	342						
Loreto	330	304	70	193	280	277	337	391	90	176	252	327							
Lucca	65	287	220	297	82	351	38	21	270	182	222								
Orvieto	190	45	206	75	140	121	205	246	242	83									
Perugia	150	129	123	64	100	176	193	230	159										
Pesaro	261	288	36	223	205	299	170	300											
Pisa	64	265	264	232	106	373	67												
Pistoia	85	250	135	280	85	313													
Rome	282	107	271	130	229														
Siena	50	151	169	126															
Spoleto	176	88	105																
Urbino	225	252																	
Viterbo	201																		

for instance, the aim is to cut across the opponent's path at all costs, edging forward threateningly and daring others to dare being more daring than you. The only riposte is to join in. It is surprising how often you will win. All holds are admitted, such as reading a big newspaper while your thin-soled shoe caresses the accelerator, all primed for the next leapette forward towards lunch. If you wait, you'll never get lunch.

It is easy to tag Italian drivers. The two letters at the beginning of their number plates give away their provincial capital. Central Italy comprises 21; the worst offenders are LT.

AN	Ancona	PG	Perugia
AP	Ascoli Piceno	PS	Pesaro
AR	Arezzo	PI	Pisa
FI	Firenze (Florence)	PT	Pistoia
FR	Frosinone	RI	Rieti
GR	Grosseto		Roma
LT	Latina	SI	Siena
LI	Livorno	TR	Terni
LU	Lucca	VT	Viterbo
MC	Macerata	SCV	Vatican City
MS	Massa		

Italian drivers are versatile. You will see the police in Rome exhibiting their skills with cinematic daring and wailing sirens every few minutes. But they pay for their ways: the casualty toll is appreciably higher than in the UK. One Italian is killed every year for every 250 *metres* of the 6,000 kilometre long motorway network. On lesser roads, the rate drops to one every 325 *kilo*metres. On a recent average, some 7,000 are killed every year in about 270,000 accidents. The slaughter is a result of the sudden prosperity: there are now 22 million cars on the roads (in 1955, there were only 1 million). The road network, being improved slowly, simply cannot cope.

You are offered small bribes for coming by car. At the frontiers, petrol coupons (*buoni benzina*), now expressed in lire, not litres, are sold at a discount of 13–20 per cent, depending on your destination. Choose the so-called 'Italy packet', because other 'packets' include coupons not negotiable in the Marches, Tuscany or Umbria. The coupons come with free vouchers for a small stretch of driving on the motorways, and a tourist card which entitles you to a free substitute car for up to ten days if your own breaks down or is in an accident. It will be provided by ACI, the Italian Automobile Club. Their telephone number, everywhere, is 116. They run main offices in twenty Central Italian towns. In Rome their headquarters is at 8 Via Marsala (next to the main station); tel. 06-49981. In Florence: 36 Viale Amendola; tel. 055-24861.

ACI also gives free tows to all foreign motorists in trouble, whether card holders or not. There is no limit to the number of times you can call them out, but the actual repairs are at your own expense.

At the frontier, ask at the ACI office for their superb, free, regional maps. They list lead-free petrol stations, camping sites and museums, and contain useful city maps. They are available in English.

The use of front seat-belts became compulsory in 1989. Motorcyclists must be helmeted. Speed limits vary according to the state of controversy between ministries. Public Works insists on lower speeds as a safety measure; Transport on higher ones to safeguard the economy; Interior and Health also have their say. The latest formula to emerge is 110 kph for cars of up to 1100 cc, 130 kph for others.

The overriding rule of the road is to cede to traffic coming from the right, except on obviously main roads in the countryside. In case of breakdown, a plastic red triangle (on sale at most petrol stations) must be set up 40 metres behind your car. In towns, watch out for signs on doors reading *Divieto di sosta* (No Parking). Indifference to this can lead to the car's removal by the police. National driving licences issued in the UK, USA, Australia and New Zealand are accepted, but they must be accompanied by a translation into Italian, available free at AA and RAC offices in the UK. Compulsory third-party insurance must be arranged at home.

● **A warning:** never leave *anything* anywhere in the car at any time. A jacket might stay on the back seat in Florence; in Rome it would walk. Boots are not inviolable. The corollary is to keep luggage light, because getting to hotels often involves trudging through pedestrian zones.

To the question, when to travel? the quick riposte is when the Italians don't. Traffic is lightest, driving greatest, views nicest and risk least during the afternoon siesta – from, say, 2 to 4.30 p.m. The best day for travelling is Monday, because most museums and galleries are closed. The worst is Sunday because everybody else is doing it, although lorry traffic is banned.

The road network in Central Italy is extensive and upkeep is good, although because of mountains the longitudes are faster than the latitudes. The backbone of the network is the heavily used A 1 from Florence to Rome, about three hours non-stop. The A 11 from the west coast to Florence feeds into it, and ranks as the most dangerous stretch in Italy. If you are striking east from Rome, an obvious route is the new A 24 to L'Aquila, used by many for reaching the southern Marches. The planned west coast motorway (A 12) fizzles out south of Livorno and does not resume until Civitavecchia. If God wishes, as the Italians say, it should reach Cecina by 1993. Between Cecina and Grosseto, the road is narrow and slow. The quickest way from Pisa to Rome is via the A 1.

The tolls exacted by the twenty-five motorway companies vary with the cubic capacity of the car. On the Rome–Florence South stretch, a distance of 255 km, a 1100–1600 cc car is charged 16,000 lire; Rome–L'Aquila, a distance of 110 km, costs 6,000 lire. A so-called *Viacard*, a motorway 'telephone card' costing 50,000 or 90,000 lire, will circumvent queues at toll stations.

Since Italy imports nearly all its fuel, petrol is dearer than in the UK or the USA. Prices waver, but in 1989 a litre of super grade cost 1,360 lire.

Petrol station opening times are less nightmarish than they once were. They still close for the siesta (except on the motorways) and they chain up their forecourt for the night at 7.30 p.m. But self-service, 24-hour stations, taking 10,000 lire notes, abound. Credit cards at petrol stations are catching on only slowly, so take cash.

Hitch-hikers have all but vanished in Italy, partly because young backpackers prefer cheap train fares to the risk; there have been cases of assault and murder by drivers. Because of drugs drivers fear attack and will almost never stop, unless the thumbs belong to two pretty girls in daylight. If you do see hitch-hikers, they will invariably be unwary young foreigners.

Car-hire has not caught on in Italy. It is much more expensive than in the US, and still dearer than in the UK, but the rates can drop if cars are pre-paid in the UK. If you hire in Italy, credit cards are accepted and no extra charge is made for a car returned in a different town. The following sample rates provided by different companies do not include Collision Damage Waiver (CDW); Personal Accident Insurance (PAI); or 18 per cent VAT:

Fiat Panda: 66,000 lire a day. 200 km free; each extra km, 330 lire.
Fiat Panda: 299,000 lire a week, plus 43,000 lire for each day extra.
Ford Escort: 59,000 lire a day, plus 700 lire a kilometre.
Ford Escort: 690,000 lire a week; unlimited mileage.
Alfa Romeo Alfa 33: 99,000 lire a day with unlimited mileage if returned to the same city; if not, 99,000 lire a day for 200 km, plus 495 lire for each extra km.

By air

Except in an emergency, air travel is not worth it within compact Central Italy.

The five main airports are Rome, Pisa, Ancona, Florence and Pescara. There are two midnightish flights daily from Pisa to Rome and vice-versa, and once-daily flights both ways between Rome and the others, except Pescara, which has no truck with Rome. In all cases, the flying time is between 50 minutes and 1 hour 15 minutes. With all the airport to-and-froing, wheels definitely win.

By train

Nature has fought a winning battle with the Italian State Railways (*Ferrovie dello Stato* or FS) and in much of Central Italy conquest has been abandoned. Half of the network is single-track. Main lines hug the coasts and paint in a backbone between Florence and Rome, following the course of the Tiber. A few whispery nerves straggle out from it towards east and west here and there and that's it. The north of Umbria and the Marches are badly served. Southern Tuscany, together with northern Lazio, are almost trainless.

But if you mean only to see the main towns, trains are the answer. They are clean, fast and sometimes punctual, but in second class, the somewhat spartan seating compares poorly with standards on British or American trains.They are classified by their turns of speed and come in six breeds. The swiftest are the inter-European expresses (*Euro-City* or EC); domestic (*Inter-City* or IC); and the *Rapido* or R, a long-distance express with a possible stop or two. The *Espresso* is not an express at all, and stops everywhere. The even more dilatory *Diretto* is another misnomer. The *Locale*, your commuter train, is more honestly named.

Italians are beginning to appreciate their trains, and the time-saving they offer, more than they once did. Increasingly, they are leaving the car in the street and defecting from buses. For instance, ten inter-city trains a day do the 316 km between Florence and Rome in 2 hours. Rome–Perugia takes 2 hours 15 minutes; Rome–Pescara 3 hours; Rome–Ancona 3 hours 15 minutes and Rome–Pisa 3 hours.

On inter-city trains, booking is compulsory. At some stations (Florence is one) American Express cards work ticket machines. But beware: the validity of tickets is not limitless. It usually varies from one to six days, depending on distance. If you arrive by air at Pisa, hourly trains take you from the terminal directly into Florence. A new line links Rome's Fiumincino airport to the city.

Although change looms, train travel in Italy is still among the lowest priced in Europe. Second class from Florence to Rome costs 24,000 lire; Rome to Pisa 25,000 lire; Rome to Ancona 23,000 lire (fast-train surcharge included).

Italians and foreigners under 26 years of age can get a 30 per cent discount by buying a cheap *Carta Verde* (Green Card), valid for one year, at travel agencies handling FS business. The over-sixties are also awarded a 30 per cent reduction if they ask for a *Carta d'Argento* (Silver Card). Families travelling together receive the same treatment with a *Carta Famiglia* (Family Card).

Tourists are entitled to highly useful unlimited travel passes, called *Biglietto Turistico di Libera Circolazione*, or BTLC. An eight-day pass costs 140,000 lire; fifteen days 168,000 lire. Another saver is the *Biglietto Kilometrico* (Kilometre Ticket). This is made out for up to five people and entitles them to twenty journeys and 3,000 km of travel – together or individually – for two months.

You won't starve on Italian trains. Most long-distance ones that travel through meal-times include a restaurant car, offering good, solid fare at reasonable prices; nearly all inter-city trains have a self-service coach. If neither is laid on, a muscular man with a basket and a bell will appear, to serve drinks and sandwiches.

By bus

Most Italians travel by bus. Buses are fleet, comfortable, spotless, remarkably cheap, and they are everywhere. You will find them perfect for excursions from a base, the only drawback being that the last return bus usually leaves fairly early, excluding dinner 'out'. In most towns, the terminus is outside the railway station and, almost everywhere, tickets have to be bought before boarding, either at the terminus or at the nearest tobacconist.

Even if you have a car, you will find the bus particularly useful in Rome: it solves the problem of getting out of the city, and then back in.

By taxi

Taxis are not expensive if drivers take the shortest routes, but often they do not. Often, too, the meters have fallen behind current tariffs and a grubby, illegible sheet listing supplements will be brandished, as other extras are barked out for pieces of luggage, night fares and the like. But in the towns of Central Italy, including Rome, almost everything is within walking distance by day. At night, radio taxis answer calls swiftly, giving you their call-sign, such as 'Tiger One', and they are an efficient way of getting home.

However you travel:

● Avoid arriving in towns too late, i.e. between 7 and 8.30 p.m.; the time of the *passeggiata*. Town centres are often banned to cars or traffic is at a standstill and hotels marooned.

● Always carry plenty of coins, essential for turning on the illumination in churches and listening to taped commentaries.

● Stock up with the tokens needed for telephone calls from bars and other public call boxes. Called *gettoni*, they cost 200 lire each and can be bought at tobacconists'. Most telephone boxes in Italy now also accept a range of coins, e.g. 100, 200 and 500 lire.

● Pick up the free maps of the town you're staying in, available at hotels.

● Bear in mind that many sights are best and most painlessly seen at night, under usually excellent flood-lighting. The sun actually obscures a lot of detail.

● Don't rely too heavily on the locals for directions. Their usual reaction is, 'Ah, the church of San Francesco! It *was* down there somewhere. Ask at the newspaper stand.'

● Take a pair of opera glasses or binoculars for art that is out of easy sight (e.g. the ceiling of the Sistine Chapel).

Where to Stay

Hotels

The tourist authorities ensure 'Glasnost' on the hotel front. They run the star-system, award the numbers, and run frequent checks. So, if you're surprised by the bills, it is likely to be because they are unusually reasonable.

Within the various categories, prices can differ greatly depending upon location. A four-star hotel near Lake Trasimeno in Umbria, for instance, may well cost a third of its equivalent in Rome. But appearances count for less than they should. You may find that the apparently prohibitive manor house hotel in the Marches, exclusive-looking and in its own grounds, is well within your means. It is *always* worth an enquiry.

On the whole, you will find the big luxury or 'modern' hotels sit outside the walls of medieval towns, which often means being out on a limb. If you want to sleep within the town, your choice will usually be limited to three-star and below. In many towns, the old traditional hotel, once the first and only, glittering and grand, now wilts with nostalgia. They are touching places to stay at, and are pointed out in the Gazetteer.

But no matter how many stars cling to hotels, they all share the same irritating lack: that of a proper reading-lamp. Italians obviously do not associate bed with a book. A clandestine bulb of adequate power is a must.

Charges usually include continental breakfast. The five-star hotels, light years away from their surroundings, can cost up to 600,000 lire a night for two, but with the loss of just one star, the pain greatly eases. Four-star hotels outside Rome charge about 160–230,000 lire in high season for two, which you may find pays for a standard of comfort and service that is becoming rare. In Rome, reckon with 250–260,000 lire in this bracket.

But the average traveller in Central Italy will be more than satisfied with three stars. Again, one star fewer saves a great deal. The card behind the door should read between 70,000 and 110,000 lire; in Rome, about 140,000 lire. 'Traditional' hotels usually fit this slot, which is the most popular. They are often family establishments with a faintly dated air; warren-like and business-like, with efficient bathrooms, and a reliable restaurant.

Two- and one-star hostelries are more spartan, but serve well as summer one-night stands. In price, there is little between them – 35–45,000 lire. The rooms may be small and/or dark; the wardrobe door might not shut; the toilet may be in the corridor; perhaps there is no lift; the floor will be of bare tiles (in the wrong colour); but they are clean and, for a fast-moving holiday, an attractive proposition.

Pensioni

Pensioni are the Italian boarding-houses, home-from-homes for polite guests run by forceful ladies with buns and commanding soup ladles. They are on their way out, even in Florence, their stronghold. Many have simply changed their name to hotel, 'because we've now got to be like other countries,' as one matron sadly explained. They were once cheaper than hotels, but she herself charged 51,000 lire for a single room with a bath. Only a few of those left impose semi-board on their guests, and most now do not mind if you can spend only one night. The atmosphere remains – antiques, parquet floor and rugs.

Conventual tourism

This is the latest cliché in Umbria for the old tradition of seeking shelter in monasteries and convents. Hit by a drop in vocations and in funds, monks and nuns are turning hoteliers to believers and non-believers. Visitors sleep in cells and the fare at the common table in the refectory is the produce of the hosts. The pioneers were the nuns at the Monastero di San Antonio in Norcia, 100 km from Perugia, at an altitude of 600 m. Eleven other institutions have now followed suit. A day's board costs about 40,000 lire. Tourist Offices usually have the addresses.

'Green' tourism

Italians are also taking to away-from-it-all holidays on farms, an already well-organised scheme. For foreigners, language could be a barrier, of course, but that should not stand in the way of London bank managers, say, milking Italian cows. Lodged in ancient farmhouses or castles being saved from ruin, guests are expected to muck in. But there is a lot more going on – from walking and riding to tennis and archery, from fishing and swimming to hunting and motocross.

For a catalogue, in Italian, write to: Turismo Verde, 20 Via Mariano Fortuny, 00196 Rome. For details on farms in Tuscany and Umbria, contact Turismo Verde at 10 Piazza Independenza, 50129 Firenze or 28b Via Campo di Marte, 06100 Perugia.

Camping

Camp-sites are numerous – there are eighty-four in Lazio alone – and very cheap, most of them shaded by pine woods along the coasts. They also congregate around lakes: fourteen are dotted around tame Lake Trasimeno in Umbria and more around Lake Bracciano to the north of Rome. But there are two camp-sites within greater Florence and four close to Rome. They compete for star ratings like hotels. Many have their own restaurants, and bowls and tennis courts, but they do look rather crowded.

A letter to the following address should produce a list: Centro Campeggiatori Stranieri, Federcampeggio, Casella Postale 649, 50100 Florence. Booking is possible through this centre: 15 May is the deadline. Otherwise, apply personally at the *Centro*, Calenzano, by exit number 19 on the A 1 motorway, 14 km north-west of Florence.

Rented villas, farm-houses and flats

These are mainly available in Tuscany and Umbria, ranging from cottages and peasant dwellings which once had cow-sheds on the ground floor, to flashy modern villas with swimming pools, domestic staff, and nasty high walls. Usually they ensure budget holidays – ideal if the family is coming along. They are let for the season or by the week or month, normally between May and October. Often, linen and cutlery are not provided. Drawbacks can be a reluctant water supply and flickering light bulbs. The heaviest concentration is in the Chianti area of Tuscany, which wags now call Chiantishire. Property can be rented through agents in the UK and US as well as on the spot.

For a list of renting agents in Tuscany, apply to Ente Turismo, 16 Via Manzoni, 50121 Florence. For foreign-let agents in Umbria, contact Camera Commercio, 40 Via Cacciatore degli Alpi, 06100 Perugia, or Camera Commercio, 6 Largo Don Minzone, 05100 Terni. No information is given by telephone. Agents should garnish their offerings with photographs of the property.

To book – or not to bother?

Part of the fun of Central Italy is that you can still roam around on spec, free of restrictive pre-arrangements. Turn up unannounced, and there is usually a room. Or, to banish worry altogether, merely have the hotel you are leaving ring up the next.

But there *are* exceptions, which are governed by no rule. It is advisable to book in Florence, for instance, in April, May and June. Beds abound there, though, in impossibly hot July and August, just when most hotels in Rome are bursting. Booking is also essential everywhere at Easter, the most crowded period. The coasts are sold out from July to 15 September. The safest, most pleasant, month for planning-haters is October.

Eating and Drinking

Bars

These outnumber *even* churches, and quicken the quickness of daytime life. Most have two doors for immediate transit: it's gulp and go. If they motion to you to sit down at the tables outside, do not mistake it for solicitude: it costs double.

If you order simply *un caffè*, or *espresso*, you will be brought a black smudge of dynamite at the bottom of a tiny cup. To obtain a larger strong, black coffee you must order a *doppio* which will be two *espressi* in one cup.

More substantial is *caffelatte*, a big glass of milk in which a *caffè* has drowned, usually drunk by Italians in the privacy of the home in the mornings and otherwise considered a beverage for undernourished foreigners. Neither during the day do they usually touch the more familiar *cappuccino*, named after the colour of the habit of the Capuchin friars – coffee topped by foaming milk sprinkled with cocoa powder. You may have interest in a *caffè corretto*, literally coffee 'corrected' with spirits – *grappa* is considered the best.

If you want your coffee hot, ask for it *bollente*, otherwise it will be served lukewarm, as per custom. Do the asking after reporting to the cash register for *il tické*. Bars are really morning places, when the *bombe*, sugared doughnuts, *brioches* and *ciambelle*, doughy circles, are piled high.

Throughout the Centre of Italy, but especially in Rome, the bars also produce excellent sandwiches, *tramezzino* – crustless, light and very fresh. Try a *tonno e pomodoro*, tuna and tomato. They also go to pains over a *spremuta di arancia* or *di limone*, fresh orange or lemon squeezed on the spot.

After dinner, Italians drop by the bar for a *digestivo*, the bravest going for a thump of *Fernet Branca*. Less purgatorial after-burners include *Averna*, concocted from a secret Sicilian family recipe, the sweeter *Montenegro*, *Ramazzotto* and *Amaro Alpino*, a drinker's drink. All of these are based on herbs and are about 30 per cent proof. *Punt e Mes*, a bitter vermouth, is also a favourite.

For a milder (20 per cent) variety, try the gently pungent *Viparo* from Umbria, a 'tonic' digestive derived from herbs and roots. For a contrast, tackle the heavyweight of the sweet after-coffee drinks, *Sambuca*, made from anise in Civitavecchia; or confront the cohort of dreg-powered *Grappas* – one of the smartest is *Carpené Malvolti*. If you go down well in the restaurant, they will present you with one of these sluggers on the house.

Restaurants

In the north, *ristorante* means exactly that. But from Florence south, including Rome, it is often a warning of costly smartness. Make instead for the *trattoria*, the typical, more modest, often family-run restaurant.

It would take research to winkle out a really bad *trattoria* in Central Italy. For one thing, it would not survive the competition; for another, the principles and ingredients of Italian cooking are so standard and simple that a cook would have to be perverse to be bad. This is so true that the quality of the cooking, on the whole, remains pretty constant; only prices fluctuate wildly. The bills decrease as you travel south: Pisa is much dearer than Rome.

By paying more, you will not necessarily eat better. On the contrary, you will often find yourself far happier in a casual and bustling family *trattoria* than in a smoother establishment with cummerbunds and wine lists. The Gazetteer picks out these homelier spots.

After all, Italy is not France. It does not cater for the fastidious gourmet; it lays little claim to refinement; and depends little on the flair of the creative chef. It does depend enormously on the freshness of ingredients, and the delights of the Italian table include hollow bread rolls fresh from the oven, crunchy lettuce crated only yesterday and sea bream landed just hours ago.

Italian cuisine depends also on simplicity; it abhors manipulation and concoction. It places a strong accent on veal and, in Tuscany, on so-called *cucina povera* (poor cooking), based on the alleged sustenance of the once-poor peasants. This includes *stale* bread. Central Italy doesn't pretend to offer the best cuisine in the country. (That credit goes to Emilia Romagna, just to the north.) But as well as being genuine, it is varied, reflecting the geography. Up in the hills, wild boar and hare figure on the menus. Around Norcia in Umbria, pork is the speciality. Florence is synonymous with huge steaks, while Rome's delicacies include tripe, brains and offal.

Half the enjoyment of eating is the watching ... and being watched. A restaurant is a seat in the stalls of the great Italian theatre. It brings out the sunnier side of the often-troubled Italian temperament. People will be as immersed in what is before them as in who is around them. Musicians will stroll in and out strumming mandolins, and pretty gypsy girls will sell roses in cellophane.

Italian menus offer three courses, often including in summer a self-service *antipasti* buffet, a display of colour and succulence not to be missed. Otherwise the first course (*primo piatto*) includes soups, such as the nutritious *zuppa di verdura*, and countless variations on the theme of *pasta*. There is the spaghetti type; long, ribbon-like *pasta* such as *fettuccine* and *tagliatelle*; broad *pasta* such as *pappardelle*; *pasta corta* (short), such as *rigatoni* and *penne* (chopped tubes); and the heavier, stuffed *pasta*, such as *ravioli* and *cannelloni*, which is baked.

The second course (*secondo piatto*) comprises meat and the expensive fish dishes, often charged in units of 100 g (*un etto*). Vegetables are always ordered separately. When it is time for dessert, proof of freshness is in the usually excellent fruit salad (*macedonia*).

If the *trattoria* also calls itself a *pizzeria*, many customers, especially the young, will order big, round pizzas only, with beer or wine. *Trattorie* are flexible and bend to whim. As opposed to French practice, they rarely offer fixed-price menus; those that do are shabby and desperate.

The *rosticceria*, now being ousted, is a clean hole-in-the-wall serving meat off the spit with side dishes and wine or beer, consumed on shelves. It is useful if you are in a hurry or broke.

Here are some of the most likely menu tempters.

First course
Ribollita: literally, 're-boil' – a marshy vegetable soup including cabbage and beans (Tuscany).

Panzanella: there is no English equivalent of this summer hors d'œuvre – dunked stale bread, olive oil, tomato, celery and onions (Central Italy).

Fettuccine all'amatriciana: tagliatelle with bacon and tomato (Rome).

Brodetto: fish soup (Marches).

Spaghetti al tartufo: spaghetti with black truffles (Umbria).

Prosciutto con melone/fichi: raw ham with melon or figs.

Second course
Cotoletta alla milanese: veal in breadcrumbs (everywhere).

Bistecca alla fiorentina: huge steaks cooked over embers (Florence).

Lombata di vitello: veal sirloin, usually excellent.

Saltimbocca alla romana: 'Roman jump-into-the-mouth' – small scallops of veal skewered to pieces of bacon with sage (Rome).

Cotoletta bolognese: veal cutlet topped by cheese and ham; children love it (everywhere).

Cervella al burro con piselli: fried brains and peas served in a small frying-pan (Rome).

Filetto di bue: ox fillet (everywhere).

Bocconcino-Spezzato di vitello: veal stew.

Cinghiale: wild boar (Tuscany).

Involtini di vitello: small stuffed veal rolls.

Porchetta con finocchio: suckling pig with fennel and herbs (Umbria).

These are the fish you are likely to encounter: *dentice*, sea bream; *merluzzo*, cod; *orata*, gilt-headed sea bream; *pesce spada*, swordfish (expensive); *rombo*, turbot; *sogliola*, sole; *spigola*, bass.

Vegetables   *Carciofi alla Giudea*: 'Jewish' artichokes, fried (Rome).
Asparagi, asparagus; *funghi*, mushrooms; *melanzane alla parmigiana*, aubergines with Parmesan cheese.

Desserts   *Macedonia*, fruit salad; *torta di ricotta*, cottage-cheese pie; *uva*, grapes; *tiramisù*, 'Pull-me-up', a light trifle with many nice interpretations; *cocomero*, watery water-melon.

Drinking

Central Italy may not be as rich in quality wines as the North of the country, but it runs to great ones even so, most from radiant Tuscany. Leonardo da Vinci thought the Tuscans should be better off for it: 'I believe', he wrote, 'much happiness descends upon those born where good wines are to be found.'

Quality, in theory, coincides with bottles labelled DOC, or *Denominazione di Origine Controllata* (Name of Origin Verified), a warranty of birth in a precisely defined area, and of an upbringing in line with strictly decreed rules, governing ageing, type of grape, strength and the like.

Greater doffing should be due to DOCG, or *Denominazione di Origine Controllata e Garantita*, a super-guaranteed warranty granted to DOCs officially picked out for special qualities. Wines marked *Riserva* should have been aged for at least three years.

These thoroughbreds should be recognisable by numbered neckbands. But some producers, fed up with alleged cases of unfair practices or impatient with tiresome rules, have deserted DOC. They advertise their superiority by perversely labelling their product, for those in the know, *Vino da Tavola*, and charge the earth for it. The practice, begun in the North, could spread.

In Tuscany, apart from *Chianti Classico* and six other DOC Chiantis, perhaps the most admired is the famous, and expensive, *Brunello di Montalcino* from Southernish Tuscany. A runner-up is the deep-red *Vino Nobile* from nearby Montepulciano. Both age handsomely.

Umbria's standard-bearer is *Orvieto*, a semi-sweet ('*abboccato*') or dry white from the high-profile cathedral town of the same name. The neglected hill-town of *Torgiano*, overlooking the Tiber south of Perugia, produces both a fulsome red and a feathery white.

Wine-growers in Lazio, the region around Rome, may not achieve greatness, but the whites from the nearby Alban hills – especially *Frascati* – have pleased the palates of Romans for centuries. The brilliantly clear, slightly bitter *Verdicchio* is the white that usually represents the Marches, but I genuflect before *Bianchello del Metauro*, a multi-hued white from the Fano area further north. The wine of the Abruzzo is *Montepulciano*, a light, widespread red with none of the nobility of its namesake (no relation) in Tuscany.

On your way around, look out for the occasional *Enoteca*, a kind of wine-bookshop where you can browse through all the liquid editions of the area. The biggest is in a Medici fort in Siena, with stock culled from all over Italy.

In practice, very few Italians order bottled wine in restaurants. To do so is regarded as eccentric, spendthrift, or disrespectful of the house. The oleaginous ink sometimes banged down in front of you in France as *vin ordinaire* hardly exists in Italy. Most *trattorie* stock wines from other regions, in dusty bottles, but serve only the local wine in brimming open flasks and are usually proud to do so. There are literally thousands of these wines, quite unashamed of being non-DOC, and most are thoroughly drinkable, many interesting, some a joy. All are far cheaper than their bottled brothers, and their variety is one of the perks of Central Italy.

So most people simply ask for red or white, depending on the area's speciality, and have a go.

Entertainment

Entertainment in Central Italy is mainly sitting around and watching. Almost exclusively, it happens outside, usually in the evening cool, or in the hope of it. Entertainment indoors is a contradiction in terms. Pleasure is whiling away dinner at an outside table, then dawdling over a drink at a pavement café as bright colours pass.

It is mingling among the throng in the Piazza Navona in Rome, having your portrait drawn, listening to the bawdy jibes of the fortune-tellers, and trying to spot the wallet-pinchers. Or leaning over the Ponte Vecchio in Florence watching the moon in the turgid dribble; or sitting on the steps of a medieval cathedral listening to a guitarist strum through a skit on the giants of the Renaissance.

Entertainment is *not* hard drinking. The bars are not designed for it; neither are the Italians. Few 'pubs' exist.

There is little nightlife. In Rome, the wing of the Church rarely sheltered levity. Now, shyly, unobtrusive doors open at the buzz of a bell, as they do more readily in Florence. Usually, for tax reasons, they are 'cultural circles', but you only have to scribble out a card to be in. They are not cheap, and sometimes unbearably dull. In the provinces, nightlife is sitting up watching television.

Festivals

During the summer, though, few days pass without some town in Central Italy exploding into life with its annual 'big day' – a pageant, some kind of race, a flag-waving competition or medieval game. Visitors sometimes suspect this folklore is laid on for their benefit; in fact, these are intensely local events, and feelings often run high as past rivalries surface with force. Often the competitions are between different wards, and you will notice from the street names that in many small cities the old divisions still exist as official addresses.

The most famous, and roughest, is of course the *Palio* of Siena, the horse races around the main square on 2 July and 16 August (the latter is better known). In Pisa, on 17 June, there is a regatta. A few days later in Florence, you can watch sixteenth-century soccer. At Gubbio in Umbria and Viterbo in Lazio, teams speed high-swaying objects through the steep streets on quasi-religious occasions. In Arezzo, south of Florence, the main square is packed in September for a joust-ing tournament between the wards, while later in the month at Gualdo Tadino near Perugia, donkey-carts race and archers compete.

Arts

On a less muscular plane, cities echo loudly to music and drama. The *Maggio Musicale* in Florence, straddling May and June, begins the year with concerts, opera and ballet. Nearby Fiesole puts on a long Sum-mer Festival lasting from June to August. *Le tout Rome* packs open-air concerts at the Campidoglio, while the July highlight in Umbria is the Festival of Two Worlds in Spoleto. Perugia lays on a rival Jazz Festi-val. The open-air opera season at Macerata in the Marches, which attracts singers of fame, runs from July to August. In picturesque squares or Roman theatres elsewhere, operas and plays may run only for a night or two. Coloured lights, loud bangs and fireworks indicate they are celebrating a saint's day.

Open-air cinema, called *Arena*, can be the answer to a hot evening. Most usually show old movies (in Italian of course), and boast an interval bar.

Sport

Golf and tennis clubs are usually hermetically sealed to transients, except at a few coastal resorts such as Forte dei Marmi and Punta Ala in Tuscany.

The west coast offers plenty of facilities for wind-surfing, with equipment on hire locally. Water-skiing is expensive, but one of the best places for it is the vast Lake Bracciano north of Rome, where canoeing is also a speciality. Underwater fishing is allowed every-where, except in harbour, and providing breathing apparatus is not used. The advised times of the day are between 5 and 8 a.m. and 6 and 8 p.m. No licence is required, but one is needed for normal fishing in inland waters. Many resorts run sailing schools.

An increasingly popular pursuit is horse-riding, especially in the Maremma around Grosseto where Tuscany's own cowboys, the *butteri*, still ride. One enterprising hotel in Montieri near Siena organises tourism on horseback, with day-trips and picnics: contact **Il Prategiano**; tel. 0566-997703.

In winter, Apennine ski resorts should never be more than two hours away, wherever you are.

Shopping

Shopping in Central Italy can be rewarding and varied, but it certainly isn't inexpensive. Do not count on bargains, although if you are in Rome during the sales, in January or June and July, you might be lucky. Florence and Rome still stand for striking design in **fashion** as well as superb, meticulous workmanship. In clothes, fabric is generally of superior quality; on the whole, fewer materials are synthetic, and you can find 'different' bright colours. In these two cities, of course, you can visit the big fashion houses. The main difference between them is in style: Florence offers restrained good taste, while Rome prizes flamboyance.

Leather is a good buy everywhere, with shoes often at very good prices. Wallets, purses, belts and bags are often very attractive. **Silk** ties and scarves, in thousands of patterns, *are* cheap. You will discover a prodigious array of **jewellery**, too, from classic rings to imaginative trinkets. And look out for objects in **straw** – hats, bags and novelties. All over Central Italy, you will find bright, cheap, often very attractive, **pottery**. The experts say the best comes from Deruta in Umbria.

Literally hundreds of different **wines** are there for the sampling, and you might want to experiment with taking home a bottle or two of sunshine for that rainy winter evening. One of the best is from Montalcino in Tuscany.

Tuscan **olive oil** is considered among the best in the world. The connoisseurs prefer the green, 'extra-virgin' oil from the first pressing. On sale at any grocer's, it comes in utilitarian tins or fine square bottles, good for recycling.

General Basics

Cinemas

Dubbing is a big industry in Italy, and virtually no Italian cinema shows films in the original language. The Italians prefer American films to their own, unless they're farces, and they refuse subtitles. Italian directors themelves use dubbing: they pick Anglo-Saxon leads for the box-offices abroad, and 'Italianise' them for home screens.

Clothing

Take light clothing, of course, but nothing in nylon or raw silk since they generate much perspiration. For the evening, light sweaters, shawls and cotton jackets are needed, since the warmest day can end in a cool breeze. This is especially true in the hills south of Rome.

If you have embassy engagements, a light black suit or gown is called for. Women will also need a shawl for churches: bare shoulders, mini-skirts or shorts (for men or women) are not on. Women should not take high-heeled shoes: they stick in the cobbles and echo in the churches. Those who walk the streets bare-torsoed are liable to fines; topless women on beaches are not.

Cultural organisations

British Council Library: 20 Via Quattro Fontane, Rome; tel. 06-475 6641. In a fine *palazzo* not far from the Quirinale, it has British authors on Italy, and a British press and reading room.
United States Information Service Library: 119a Via Veneto, Rome; tel. 06-46741. It is inside the Embassy.

Documents

Citizens of EC countries, Australia, New Zealand and the United States require only a valid passport. A stay of up to three months is allowed, after which a Stay Permit (*Permesso di Soggiorno*) is required. This can be prised out of Police Headquarters (*Questura*) after a patient siege.

Electrical current

A few years ago, each home ran on two voltages, but now 220 volts is standard. Plug pins are round.

Embassies and consulates

Britain: 80a Via XX Settembre, Rome; tel. 06-475 5441 or 5551, 24 hours a day. A ten-minute walk from the station, the Consulate (usually open 9.30 a.m.–12 noon and 2–4 p.m.) is inside the Embassy, a controversial creation by Sir Basil Spence started in 1968, reactions to which range from shame to delight.
Canada: 27 Via G. B. De Rossi, Rome; tel. 06-855341/2/3. This is in a quiet lane off the Via Nomentana; ask for the Villa Massimo.
Ireland: 3 Largo Nazareno; tel. 06-678 2541, near the Trevi Fountain.
United States: The massive fortified Embassy, in the heart of the Rome of *La Dolce Vita*, is at 119a Via Veneto, Rome and the Consulate (open 9.30 a.m.–5.30 p.m.) is next door at 121. They have the same telephone number, 06-46741.
Australia: 215 Via Alessandria, Rome; tel. 06-832721. Beyond the walls, this is close to the British Embassy in the Via Nomentana area. The Consulate is in the same building.
New Zealand: 28 Via Zara, Rome; tel. 06-851225. The Embassy and Consulate are together, just a few steps from the Australians.

Health

Italian doctors can be excellent; in an emergency, help comes quickly; the big hospitals are well equipped; the medical staff is usually highly qualified. So you may not die, but conditions can often be appalling.

Under EC agreements, EC citizens have the right to free treatment in Italy, including major surgery. If you fall really seriously ill, you will receive superb treatment in the really big hospitals, such as the rambling, old-fashioned *Policlinico* in Rome. However, this is often seen by Romans as a byword for the worst in Italian state medicine, cockroaches and all. That is the problem: if you are only *quite* ill, you are liable to see them, and find no bell-push. The alternatives would be to fly home, or elect a private hospital where rates, though high, are less than in West Germany or France. Examples would be the *Ospedali Riuniti di Santa Chiara* in Pisa, and the *Salvator Mundi* in Rome (all the foreigners go there).

The First Aid (*Pronto Soccorso*) departments of the big hospitals are efficient and friendly. If you must have an X-ray, for instance, or an injection against toothache, they will oblige for a derisory sum.

There are no local afflictions to guard against in the Centre, and no dangerous fauna. In low-lying country areas, mosquitos can be a hazard, so take insect-repellent. Those who start out by lying under the direct sun for more than fifteen minutes will fall ill at once, with shivers, nausea and constipation. Initially, avoid the beach until after 4.30 p.m. To contract direr ills, swig wine on the beach while sunbathing.

As a precaution, drink bottled and not tap water, as the Italians do. If you order mussels (*cozze*), ensure that they are piping hot.

Pharmacies are well stocked, and lax about the need for a prescription: if you present your old bottle or pack, they will usually hunt down the equivalent. They work their shutters in concert with the shops, but all post notices of where to find chemists after hours. You will then be served through a peep-hole in the main door – a precaution against assault.

Insurance

Arrange all insurance, personal and for the car, at home. Italian insurance companies are not to be disturbed. Rates are high and claims, when attended to, are emasculated.

Laundry and dry-cleaning

Most hotels provide an efficient overnight laundry service, though charges are steep. Dry-cleaning can take thirty-six hours. Launderettes and the *bella figura* could never co-exist, so there are few. But things dry quickly, and the secret solution is a rub-dub in the hotel and a small travelling iron.

Money

The currency unit is the lira (plural lire). Coins come in denominations of 10 (now rare), 50, 100 and 500; banknotes in 1,000, 5,000, 10,000, 50,000 and 100,000. Avoid the 100,000 lire notes if possible, as it can be hard to find change. There has always been a bizarre shortage of small change in Italy, especially of coins, which you should hoard jealously.

Italy does not shine on money services; only the banks offer acceptable exchange rates, and that involves a wait. Hotels take a good cut, as the very few money-changers do. If the banks are shut, travellers' cheques (strongly recommended) and currency can be changed at the often crowded American Express offices in Rome (Piazza di Spagna) or Florence (Via Guicciardini), both usefully open on Saturday mornings. Cash-dispensers that take Visa cards are operated (if working) by the Banca d'America e d'Italia; in Rome, try their branch at 4 Largo Argentina. If you are still stuck, try Rome's *Stazione Termini*, where the exchange office is open on Sunday mornings.

Foreigners are allowed to take out of the country up to 1 million lire in banknotes, and up to 2.5 million lire's worth of foreign currency without declaring it. Anything over that amount has, in theory, to be declared, but the limit is 10 million. Any amount of money may of course be brought *in* to the country, but the Bank of Italy says that if you plan to take money out again, a declaration must be made when you arrive.

Credit cards have been slow to catch on, but most three-star and many two-star hotels accept them. However, many restaurants (especially the smaller ones) do not, and even if they do they would much prefer cash. Signatures in Italy arouse profound suspicion. Many hotels prefer Eurocheques to credit cards because they are cleared faster.

Foreign currency causes great confusion; Italians will look through the sporting papers for exchange rates. To pay with it is tantamount to throwing it away. It is usually accepted only if you obviously have no other means of paying.

Newspapers, television and radio

Newspapers: in Italy these are virtually always 'political', in that they are financed by, reflect, promote or prefer a given Italian party or interest group. The Anglo-Saxon ideal of impartiality has made little headway in Italy, where the interest is in what to make of the facts, not in the boring raw material.

The paper nearest to the ideal is *La Stampa*, published in Turin and owned by the Agnelli (Fiat) group. Milan's *Corriere della Sera*, for long the rigorous standard-bearer of Italian journalism and the most respected abroad, has lost its halo after political upsets. In such a fiercely localised country, national newspapers have found it hard to come into being, though an exception is *La Repubblica*, a verbose and racy pro-left Rome tabloid with a circulation of over 800,000 – the highest in Italy and unprecedented. Otherwise, papers tend to be regional, and one of the best is *La Nazione* of Florence. More sensational is *Il Messaggero* of Rome, once establishment and now left-wing, with a run of 300,000. British-style pin-up tabloids do not exist.

In Florence and Rome, same-day British dailies are on sale and the *New York Herald Tribune* prints in Rome. English-language newspapers in Rome have faltering lives, but *Wanted in Rome*, a give-away with sprightly vignettes on the Roman scene, could be a stayer.

Television: the 'State' channels, as already explained (see page 22), are in fact run by the political parties. Technically the old RAI monopoly remains because the would-be competition, the private stations, are prohibited from transmitting on a national scale. The bigger ones, such as *Canale 5* and *Italia 1*, get over the ban through simultaneous taped local broadcasts. The smaller ones do not, and are content with advertisements and old American footage.

Radio: reception can be fickle, but the BBC World Service broadcasts on medium wave on 648 metres (clearest late at night), and on short wave on 19 metres in the mornings and on 49 metres in the evenings. Tele Montecarlo relays American CBS Evening News early in the morning and Vatican Radio broadcasts news in English on medium wave.

Opening hours

Banks open twice daily from Mondays to Fridays; as a rule, from 8.30 a.m. to 1.35 p.m. and after lunch from 3.30 to 4 or 4.15 p.m., but they periodically tamper with the timetable. If you arrive during the final fifteen minutes, you may be refused admission.

Shops have two lives a day too, except the Upim department stores, which are open all day. Many shops, especially clothing shops, close on Monday mornings. Otherwise, they trade from 9 a.m. to 1 p.m. and from 3.30 or 4 to 8 p.m., including Saturdays. Grocers, fruiterers and butchers take a half-day off on Thursdays in winter and on Saturdays in summer. Open-air markets begin at 7 a.m. and sweep up around 1 p.m.

The opening times of museums, galleries and churches are a maddening topic typified by anarchy. The State, the Municipalities and the Church do not consult and they close down at will. Timetables in one town bear no relation to those in the next. Even in the same town, all is flux, depending on funds, unions and seasons. Every generalisation is riddled with exceptions. Rashly, then:

● Most state and municipal museums are closed on Mondays.
● Most open only for half-days, usually from 9 a.m. to 1 or 2 p.m. Exceptions are the Uffizi Gallery in Florence, open continuously 9 a.m.–7 p.m. (9 a.m.–1 p.m. on Sundays), and the San Matteo National Museum in Pisa (the same timetable).
● On Sundays, museums on the whole close one hour earlier than during the week.
● State museums also close on 1 January, Easter Day, 25 April, 1 May, 2 June (if a Sunday, otherwise the first Sunday in June); 15 August and 25 December.
● Cathedrals and churches close earlier in the mornings than the museums. It is safest to presume that the door clangs to at noon. But they *usually* re-open later, often between 2.30 and 4 p.m. to close at 5 or 6 p.m. (a grey area). Exceptions are San Marco in Florence, which is unwont to re-open in the afternoons. Siena Cathedral, on the other hand, remains open from 9 a.m. to 7.30 p.m.

Post offices

Main post offices, often in the dead centres of towns, stay open throughout the day until 8 p.m., but close for the weekend at Saturday noon. Branch offices close at 1.50 p.m. for the day (11.50 a.m. on the last day of the month).

Not surprisingly, they are often packed. If you are simply after stamps, buy them instead at any tobacconist (*tabacchi*). To speed letters, send them *Espresso* (for 3,100 lire), dropping them into the yellow boxes: it is worth it. In Rome, many use the Vatican Post Office, which is far faster than Italy's.

Siesta

It is pointless trying to do anything during the siesta, the immovable divide of the Italians' day and their solution to summer. It lasts from about 1.30 to 3.30 p.m. at the earliest, the time when the first shops re-open. More usually, it goes on until 4.30 or 5 p.m. In this sacrosanct period, human communication ceases. The way to wreck a friendship is to phone; the way to be noticed in a hotel is to strum a guitar. The way to live with it is to sleep or drive. In theory, civil servants are supposed to straggle back to their offices and yawn there till 8 p.m. Some do not. Any business *has* to be done in the morning.

Telephone

Italy's prefix for incoming calls is 39.

For police and other emergency services that cannot be reached directly: 113.
Ambulance: 5100.
Fire: 115.

The exchange codes for the main towns covered in this book are:

Ancona	071	Montepulciano	0578
L'Aquila	0862	Narni	0744
Arezzo	0575	Norcia	0743
Ascoli Piceno	0738	Orvieto	0763
Assisi	075	Perugia	075
Bevagna	0742	Pesaro	0721
Città della Pieve	0578	Pienza	0578
Civitavecchia	0766	Pisa	050
Cortona	0575	Pistoia	0537
Fabriano	0732	Pitigliano	0564
Fano	0721	Prato	0547
Fermo	0734	Recanati	071
Fiesole	055	Rome	06
Florence	055	Ronta	055
Foligno	0742	San Gimignano	0577
Grosseto	0564	San Miniato	0571
Gubbio	075	San Sepolcro	0575
Jesi	0731	Sarnano	0733
Livorno	0586	Senigallia	071
Loreto	071	Siena	0577
Lucca	0583	Spello	0742
Macerata	0733	Spoleto	0743
Massa Marittima	0566	Todi	075
Montalcino	0577	Urbino	0722
Montecatini	0572	Viterbo	0761
Montefalco	0742	Volterra	0588

Most hotels have direct dialling. To telephone home, dial the outside line (often 9), followed by 00 (international lines) and then for the following countries:

UK: 44 (cost per minute 1,400 lire)
To reverse charges: 15.
USA and Canada: 1 (cost per minute 3,700 lire)
To reverse charges: 170.
To call the US direct from Rome either collect or with a calling card:
172 1011.
Australia: 61 (cost per minute 4,900 lire)
New Zealand: 64 (cost per minute 5,080 lire)
To reverse charges: 170.

Time differences

'Official time', as the Italians call the deviation from 'God's time', is one hour ahead of universal time in winter. From the end of March to the end of September, it is two hours ahead, although still only one hour ahead of British Summer Time.

In the USA, Eastern standard, it is six hours earlier; in Australia (Sydney) nine hours later, and in New Zealand eleven hours later.

Tipping

The Italians tip less generously than foreigners and their example should be followed. There are no set rules but, on the whole, the concept of a service charge *and* a tip is only a glint in the eye of the waiter.

Practice varies, but often when dealing with unworldly foreigners, restaurants add 10–15 per cent to the bill in writing. Italians would leave nothing extra; if you are embarrassed, leave only the small change in the plate or 1,000 lire maximum. If you make a habit of going somewhere, they will eventually leave all the service up to you, as they should. Then 10 per cent will delight. Restaurants do not delight in giving you an official bill (*Ricevuta fiscale*) as they are meant to, since they are spoors the taxman can follow. If they decide you can do without one, the bill can pleasantly shrink.

In bars, it is done to leave 100 lire for each coffee or drink. The hotel porter is worth 2,000 for lugging bags to your room, and the doorman 1,500 for whistling up a taxi. The receptionist would receive 5–10,000 only in cases of special helpfulness – arranging a restaurant or a tour, for instance. Otherwise a mere *arrivederci* will do.

Italians do not tip taxi-drivers unless they help with luggage or old people.

Toilets

You will be convinced at first that Italians have no bladders. The few public toilets that once existed have been boarded up ever since their guardians stalked off with higher ideas. You manage in the bars. By law, their owners are required to allow the public to enjoy their facilities without being customers. Dark and cramped, they are passably clean as a rule, although it is always useful to have been studying the local press beforehand. The majority are orifices in the ground between foot-holds; vigilance over the hip-wallet is wise.

More conventional postures come with the larger restaurants, where hygiene standards are usually a point of honour.

Some Italian

Numbers

One	Uno	Thirteen	Tredici
Two	Due	Fourteen	Quattordici
Three	Tre	Fifteen	Quindici
Four	Quattro	Sixteen	Sedici
Five	Cinque	Seventeen	Diciasette
Six	Sei	Eighteen	Diciotto
Seven	Sette	Nineteen	Diciannove
Eight	Otto	Twenty	Venti
Nine	Nove	One hundred	Cento
Ten	Dieci	Two hundred	Duecento
Eleven	Undici	One thousand	Mille
Twelve	Dodici	Two thousand	Due mila

Around the town

I am	Io sono
We are	Noi siamo
My name is	Mi chiamo
I'm looking for	Cerco
Help!	Aiuto!
Thank you	Grazie
Please	Per cortesia
Good morning	Buongiorno
Good night	Buona notte
How much is it?	Quant'è?
Where is . . . ?	Dov'è?
I like	Mi piace
I don't like	Non mi piace

What is it?	*Che cos'è?*
I'm lost	*Sono perso*
I'm unengaged	*Sono libero*
What's your name?	*Come ti chiami?*
Where are you from?	*Da dove sei?*

Open	*Aperto*
Bus	*Autobus*
Toilet	*Bagno*
Beautiful	*Bella*
Ticket	*Biglietto*
Ugly, awful	*Brutto*
Avenue (in centre)	*Corso*
Centre	*Centro*
Old town	*Centro storico*
Church	*Chiesa*
Closed	*Chiuso*
Cathedral	*Duomo*
Dinner	*Cena*
Stamp	*Francobollo*
Crescent	*Largo*
Parking	*Parcheggio*
Square	*Piazza*
Police	*Polizia*
Don't mention it	*Prego*
Breakfast	*Prima colazione*
Post Office	*PTT*
Too much!	*Troppo!*
Station	*Stazione*
Street	*Via*
Avenue	*Viale*
Alley	*Vicolo*

In the restaurant

Meat	*Carne*
Steak	*Bistecca*
Ox fillet	*Filetto di bue*
Pork	*Maiale*
Veal	*Vitello*
Fish	*Pesce*
We would like a table for two	*Cerchiamo una tavola per due*
Can we have the menu please?	*Ci dia il menù per piacere?*
House wine	*Vino da casa*
What's good tonight?	*Che c'è di buono?*
First course (pasta etc.)	*Primo piatto*

Main course	Secondo piatto
Side dish	Contorno
What's for the last course?	E per dopo?
Could we have the bill please?	Ci dia il conto per cortesia?

For typical names of dishes in Italian, see under 'Eating and Drinking' (pages 51–2).

In the hotel

Have you a room please?	Cè l'ha una camera libera per cortesia?
How much is it?	A quanto viene?
Is breakfast included?	E incluso la prima colazione?
Double-bedded room	Camera matrimoniale
Twin beds	Due letti
Single room	Camera singola
With shower	Con doccia
With toilet	Con bagno
Lift	Ascensore
Key	Chiave

In the car

Car	Macchina	Break-down service	Soccorso stradale
Petrol	Benzina	Accident	Incidente
Tyres	Gomme	Insurance	Assicurazione
Bonnet	Cofano	Traffic light	Semaforo
Boot	Portabagagli	One way	Senso unico
Clutch	Frizione		
Brake	Freno		

The arts

Picture gallery	Pinacoteca	Triptych	Trittico
Museum	Museo	Sculpture	Scultura
Ticket office	Biglietteria	Marble	Marmo
Room	Sala	Wood	Ligneo
Picture	Quadro	Romanesque	Romanico
Canvas	Tela	Renaissance	Rinascimento
Wood panel	Tavola	Masterpiece	Capolavoro
Polyptych	Polittico		

Glossary

Baroque A florid, festive, theatrical style of architecture and sculpture, imprinted with fantasy, typical of seventeenth-century Rome.

Basilica Originally a Greek and then a Roman term for a large, oblong, vaulted public hall, usually supported by rows of columns, dedicated to the administration of justice and business. The halls then became the model for Christian churches, although today a basilica is a special church with a papal throne.

Comune In modern Italian, the town hall, but also used here to mean the independent medieval city or the general medieval movement towards autonomy.

Dossal The upright back of the altar, often decorated. Panels provide repositories for relics, statues and the like.

Gothic Gothic architecture (1150–1400) began vying with Romanesque in Italy in the mid-twelfth century. It began in the Ile de France; its apex is Chartres Cathedral. Imported into Italy by the Cistercians, it was then taken up by the Franciscans. In the original Gothic, the weight of the superstructure did not rest on the walls, but on vertical shafts. The main feature is the upward thrust and its attendant feeling of airiness. Others are ribbed vaults, pointed arches, and richly decorated façades with double spires and triple doors. The Italians, with too much sun for true verticality, refused to get the hang of it. They stunted it with horizontal lines, and went for detail to produce a gothicised Romanesque. Examples can be seen in the cathedrals of Siena and Orvieto.

Loggia An arched structure, open on one or more sides supported by pillars. In the medieval period, these stone canopies were meeting-places for guildsmen. The term can also apply to a series of arched arcades.

Medieval Arbitrarily, the entire period from the end of the Western Empire in 476 to the early fifteenth century.

Municipium A city annexed by Rome which usually enjoyed second-class Roman citizenship – i.e. it had no political rights.

Palazzo Not 'a palace': in modern Italian it can mean a slum tenement or an office block. In this guide it is often a striking building of a medieval city-state, for instance the *Palazzo dei Priori*, the seat of government of the 'Priors', leaders of the main trades guilds. Called *Signori*, they became corporately the *Signoria* in Florence. The *Palazzo del Podestà* is the headquarters of the Chief Executive, an outsider called in to assume government for a two-year spell. He brought his own staff and appeared at the start of the twelfth century, usually when a city's elected *Consoli* admitted incompetence to rule themselves. The *Palazzo (del Capitano) del Popolo* was the seat of the 'Captain', the chosen protector of the power-hungry 'people', conscious of their rights after wars with more senior citizens. He often headed an administration parallel to the Podestà's, but from a separate building.

Pediment   Triangular crowning to a portico.

Polyptych   Painting of four or more folding panels.

Predella   The bottom line of a polyptych, a long strip of scenes often filling in the biography of the personages above it; also the base of an altar piece, with a similar function.

Quattrocento   Literally, 'the four hundred', meaning the years from 1400 to 1499 (the Italians much prefer cardinals to ordinals), hence the fifteenth century. *Cinquecento*, on the same principle, is the sixteenth century.

Renaissance   This is controversial. In this book, it is taken to mean a period of about two centuries, ending with the death of Michelangelo in 1564. It was a flowering of the arts that sprang from a fascinated, sometimes uphill, re-imagination of the classical world, mainly Rome's, and a re-discovery of a man with a body and mind of his own.

Romanesque   Architectural church style dominant between the year 1000 and the early twelfth century, first developed in Lombardy whose builders then moved south. Considered to embody a revival of values in the wake of the barbarians, Romanesque is partially a harkback to the buildings of ancient Rome. Its features are a grandiose conception, pyramid façades, pillared upper galleries, rose windows, often detached bell-towers, and narrative sculpture setting down history and doctrine.

Tondo   Circular painting, usually on canvas or a panel.

Triptych   Altar piece of three hinged panels telling one story.

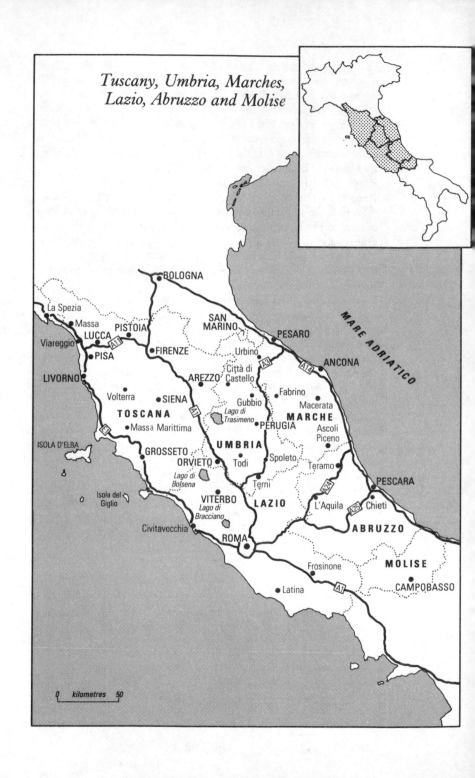

Tuscany, Umbria, Marches, Lazio, Abruzzo and Molise

Gazetteer

Introduction

The regions The five regions of Central Italy – Tuscany, Umbria, the Marches, Lazio, and Abruzzo and Molise – have very separate identities. They are different countries. A boundary is crossed and, with theatrical abruptness, the entire scene changes. The landscape is foreign; so are the colours, the town squares, the faces, the paintings in the galleries.

Tuscany, though far more varied in itself than its popular image suggests, is, in cinematic terms, the panning-shot – all undulating countryside often green with olives, big-screen horizons, sweeping views of plunging valleys from sharp ridge-lines. The people can be tough.

In Umbria, you rarely see so far. The hills wear forest like fur, and enclose you. Except for its two big valleys, its countryside is strangely personal and gentle. It is the land of mystics. The people are quiet.

In the Marches, 'Italy' is unrecognisable. This is a long coastline with a choppy hinterland of naked hills scattered about like marine bollards. Endless valleys slosh around them. The people do not look a bit Latin.

Lazio, or Latium, is Italy's most assorted and newest region. Although centred on the mournful plain around Rome, it is, surprisingly, 80 per cent hilly or mountainous. It takes in the arid Sabine hills to the north-east and, in the south-west, malarial marshes drained under Mussolini. The people do not know who they are.

Abruzzo and Molise is dramatic mountain country, a soaring wilderness with the highest villages in Italy. Peaks dominate. Parts resemble Switzerland. It has bears, snow and no art. The people are reserved and distrustful.

Routes This guide begins in Pisa. That may sound slightly unconventional, but it is based on the assumption that, apart from sun and sea, the main attraction of Central Italy is its exorbitant treasure-hoard, and that great interest lies in following its flowering from start to finish. It was in this snoozing coastal town that the whole artistic awakening in Central Italy began – because of money. Here started the recovery from the Dark Ages, which in Italy were truly dark, because she had had the farthest to fall. Pisa also happens to have a convenient airport.

By stages, the text follows the waking process to Florence where it explodes into the magnificence of the Renaissance. It winds up with the 'transfer' of the Renaissance to Rome, with its flowering of Baroque. It then dwells on the start of the entire cycle – ancient Rome. The artists of the second millennium were for ever checking back on her example.

On the way down to Rome from Pisa, the guide meanders through the regions, each of which denies there was any academic scheme to things, and tells its *own* story to prove it. Their cities remained in the Middle Ages, and their superb medieval towns will take up much of your time.

The most striking are Siena, Perugia and Orvieto; San Gimignano near Siena is high upon the list, but too many others have awarded it the same position. Off this track lies Massa Marittima in the Maremma of Tuscany, a secret gem and, in the extreme south-west of Tuscany near Lake Bolsena, some find little Pitigliano unsurpassable.

Renaissance Italy means, essentially, Florence, Urbino in the Marches, Rome and, down the list, Montepulciano, west of Lake Trasimeno with its gory associations.

Since Roman Italy *is* Rome, this guide is scant about the impact of Rome beyond itself.

Naturally, Pisa, Florence, Siena and Rome will form the star quartet of any visit. Florence, by the way, can be a trap: its galleries impose a sense of duty which, fulfilled, can dull your palate for all the rest. And the rest is rich.

In many towns mentioned here, you could easily spend two or three nights for relaxation but, except for Florence, Rome and perhaps Siena, the actual sights will rarely detain you for more than a night. Florence is worth three at least and Rome five.

If this is your first trip, the Marches and Abruzzo are dispensable extras, fascinating as they both are. But if you want to spend part of your stay driving through untouched mountain scenery, Abruzzo will certainly be your goal. Neglected Lazio is not so disposable, chiefly because of its fascinating places not far from Rome.

For those who want to dilute the past with sea, resorts are listed under separate headings for the east and west coasts. The Italian Health Ministry has passed 88 per cent of the beaches as fit for swimming.

A tour that would exhaust the highlights of Central Italy would exhaust a mule. Planning a route unfortunately must be an act of violent elimination. Many decide on the 'big four' and then explore one region only.

This is the marathon route, which would still leave out a lot: Pisa – Florence – Siena – then far to the north-east through Arezzo for San Sepolcro to see Piero della Francesca – further north-east for Urbino and the Ducal Palace – to Fano on the Adriatic – inland, partly along the *Flaminia*, to see dramatic Gubbio – down into Perugia with side trips to Assisi and Spello – Spoleto – and finally the run down to Rome.

Here is a more compact route: Pisa – Lucca – Florence, with side trips to Siena and San Gimignano – Perugia, as a base for northern Umbria – Todi – Orvieto – Viterbo – the coast past the Etruscan tombs at Tarquinia – south along the *Aurelia* for the big Etruscan necropolis at Cerveteri – Rome.

Tighter still: Pisa – Florence – Siena – Montepulciano – Orvieto – Pitigliano – through the wild Maremma – the beaches at Monte Argentario (Orbetello) – the coastal Etruscan places – Rome.

If you kick off in Rome, a quick survey would be: Rome – Orvieto – Perugia – Gubbio – Cortona – Siena – Florence – Pisa. Rome could also be the launch for Abruzzo and the Marches. The 'new' A 24 motorway towards L'Aquila is the key.

Restaurants Since dinners can boost or ruin a stay, a word is needed about the guidelines behind the choice of restaurants in this book. One basic assumption is that your favourite sport is not money-throwing. Expensive restaurants are mentioned only if they are particularly worth it, and some are. Quality in Italy does not automatically improve with the price; often the contrary happens. In the restaurants listed, your bill should be 'contained'.

Another assumption is that, being in Italy, you will want to dine like Italians, with Italians. A proper restaurant in Italy has little in common with an Italian restaurant abroad. They are much more laid back. Initially, you may be surprised by the choice, since it includes places with the television on and the family, plus children, around the table. This should be clear from the text.

If the listings for each town are not extensive, the reason is human frailty. Each one has either been personally sampled by your author or strongly recommended by reliable sources on the spot, which does restrict the range. Into which of these two categories a restaurant falls should also emerge from the wording. *Buon appetito!*

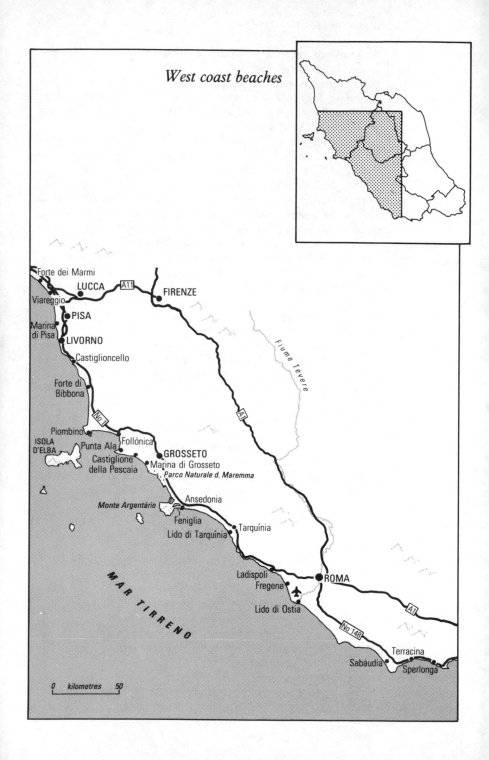

West coast beaches

Forte dei Marmi
LUCCA
A11
FIRENZE
Viareggio
PISA
Marina
di Pisa
LIVORNO
Castiglioncello
Forte di
Bibbona
No 1
Piombino
ISOLA
D'ELBA
Punta Ala
Follónica
Castiglione
della Pescaia
GROSSETO
Marina di Grosseto
Parco Naturale d. Maremma
Ansedonia
Monte Argentário
Feniglia
Lido di Tarquínia
Tarquínia
Fiume Tévere
A1
Ladispoli
Fregene
ROMA
Lido di Ostia
No 148
A1
Terracina
Sabáudia
Sperlonga

MAR TIRRENO

0   kilometres   50

Beaches

West coast

With few, if any, rivals in the Mediterranean, the west coast is the longest-running spectacular in Italy, its sudden vistas making even jaundiced travellers reach for a breath. The scenes switch rapidly – from the tiny cove at the foot of a cliff to endless pine-fringed sand, from a mountain tumbling into blueness to a restful bay.

Of course, it plays to a full house, so avoid August, if at all possible. The following is a guide (north–south) to some 'secret' places with poor audiences, and an indication of what to avoid.

Forte dei Marmi   Some 35 km north of Pisa, this is the smartest resort on the Tuscan coast, with a manicured beach of fine sand, villas of the wealthy among the pines, and famous nightclubs. It is a favourite of the Agnelli family. It offers sailing, horse-riding and golf.

Viareggio   Next-door to the south, this is Benidorm Italian-style – i.e. less coarse. It is the biggest and most popular seaside town in the country, set among pine woods with two hundred hotels and ten camp-sites.

Marina di Pisa   Now a crowded, unlovely Pisan suburb with a mean, rocky beach. It is noted for its fish restaurants.

Castiglioncello   A picturesque resort of bays and cliffs south of Livorno, with 2 km of sand and rocks. The drawback is that it is packed.

Forte di Bibbona   11 km south of Cecina, this village has seven hotels and an extensive soft-sand beach against a pine-wood backcloth in reclaimed swamp land. It has five camp-sites.

Follonica   This is an ugly place, with a crowded strip of beach and dirty water. If you have come down from Massa Marittima in need of change, do move on to:

Punta Ala   This is 20 km further on, at the tip of the sweeping Gulf of Follonica. Take the SS 322 and turn right at Pian d'Alma. It is an exclusive residential resort, smothered by pines, adopted by polo-playing Milanese. Park under the trees to your right before you arrive and walk through them; they conceal the Gulf.

Riva del Sole   17 km south of Follonica on the SS 322, this holiday bungalow village was founded in the 1950s by Swedes for their sun-starved countrymen. It even runs to a Swedish vice-consul, but its large four-star hotel is open to all; tel. 0564-933625.

Castiglione della Pescaia   5 km further on, this is a well-heeled fishing village for reasonably heeled Italians. Towered over by its walled medieval quarter and fifteenth-century fort, it is the door to a splendid 'confidential' beach. Whereas unsightly bathing establishments flank both sides of the township, just to the south is an immense fenced-off pine forest. Tracks through it lead to almost deserted fine sand and clean water, with no man-made structure in sight.

Though it is like climbing a flagpole, don't miss the fort. This gives perhaps the most sweeping view of the entire coast.

The four-star **Hotel L'Approdo** is the smartest: 29 Via Ponte Giorgini; tel. 0564-933466. A few yards away is the older **Hotel Roma**, 14 Via C. Colombo; tel. 933542. The three-star, fairly priced, **Miramar** at 35 Via Veneto, tel. 933524, overlooks the beach. All of these have restaurants, which are recommended in preference to those in town, which are a rip-off.

Marina di Grosseto   A concrete slum.

Principina a Mare, 5 km further on, is a residential holiday township beneath the pines with powdery sand and dunes on the edge of the 15 km long Maremma Nature Reserve. Dead, but also dead quiet! The two large hotels have sensible full-board rates: the four-star **Hotel Principe**, tel. 0564-34598, and the three-star **Hotel Grifone**, tel. 34300.

Monte Argentario, 30 km further south, is the picture-postcard playground of Italy's rich. Once an island, it is now linked to everyday life by two natural causeways and a dyke. In the pretty pirate harbours of Porto San Stefano and Port'Ercole, occupied by the Spanish for 150 years, masts sway gently and bangles click on slim wrists. Caravaggio died here, in 1610. A fine, long, sandy beach is on the southern causeway, called *Feniglia*.

Ansedonia   A steep promontory overlooking the southern causeway, conserves the ruins of **Cosa**, once a flourishing Roman trading centre, laid to waste by the Visigoths. The trees also hide a maze of millionaires' villas. The rocky beach is tiny.

Decent beaches now disappear until well south of Rome. **Lido di Tarquinia**, **Ladispoli**, **Fregene** and **Ostia**, the seaside of Rome, are lower-income resorts happily dedicated to noise, chaos, *bambini*, crowding, bathing cabins, black sand and muddyish sea-water.

Il Buco is the unofficial name for a long stretch of beach, 8 km south of Ostia, screened from the road by bushes and dunes, thronged by Rome's nudists, gay and female. The beach is litter-strewn, the sea like minestrone.

Sabaudia, about 90 km south of Rome below Anzio, is a soulless Mussolini new town, built in 1933 on a coastal lake amid ordered greenery. It is frequented by older Romans who appreciate clean beaches and water as well as staid tranquillity.

Sperlonga, 110 km from Rome, just after Terracina, is a natural jewel, a whitewashed Italian casbah. There are two long, sandy beaches, overlooked by hills and a (now arty) medieval township of steps and covered alleys on a sheer spur. The ancient Romans turned its coastal caves into 'places of pleasure', as they say. Tiberius was one of those Romans, as the ruins of the cave named after him bear witness. The setting of the southern beach, skirting a sweeping bay, has been wisely left intact, and the water is limpid. It is, unfortunately, crowded in August but less so mid-September. There are also hidden beaches beneath the cliffs between Sperlonga and the medieval **Gaeta**, 18 km south. The **Hotel Aurora** overlooks the sea; tel. 0771-54114/54014.

Adriatic

The beaches of the east coast are the northern Europeans' new invasion route, although 80 per cent of the forms on the sand belong to Italians, especially from Umbria. Some 170 km long, the coast of the Marches is dead flat; except at two points only, the hills keep their distance, and it is mainly bathing-establishment territory, choked by umbrella plantations (the Italians deal with the sun by avoiding it). You pay to enter.

The Adriatic is sick, polluted by industrial waste and fertiliser chemicals seeping into it from the Po, where an unpleasant, but apparently unharmful, jelly-like kind of seaweed rises to the surface. Stringent laws are now on the books to purge the Po, with funds earmarked. Whether the many authorities and interests involved are able to co-operate to enforce them remains to be seen. The water does improve with progress south.

Pesaro is one of the places where the hills come down to the sea. The modern adjunct of this ancient city is a serried procession of see-through three-star hotels along an extensive beach. Sedate, quiet, it deliberately caters for older people, and is favourite with the British. The Tourist Office is at 164 Viale Trieste, 61100 Pesaro; tel. 0721-69341. For recommended hotels, see page 197.

Fano, 11 km further south, was once a resort for the idle rich of the 1930s. Its two beaches, the southern one pebbly, are more part of the town than at Pesaro. Its *riviera* stretches south for 20 km, dotted with twenty-one camping sites. The Tourist Office is at 10 Viale Cesare Battisti, Fano; tel. 0721-803534. For recommended hotels, see page 198.

Senigallia, 24 km further on, is unashamedly the biggest resort town in the northern Marches. Its 120 hotels march down the prom in close order, slightly dated. But the beach goes on for 7 km with long

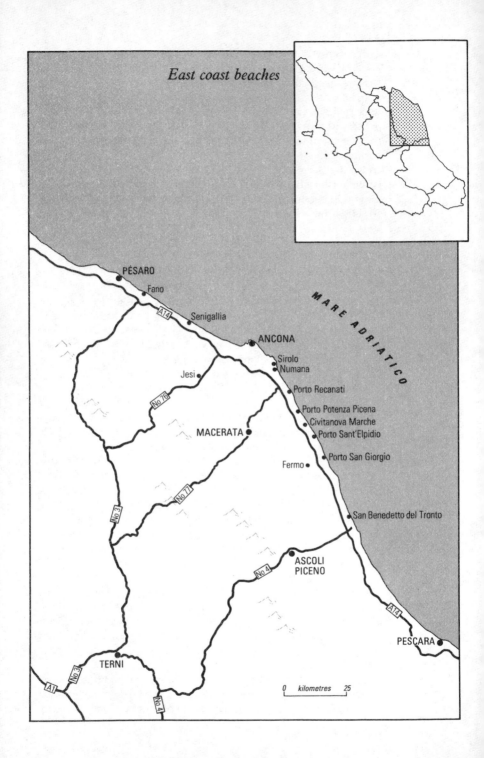

East coast beaches

M A R E   A D R I A T I C O

PÉSARO
Fano
A14
Senigallia
ANCONA
Sirolo
Numana
Jesi
Porto Recanati
Porto Potenza Picena
Civitanova Marche
MACERATA
Porto Sant'Elpidio
Porto San Giorgio
Fermo
San Benedetto del Tronto
No 76
No 77
No 3
No 4
ASCOLI
PICENO
No 3
A1
A14
PESCARA
TERNI
No 4

0   kilometres   25

'free' chunks and camping sites. It aims at the Italian middle class, with 'Nights' and clock-golf. The Tourist Office is at 2 Piazzale Morandi, 60019 Senigallia; tel. 071-62150.

Where to stay The smartest hotel is the four-star **Larche**, 20 Lungomare Marconi; tel. 071-6113. Or try the three-star **Adriatico**, 69 L. D. Alighieri; tel. 61451, or, also along the promenade, the **Metropol**, Lungomare L. da Vinci; tel. 65576.

A two-star hostelry on the same stretch is the **Nettuno**, 19 L. L. da Vinci; tel. 61481.

The beach fizzles out north of Ancona, the second place where high ground abuts the water. Below the bulge lies **Sirolo**, a manicured suburbia atop the cliffs, with three camp-sites. Next door is rather chic **Numana**, a small place ringed in by hills, with a fine pebble beach curving off into the distance for 5 km. The Tourist Office is at 14 Via Marcello Marini, Ancona; tel. 071-201980.

Where to stay The smartest hotel is the four-star **Numana Palace**, tel. 071-930156 (no address needed). There are also the three-star **Scogliera**, tel. 936152 and the two-star **Gabbiano**, tel. 937114.

That ends the coastal variation. At **Porto Recanati**, 10 km further down, the first buildings went up in the thirteenth century, and it remains a bit old-fashioned and down-at-heel.

Where to stay **Enzo**, 21 Via Matteotti; tel. 071-97684.

Royal, 1 Via dei Pini; tel. 979 6446. Three-star.

The crowds and the kids are at Porto Potenza Picena, Civitanova Marche, Porto San Elpidio and, above all, at **Porto San Giorgio**, the harbour of ancient Fermo, up in the hills. This sprang up around a thirteenth-century village, and takes pleasure craft.

Where to stay The only four-star hotel is **Il Timone**, 61 Via Kennedy; tel. 0734-49536. On the prom is the three-star **Piceno**, Lungomare Gramsci; tel. 678001.

The biggest, most modern resort of the Marches is **San Benedetto del Tronto**, some 90 km south of Ancona. It is pure tourist industry: an endless line of 124 modern hotels, mostly three-star, with 20,000 beds. It has pretensions to exotic elegance. It is smothered by palm trees, and offers shady walks. *No* dodgems. Its guests are 85 per cent Italian. It offers 5 km of beach and, for once, clean water.

Where to stay The choice is bewildering. All the hotels are near the sea, but some are a hike from the harbour and the centre.

The four-star **Ambassador** is at 5 Via Cimarosa; tel. 0735-659201.

The equally-starred **Sabbiadoro** (Golden Sands) is at 46 Lungomare Marconi; tel. 81987.

In the three-star class there are the **Michelangelo**, Viale Rinascimento; tel. 659715; the **Beaurivage**, 92 Viale Europa; tel. 81682; and the **Camiscioni**, 32 Viale Trieste; tel. 85603.

The many two-stars include the **Olimpo**, 78 Viale Europa; tel. 82194; and the **Persico**, 5 Viale Rinascimento; tel. 656334.

Tuscany

Bagni di Lucca •

Pistoia •
Montecatini
Terme •
Prato •

LUCCA •
Poggio a Caiano •

Borgo
San
Lorenzo •

Fiume Sieve

Pratolino •
Fiesole •

Rufina •

Caprese
Michelangelo •

Vinci •
Cerreto Guidi •

FIRENZE •

Fiume Arno

San Sepolcro •

PISA •

Fiume Arno

No 67

Empoli •

Impruneta •

Anghiari •

San Miniato •

San Casciano
in Val di Pesa •

Fiume Greve

Greve in
Chianti •

Arezzo •

Monterchi •

LIVORNO •

Certaldo •

Radda in Chianti •

A1

San Gimignano •
Colle di Val d'Elsa •

Monteriggioni •

Cortona •

Volterra •

Abbadia Isola

SIENA •

Larderello •
Castelnuovo di Val
di Cecina •

No 2

Sinalunga •

COLLINE METALLIFERE

Montepulciano •
Pienza •

Montalcino •

Chiusi •

Massa
Marittima •

San Quirico
d' Orcia •

Roccatederighi •

No 223

Fiume Orcia

Montepescali •

GROSSETO •

Sovana •

_Parco Naturale
d. Maremma_

Pitigliano •

ISOLA D'ELBA

No 1

0   _kilometres_   30

Isola del Giglio

Tuscany

Introduction

Tuscany *is* Central Italy.

It can, and does, speak for the rest. It cannot claim to have Rome in its orbit, of course. Rome has Roman ruins, the Papacy, and Baroque art. But the Tuscans have all the rest.

Tuscany is the biggest region in the Centre and, in terms of treasure, by far the wealthiest and most varied in Italy. Nowhere else have you so much wonder to wonder at and so much to do – from swimming off deserted dunes to being jostled by crowds in a gallery. In one morning, you can gaze out over vast panoramas and contemplate the works of a neglected genius in the quiet of his home town.

Unlike other regions, Tuscany has always had a sharply defined identity, a sense of unity. When it was much bigger than it is now, it more or less coincided with Etruria, the land of the Etruscans, from whom it gets its name. The Tuscans carried forward their forebears' love of art and expression. It was they who brought about the huge innovations that revolutionised the old way of looking at life. Out of their crucible, you could almost say, emerged the West. You can see the very first stirring of Western art in the painted crucifixes and altar pieces in the museum at Pisa. Tuscany produced Giotto, the father of modern painting.

Tuscany also produced Italian – in the person of Dante. His language in *The Divine Comedy*, nearly seven centuries old, is still basically today's, although the now vaguely accepted catchword for modern spoken Italian is 'Tuscan tongue in Roman mouth.'

Tuscany is dotted with imperative medieval towns, grand and aloof. It is the region of the Renaissance, and Florence. The only other city like it was ancient Athens. Here lay patronage of art began. This identity is reflected in almost every village; stop anywhere and you will light upon *something* that delights – a Paleo-Christian church or a hidden picture-gallery.

History

Tuscany can stand both for Central Italy's violent past – the razed town, the dripping dagger, the warring families, the small-town fanaticism – and for the Italy of today, facing pollution, urban sprawl, sudden wealth and the open market of 1992.

Here you will still travel roads laid down by the Romans – the

Aurelia and the *Cassia*. Florence was then *Florentia*, 'The Bountiful One'. After the butchery of the population by invading Goths, the fair-haired Lombards streamed down into Italy with their wives and household effects. For two long centuries, they ran Tuscany as a duchy from Lucca, and the masons who later built the Romanesque churches were their descendants.

When Charlemagne, acting for the Pope, routed them in battle, he annexed Tuscany to his Empire and ruled through viceroys. But with the death of the last, the formidable Countess Matilda, central authority in Tuscany melted and the restless cities grabbed independence. Nobles and bishops were stripped of power and the new republics were born.

Most of the splendid medieval city centres in Tuscany went up in the twelfth and thirteenth centuries during the new era of assertiveness, wealth and stormy civic life. The perfect outlet for the rivalry between the cities was the epic struggle between Church and State. Tuscans sided with one or the other as a pretext for striking the nearest enemy, or to wheedle favours out of Pope or Emperor. Their land became a chess-board of competing interests. Despite fickleness, Florence (on the whole) was Guelf; neighbouring Siena was Ghibelline. Lucca was Guelf, so aggressive Pisa nearby shouted for the Emperor.

Pisa was once Tuscany's most powerful city, but she faded away with Florentine expansionism. In 1125, Fiesole was razed to the ground. Other moons sucked into Florence's orbit were also frizzled: Arezzo, San Gimignano, Volterra. Pisa, the arch-rival, buckled under in 1406; Siena much later.

But the turbulence of democracy was tiring and, one by one, the republics opted for a quieter life under a strong man, or *Signore*. In Florence, the name was Medici, a dynasty that ruled Florence for three centuries. Initially, they were intellectuals – rich, scheming, talented. Without them, the Renaissance seems almost unimaginable. At first they governed in the guise of ordinary citizens. But in the sixteenth century, a Medici Pope named one of them a duke, and one-man rule was formalised for good. When the line ran out in the eighteenth century, Tuscany was, grandly, turned over to the Hapsburgs.

For four centuries, Tuscany had been the motor of Italy, in the vanguard of Europe, and the heritage she amassed is still astonishingly intact. Pisa produced a triumph of Romanesque architecture by seeing it through a Pisan prism. This was where chisels first brought 'Italian' sculpture to light, and you will find great crucifixes there betraying the first stirrings of the 'new art' in painting.

The scene then shifts to Siena, the great little Gothic city of Tuscany, where the very special Sienese school – all gold and serene Madonnas – was already prolific in the thirteenth century, and teaching Florence something.

But in the fifteenth century, Florence dominated absolutely. Donatello was the new giant of sculpture; the Renaissance architect Brunelleschi was at work; Botticelli was all the rage, and Michelangelo had not yet moved to Rome.

Tuscans and their land

The 3½ million Tuscans outnumber Romans by a small margin, but the other peoples of Central Italy by far. They are 'superior', stingy, a bit racist, practical, brusque, hard-working, fair and untheatrical, talented and creative, with solid peasant stock behind them. But today only 10 per cent of them work in agriculture. Many former farmers are now in ship-building, chemical and service industries. Thousands are still craftsmen. The Communist Party dominates the region.

Tuscany is a country in itself, immensely varied; Tuscans may have a united outlook on things, but no one part of their land is quite united with another. There are two common denominators, though. Tuscany's hills and minor mountains, quilted with woods or splashed with the green of the olives, are more or less educated: they are never rough or haughty and rarely jagged, but rounded, curvaceous, often with the grace of waves. Only a tenth of Tuscany is flat. And in Tuscany nature is trimmed to the needs of man. The human hand is everywhere; little is left to chance. The Tuscans claim, with some smugness, that their treatment of nature never transgresses the tenets of good taste, as they put it. Otherwise, it is every hill for itself.

Orientation and where to go

In the north-west, the sheer Apuan Alps look down on the sea from close quarters. Then comes the broad, boiling basin between Pisa and Florence: though the river Arno skirts it, they have found no real name for this part; I suggest the Ellipse. The Mugello is the Florentines' great natural park to the north, a fresh, green basin rimmed by mountains and named after the Apennine range overlooking it. Eastern Tuscany is known by its river valleys: they are the Valdarno (Valley of the Arno), superseded lower down by the Val di Chiana (both are followed by the A 1 motorway) and, in the extreme east, the Val Tiberina.

Neither has anyone come up with one word for what is to the west of Chianti-land: the huge expanse of wilder, untidier hill-country stretching to the sea. It evades definition. Here, Tuscany can mean graceful and rounded hill-country, near Siena; it can be a forlorn place with cracked, unpeopled hills of clay, or grandly remote with sweeping contours as it is around lonely Volterra.

Southern Tuscany has the grandiose, often empty landscapes roughly south of Siena, where you are frequently on the roof, commanding vast, breathtaking panoramas from sinuous ridge lines, or else gazing up at medieval fortified villages clinging to the tops of hills. The Maremma, on the other hand, is the vast, thinly populated coastal plain in the extreme south-west run by Grosseto, once malarial and desolate, backed by mountains, where a few wild boar still root about, together with the last of Tuscany's 'cowboys', the *butteri*.

For many, Tuscany is at its most beautiful in the Chianti region, almost the emblem of the Tuscan countryside and certainly the most popular. The pastime, of course, is wine-tasting. But there is a fiercely medieval Tuscany, too, where the fascination is with halted time up in those scattered hill settlements, still almost exactly as they were in the thirteenth or fourteenth century, when the obsession was defence. They are mainly in what was the old, and large, Republic of Siena, to the north-west of the city, where the medieval standard-bearer is bold San Gimignano; or down to the west of the Val di Chiana.

The least-known part of Tuscany is the Maremma, but it is being discovered and is worth exploring. The townships not to miss down there are Pitigliano and nearby Sovana. If you want to witness the Renaissance at work in the countryside, the main objectives will be Montepulciano, amazing little Pienza, and Colle Val d'Elsa.

Apart from Florence, Siena and Pisa, the main artistic towns – *città d'arte*, they are called – with striking medieval squares, sculpture and painting to show, are Lucca, San Miniato, Pistoia, Prato, San Gimignano, Massa Marittima and, hard up against the border with Umbria, little San Sepolcro. But nearly every little church you come across hides a rare fresco or canvas.

Finally, it would be a pity to miss the monastery of Monte Oliveto Maggiore, just to the south of Siena with a famed fresco cycle, and the remote, perfect Romanesque church of Sant' Antimo, south of Montalcino.

Food and wine Tuscan cooking is simple, unpretentious and country-like, based on thoroughly fresh ingredients, olive oil and hill-country winters. It tends towards game, and some palates may miss lightness. Specialities include: Florentine bean soup (broad beans in oil with onions, garlic, black cabbage, celery and tomato sauce); *Pappardelle alla Lepre* (lasagne with a savoury sauce made from fillet of hare); Florentine mixed fry (brains, sweetbread, artichokes, aubergines and lamb chops with an egg browning); sweet and strong hare (cooked in a sauce of vinegar, sugar, egg and chocolate).

Tuscany's wine is Chianti, a generic name for a score of wines, both red and white, bottled in and around the original Chianti Classico area. But for many the greatest wine in Tuscany is the ruby-coloured Brunello from Montalcino. Another lordly wine is that of Montepulciano, and many swear by the dry-white Vernaccia from San Gimignano (for details, see under each town).

The other DOC (certified origin) wines in Tuscany are: Bianco di Pitigliano (in Maremma); Elba Bianco; Elba Rosso; Rosso delle Colline Lucchesi (Hills of Lucca); Montecarlo (nearby); Parrina (south of Grosseto); Bianco Vergine Val di Chiana (near Montepulciano); Carmignano (between Florence and Pistoia); Bianco Val di Nievole (south of Pistoia); Montescudaio (inland from

TUSCANY

Cecina); Morellino di Scansano (Maremma, south-west of Grosseto); Bianco Pisano di San Torpé (south-east of Pisa); Candida dei Colli Apuani (Apuan); Pomino (near Rufina, east of Florence); and Bolgheri (near the coast south of Cecina).

Northern Tuscany

Pisa

This is the door to Central Italy, a sleepy town (population 100,000) of arcades and small squares straddling a sharp bend in the river Arno. Many visitors simply snap the Leaning Tower and race off to grander Florence, which is a pity. Pisa merits a good look and an overnight stay.

Getting there
Pisa airport, *Galileo Galilei*, is the convenient starting point for Central Italy. British Airways and Alitalia fly in and out daily. The cheapest summer (July–September) return flights from London in early 1989 cost £193. Half a dozen charter companies also use the airport, but they do not charge much less. They are CIT; Global; Pegasus; Pilgrim Air and Solemar (Glasgow).

Daily flights from New York connect via Rome; arrivals from Sydney to Rome can pick up Pisa flights three times a day.

An advantage of Pisa is that it is less plagued by strikes than other Italian airports: it is shared by the military, who take over if civilians stop work.

Airline officials strongly warn against using Pisa on summer weekends because of charter congestion. Opened in 1966, the airport is now being enlarged. On the return trip, they urge use of the new check-in terminal at Florence station which gives you the first call on seats.

To the right of the arrivals hall, seven **car hire** firms vie for custom: Hertz, Europcar, Maggiore, Avis, Eurodrive, Budget and Interrent. All let you leave the car in another place. Collision Damage Waiver is recommended, covering you against damage to car.

Uniquely in Italy, **trains** wait outside the back door of Pisa airport. Hourly they speed off to Florence, stopping after five minutes at Pisa Central station. They also go to Lucca, Montecatini and Pistoia. **Buses** leave every eight minutes for Pisa Central, taking six minutes.

Booking: British Airways (in Florence): tel. 055-218655. Alitalia (in Pisa): tel. 050-501570.

By car
Pisa sits on the coastal road, the *Aurelia* (SS 1), 64 km south of La Spezia. It is 490 km up from Rome on the same road and a left-turn off from the A 12 Genova–Livorno motorway. By motorway from Nice takes roughly four and a half hours.

85

By train | On the main west coast line, Pisa stops fast trains from the Riviera, Northern France and Switzerland, including the Paris–Rome *Palatino*, which otherwise snubs Tuscany. From Rome, two daily inter-cities take three hours. There are commuter links to Florence, and you should change at Empoli for a single-track section to Siena.

A seafaring power | The astounding artistry you will find in Pisa would never have happened if the city had not once been a powerful and feared maritime republic, a master of the Mediterranean. Power brought it wealth it had to show off, and a new style.

Before it silted up, its port was a major naval base under the Roman Empire. But Pisa really made its name as a naval power by crushing the spread of the Saracens in the Mediterranean. It chased them out of Sardinia in the eleventh century and then its great fleet defeated them at Palermo. Next it craftily supplied the transport for the First Crusade. That led to colonies and trade, and a gift from the Pope in the form of Corsica. It also backed the German Emperors, to be rewarded with much Italian coastline.

In the twelfth and thirteenth centuries its ships, raiding parties and merchants were everywhere, from Constantinople and Egypt to Spain and North Africa, especially Tunisia. This was Pisa's Golden Age; already the proud city fathers had chosen to build a cathedral which would cry out glory for good. They could never have dreamt that they would succeed so well, or that in the twentieth century, Pisa would still be the melting-pot it was then: 'The city runs foul with pagans,' a twelfth-century reporter noted. 'Turks, Libyans, Parthians and loathsome Chaldeans sail along her shores.'

But glory faded fast. First the Pisan fleet was sunk in a sea-battle with Genoa, which inflamed violent local feuding. Chronic dissension ensued. Strong men were hired and fired. Finally, after a long siege in 1405, Pisa was defeated by Florence, which was desperate for a sea port; it swallowed up Pisa for good in 1509. Since then the city has been asleep, cosily wrapped in its past. But its creative spirit had withered away long before, money and confidence gone.

Today, Pisa lives off unseen industry, tourism and young people: they attend the second oldest university in Italy after Bologna, and the army training centres. You will also see American servicemen from a nearby supply depot. The town council is left-wing.

A proverb goes: 'Better a death in the house than a Pisan on the threshold!' That was when its raiders were known for looting, pillage and indifference to maidenhood. A little of this still sticks: they are considered rude and a bit rough, but quick to help those in need.

What to see

The Cathedral complex | In the Campo dei Miracoli (Field of the Miracles), a grassy oasis on the northern bank of the Arno just within the far walls, is the Cathedral. It looks dismantled: the baptistry and the bell-tower stand apart. Work began in 1064, the first shell-burst of a new, creative age.

At first sight, the dazzling symmetry of the group blots out the tourist occupation army, the stalls, the vendors. It has been called a poem in space, a giant's chess-board. Medieval architecture sought, above all, to cause wonder, to move the soul, and nowhere else in Central Italy does it succeed on such a scale and with such harmony.

Why did they build so far from the centre, virtually in the suburbs? The current theory is simply lack of space anywhere else. They put it on the site of an ancient cemetery, where Longobard skeletons still surface.

This is the prototype of Pisan Romanesque architecture – a blending of the robust style of the post-barbaric revival and the taste for things Oriental developed by the sea-roaming Pisans. The festive stripes of marble, those upper galleries of small pillars, the pyramid façade, and a dome faintly reminiscent of Istanbul are the hallmarks. They set a trend far and wide.

The Leaning Tower

You buy a token and push through a turnstile, as if it were a fun-fair novelty. People who take the 294 steps too fast will feel they are being tipped into the void with no right of appeal. The Tower's seven storeys and belfry lean to the south 5.3 metres away from the vertical. The seventh storey overhangs the first by 2.97 metres. It is 54.8 metres high if measured on the north side and 55.65 metres on the south. In 1988 it leant over further by 1.29 mm; it has budged by the same amount yearly for the past sixty years. At that rate, the experts claim, and if other factors remain constant, it will be another 200 years before it keels over. They declare there is no cause for alarm.

But the lean has always foxed them. They quarrelled among themselves for centuries over whether it was deliberate, for instance. The agreed answer today is: partly. But not from the outset. It was started in 1173 in good faith, but twelve years later, when the builders had reached the third landing, the ground suddenly caved in. Work was suspended for ninety years.

Records of the time pass over the disaster in silence, as if the stunted thing had brought shame to the city. But then, with a leap of the imagination, they decided to go ahead again and build at the angle nature had suggested. Work was stopped at the seventh storey in 1286 when a test revealed a further alarming tilt. They took courage again and, a century later, the belfry was gingerly added.

The belfry weighs 750 tons, and periodically somebody suggests removing it to lighten the burden; decapitation of the tower is one of the ideas usually put to dithering committees convened every year or two. Another is to prop it up with ugly buttresses; a third is to stiffen the clay beneath it. The committees just listen.

The Tower was not the first cylindrical one in Italy, but the circular colonnades and the animated spiralling effect, brought about by 180 small columns, were absolutely new. Its lean in fact deflects from what a Pisan academic calls 'one of the most original works of art in the Europe of the Middle Ages.' It is Islam italianised. And matching

The Baptistry

detail binds it perfectly to the rest of the group.

Begun in 1152 when Pisa was at the height of her power, the circular Baptistry was made to resemble a great bejewelled crown. It matches, perhaps too carefully, the Cathedral, but nowadays it is mainly seen as a monument to Nicola Pisano (1200?–1284), considered to be the first modern sculptor. This genius revived the forgotten art and prepared the way for the sculpture of the Renaissance and for Michelangelo. He and his helpers did many of the human and animal heads, the busts of saints above the upper colonnade, but his masterpiece is the hexagonal pulpit inside, atop granite pillars resting on lions. The thronged five upper panels tell the New Testament story and conjure up the Final Judgement.

Nicola's inspiration was classical; he was among the first sculptors to go back to learn from Latin and Greek models, and his three-dimensional figures do indeed have a classical air, although they were brought up to date and moulded unmistakably on Tuscans. This pulpit is for many the apex of Tuscan Romanesque sculpture. The Pisans so valued it that they immediately passed a bye-law to have it permanently guarded.

The Cathedral

Buscheto, the architect who began the Cathedral, is buried (literally) within the vivid, encrusted façade. Inside, Pisa's Islamic dimension is most outspoken in the grandiose arches holding up the cupola. But what most matters, again, is the pulpit, this time the work of Nicola Pisano's son Giovanni (1240?–1320). It took him eight years and he finished it fifty years after his father's.

But despite such a short gap, the style has utterly changed: Romanesque has vanished. This pulpit ranks as a highlight of Gothic sculpture in Italy, and is highly emotional. Look, for instance, at the dramatic panel of Herod surveying scenes of horror as his men flail their way through the desperate mothers. In the Last Judgement, the damned rejected by the angels tumble into the mouths of monsters.

Hard by hangs a grimy chandelier known as 'Galileo's Lamp'. Tradition has it that Galileo, Pisa's most renowned son, kept watching it as the sacristan set it in motion by lighting it. And so he hit upon a notion that bred his law on pendulums, which relates the extent of the sway to the length of the swayed. Kill-joy experts dourly argue that the lamp was put up later.

The monumental cemetery

Skirting the city walls, this marble rectangle encasing the green of the old cemetery, started in 1277, once housed perhaps the greatest collection of fourteenth- and fifteenth-century frescoes in existence. But in July 1944, an American shell fired from 9 km south of the Arno (then the German front line) set its roof ablaze during curfew, and most of them were lost for good. You can see something of what was saved and restored, including the striking *Triumph of Death*, in which a fourteenth-century nobleman, out hunting with his ladies, suddenly comes upon a terrifying scene of tombs and devils.

The Cathedral museum

Close to the Leaning Tower, the carefully arranged *Museo dell'Opera del Duomo* is a natural follow-up to the Cathedral complex: it's the haven for threatened sculptures once outside. So you get a rare close-up of the bigger figures by Nicola Pisano and especially by his son Giovanni. There is also work by another family, Andrea Pisano (1273–1349), and his sons Nino and Tommaso. Between them, these five artists from Pisa dominated Italian sculpture for almost two centuries, until domination by Florence throttled the Pisan spirit. Giovanni Pisano's most popular composition, a Madonna and Child in ivory, is in room 9. From the museum, once a nuns' cloister, there are also unusual close views of the Leaning Tower.

National Museum of San Matteo

When Pisa was powerful, painting bloomed in profusion, and a 15-minute walk away, on the north bank of the Arno, this former Benedictine nunnery puts on one of the richest displays of twelfth- and thirteenth-century painting in Tuscany. It is in the Piazza San Matteo, Lungarno Mediceo.

Go via the most unusual square in town, the Piazza Cavalieri, the political centre of Republican (i.e. 'free') Pisa, with half a dozen getaways. The weirdly striking *palazzo* with the outside staircase, smothered in graffiti, was designed by the Medici as headquarters of a new (sixteenth-century) order of knights, St Stephens, which were set up to rid the coasts of Moorish pirates. In the *palazzo* opposite, a commander of the Pisan fleet was starved to death with his sons and nephews, accused of plotting a coup d'état. Dante put him in Hell.

In the (rather crude) museum, the earliest paintings are great crucifixes, brought in from churches damaged in the Second World War. The best known, upstairs left, are by Giunta Pisano, an innovator who stresses Christ the human being, the first official painter for the Franciscans who, after all, 'domesticated' God.

Other Christs are 'triumphant' with wide-open eyes and serene features. One of the Gallery's treasures is from much later on – a polyptych by the Sienese court painter Simone Martini. After defeat by Florence, Pisan painting withered away as well.

As for sculpture, besides more Giovanni Pisano, you will find a lovely so-called Madonna with Milk, in gilded marble by Andrea and Nino Pisano, and a bronze bust of a saint by Donatello, one of his first works, which came to Pisa as a gift.

Where to stay

Top range

Hoteliers all urge booking ahead in the summer.

The best, and dearest, hotel is the modern four-star **Cavalieri**, conveniently facing the station and widely known for its excellent restaurant: 2 Piazza della Stazione; tel. 43290.

Next best is the nearby four-star **D'Azeglio**, 18 Piazza V. Emanuele; tel. 500310.

Yards from the Cathedral is the four-star modern, but slipping, **Grand Hotel Duomo**, 94 Via Santa Maria; tel. 561894.

Mid range

Overlooking the Arno is a faded old lady, the nineteenth-century three-star **Royal Victoria**, once *the* hotel, where the Duke of Wellington stayed (ask for room 212). It is at 12 Lungarno Pacinotti; tel. 23381.

A well-spoken-of hotel, near the Cathedral, is the **Villa Kinzica** at 4 Piazza Arcivescovado; tel. 560419.

Bottom range

In the same piazza, Arcivescovado, at no. 1, is the one-star **Gronchi**; tel. 561823.

Where to eat

All agree that the best place for Pisan cooking is **Da Bruno**, in the Via Luigi Bianchi; tel. 550964 (closed Monday evenings and Tuesdays). It is friendly and professional under straw lampshades, with jugs and plates on the walls. The fare is robust, rich and unambiguous. Specialities include baked lamb, chopped boar and Pisan soup.

More aloof, in the same area, but business-like is the **Emilio**, at 26 Via Roma; tel. 26028 (closed Mondays). It is patronised by the local football team, as the photos testify.

Also recommended is the **Sergio**, near the river at 1 Lungarno Pacinotti, tel. 48245 (closed Sundays and Monday lunchtime).

The most reliable of the more economical places near the Cathedral is the **Ristorante Duomo**, 70 Via Roma; tel. 582325 (closed Mondays).

Tourist Offices are at Piazza Duomo (near the museum); tel. 560464, and at 42 Lungarno Mediceo (by the river); tel. 20351.

Livorno

Few would recommend a long holiday in Livorno (Leghorn), 20 km south of Pisa, Tuscany's main port and a bastion of the Italian Communist Party, which was founded there in 1921. But it is a hotel kitty and transit point: ferries leave for Corsica, Elba and Sardinia.

Allied pilots blew up Livorno's history in 1943–5; it is now a rehash. It was built by the Medicis as a 'new town', perhaps the first in Europe, to give Tuscany a new outlet to the sea after the silting-up of Pisa. You can still stroll around their Royal Moat and through a quiet canal quarter called 'New Venice'. A massive Medici fortress of 1650 dominates it. In part, Livorno flourished because of foreign communities, including a hefty British contingent, initially attracted by a 1593 constitution guaranteeing asylum to all fleeing persecution.

Italy's spruce Naval Academy hides in the leafy southern suburb of Ardenza (your author once taught there). Byron and Shelley both lived thereabouts, understandably: the coastal rocky inlets and cliffs to the south are wild and beautiful.

Where to stay

The **Boston** is close to the port at 40 Piazza Mazzini; tel. 882333. It is small and efficient; insist on a back room.

The **Gran Duca**, facing the port entrance at 16 Piazza Micheli; tel.

32024, is more rarified, but refuses credit cards.

Both are three star.

Where to eat

The **Angelo d'Oro**, close to the Hotel Boston, is cheap, football-mad and family (closed Wednesdays).

La Cantinetta is on Via Bassa; tel. 886153.

Topsy, in Piazza Luigi Orlando, left of the Boston, is a decent disco open till 3 a.m.

The **Tourist Office** is at 6 Piazza Cavour; tel. 33111.

The 'Ellipse'

Between Pisa and Florence this odd feature, 80 km long with two lots of hills at either end, is one of the most intensely cultivated and populated stretches of Tuscany, as well as a rare tedious bit. But it is flanked by great, arresting cities of ancient importance. The river Arno defines its southern side, together with the rather painful SS 67 linking Florence and Pisa. If you are in a hurry for Florence, take instead the curving A 11 motorway, which traces the Ellipse's northern edge, passing by Lucca and Pistoia.

Lucca

Lucca is only 21 km north-east of Pisa, but really it is light-years away. It has no equivalent in Central Italy: you sense its seclusion and 'difference' at once, and soon its snobbery. Little has changed over the years. The people are so jealous and proud of their past that within their perfectly preserved walls all modern building has been banned for years.

Lucca is agreeably off the tourist caravan routes, and has kept to itself despite its vulnerable position as a kind of 'island' in the mouth of a lush plain. It lay once on the main pilgrim route from France to Rome via Viterbo. Predatory Florence was only some 80 km away to the east. Today, frequent trains link Lucca to Florence, Pisa and Viareggio, 79 km away by road.

Despite its propinquity to Florence, Lucca stood its ground for a long time. The Longobards had made it the very capital of Tuscany. Later, unlike any other city you will visit, it managed to hang on to autonomy for four long centuries. It was the only city in Tuscany not to submit to Florence. But then Napoleon handed it to his sister, Elise.

Today, it is a wealthy place, although its citizens hide the fact. They came into riches by siding with the Teutonic emperors; in exchange, they won trade routes throughout Europe for silk and banking services. Their links were with Flanders; they *never* mixed with Tuscans.

The *Lucchesi* have a reputation for being ultra-conservative. Neighbouring towns are Communist strongholds, but theirs is a Christian Democrat redoubt. Until the turn of the century, families from slatier towns sent their daughters to Lucca to be taught social decorum in 'better' families. Certainly, they are the most softly spoken Italians you will hear. Decibels climb with the descent south, but Lucca had one very vocal son: the composer Giacomo Puccini. You can see his birthplace in Via Poggio.

What to see

San Michele

Like Pisa, Lucca enjoyed its heyday in the twelfth and thirteenth centuries. The most incredible and flamboyant outcrop is the exuberant Church of San Michele, in a grand square of the same name which it has all to itself. This show alone justifies a visit. Built above the old Roman forum in 1143, it is medieval psychedelic, with clashing columns of Blackpool rock, four galleries of riot, a kind of sculptural funfair and the lot topped by a huge Archangel Michael.

Utter theatre it is – and inside, utter vacuous gloom. Technically, it comes under 'Pisa–Lucca Romanesque'. Symonds, the colossus of nineteenth-century art historians (today rebuffed), dryly points out disapprovingly that Romanesque is often more bizarre than beautiful.

The Cathedral

Behind the Romanesque façade of the Cathedral of San Martino there is not a void. Many Italians drop in at Lucca, in fact, solely to gaze upon the tomb of the young and beautiful Ilaria del Caretto, the second wife of a local fourteenth-century strongman. She lies in the far left-hand corner of the lofty Gothic interior in a fine marble garment, watched by her puppy, almost radiant with serenity. She was fashioned three years after her death by the Sienese sculptor Jacopo delle Quercia (1374–1438), and her tomb ranks as an early Renaissance masterpiece.

The blackened wooden Christ in the marble temple in the nave is the most revered image in Catholic Lucca. It is the *Volto Sacro* or 'Holy Face', an eleventh-century effigy said to have reached the nearby coast from the Levant aboard a ship without crew or sails. A dispute over ownership broke out, so they placed the *Volto* on an ox-cart to see which way it would go. The beasts plodded towards Lucca. Every 13 September, the Face, mentioned by Dante, is paraded through the streets.

The tower houses

Lucca still abounds in fortified dwellings: in the days of feuding families and gang warfare, domestic safety depended on poor access and high towers. The best idea of Lucca is to be had from the top of the finest tower. The fourteenth-century, 36-metre high *Torre Guinigi*, at the house of the family of Ilaria's husband, is in the street of the same name, the best-preserved in the medieval quarter. It is reached along Via Filungo, the city's Bond Street, where even the shop interiors demonstrate resistance to change.

From the top of the tower, you can make out Lucca's emblem among the jostling red roofs – the lemon-shaped Roman amphitheatre. Medieval tenements occupy the old seating arrangements, and the old arena, now cleared, is a market place. At night, it echoes eerily.

The ramparts

Lucca's encircling groves of trees trace its totally intact walls which, the *Lucchesi* admit, have done much to mould their outlook. They seriously render up thanks to the walls for saving them from the ills afflicting other Italian towns today – jerry-building, drugs, pollution, the erosion of tradition. You can walk around them on the top. They are Lucca's third lot of walls: the massive San Gervasio gate and a stretch of moat (Via del Fosso), now in the city, are all that is left of the medieval belt.

The costly decision to replace it was a measure of Lucca's determination not to be gobbled up by Florence like other towns. The old walls would not have withstood artillery. Begun in 1544, the eleven stout curtain walls were not completed for 101 years. Thirty metres thick at their base, they sprouted 126 cannons placed in the ten jutting bastions; the casemates are still there. But they never echoed to a shot fired in anger: deterrence worked.

Where to stay

The only three-star hotel within the walls is the roomy, old-fashioned, rather spartan **Universo**, Piazza Puccini; tel. 43678.

There is a smaller two-star, the **Ilaria**, 20 Via del Fosso; tel. 47558, and the two-star **La Luna**, 12 Corte Compagni; tel. 43634.

Just outside the walls is the three-star **Celide**, 27 Viale Giusti; tel. 954106.

Where to eat

One reason in itself for a stop in Lucca is the **Buca di Sant' Antonio**, 3 Via della Cervia; tel. 55881 (closed Sunday evenings and Mondays). One of the most exquisite restaurants in Central Italy, and far from exorbitant, it was founded in 1782. Under festoons of hams and copper pots, the specialities – grinder soup, kid goat on a spit, chestnut cake – are a delight to eat. The service is superb.

A popular, bustling, tucked away, 'in' place for local 'poor peasant' cooking of the past is **Da Giulio**, 29 Piazza San Tommaso; tel. 55948 (closed Sundays and Mondays). Booking is advised. Examples of the hardy fare are spelt with lentils; cod with onions; tripe and vegetable pie – as a dessert!

Bagni di Lucca

One of the great spa towns of Europe in the last century is 23 km to the north. A leafy, spread-out resort with villas and a once-famous casino, it was famed even in the early Middle Ages for what its hot springs could cure – from rheumatism and arthritis to gout and obesity – in water and mud baths. Byron and Shelley stayed here, and other Brits now repose in the 'English Cemetery'. Today, it is fading, and frequented mainly by the less well-off on national health cures.

Montecatini Terme

Now, by far the most fashionable watering place in Tuscany, favoured by the better-off, is further on, 47 km from Pisa. Tree-lined avenues, parks, turn-of-the-century staid hotels, smart shops and cafés compose its genteel atmosphere. Once the private property of the Medici, it is a summer home for sufferers from liver ailments.

Montecatini Alto

High above it, 5 km away and reachable also by cable-car, is the old town, a popular night-spot for the no-longer-adolescent down below. Its stage-like, sloping square, overlooked by a floodlit castle, becomes

Where to stay

a big outdoor café at night, noted for its breeze and off-hand service.

A cheap one-star hotel, **Bellosguardo**, a former villa untouched since before the Second World War, is a superb look-out post over the Ellipse; tel. 78637.

Pistoia

Half-way between Lucca and Florence, 37 km from Lucca on the A 11, Pistoia is now a quiet, largely modern, agricultural centre with a population of 90,000. It was one of the first cities in Italy to draw up a 'democratic' constitution, in 1177. It was Ghibelline, and its star shone brightest in the thirteenth century, when its banking houses operated in France and lent to royalty. But under repeated attack and siege, by Lucca and Florence, it finally succumbed to Florence in the fourteenth century, by which time it had the most foul repute in Italy for thuggery, murder and anarchy. Appropriately, 'pistols' are named after the town, a word originally used for the nasty little stilettos that everybody carried. Then they thought up the hand-guns.

What to see

The Cathedral altar

Despite its apparent oneness, the magnificent silver altar in the Chapel of St James is the work of numerous artists spanning three centuries to 1456. It began as a small painted altar-piece, built to honour a relic of the saint. It was damaged, replaced in silver, and continually added to over the generations, to become a mirror of these Tuscans from the early Gothic period to the Renaissance.

It is home to 628 figures. The earliest ones are Old Testament prophets attendant upon Jacob in the first two rows of the dossal. The finest are on the left side. The Renaissance architect Filippo Brunelleschi probably sculpted the vigorous upper saints and prophets.

Sant' Andrea

A pulpit by Giovanni Pisano is in the homely churchette of Sant' Andrea, in Via dell'Andrea, completed a year before he began his pulpit in Pisa. He has caught all his characters in moments of unguarded emotion: here what was soon to be called, even then, 'realism', heralds the Renaissance far ahead of painting.

Palazzo del Comune

The hefty cube of the Palazzo was originally Guelf, and therefore ignored under Ghibellines; it had to await the fourteenth century for attention. Its halls are adorned with blood-curdling battle-scenes.

Where to stay

Close to the Piazza del Duomo is the three-star **Leon Bianco**, 2 Via Panciatichi; tel. 26675/6.

Prato

To many Italians Prato means 'Industry – To Be Avoided', but beneath the grime there is gold-dust, though perhaps better prospected *after* Florence. One ploughs past pylons, factory gates, blank walls and surprising modern art to debouch abruptly into a pristine *centro storico*.

It has the biggest, lemon-shaped, old **market square** in Central Italy. There is the so-called **Emperor's Castle**, clean-lined and angular, ordered by the Emperor Frederick II to put heart into the local Ghibellines and, on account of its imported Teutonic design, unique in Central Italy. Next to it, the refined church of **Santa Maria delle Carceri** is all Renaissance proportion in the form of a Greek cross, by the Renaissance architect Giuliano Sangallo.

Cathedral   But the climax is the little striped Romanesque Cathedral in the main square. Laughing children dance around a singular, canopied, fifteenth-century wall-pulpit, a jolly joint creation by Donatello himself and Michelozzo. Inside, it not only demonstrates in its naves and cloister Prato's very own version of Romanesque, a coloured variation on Pisa's, but sends up a hymn of its own to the Renaissance.

In the choir, Filippo Lippi left his masterpiece, a biography of the life of St John the Baptist, a vivid cycle that took him fourteen years, one of the highlights of the early Renaissance. Agnolo Gaddi frescoed the Chapel of the Holy Cincture, telling how a girdle given by the Virgin Mary to St Thomas was then entrusted to an old priest whose female descendant married a man from Prato, who had the relic mailed by sea to his home town . . .

Paolo Uccello has a fresco in the Cathedral museum.

The tall Palazzo Pretorio is a captured king in the tightly ordered Palazzo Comune, packed with Florentine painting from the fourteenth and fifteenth centuries.

Where to stay   The most central is the two-star, old-style **Stella d'Italia**, 8 Piazza
and eat   Duomo; tel. 27910.

More comfortable and distinctive is the three-star **Flora**, 31 Via Cairoli; tel. 20021.

A simple, reliable, but hot, place for dinner is **Lo Scoglio**, 42 Via Verdi; tel. 22760 (closed Mondays).

Poggio a   To inspect a splendidly elegant Medici palace, go just 8 km south of
Caiano   Prato to the SS 66. For the self-deprecating people of Prato, saddened by the grime, this is *the* local sight. Built in 1479 by Giuliano Sangallo for none other than Lorenzo the Magnificent, it became, with its regal outside staircase, the trend-setter for Renaissance *palazzi* all over.

San Miniato   Roughly half-way between Pisa and Florence on the slow SS 67, San Miniato could lay claim to being the most enchanting, secluded and trim medieval township in the whole area. It was named by a group of Longobards after a Roman soldier-saint they admired who, after being decapitated, had waded across the Arno with his head in his hand.

Prato del   Draped over a horse-shoe of hills, its tree-shaded main square,
Duomo   called Cathedral Meadow is quite removed from the rest – very high-

table. For its mix, it is also unique in Central Italy. The simple Romanesque façade of the Cathedral (forget the inside), with its massive, original bell-tower, faces a seventeenth-century Bishop's Palace, next to which a tower belonging to the vanished twelfth-century Palazzo of the Emperor's Vicars is incorporated into a restaurant.

Rocca   San Miniato was where the Teutonic emperors put up on their way down to Rome or contest, and you can well see why by looking at the Fortress built by Frederick II. Only a tall tower remains, but from there you can take ocular possession of a huge chunk of Tuscany, bracketed by the sea at Livorno and Viareggio, Volterra to the south and the mountains beyond Prato to the north-east.

Museum   The Museum, to the left of the Duomo, is worth a visit. It guards a bust by Verrocchio, a grief-laden *Crucifixion* by Filippo Lippi, and clear, detached frescoes from the church of San Francesco.

San Francesco   The church itself is 200 metres down the hill, a monastery founded by the saint himself when he came to preach peace at the Fortress in 1211. The two cloisters beat the church.

Where to stay   The three-star **Miravalle**, up on the Meadow, is the only possible choice: 3 Piazza Castello; tel. 418075.

Empoli   A few kilometres further along the main road, this industrial centre (population 45,000) on a twist in the Arno specialises in glassware; its appearance is deceptive. Its unprepossessing shell conceals a pleasant, arcaded old square, Piazza Uberti, watched over by a small, rather unusual Cathedral, a subdued geometrical game in black and white. If you are travelling from Pisa, this will be your first taste of how the unemphatic Florentines toned down the Romanesque style. Empoli belonged to a line of tired, debt-ridden feudal counts and swore allegiance to Florence early on, in 1182.

Vinci   Leonardo da Vinci left relatively little behind in Central Italy, so his nearby birthplace, and the fascinating display there of some of his inventions, have a real rarity rating. Only 11 km north of Empoli on the road to Pistoia, the display is in the village castle, home of the Guidi, who owned Empoli (open 9.30 a.m.–12 noon; 2.30–6 p.m.).

The models on view are modern reconstructions of his inventions, based on the numerous detailed drawings he left behind. They do something to bring home the enormous span of his curiosity, and the very practical side of his romping imagination. It is thoroughly uncanny how the man anticipated modern times. He foresaw the helicopter and the diving suit, as the models prove. He dreamed up the tank as well, in the form of a kind of tortoise-shell on wheels. He had ideas for a paddle-steamer and ball-bearings, but what steal the show are his contraptions for human flight.

From the castle, the unfolded Tuscan countryside still looks much as it must have done to him. His actual birthplace was at Anchiano, 2 km away, but the village church of Santa Croce in Vinci still has the font in which he was baptised.

Cerreto Guidi

The reason for a whistle-stop 5 km away to the south-west is a handsome, open, sixteenth-century Medici villa, built on top of a castle belonging to the bankrupt Guidis, who sold the village to Florence. Access is via uncommon, grandiose ramps over former stables, and portraits of the Medici dynasty hang in the stately, decorated rooms. You can gaze out over the valley of the Arno and easily pick out the tower of San Miniato.

Florence

Central Florence today is still more or less the same small city that in one brief spell cast the mould of the modern mind. Despite developers and roaring motorbikes, it still embodies the Renaissance, and speaks its language with a clarity heard nowhere else. Because of its compactness the sheer density of its riches is unsurpassed anywhere in Italy. You can walk right across it in thirty minutes. The spectacle is blinding, almost daunting. Masterpieces are as ubiquitous as bars. Admirers are quickly dazed.

A Florentine doctor, a hospital psychiatrist, now specialises in an apparently very real variety of cultural shock, first described by Stendhal who became unable to walk after being dazzled by Santa Croce. The doctor lists other symptoms of *Stendhalismo*, as she calls the ailment: palpitations, dizziness, loss of identity, violent headaches. Her first case was a girl lying in a faint outside a church. There is just far too much of it. Beware!

Florence needs four days at the very least – that will give you a look at a representative fraction. But the looking is far more enjoyable for being watered down by exploration: within a radius of 100 km of Florence, the relaxing Tuscan countryside is scattered with things to see – hill-towns, frescoed churches, vineyards, vast horizons, long menus.

When to go

If possible, avoid August, when the city bursts with the entirety of European youth. It is hot, airless and sticky and the Florentines have all left. Many restaurants are closed and the better hotels empty. By far the most pleasant months are May and June and then September to October: not too hot for looking, warm enough to lounge. Winter can be very cold.

Getting there

By air

Tuscany's international airport is Pisa. From the airport, there is an hourly train service to the heart of Florence. The new air-terminal for the return trip is on platform 5 in Florence railway station, with final destination check-in possible. The train journey takes an hour.

By car

From France and Genoa, turn off the A 12 just before Viareggio. From Rome, leave the motorway at Firenze Sud, then follow Viale Europa into town.

By train

There are direct trains from Paris (with connections from London),

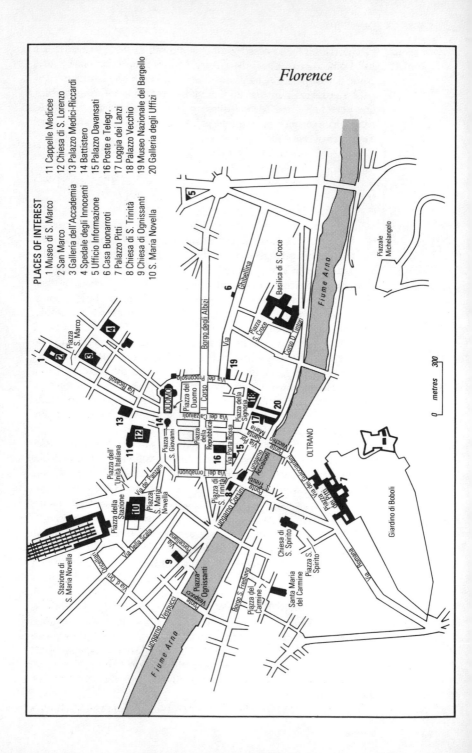

Florence

PLACES OF INTEREST

1 Museo di S. Marco
2 San Marco
3 Galleria dell'Accademia
4 Spedale degli Innocenti
5 Ufficio Informazione
6 Casa Buonarroti
7 Palazzo Pitti
8 Chiesa di S. Trinità
9 Chiesa di Ognissanti
10 S. Maria Novella

11 Cappelle Medicee
12 Chiesa di S. Lorenzo
13 Palazzo Medici-Riccardi
14 Battistero
15 Palazzo Davansati
16 Poste e Telegr.
17 Loggia dei Lanzi
18 Palazzo Vecchio
19 Museo Nazionale del Bargello
20 Galleria degli Uffizi

Marseilles, Munich and Vienna. Ten inter-cities daily link Florence and Rome in two hours flat. Trains are available for Arezzo and Perugia, too.

Buses

The two main bus stations flank the railway station. To the right, with your back to the buffers, Sita buses leave regularly for Siena, less often for Volterra. To the left, over the road, Lazzi buses leave for west coast towns, from Viareggio down to Grosseto.

Useful addresses

The main **Tourist Office** is at 16 Via Manzoni; tel. 247 8141/5. Another is at 15 Via Tornabuoni; tel. 216544/5.

● **British Consulate**, 2 Lungarno Corsini; tel. 284133, 212594.

● **US Consulate**, 38 Lungarno Vespucci; tel. 298276.

● **Australia**: no consulate.

Getting about

Florence is astride the Arno, but nearly all its riches are amassed on the north bank. The south bank is known as Oltrarno (Beyond the Arno), and is popular, the equivalent of Rome's Trastevere. The city is laid out on the grid system of the ancient Roman camp (*castra*) it once was: this is the foundation of its logic.

The geographical centre is the Cathedral, but the modern centre is totally foreign to the 'real' Florence. This is the ill-conceived Piazza della Repubblica, a late nineteenth-century creation once written off as 'a German beer-drinking square'. It is utterly out of place.

The Florence 'look'

The proper Florence hems the centre in. Much of the city is now pedestrianised, which is fortunate since walking is the only way to see it. The chances are that a Renaissance man would recognise pretty easily what you see today. This might be the city of the Renaissance, but he would doubtless remember that Florence still nurtured much of the mistrust and wariness of the Middle Ages. The Renaissance *palazzi* you pass bear witness to it: wearing those great black eaves like eyelashes, they are more like fortresses than homes. They exude defensiveness. The lower parts of these stately masses are unwelcoming blank wall, made out of rough-hewn blocks. The door-ways are mean and narrow; the windows high up and out of reach – those closer at hand have stout iron gratings clamped over them.

Here there is little of the refinement of the Renaissance *palazzi* in Rome. These stout affairs are built-in memories of strife, street-fighting and blood. They are loftily male; prettiness is not Florence's strong point.

Yet they are also monuments to sobriety and decorum, as is the whole of Florence. The city is all of a piece, intolerant of deviation. The dominating greyish-brown of its stone partly accounts for the unity; so does the uniformity of its treeless streets – narrow, long and straight, and all on the level so that it is easy to lose your bearings within the city's small compass. This Renaissance sanity provides people with a bridge into Italy. Its rationality is recognisable, whereas the chaos of Rome is not.

History

How a quarrelsome city whose population was never more than

Background to greatness

80,000 could, in barely one century, produce an explosion of genius that shook the world is a mystery that may never be solved, but one reason was certainly gold – and the use of it by patrons. In the thirteenth century, Florence's bankers were the most powerful in Europe. Her coin, the florin, was international tender. Florentines, like Dante's father, were moneylenders, and also cloth and woollen merchants with far-flung markets, which brought more gold tumbling in.

The Medicis

The Medici dynasty also had gold, and owned or promoted much of what you see in Florence today. They were bankers, too; at first to the Popes. They dealt craftily across Europe, and enjoyed a monopoly in the production of alum, vital to the city's textile industry. They came to power on the crest of weariness, after some three centuries of inter-family and class warfare, coups d'état and murder, all dictated by everybody's abhorrence of being bossed. An Italian historian of the time diagnosed Florence as suffering from a passion for equality combined with every family's determination to be on top (he could have been pontificating on Italians today).

One victim of these internecine hatreds was Dante. Now you will find quotations from his *Divine Comedy* (begun in about 1307) larding street-corners, but Florence was hardly grateful to him in his lifetime. He was hounded out of the city for favouring the faction that opposed the Popes' temporal power. He branded Florence 'an evil stepmother'. 'Rejoice Florence!' he thundered. 'May your name resound throughout Hell!'

Florence's support of the Papacy brought it even more wealth and privilege. And although they subjugated their main Ghibelline enemies – Pisa and Siena – by force, the Medici were not soldiers. More typically, they conquered their neighbours by sending out mules laden with gold.

Originally of peasant stock, they floated to the top initially through cultivated popularity, which they maintained through shrewdness, ballot-rigging and tact. For a century, they posed as private citizens with no official title.

They were the greatest patrons of the arts Europe had ever known. They financed the Renaissance – out of guilt over their rise to power, some think – and were an essential part of it. Cosimo the Elder, who inaugurated their disguised dictatorship in the 1430s, restored the study of Greek, read Plato and, with architects and sculptors such as Donatello under his protection, was responsible for the first Renaissance buildings in Florence.

But the champion of the Renaissance, the symbol of Florence at its most glorious, was his grandson, Lorenzo the Magnificent, an accomplished poet with the looks of a prize-fighter and the benevolence of a saint. He was two years older than Botticelli, who was just one of a brilliant circle who enjoyed his munificence and friendship. He took a

15-year-old boy into his house to be treated as one of the family: his name was Michelangelo.

Lorenzo the poet lamented the transience of things. And so it proved. His son Piero, known as 'small brain', fraternised with the invading army of the French king, Charles VIII, and was chased out by a furious populace.

Savonarola

You can visit the monastery, still intact, whose prior then took over the city, foretelling its doom unless it renounced wickedness. Under the fanatic monk Girolamo Savonarola, the populace elected Jesus Christ the leader of Florence. But four years later, in 1498, they burned the monk.

His prophecy, however, came true. Under a deal with a Medici Pope, the Spanish troops of Emperor Charles V laid siege to Florence for a year (Michelangelo was Master of Fortifications). Betrayed by their own commander, the Florentines surrendered.

The end

A new Medici master thus installed with the title of Duke (the first of many) was the bastard son of an Arab slave woman. It was 1530, and the beacon for humanity known as Florence began to dim. Under the Spanish Inquisition, Plato was banned on pain of death.

Florentines

The Florentines, rather smugly, agree with the world that they are the cultural snobs of Italy. They enjoy their willed parochialism; they believe they deserve a place apart. After all, they enlightened Europe's barbarians: who else in the second millennium has such an heirloom in its drawers?

In Florence, the Renaissance is still dinner-table talk. The style is still there, even in thin-walled suburban homes. They eschew the florid, and prefer the composed. They define themselves willingly: 'We're unsociable,' they tell you. 'We're quarrelsome and proud.' One senior civil servant told me: 'We're difficult. We argue. I suppose we don't smile too much. But I think you can say we're dependable.' And outsiders agree. According to a diplomat, 'They're brusque and tough. But they can become good friends. They work hard, and once they've agreed on terms, they're scrupulous.' Their most prominent English resident claims: 'They're straightforward and honest, perhaps a bit hard, but very practical, with a great sense of what life is about. You find it in their proverbs, which are profoundly true.'

They are also unbelievably fractious, as they always have been. Today, four full-blown rows are currently raging:

● The most visceral is over a plan to build a great satellite town on land jointly owned by a big insurance company and the Agnellis. Promoters of the scheme contend that it would ease pressure on the old centre and create a Florence ready for the twenty-first century. Detractors, including the Green parties, counter that it would spell the desertion and death of today's Florence.

● Linked with this is disagreement over tourist policy. Many deplore the changes induced by mass tourism. The once-elegant centre, they object, is being turned into a camp-site for day-tripper battalions; pizza places are ousting bookshops. Florentines are being chased away from the centre; only 41,000 remain, as against 90,000 fifty years ago. Day-to-day life is vanishing: 'Try and find a butcher's shop in the centre,' a local journalist complained.

Really, the argument is over the new brand of tourists – the poor young. Loaded like sherpas, swinging plastic mineral water bottles, they dominate the reserved streets. The burghers claim that they leave only litter behind; others that they take memories away with them, and that when they are richer they, or their children, will return.

● A third disagreement is over whether Florence should have a decent airport and, if so, where. The present one is still at field stage. With this issue, the old rivalry with Pisa re-surfaces.

● But perhaps the most disturbing quarrel of all is over the Arno. Despite an avalanche of learned studies, virtually nothing has been done to stem a repetition of the 1966 flood. One idea was for dykes upstream. Some claim that against fickle nature no defence exists; others retort that it does, but will take forty years to marshall. Meanwhile, the Arno has reached disaster level at least once since.

The Renaissance

This is the basis of the Florentines' cult of themselves. Some scholars brand the very term a misnomer: how can something completely new be called a 're-birth', they ask. Another school objects to it because the new-born spirit was promptly killed off by the Counter-Reformation. In this book, the word is used conventionally to mean the cultural revolution spanning about one and a half centuries from the death of the Tuscan poet and classicist Francesco Petrarca in 1370 to the death of the artist Raphael in 1520.

The essence of the Renaissance is often seen as the expression of a new individualism, fostered by the breakdown of central authority. In the arts, it began as a search for a new model, which led to the re-discovery of ancient Rome, a furious revival of classical studies, and a search for lost rules. The Italians began turning back to their Roman heritage; it is staggering how much of it had been lost. To revive it, Renaissance man often had to start from scratch again.

Mythology and paganism were re-imagined, and a totally new outlook, based on rationality, emerged. In the political vacuum of the times, the spiritual stranglehold of the Church withered away and so the Renaissance was also the discovery of the pleasure of living: men found the earthly paradise denied to them so long by the stern medieval monasteries. Renaissance Christianity, therefore, is of a humanised variety. Often artists try to show that Christianity and paganism can co-exist; is a search for a new synthesis.

In architecture, the Renaissance meant the clean line and geometrical harmony. The circle came to be seen as the perfect shape. As if to re-create order where none existed, to paper over the anarchy, an obsession emerged with utopias and the lay-outs of ideal cities. In sculpture and painting, artists sought an escape from formalism and a new way of handling space. They celebrated nature and the human form, accurately observed.

Once, the artists' sole patron had been the Church, and the only near nudes allowed were the body of Christ and Adam and Eve, the latter pair always depicted as cringeing. But when lay patronage emerged, a whole new period of secular art began. Delight in the naked body and in physical beauty marked it out from anything else in the Christian era.

The Florentine Masters

Cimabue (1240–1302). Little is known of his life, but he began as a Florentine protégé of the Papal court in Rome, and later went to Assisi at a time when it was becoming the biggest artistic work-site in Central Italy. Famous in his own lifetime, he worked within the Byzantine tradition, but began to Westernise it. He infused humanity and drama into the frigid elegance of his mould. He was one of the very first of the moderns, perhaps preceded only by Giunta Pisano of Pisa.

Giotto (1267–1337). The son of a farm labourer who had moved into the Florence area, he was one of a new flood of rural immigrants disliked by Dante because of their 'stink'. He had four children, worked in Florence, Rome and Assisi, and became so rich that he employed six solicitors in Florence to hunt down his debtors.

He went far further than Cimabue and, though he too at first worked within the then popular Byzantine tradition, he eventually trumpeted out a new kind of painting that set the trend for centuries. 'He turned Greek [Byzantine] into Latin,' Italy's medieval story-teller Boccaccio said of him. Given his humble background, he was powerfully impressed by the lightning spread of the Franciscan movement, the 'people's church', which legitimised his popular, contemporary approach.

His religious world is tangible, his characters down to earth, and he indulged an eye for the telling, prosaic detail. Technically, he overturned the Byzantine reviewing stand, with those bored stares, and had his people relating to each other. He introduced the headline, which kept the rest of the story subordinate.

Brunelleschi (1377–1446). The foremost architect of the Renaissance, he is best known for his 'miracle' – the great dome of Florence Cathedral. He also designed the church of San Lorenzo and the Pitti Palace. He was the first ever drawing-board architect, who preplanned with maths and measures. His example and influence produced the (more or less) single face of the Florence of today. He was a close companion of Donatello.

Donatello (1386–1466). With Brunelleschi, he travelled to Rome to measure and sketch what remained of the ruins and art of antiquity. Much of this still lay buried at the time and it is said of Donatello that he revived classical sculpture without seeing hardly anything of it. He transcended idealisation; his realistic figures can be contorted by emotion. A prolific artist, he was overshadowed only by Michelangelo.

Botticelli (1445–1510). Son of a tanner and apprenticed first to a goldsmith (as most Renaissance artists were), Sandro Botticelli was rated less highly in his lifetime than he is today. His *Spring* (in the Uffizi Gallery) is now considered the very epitome of the Renaissance. His characteristic is a delicate clarity of outline. A Neo-Platonist, he romanticised classical mythology, and was deeply affected by the teachings of Savonarola.

Leonardo da Vinci (1452–1519). Born at Vinci near Florence, this painter, architect, sculptor, engineer, inventor, botanist and anatomist has left relatively little in his native city. He painted the *Mona Lisa* in Florence (she was the wife of one Francesco del Giocondo). Superbly handsome, generous with money and a physical Titan, he was no friend of Michelangelo.

Michelangelo (1475–1564). Scornful, unsociable, demanding of himself, ill-tempered, tortured by solitude and by his art, Michelangelo saw a rival in Leonardo, and developed a profound hatred for him. He refused helpers of any standing, spent his long life between Florence and Rome and, like Leonardo, finished little of what he started.

For some, this was simply because, as a perfectionist, he was rarely satisfied with his work. For others, his *non finito* was deliberate, a means of suggestion. Others still see in it his conception of the artist as god: it is the act of creation. Most of his sculpture is in Florence.

Raphael (1483–1520). Raphael was not a Florentine, but was born at Urbino in the Marches. He spent only four years in Florence, arriving when he was 22, only weeks after Michelangelo had unveiled his *David*. Although he, too, is best known for his work in the Vatican, he is today well represented in Florence. A man of beauty and grace with a flair for friendship and amours, he knew little of the inner torment of a Michelangelo. It has been said that he simply perceived the world as beautiful, and put down what he saw. After his premature death at 37, perhaps from malaria, myth and superstition clung to him as to a mortal god. People whispered about an alikeness to Christ; the claim that he was born and died on a Good Friday aided the aura.

Vasari (1511–1574). You will come across the heavy hand of Giorgio Vasari of Arezzo all over Florence. As the official Medici court painter, he has failed to muster much acclaim. But as the author of *The Lives of the Artists*, first published in 1550, he is indispensable – informative, amusing, sagacious and well pleased with himself. He is still the standard crib on the Renaissance. He was a younger friend of Michelangelo, whom he lionised and adored.

The work of these artists is in some forty museums and churches in Florence. It would be ruination to try and see even a majority of them. The eyes glaze over quickly. The solution is to concentrate on four or five at most. Florence is not superior to anywhere else in the matter of opening times (see General Basics, page 61). The Tourist Office some-times prints a list. As a rule, the Uffizi Gallery is open 9 a.m.–7 p.m. on weekdays, except Monday.

Don't forget: painting and sculpture can look all the better after a break – a side-trip to Siena or San Gimignano; shopping, or just stroll-ing around. Florence is more than museum-cruising.

What to see

Ponte Vecchio

After arriving in Florence, most people almost automatically stroll towards the Arno to check that the symbol of the city, the Ponte Vecchio, is still there – only to find everybody else doing the same. The higgledy-piggledy fourteenth-century 'Old Bridge' humps it over the Arno at its narrowest point and for two centuries bore butchers' shops. But then a fastidious Medici ruler had them chased away as unsightly, and replaced by jewellers, still flourishingly there. Their overhanging shops reflected their ideas on space-saving. Pick-pockets delight in this bridge.

Piazza della Signoria

Then in two minutes you are in the 'Square of the Sires', the centre of the city's political life since the Middle Ages. (In 1989, it was a mess, being re-paved after excavations.) Nobody claims that this rather clut-tered, oddly irregular, square is one of the beauties of Italy, but its fort-like **Palazzo Vecchio** is the most commanding and stylish civic structure in Tuscany. It went up very early in the fourteenth century, and was conceived by Arnolfo del Cambio to house and protect the city's nervous Priors who, during their statutory brief terms of office, never left it.

From its slim, off-centre needle of a tower (35 metres high), a daring creation, guards watched out for trouble in the streets, with an excel-lent view. Its mast bears the Lion and the Lily, the emblems of Flor-ence. Later, the first Medici Dukes moved in. Today it has reverted to what it first was – the Town Hall.

Somebody has remarked on what a violent square this is; it is virile and no hymn to sweetness. Michelangelo's *David* once stood where a copy now stands, to symbolise the Florentines' insistence on free-doms. To its side, Donatello's sanguinary *Judith and Holofernes* was another warning about the fate of those who tampered with them.

The graceful fourteenth-century **Loggia dei Lanzi** – so called because a Medici kept a detachment of Swiss lancers there to intimi-date his subjects – is but a refuge for further bloodiness. On the right, the Romans are raping the Sabine women; notice the horror scene on the pedestal, easily the best-known figment of the sixteenth-century Giambologna's imagination. On the left, Perseus holds high the drip-ping head of the Medusa as gore gushes from her neck. The author of this masterpiece has signed himself on Perseus' sash: Benvenuto Cellini, the Florentine philanderer, goldsmith and murderer.

The Loggia was built especially as a setting for public occasions, such as the election and proclamation of the Priors. In the sixteenth century twenty-six such loggias dotted Florence, so that passers-by could stare upon the family happenings of the rich, their weddings and banquets.

You are now on the doorstep of the biggest State art gallery in Italy.

Galleria degli
Uffizi

Italy's shrine to painting houses the finest collection of Florentine Renaissance pictures in the world. Though it does not close for siesta on its open days, it is still often a scrum: more than a million pairs of feet a year shuffle through its forty-five rooms. Of course, it is impossible to take it all in during one visit. The only way is to be drastically choosy; what follows should speed the winnowing.

'Uffizi' is an old variant of the modern *uffici*, offices. This sober, U-shaped building, designed by Giorgio Vasari in the mid-sixteenth century, was originally an office block for judges and civil servants under the Medici dynasty. The Grand Dukes later had it enlarged so that the family's scattered treasures could be gathered under one roof. The widow of the last Medici Duke, Anna Maria Lodovica, played out the family with a final grand flourish: in 1737 she bequeathed the contents of the Uffizi and the family's other treasures to the Tuscan State, with the proviso that they must never leave Tuscany. Her idea was to prevent the treasure falling into foreign hands, but during his Italian visitation Napoleon tore into it and many pictures are still in the Louvre. Florentines wring their hands over his thievery to this day.

The Uffizi is rather a school-masterish place. It sets out Italian painting from the thirteenth to the eighteenth centuries in strict chronological order, playing off one painter against another to teach us who influenced whom and who proved the brighter.

Its prologue, in the first room on the left, is a juxtaposition of two thirteenth-century enthroned Madonnas, the one facing you by **Giotto**, that distant patriarch of Western painting, and the other, to your right, by his benevolent teacher, **Giovanni Cimabue**. Every Italian schoolboy learns how Cimabue 'discovered' Giotto in the countryside when he caught him as a young boy scratching the picture of a sheep on to a stone. He was so impressed, he at once had the boy's father allow him to come to Florence and be his apprentice.

Giotto was a close friend of Dante, who immortalised Cimabue in Purgatory. 'Cimabue,' he wrote, 'thought that in painting he had the field to himself, but now Giotto's all the rage and the fame of the former has dimmed.' Although indeed thoroughly eclipsed by his pupil, Cimabue started the great revolution against the stylised, imported Byzantine style which had been in fashion since the ninth century. Giotto then broke the Byzantine mould for good. A trip to Assisi will disclose much more of the two men's work.

And it would take a trip to Urbino in the Marches to communicate with the Duke of Montefeltro, whose renowned easel portrait by **Piero della Francesca** is in room 7, dedicated to the early Renaissance. The 'imitation' hills in the picture are the quite real ones of the Marches, and they serve to trumpet out Piero's mastery of perspective (see San Sepolcro on pages 152–4 for more; Piero's main work, at Arezzo, was unfortunately under restoration in 1989).

A highly successful hired sword turned philosopher and patron of the arts, the Duke of Montefeltro was arguably one of the most forceful personalities of the Renaissance and his court at tiny Urbino was one of the dynamos of that cultural revolution. He apparently acquired his remarkable nose after losing his right eye in battle and ordering his surgeon to allow his left eye a full field of vision, so that the fighter could still fight. Pundits in Urbino, however, gave me a less heroic version: he lost both eye and the nasal segment to a lance in a jousting tournament when he was 28.

Perspective was one of the rediscoveries of the Renaissance, and nobody was more tormented by its problems than **Paolo Uccello**, whose *Battle of San Romano* is a rigorous demonstration of how to beat them. He owed his name to his partiality for painting birds, *uccelli.*

The Uffizi is telling us by this time that painters were turning from the sacred to the profane. In room 10, the biggest in the gallery, you will find the man held to epitomise the 'pagan' side of the Renaissance – **Sandro Botticelli**. The Gallery's curators say he is by far their biggest draw. He is a young person's painter. Today's Florentines like to see in him 'love and dreams before they vanish' – a melancholy Romantic, three centuries ahead of cue.

Modern experts, however, see his work as the apex of a new, élitist trend in fifteenth-century Florence. Painting was no longer as accessible to ordinary people as earlier in the Renaissance; it was now being aimed at the court, infused with rediscovered mythology and a Neo-Platonic outlook, which was in vogue under Lorenzo the Magnificent. This was 'literary' art, incorporating the findings of those enthusiastic Humanists.

It was not 'easy' then and it still isn't. Generations of critics have been locked in argument over what Botticelli's *Primavera* is actually *about.* For some, the aerial figure on the right is the genie of death pursuing Simonetta Vespucci, the beautiful creature loved by Lorenzo's brother Giuliano before he was murdered in a plot. She died of consumption in 1476. Other critics claim the figure is Zephyr, starting by his touch the awakening of Spring. The picture was commissioned by the Medicis; so was the even more celebrated *Birth of Venus*, and this time the figure being gently wafted to shore in a shell is known almost for certain to have been modelled on the poor Simonetta.

These two pictures, with their poetry and purity of line, are usually regarded as marking the pinnacle of the Renaissance before the advent of Michelangelo. But what won Botticelli instant celebrity in his own day was his *Adoration*, because he placed three generations of Medici among the spectators. In the foreground on the left, leaning on his sword, is the great Lorenzo; the figure in the yellow cloak on the right is Botticelli himself.

Botticelli, and his Florence, change in room 10. The fragility of his world proved too real, and his small masterpiece *Calumny*, hard to see under the glass, is the work of an older, disturbed man under the spell of the stern preachings of Savonarola. It is stylised hysteria, as the donkey-eared King heeds the counsels of Ignorance and Suspicion, while hooded Calumny drags forward a naked youth, Innocence. Converted by the monk, Botticelli abandoned painting. It is said that had it not been for his friends, he would have died of hunger.

We are given another lesson in room 15 where Andrea del Verrocchio is cruelly compared with **Leonardo da Vinci**, his pupil. The kneeling angel on the left of Andrea's canvas, done in profile, was painted in by Leonardo and when the good Verrocchio saw it, they say that he felt so shamed that he swore never to paint again – and didn't. He was really a sculptor.

In the octagonal **Tribuna**, built as a showcase for the Gallery's gems before re-arrangement, the light pours down on the statuary, especially on the so-called *Medici Venus*, a Roman copy of a Greek original. For generations, this was the sex symbol of Florence.

From the end gallery overlooking the Arno, you will see the red-tiled covered corridor used by the Medicis to walk from the Uffizi across the Ponte Vecchio to the Palazzo Pitti, their new home after the Palazzo Vecchio.

Many tend to overlook the classic sculpture and the marble Emperors in the Uffizi, but they do show what a long road the men of the Renaissance had to follow to catch up again after the near-obliteration of art in the really very Dark Ages.

In room 25, the first in the other wing, is the only known panel-painting executed by Michelangelo. Note the muscularity of his Madonna: 'He has made the Virgin a man,' they all say. Its provocative contrast is a bold Renaissance assertion that pagan antiquity, symbolised by rather casual male nudes, can co-exist with Christianity, a view also held by the Duke of Montefeltro.

The fellow-artist whom Michelangelo could not stand is next door. Here the contrast is between the self-portrait of **Raphael** and his portraits of the ambitious Pope Leo X (uncle of Lorenzo de' Medici) and Pope Julius II, the Pontiff whose relations with Michelangelo were so often tense. These two Popes presided over the final, Roman, phase of the Renaissance.

Further on, in room 28, the temptress *Venus* with her lap dog waits, in no apparent hurry, to be dressed by her maids. The Duke of Montefeltro commissioned her from **Titian**. **Tintoretto** is in room 35 and, after the enormous works by **Rubens**, **Caravaggio** almost startles with his *Sacrifice of Isaac* in room 43. His ambiguous *Young Bacchus* is always brought up in the same breath as his alleged homosexuality.

It all ends rather sadly with **Rembrandt,** showing himself both as a young and as an old man.

Cathedral   The real heart of Florence is its alarming Cathedral complex; the sense of measure about Florence does nothing to warn you of the extraordinary apparition. It looms up, all of a sudden, like some enormous zebra trapped in a play-pen. Then, at second sight, enveloped in swirling traffic and fumes, it turns into a psychedelic railway station, exuding about the same amount of holiness.

Size, in fact, was the whole aim. It is Arnolfo di Cambio's greatest legacy, and he was instructed by the Priors, in 1294, to transform the old cathedral into a church of 'a magnificence unsurpassable by the wit or industry of man.' They wanted it to demonstrate 'the magnanimity and wisdom' of the Florentines. Their real purpose, it is now thought, was to outdo even Imperial Rome.

Behind the fourteenth-century marzipan façade, you enter the vacuous gloom of the third longest church in the world, pipped only by St Peter's in Rome and St Paul's in London. Its real magnificence, though, is **Brunelleschi's dome,** the era's biggest architectural triumph. Nothing of its magnitude had been attempted since the Empire, and nobody was quite sure how to go about it. By 1418, the whole place was finished, except for a cavity 40 metres across waiting to be capped. Brunelleschi fought off his rivals. He was distrusted and doubted, but in Rome he had wheedled secrets out of the Pantheon and other ancient remains.

He flabbergasted everyone by raising the beehive dome without cumbersome scaffolding, using instead a new-fangled lift worked by an ox. It was cheap. His real scoop, though, was a cupola without visible means of support. The trick was to double it: it is two skull-caps, one within the other – the inner one is the real crust, while the outer one is a parasol to hide the struts. There is an airspace between the two, which stalwarts can climb up through (there are 463 steps).

The whole thing took Brunelleschi sixteen years. As a reward, they buried him in the Cathedral, a fact discovered only recently.

The bell-tower outside is called 'Giotto's' because he began it but, after the dome, the second marvel of the Cathedral is the East Gate of the octagonal **Baptistry,** the one facing the marzipan. The ten panels (some probably being restored) took the Florentine sculptor **Lorenzo Ghiberti** twenty-five years. In a famous remark, Michelangelo described these doors as 'so beautiful that they would do well for the doors of Paradise.' They read from the top left, horizontally, starting with Adam and Eve. They announce that Renaissance sculpture has come into its own: all traces of Gothic stiffness have gone.

The son of a goldsmith and master of Donatello, Ghiberti spent his life at the Baptistry. He was in his twenties when they awarded him the contract for the North Gate (to the right of the East), after he won a famous competition in the first year of the fifteenth century.

Ghiberti's sculpture has been called 'painting in bronze'.

The Baptistry itself, once the Cathedral before the title crossed the road, is the oldest building in Florence, perhaps going back as far as the fifth century. For many Florentines, it is their favourite. Dante was baptised here. The most grandiose scene to emerge from its soft glitter of thirteenth-century mosaics is a giant Christ presiding over the Last Judgement.

Museo dell' Opera del Duomo

As in other cathedral cities of Central Italy, precious works once in or about the Duomo are now kept in the museum, well worth a visit. It is behind the apse at 9 Piazza del Duomo; open 9.30 a.m.–1 p.m., 3–5.30 p.m. (10 a.m.–1 p.m. on Sundays).

On the ground floor lies the paraphernalia Brunelleschi used for his dome. On the way up is a *Pietà* smashed to bits by a dissatisfied Michelangelo, and pieced back together 300 years later. He is said to have sculpted his own face as Nicodemus. Upstairs there is Donatello's riotous choir loft and, above the merriment, his chillingly haggard Mary Magdalen. Among the figures brought in from the bell-tower niches are his equally candid rendering of the skull-shaven Old Testament prophet Habbakuk.

Galleria dell' Accademia

After the over-view at the Uffizi, the most pleasant way around Florence is to seek out its artists individually. Logically, the first call is on **Michelangelo** at the Accademia, at 60 Via Ricasoli, near the Cathedral.

The first Academy of Arts in the West, for a century it has been synonymous with the creator of *David*. For safety's sake, the sculpture was moved into his special apse from his traditional place outside the Palazzo Vecchio in 1873. It may seem like the rush-hour, as everyone elbows forward to gaze up at the 4.1 metre-tall apparition.

Michelangelo intended him to stay for ever in the Piazza della Signoria, as a talisman for the everlasting freedom of Florence. The protector of the children of Israel, *David* was meant to remind the rulers of Florence of their duty; they didn't look.

It is the work of a man of only 26, which grew out of a great chunk of marble left derelict in the yard of the Cathedral Works Office. The stone seemed of no use to anyone since some incompetent had botched a job on it and left it ravaged. Michelangelo badgered the civil servants for it. He saw he could bend to the damage and work around it. He got it – and *David* was born of errors.

The adoring Vasari commented: 'Obviously, nobody who has looked upon the *David* of Michelangelo would want to see anything else by anyone, be he alive or dead.' It established Michelangelo as the greatest sculptor of his age, and explains why Pope Julius II then summoned him to Rome to fashion a tomb for him that would be the centrepiece of the new St Peter's he had ordered.

'I lost all my youth because of that tomb,' Michelangelo bitterly wrote later. He spent forty years fretting over it, but never finished it –

because of rows with the Pope, the envy of his enemies, fresh commissions, such as the Sistine Chapel, and then the Pope's death.

The little he did for the tomb include the sculptures of the so-called *Captives* you see in the hall of the Gallery. They were meant to have been among other prisoners manacled to figures holding up the tomb with their heads. They would symbolise the provinces that were brought under Papal subjugation, and the destiny of the arts after the death of a Pope regarded as the greatest patron the new Europe had known. They superbly embody Michelangelo's credo that the sculptor was not one who imposed his will upon the marble, but one who liberated an idea already within it. His *Atlas*, bowed down under the sky, seems to be wading out of matter as if ready-made. The *Captives* also bear out the reputation he built up even during his lifetime as a genius who completed little of what he began.

Some critics suspect that the supported Christ with the roped groin, known as the *Palestrina Pietà* (after a town near Rome) is not powerful enough to be by Michelangelo.

It is not worth looking upstairs.

Medici Chapels An older and more tragic Michelangelo produced the celebrated sculptures in the nearby Medici Chapels, behind the church of San Lorenzo with the entrance in Piazza Madonna degli Aldobrandini. They are in the New Sacristy, commissioned by the Medici Pope Clement VII, the bastard son of Lorenzo the Magnificent's slain brother. This was to be the Medici dynasty's mausoleum, but again Michelangelo left it unfinished, this time for heaviness of heart.

Gloom and torment pervade his creation, a mirror of his despair and sorrow over the fall of the Florentine Republic and the woes of Italy. He worked on it for thirteen years, on and off, but as he did the soldiery of the Empire sacked Rome and the last five years he spent chipping away in the Sacristy followed the fateful siege of Florence of 1530. He had designed and strengthened the new fortifications.

He leaves little doubt about his frame of mind. The doom-laden figure on the left is Lorenzo, grandson of the Magnificent, an ideal portrait taken to symbolise Thought, as his attitude rather suggests. Beneath him, over the tomb, lie the allegorical figures of the male Dusk and the female Dawn. The latter is usually considered as one of his three greatest triumphs (the other two, *Moses* and his *Pietà*, are in Rome). For her, waking is pain and unpleasantness, the returning memory of what has happened to Italy.

On the opposite tomb lies Night, grieving in her sleep, a terrible image of resigned sorrow. Michelangelo confirmed that he was thinking of politics when he made her, writing at the time: 'I am glad for sleep and all the more so for being in stone, because as long as ruin and shame persist, not to see, not to hear is, for me, a great fortune. So do not wake me up; keep your voice down.' Her partner is the male Day, still struggling free of the marble. The heroic presiding statue, repre-

111

senting Action, is Giuliano, the Magnificent's youngest son.

Here, too, you will notice, Michelangelo's women are hefty, strangely masculine ladies – as if, one critic suggests, fragile, virginal females would have been too frail to convey his emotional force.

He was in a hurry in the Sacristy. He left chisel-marks and while shaping his cross-legged Madonna he left two versions of the Child's right forearm. When his task-master, Pope Clement, died in 1534, Michelangelo downed tools, left Florence and never returned.

San Lorenzo   The church of San Lorenzo was the parish church of the Medicis. You would expect a splendid sight, yet its face-without-a-skin, looking down on the market stalls, verges on the unseemly. It is yet another case of Michelangelo not concluding something. He was instructed to invent a façade for the church by the Medici Pope Leo X. He reluctantly produced a model, complaining that he still had work to do on the great tomb at St Peter's for Pope Julius, Leo's predecessor.

The project was fated. First, the workforce he had assembled vanished when he insisted on supervising them all single-handed. Secondly, Leo wanted special marble, and Michelangelo wasted several years planning a mountain road to transport it. Thirdly, war sponged up the money allocated for it, and fourthly, Leo died.

But Michelangelo left his imprint as a revolutionary architect at San Lorenzo nonetheless, in the form of the **Laurentian Library**, designed for the Medicis' collection of manuscripts. A door off the left aisle leads to a cloister and the staircase is on the right. In the so-called Vestibule, shaped like a dice, with a triple staircase, he took unheard-of liberties with sacred Renaissance rules, and so paved the way for Baroque. A modern Italian critic writes of the double columns embedded into the walls: 'What else are they if not disfigured statues rendered abstract, or geometric bodies about to become human?'

No wonder the public found him difficult, a kind of Florentine Picasso.

But the heartbeat of the Renaissance is almost audible in San Lorenzo, its pulse in the **Old Sacristy** (in the far left corner), a hymn to **Brunelleschi**. This exact cube, capped by a done, is one of the very first expressions of the Renaissance and, to many, the most pleasing. It is his first entire church, the result of calculated harmony. The nave, for example, is exactly twice as high as it is wide.

The two bronze oblong **pulpits** were the last works of the then elderly **Donatello**.

Museo   But the main domain of Donatello is the Bargello, once the most
Nazionale   sinister building in Florence, now the National Museum of Sculpture,
del Bargello   hard by the Piazza della Signoria, at 4 Via del Proconsolo; open 9 a.m.–2 p.m.; closed Mondays.

The Bargello was the residence of the Chief Constable, who lived above the shop. From the sixteenth century onwards, it also accommodated a prison, torture chambers, a law court and police spies. The well, centre stage, is where the scaffold once stood. When a head rolled, they would toll the big bell in the tower.

To the right of the entrance on the ground floor, there is more Michelangelo, including his bull-necked *Brutus*, his study of a politician sculpted in bitterness in Rome where he was living with other Florentine exiles.

You will also find the model for **Benvenuto Cellini**'s dramatic *Perseus* in the Loggia dei Lanzi, as well as the original bas relief belonging to it showing Perseus liberating Andromeda. Cellini's real reputation rests on his racy autobiography – that of a murderer, wencher, swordsman and a jeweller without equal. It is the most vivid picture of sixteenth-century Italy we have.

Donatello is in the Great Hall on the first floor, once the cellblock. He pulled the blind on medieval sculpture and his break with the past sings out from his *St George*, begun in 1415 when he was 29, at the behest of the Armourers Guild. The young saint's vibrancy and lofty composure apparently caused a stir. 'It is as if there is the movement of life under the marble,' they marvelled. The bas relief below marked his novel discovery of very low relief, which made for the illusion of movement.

His saucy, long-haired *David* in bronze, dominating the Hall, came to life when Donatello was middle-aged. This is the first free-standing nude of the Renaissance, his most ambiguous work, and was thought to have been modelled on a Florentine urchin. Some claim to see the moral decadence of the times mirrored in it. It certainly contrasts tellingly with the earlier, graceful, bodiced *David* done in marble when he was 22.

When he was only 16, he had been allowed to sit in on the panel adjudicating on the competition for the doors of the Baptistry. The samples submitted are on the wall in the Hall. The set subject for the test was the Sacrifice of Isaac, and they had whittled down the five candidates to Lorenzo Ghiberti, Donatello's master, and Brunelleschi, to become his close friend. The latter's entry on the left is odd – despite the drama of the moment, those present seem amazingly casual: two attend to their feet and the ram scratches its ear. Ghiberti spared us the goriness and *his* people pay attention. He, as we know, won.

Donatello lived to be 80, never short of commissions, and a favourite of Cosimo de' Medici. He was generous with his earnings: it is told how he kept money in a basket slung from the ceiling and let friends dip into it whenever they would.

Palazzo Pitti

This huge, barrack-like place beyond the Ponte Vecchio, Oltrarno is where to enjoy the sunny disposition of **Raphael**, now a bit out of fashion. If the Palace looks a trifle out of place in a city of due proportion, that's because it was ordered by a rich fifteenth-century banker, Luca Pitti, who wanted to upstage the Medicis. But he ended up in ruin, and Cosimo I bought the uncompleted edifice, later to become his own dynasty's new residence. Today, it is the home of the Florence fashion shows.

The collection is in the **Palatine Gallery** (open 9 a.m.–2 p.m.; closed Mondays) on the first floor, to the left at the top of the stairs (the rooms on the right can be ignored). Unlike the Uffizi, the Pitti doesn't lecture. Here, the Medicis' pictures are arranged as they would be in a private collection, with an eye only for pleasure. The sumptuous rooms with their splendidly frescoed ceilings are named after the gods.

Treasures abound, including an unsightly sleeping *Cupid* by Caravaggio in Jupiter's Room.

Titian holds court in the first two rooms, Venus and Apollo. His *Portrait of a Gentleman*, with a troubled, introspective look, otherwise known as 'The Man with the Grey Eyes', is believed to have been inspired by the Duke of Norfolk. It is in Apollo's Room.

Raphael starts in Jupiter's Room, the former throne room. His *Donna Velata* (*Veiled Woman*) is thought to picture a Roman brunette who often modelled for him, known as 'the baker's daughter'. She is supposed to have sat for the most popular portrait in the Pitti, his tender *Madonna della Seggiola* (*Madonna with the Chair*) in Saturn's Room; the face is still recognisable in Rome's Trastevere today.

Raphael was not averse to a little light plagiarism. Experts presume, from the hands of *Maddalena Doni* in the same room, that he must have had a peep at Leonardo da Vinci's *Gioconda*, while she was being painted in Florence. An interesting Raphael, easily missed, is his *Pregnant Lady*, next to the exit in the Iliad Room.

Your legs permitting, it is now worth climbing up through the ordered **Boboli Gardens** behind the *Palazzo*, because they set out so boldly the High Renaissance view that nature was preferable in an unnatural state. Trees and shrubs are regimented like troops.

Overlooking the gardens is the formidable Belvedere Fort by the Grand Duke Ferdinand I, with defensive buttresses pointed at his citizenry below. There is a panoramic bar on the way, and the view of Florence from it is spectacular. One sees how totally the city is dominated by Brunelleschi's dome. It must have been from some such vantage point that Michelangelo is said to have looked down upon the Cathedral and declared: 'I'm going to Rome to make you a sister – bigger, yes, but not more beautiful!'

Santa Maria Novella These sights are the core of Florence. You will have done it cursory justice. Much more remains, but you need more time if you are not to suffer indigestion. If you have it, do see Santa Maria Novella (next to the station) for a lighter look at the Renaissance. Behind the high altar, the frescoes by **Domenico Ghirlandaio** compose a back-copy of a glossy, late fifteenth-century society magazine. They are bursting with detail and happy touches. A modern gloss on the lives of the Virgin and St John the Baptist, they feature everybody who was anybody in Florence at the time.

They are a revelation on contemporary fashion, too, especially ladies' headgear, which steals the show in the scene of the Baptist's birth. Note the hurried late-arrival holding on to her fruit like a hat – a nice guess at what came next! Though pooh-poohed by the purists, these cameos proved hugely popular. Among the artist's helpers was an often insolent 16-year-old boy who would insist on correcting his drawings. He was called Michelangelo.

The church was begun by the Dominicans in the late thirteenth-century as a counter-weight to the Franciscans' Santa Croce. Because the Dominicans' rather academic style of preaching targeted the educated, they made their church smaller. An optical illusion hides by how much: the pillars march towards the altar with decreasing gaps between them, making the nave seem longer than it is.

To the left of the main altar hangs the famous wooden crucifix carved by **Brunelleschi** after being challenged by a mortified Donatello to improve on one he had done. The architect of the Duomo's dome had derided his friend's Christ as 'a peasant'. When he saw the result, Donatello admitted defeat.

In the adjoining so-called **Spanish Chapel**, outside and to the left of the church (open only till 12 noon), the dwarfing frescoes by **Andrea di Firenze** are serious dissertations on the Dominican way to spiritual salvation in the mid-fourteenth century. On the right, for instance, the black-and-white dogs tearing into wolves symbolise Dominicans dealing with heretics.

Santa Croce   At first you may wonder at all the fuss over the church of Santa Croce, in the piazza of the same name, just east of the Palazzo Vecchio. Like San Lorenzo, it gets off to a bad start. Built to pack them in, this great barn – the biggest Franciscan church in Italy – was until the 1950s a national pantheon. The first sight on the right is the hideous tomb of Michelangelo, wrought by his admirer and friend Vasari. Just as rhetorical is a cenotaph to Dante, which is no compliment to the poet's astringency (he is actually buried in Ravenna). Galileo, Machiavelli and many others lie here.

The Franciscan founders would not only have been shocked by Vasari's heavy hand at art. Santa Croce was once ablaze with four-teenth-century frescoes; bowing down to orders from Cosimo I, he had them all wiped out. The heavy altars in the aisles, which clash with the church's simplicity, were his idea as well.

Giotto's frescoes, thank God, survived. They are in the tiny chapel to the right of the main altar, and were found only a century ago – then to undergo 'improvements'. These have now been removed, exposing the originals. His masterpiece, *The Death of St Francis*, with its extraordinary play of hands, is almost intact.

The vivid frescoes smothering the other chapels on the right are by the hand of Giotto's most faithful pupil, Taddeo Gaddi and his son Agnolo.

Outside on the left is the door into the cloisters. The far end of this little oasis of quietness is framed by the portico of the **Pazzi Chapel**, revered by many as the apotheosis of **Brunelleschi**, surpassing even the Old Sacristy in San Lorenzo. Based on the concept of the circle as the nearest shape to perfection, it is almost an abstraction.

The main interest in the museum on the way out is a great, damaged crucifix by **Cimabue**, the most eminent casualty of the 1966 floods.

San Marco   At the northernmost edge of central Florence, in the Piazza San Marco off Via Cavour, is the Dominican monastery of San Marco and the mystical world of **Fra Angelico**. Here, the aura of monkish life withstands daily invasion. This is where Savonarola, the Prior, was grabbed and dragged off to be burnt at the stake in the Piazza della Signoria on 23 May 1498. You can still see his cell. Before him, the Prior was Fra Angelico, from nearby Fiesole (1387–1455).

Although born a century after Giotto and a contemporary of Uccello, Fra Angelico is far removed from the worldliness of the Renaissance. This devout friar painted no naked bodies; everyday life does not exist for him. While Uccello pored over perspective, Fra Angelico serenely painted away at the contours of the soul. He seemed to paint visions rather than real people. His renunciation of the world even led him to turn down a Papal offer to be Archbishop of Florence.

The monastery is now his one-man show, beginning in the Pilgrims' Hospice, on the right of the entrance. Of his thirty-five scenes from the life of Christ, one admirer wrote: 'He painted here with his breath.' Across the cloisters in the Chapter House, his enormous *Crucifixion*, so intensely painful yet so restrained in its composition, is regarded as his finest work.

At the top of the stairs to the first floor, you are confronted by the friar's most popular piece, the *Annunciation*, in a Renaissance porch. It is the prelude to the forbidding atmosphere of the forty-four spartan cells, relieved only by the frescoes. On the whole, those on the right are Fra Angelico's and those on the left his pupils'.

Ospedale   Hard by San Marco is the Piazza Santissima Annunziata, flanked
degli   by the colonnades of the Hospital of the Innocents, the first emergence
Innocenti   of Renaissance lay architecture in Florence, designed by Brunelleschi. Interspersed between the arches, terracotta babies in swaddling clothes cry out for help. It was founded in 1495, the first foundling hospital in Europe. Offspring were deposited, anonymously, in a kind of rotating letter-box under the arcades on the left.

How did they   The superly restored interior of a wealthy patrician family's dwell-
live?   ing gives an insight into everyday fourteenth-century life. The **Palazzo Davanzati** is at 13 Via Porta Rossa, which runs south from the Piazza Signoria.

Casa Buonarroti Admirers of Michelangelo will be unable to miss 70 Via Ghibellina, near Santa Croce, a fine house bought by the artist for his family, where some of his drawings, clay models, and early marble reliefs are on display, including an animated *Battle of the Centurions*. Among the drawings are meticulous sketches for figures in the Sistine Chapel, and there is a tortured model for a 'Fluvial God'.

Palazzo Medici A delightful, gossipy, fifteenth-century fresco cycle by **Benozzo Gozzoli** decorates the chapel in this massive *palazzo* at 1 Via Cavour (near the Cathedral), built for the Medici family in 1440. His *Going of the Wise Men to Bethlehem* was based on an actual procession held in Florence and has snaps of all the participants, among whom were members of the Medici family, including a 15-year-old Lorenzo the Magnificent.

Santa Maria del Carmine The frescoes of **Masaccio** at the church of the Carmine in Oltrarno have been under restoration for some time, and cannot be seen.

Dante's House Ignore the so-called house of Dante. It's not.

What to do Florence is no 'fun' city. No city in Central Italy really is. There is no or little nightlife, at least for outsiders. After dinner, Florentines with time to spare wander over to the Piazza Repubblica, between the Piazza della Signoria and the Cathedral, and have a coffee or *amaro* at the unlikely named Café Paszkowski or at one of its three plush rivals. This square is the only real sitting-and-watching place in Florence. The tables are not cheap.

Young people content themselves with the Ponte Vecchio, which nightly plays host to a kind of international youth congress. They play guitars; sing; trade drugs; New Yorkers meet Poles; East Germans meet Westerners. To jaundiced eyes, it can be an encouraging or an untidy sight. In nearby streets, crowds gather around tumblers, clowns and young magicians.

The Tourist Board realised that this was not enough. As a timid start at making amends, it now usually opens each municipally-run museum for three or four evenings a month, from 9 to 11 p.m. Admittedly, these establishments include the Florentine Museum of Pre-History and one on the History of Science. But there are star turns: the Cathedral Museum; the Casa Buonarroti and the Palazzo Vecchio. A brochure is available from the Tourist Offices.

Festivals There are concerts, too, including the now established *Maggio Musicale* (Musical May) in the *Teatro Comunale* and the *Teatro della Pergola*, which extends into June. The amorphous *Firenze Estate* (Florence summer) promises unspecified events in various places from June to September. Better known is the *Estate* up at Fiesole with music and drama performances, some in the Roman amphitheatre, dotted around between June and August.

Shopping The best buys are jewellery, leather, umbrellas, pottery, paper and olive oil. Quiet bargaining is the norm; it produces modest results.

Arguing will produce none. You would be lucky to hit on real bargains nowadays, but shopping in Florence is still rewarding because quality is still as high as the style, and the craftsman is king.

The goldsmiths' shops on the Ponte Vecchio burst with expensive **jewellery**, with the emphasis on gold, coral and pearls, but you can also dig out less expensive trinkets.

Leather is sold everywhere; Florence has a greater variety of shoes than anywhere else in Italy. Gucci and Ferragamo began in Florence, and their elegant shops, with clothes for men and women, as well as shoes, purses, handbags and luggage, are well worth looking at. Both are on Via dei Tornabuoni, the Bond Street of Florence, along with the other big Italian fashion houses. The street, the most fashionable in Florence and named after the astute mother of Lorenzo the Magnificent, is the continuation of the Ponte Santa Trinita, the next bridge along from the Ponte Vecchio, going *away* from the Uffizi.

Slightly less expensive leather is to be had at the Leather School attached to Santa Croce. Students there learn how to make Florentine purses and notebooks stamped with gold, in addition to handbags, luggage and leather clothing. Big-name designers sometimes commission their work; the students' prices are lower than their patrons'.

In the alleys around the Via dei Tornabuoni, notably the Borgo San Jacopo and the Via Porta Rossa, and around the Duomo, scores more shops offer leather goods through the whole gamut of prices.

Via Por Santa Maria is a good place to find less expensive **gloves** and **silk scarves**. Also look for brightly coloured cotton **umbrellas** with wooden handles, and for **terracotta pots** as you wander.

Many shops, as well as outdoor market stalls, will show you Fendi or Vuitton look-alikes at bargain prices. Don't believe the labels, but the goods are well worth scrutinising, because the workmanship is often excellent and the prices too. The designs are similar to the real thing.

One famous open-air **market** is the late Renaissance Loggia del Mercato Nuovo (New Market), between Via Porta Rossa and Via Por Santa Maria, also known as the market of the Porcellino, after the popular seventeenth-century bronze boar drinking among toads and grass-snakes at its edge. It does a brisk business in fake brands, as well as in straw hats and bags, embroidered blouses, tablecloths and objects of gilded or painted wood. The *putti*, little cherubs, are charming.

The other market, outside San Lorenzo, runs more to cheap clothing and leather, with no pretensions at all. The *Officina* at Santa Maria Novella sells its own preparations of perfumes, soaps, lotions, shampoos and pot-pourri in a restored former chapel in Via della Scala, near a church of the same name.

Shops selling Florence's distinctive **marbled paper** are all over the centre.

**Where to
stay**

The mere fact that there are 359 hotels in Florence, half of them one-star, shows how crowded it can become. It is already crammed by late April. Its wealthier visitors, including Americans, are not as numerous as they once were, so the better hotels are emptier than the down-market ones – above all, in suffocating August.

Given such a massive choice, these recommendations must be very selective. Hoteliers all advise booking in advance.

Top range

Perhaps the best and most central 'traditional' hotel is the five-star **Savoy**, Piazza Repubblica; tel. 283313.

Its rival is the elegant, leathery, spacious **Excelsior**, 3 Piazza Ognissanti; tel. 264201. Overlooking the Arno, it usefully faces a guarded car-park.

Facing the station is the long-established, efficient, huge **Baglioni**, Piazza Unità Italiana; tel. 218441.

Via della Scala, near the station, has a row of seedy hotels, but a stylish one with big duplex rooms and a small swimming pool is the four-star **Croce di Malta**, 7 Via della Scala; tel. 282600.

Two modernised four-star hotels overlooking the Arno are the **Berchielli**, 14 Lungarno Acciaiuoli; tel. 264061; and opposite, almost *in* the river on the south side, the smart, well patronised **Lungarno**, 14 Borgo San Jacopo; tel. 264211.

A cheaper four-star near the Duomo is the delightful **Monna Lisa**, 27 Borgo Pinti; tel. 247 9751. This small Renaissance palazzo with frescoed ceilings and great charm is much in vogue. Ask for a room giving on to the courtyard (*cortile*).

Mid range

Traditionalists will adore Florence's oldest hotel, the three-star **Porta Rossa**, allegedly dating from 1386, and right in the heart of the city at 19 Via Porta Rossa; tel. 287523. It has creaking parquet floors, huge halls, belching plumbing, vaulted ceilings and off-hand charm.

In a quiet side street near Santa Croce is the **Dante**, Via San Cristofano; tel. 241772. It is recommended by locals.

Aprile, 6 Via della Scala (near the station); tel. 216237, is a fifteenth-century Medici palazzo fully renovated. Friendly and tasteful, this has won acclaim.

Hermitage, 1 Vicolo Marzio; tel. 287216, is only yards from the Ponte Vecchio. Its roof-top terrace has great views of the centre.

Modest but up to date is the three-star **Hotel Rapallo**, 7 Via Santa Caterina d'Alessandria (near San Marco); tel. 472412. It has room safes.

Bottom range

A handy small two-star is **Hotel Consigli**, 50 Lungarno Vespucci; tel. 214172.

Also central, near the Pitti Palace, is **La Scaletta**, 13 Via Guicciardini; tel. 283028.

Near the railway station: **Madrid**, 59 Via della Scala; tel. 282776.

You may prefer to do as they all once did and stay in that typically Florentine institution, a *pensione*. Alas, officially, the 'rooms with a view' no longer exist – the Tourist Board has renamed them all 'hotels' and given them stars. Unofficially, they do still exist, posing as *Hotel Pensione*. But beware: some still stick to their *pensione* habits and can shut you out at night if you do not ask for the key.

A pleasant one, with the atmosphere of a private house and a visitors' book, and in the smartest street, is the **Tornabuoni Beacci** (three-star) on the top floors of 3 Via Tornabuoni; tel. 212645 or 268377. Booking is a must.

In the same street, with quiet back rooms and the same intimate feel, is **Residenza**, 8 Via Tornabuoni; tel. 284197 or 218684.

E. M. Forster's *pensione* has been identified as the **Jennings-Riccioli**, 7 Corso Tintori; tel. 244751. It now has three stars.

Where to eat

Florence has as many restaurants as street corners, and the ones the Florentines prefer often offer a somewhat bohemian, deceptively rough-and-ready atmosphere, together with bountiful 'peasant cooking'. It is a little heavy for some tastes, and is often deliberately rudimentary – fare for ruddy, impoverished peasants on a winter night. Needless to say, it is usually excellent, and the steaks in Florence, noted for their size, are famed. That said, gastronomically, Florence isn't Paris.

Listed here are a sampling of the 'in' places in 1989. Many still *do not* accept credit cards.

Cantinetta Antinori, 3 Piazza Antinori (at the end of Via Tornabuoni; closed Sundays). Off the fifteenth-century courtyard of the famous Chianti family *palazzo*, this is an ideal lunch place, where you construct your fare from ingredients grown on the Antinori estates.

La Baraonda, 67 Via Ghibellina (near Santa Croce; closed Sunday evenings); tel. 234 1171. Bustling, friendly, solid and reasonable.

Trattoria Coco Lezzone, 26 Via Parioncino (near Piazza Santa Trinita; closed Tuesday evenings and Sundays); tel. 287178. This is like dining in a packed lavatory, but it's worshipped. Be prepared to queue.

Cibreo, 11 Via Macci; tel. 234 1100 (closed Mondays). Locally recommended.

Ristorante Di' Fagioli, 47R Corso dei Tintori (closed Saturdays and Sundays); tel. 244285. A typical, serious eating place with few frills. Try the *involtini di Gigi*.

Il Latini, 6R Via Palchetti (near Piazza Goldoni; closed Mondays and Tuesday lunch); tel. 210916. This *is* eating *alla Fiorentina*. Boisterous, crowded, communal tables, shared wine, only apparently haphazard under the hanging hams. This is where to test the steaks.

Ristorante da Otello, 36R Via degli Orti Oricellari (near the station; closed Tuesdays); tel. 215819. Far less typical; bland, quiet and courteous.

Ristorante Ottorino, 12 Via delle Oche (near the Duomo; closed

Sundays and all of August); tel. 218747. Smart, slightly expensive, professional and discreet in a modernised rustic setting. Here you can talk.

Sabatini, 9 Via Panzani (very near the station; closed Mondays); tel. 282 802. A commodious, traditional, aloofish, quiet establishment. It used to be the best. It is expensive.

Sostanza, 25 Via Porcellana (near Ognissanti; closed Saturday evenings and Sundays); tel. 212691. A rowdy variation on Il Latini. Not a bit smooth, but much loved.

Many Florentines, to escape tourists and menus in English, are increasingly crossing the river to eat in peace in Oltrarno. You could do worse than roam around in their tracks. Try the downstairs **Trattoria Capponi**, 26 Borgo San Frediano (over the Vespucci Bridge; closed Tuesdays); tel. 292130.

Fiesole

Instant relief from the rigours of Florence is to be found up in its over-looking hill-town, an airy place, once Etruscan, which immediately puts Dante's city into perspective in the superb context of its huge river valley. You can lounge around outside at café tables. Some people prefer Fiesole to Florence as a base to stay. It is 14 km away from the city and 295 m above sea level.

Getting there

Take the number 7 bus from Via Cerretani, near the Cathedral, or at San Marco. The grinding climb up through the olives and umbrella pines takes twenty-five minutes.

History

Fiesole's Etruscans were subdued by the Romans in 283 BC, but it was not until the town turned against them in the 'Social War' that they put in a garrison. This was the seed of a fully-fledged Roman city, which roosted it over the entire region before being slowly out-shone by the rival down in the valley.

What to see

San Francesco

The truly revealing view of Florence emerges after a toil up the narrow Via San Francesco from the bus terminus. The sight rewards the effort. There is a small Franciscan monastery and church at the top, once the site of an Etruscan-Roman necropolis 'destroyed by the Florentines', as the notices put it, in AD 1010. The friars' museum includes a piece of original Etruscan wall.

Roman ruins

Back down at the terminus behind the originally eleventh-century Cathedral is the entrance to a fair-sized Roman amphitheatre, in itself a balcony for another spectacle of gently interlocking hills in the distance. Behind the theatre to the right is a sophisticated Roman bath complex. The rectangular cavity you first come across was a swimming pool. The awning in the right-hand corner covers the boiler-room, as the two circular 'wells' perhaps suggest. The three arches composed part of a *loggia* built over the Etruscan boundary wall.

Where to stay The most convenient hotel, in the terminus square, is the three-star **Aurora**, 39 Piazza Mino; tel. 59100. Among five other hotels is the two-star **Villa Bonelli**, 1 Via Francesco Poeti; tel. 59513.

The Mugello

The Florentines delight in the Mugello as a lovely back garden, an escape from summer in the city, ideal for day-trips (so avoid it at weekends). If you are in Tuscany for the first time, it will not be on the 'must' list, its main attraction being impressive scenery – verdant, mountainous, thickly forested, watered by bubbling brooks and at times almost alpine. Vineyards alternate with laden orchards.

It is a very bumpy hollow, 30 km across between the Apennines and the hills north of Florence. The river Sieve curves through it before joining the Arno upstream from the city. To reach it, climb up the SS 65, which heads north for Bologna, or break off the A 1 for the same city at Barberino.

Barberino di Mugello The township, once ruled from a hidden twelfth-century castle 1 km away, is no prize-winner. But curiously its fifteenth-century Palazzo Pretorio is barely distinguishable from the other *palazzi* forming the town's vast horse-shoe square, a kind of Italian 10 Downing Street – that's a new one.

Pratolino If you choose the SS 65, you will first reach Pratolino, 12 km out of Florence. It is synonymous with the **Villa Demidoff**, so called after its last owner, a Russian prince. It is a vast park and nature reserve among rolling hills and meadows laid out by the Medici Duke, Francesco I, around a rather prosaic, closed villa built for his mistress and later wife, Bianca Capella. A favourite with fleeing Florentines, it is the magnificent backdrop for summer concerts, and they call it the 'Laboratory of Marvels'. Fifty-three types of bird have been spotted within its confines, but literally the biggest marvel is the so-called **Colossus of the Apennines**, a huge, bearded, squatting giant by the late Renaissance sculptor Giambologna, one of the great outside ornaments of the time.

San Piero a Sieve To get the Mugello's geography right, a massive, high-altitude Medici fortress, open to the public, is an aid. To get to the sixteenth-century **Fortezza di San Martino**, take the steep track that flies up from the old quarter of this crossroads township 25 km from Florence (where the SS 65 meets the SS 551). It is in good shape, with underground chambers and gun emplacements. Its cannon could traverse the horizons, with the subjects of the Medicis for miles around within easy range. It is a popular outing for the locals.

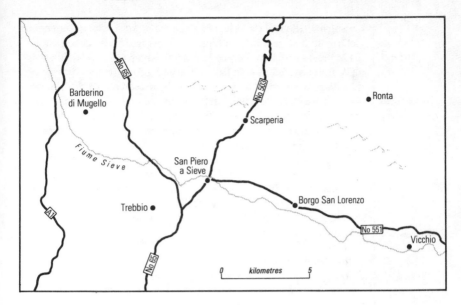

The Mugello

Castle of Trebbio

So are the meadows and shady cypress trees below the earlier, elegant Renaissance castle perched still higher on the opposite side of the valley, designed by Michelozzo Michelozzi. The castle itself is occupied and closed to chance visitors. It is reached via a track off the SS 65 near San Piero.

Scarperia

Borgo San Lorenzo, the 'capital' of the Mugello, was hit by an earthquake in 1919 which left little to see. On a high platform above the valley, on the SS 503, Scarperia (population 5,000) is the only township with real character, mainly because of its very mean Palazzo Pretorio in the main street. The elegant façade is only a front for a stout, skirted oblong of defiance. If it vaguely recalls the Palazzo Vecchio in Florence, that is perhaps because Scarperia was founded by Florence in 1306, as a forward defence position against would-be predators from the north. A century later, in fact, it did repel a siege by a force despatched against it by the Archbishop of Milan.

Opposite the *palazzo* is the frescoed church of a former monastery and, to the left, its simple cloister.

Vicchio

On the way out of the Mugello along the SS 551, Vicchio is a sleepy, nondescript place with the hooded figure of Giotto presiding over the main square. He was born in the next-door village of **Vespignano**, and a yellow tourist sign points the way to the isolated birthplace of 'the restorer of Italian painting' as the plaque has it (open p.m. only at weekends, Tuesdays and Thursdays). It was hereabouts that he was 'discovered' carving by the old Cimabue. Beato Angelico was also born in Vicchio and there is a fragment of a house where Benvenuto Cellini often stayed. But nothing of all this fame has rubbed off.

Rufina

On the way back to Florence along the River Sieve, there is a strikingly alpine stretch – with firs, valley and glinting river – just before the village where they produce one of the most widely sold Chiantis.

Where to stay

If you are stuck for a hotel in the Mugello, make for one of the four big ones at **Ronta**, where the Florentines park their grannies for summer. It is 6 km north of Borgo San Lorenzo on the road to Faenza in a tight alpinish valley at 450 metres.

The first of the (undistinguished) four is **Hotel Parco dei Fiori**, 72 Via Faentina; tel. 840 3067. The local hospitality derives from pre-war years when Englishmen would spend the July–October 'season' here, until American bombs gutted the big *pensione* where they all stayed.

Chianti

For many, especially for its many British and other foreign residents, Chianti *is* Tuscany, a ravishing world of quietness, with smooth, gently ascending hills cloaked in woods, disciplined vineyards, olive groves flashing in the sun and lonely castles. Yet it is domestic too, the familiar background to so much Italian painting.

This world is so many people's image of what Italy as a whole *should* look like, but it is far from huge, being simply the stunning hill-country between Florence and Siena where Chianti Classico comes from. At first, coming from Florence, Chianti is gentle and lush, slopey rather than hilly, but then it mounts like a breaker, with deep valleys barrelling forward through high and rounded hills.

Getting there

A car is almost essential. If you start out from Florence, cross the Arno over the Ponte Carraia, head for Porta Romana, and then at the messy big junction take the 70-km long SS 222, known as the **Chiantigiana**. This meanders tightly through the Chianti world, ending in Siena.

Otherwise, Sita buses from Florence follow the SS 222 too, as well as the Cassia (SS 2), less interesting because it skirts Chianti's heart. Inter-town buses also exist.

History

Settled by Etruscans and then Romans, Chianti became a feudal possession of the big family with which it is still associated today as early as the eighth century. They are the Ricasolis, who live in the solitary Castello di Brolio to the north-east of Siena, descendants of the original feudal lords, the Firidolfi (see page 125, under 'Wine'). Theirs is just one of the many sturdy castles peppering the hills, defence positions constantly fought over by Florence and Siena in the twelfth century during a protracted power struggle. The road to take to inspect

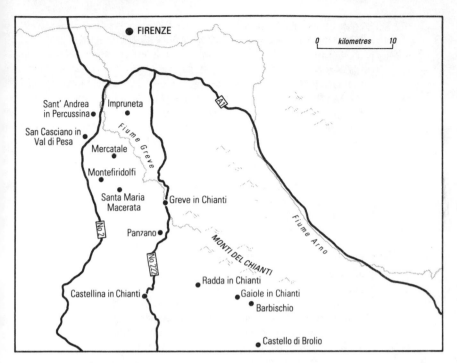

FIRENZE

kilometres 10

Sant' Andrea
in Percussina

Impruneta

San Casciano in
Val di Pesa

Mercatale

Fiume Greve

Montefiridolfi

Santa Maria
Macerata

Greve in Chianti

No.2

Panzano

No.222

MONTI DEL CHIANTI

Fiume Arno

Castellina in Chianti

Radda in Chianti

Gaiole in Chianti

Barbischio

Castello di Brolio

Chianti

these fortresses is the SS 408, dubbed 'Road of the Castles' (*Strada dei Castelli*). The tourist people have worked out coloured itineraries for tracking down the others, but they are confusing and unhelpful.

Florence won the struggle, and in the next century the word Chianti appeared for the first time when she formed the so-called 'Chianti League', one of several into which the Florentine Republic was split. The township of Radda won leadership in the fifteenth century, and still is the capital today. But Chianti now, finally, belongs to Siena.

Wine

The nicest pastime in Chianti is sampling the wine – free. There are no firm rules, and just because the estates are clearly signposted does not automatically mean they will let you examine (*assaggiare*) their product. If they announce they sell wine on the spot (*Vendita Diretta*), then you can. In the townships, look for *Enoteca*: some allow sampling only if asked; some refuse; others positively invite you to sip.

The most enterprising estate is the hidden Castello di Brolio, an 8-km crow's-flight south of Gaiole (turn left off the SS 408 on to the SS 484). It passed into the hands of the Firidolfi family in the twelfth century; destroyed by the Aragonese, it was rebuilt as one of the first Renaissance fortresses in the fifteenth century. Visitors are allowed in to see the high pentagon of walls and the chapel only, driving up a steep gravel drive through sombre cypress trees. At the foot of the hill below the castle, along the road for Marcellino-Monti, the family has thoughtfully set up a reception centre in the production depot. It handles tasting, buying and guided tours.

It is to Brolio that the world owes Chianti. In the last century Baron Bettino Ricasoli, a former Italian Prime Minister, brilliant, cross-eyed and very jealous, snatched his wife away from a ball in Florence because a young man had made a pass at her, and drove her through the snow to the castle where he stayed with her, to spare her similar attentions, for ever.

The Baron killed his time wine-doodling, and finally hit on a mixture of grapes that proved hugely popular and was imitated by all. 'You are now in the land of the Black Cockerel,' the notices say as you enter Chianti Classico, and the *Gallo Nero* is on the neck labels.

Seven other kinds of Chianti also exist, in a large area all around the Classico, some from quite far away. They are: Chianti Montalbano; Chianti Rufina; Chianti Colli Fiorentini; Chianti Colli Senesi; Chianti Colli Aretini (Arezzo); Chianti Colline Pisane; and, simply, Chianti.

Chianti is for drinking both young and old. The young wine goes into the typical flasks; the old into bottles. When aged for at least three years in oak butts, it is entitled to the honour *Riserva.*

Nowadays about 45 per cent of Chianti finds its way down foreign throats; the Chianti Wine Growers' Consortium has pronounced 1983 and 1986 the best recent years, and many would judge the best Chianti to be Brolio Riserva.

Greve in Chianti The mini 'capital', 25 km south of Florence on the SS 222, is a charmer named after the river running past it; it is built on the site of its burned-down castle. Its novel main square is an almost perfect isosceles triangle flanked all around by arcades which are also flowered terraces. One *Enoteca* is at the point of the triangle and there is *Vendita Diretta* just outside the township.

Panzano The Chianti Consortium run a serious, signposted *Enoteca* at nearby Panzano, at the top of the valley.

Radda in Chianti But the most enticing township must be Radda in Chianti, off the SS 222 to the east. From high up, it looks out over a regal swell of wooded hills stretching to the horizon. It is run from a handsome sixteenth-century Palazzo Podestà, opposite an odd fifteenth-century church with a semi-circular picture frame for its upper façade. Here, two *enoteche* invite you in, belonging to the Vigna Vecchia estate and the local wine co-operative.

Gaiole in Chianti Down in a hollow encircled by low hills, Gaiole is less eloquent, even dull, but tasting is done, especially at tables outside *Vecchie Cantine,* just as you drive in.

Barbischio What makes up for its plainness is this astonishing crow's-nest five minutes away, with a whole valley below it. A restored tower denotes its departed castle. There is no tasting here, not even a bar.

Castellina in Chianti

The remaining centre is a husbanded one-street village 578 metres up, with a fake Romanesque church and a done-up fort. It is recognisable from a distance because of a nasty, humming, cattle-feed factory. Ten estates are thereabouts, but in the village only one, La Castellina, will offer you a glass, on demand.

Visually, Western Chianti is not in the same league (if time presses, it is perhaps better left unknown).

Impruneta

About 15 km south of Florence comes the town named after a medieval sanctuary known as St Mary in the Pinewood. It consists of a huge sloping square, commanded from below by the low-slung church of **Santa Maria** with a fine thirteenth-century bell-tower. The original church (the present façade is seventeenth-century) was built three centuries earlier to shelter a Byzantine image of the Virgin found during the ploughing of a field; the oxen knelt when they stumbled upon it. Kept at the altar, it is flanked by two chapels designed by Michelozzo, both brightened by gleaming terracottas, unmistakably by Luca della Robbia.

Sant' Andrea in Percussina

Then, a few km due west of the town, off the Cassia below Tavarnuzze, the now restored villa where Niccolò Machiavelli did his writing awaits visitors. It is in the clearly signposted hamlet of Sant' Andrea. The former emissary of the Florentine Republic retired to his property here, which he called his **Albergaccio** (Bloody Inn), after being sent into exile by the Medicis for a year: they had returned to power with the help of Spanish troops in 1512 and at once suspected him (wrongly, it seems) of subversion. Though he grovelled, they never gave him another post. As he wrote to a friend, he would spend afternoons arguing over dice with the locals in the tavern, and the evenings 'holding discourse' with Roman historians, and composing. Here he wrote *The Prince* and *On the Art of War*.

San Casciano

The attraction of nearby San Casciano is the wealthy little Tuscan Gothic **Chiesa della Misericordia** in Via Morrocchesi. It boasts a painted crucifix by Simone Martini, another by Donatello, and a vivid wall-pulpit by the fourteenth-century sculptor Giovanni Balduccio.

This could be a chance to dip into the vineyards on the east of the River Greve. Make for the smart 'in' village of **Mercatale** (outside tables), but turn off beforehand for the microscopic **Montefiridolfi**. Beyond, the scenery becomes almost English, very quiet, and the road runs actually through the vines, past the discreet farm of the Antinori estate, one of the big Chianti producers. It fizzles out in another minute hamlet called **Santa Maria Macerata**, with a tiny church bracketed by cypress trees.

Siena

If Florence is the domineering male of Tuscany, Siena is the estranged sister, bejewelled and gentle, lost in a dream, perfectly preserved. To her admirers, she is quite simply the most beautiful city in Tuscany. Dickens found her 'dreamy and fantastic' (though he preferred Verona). Siena does belong to a vision, utterly divorced from today. Seen from a distance, she is a medieval fantasy in the middle of nowhere, with crazy zig-zag walls wrapped around a huge carcass of a Cathedral and a tower as tall as a Dolomitic peak.

Like a vision, Siena happens at once. Suburbs and mess are absent: there is countryside – and then Siena. Once inside, the sense of having shut out the world is strong. What strengthens it is: no traffic.

Her difference from Florence strikes home at once. No two cities in Central Italy have been divided by deeper enmity and bitterness for so long; they had, and have, nothing in common. If Florence is the straight line, Siena is the curve. Florence is Renaissance; Siena is Gothic – when the Renaissance came, she looked the other way. Artistically, Florence pioneered a highway, Siena a rather special by-way, and far earlier. The rich Sienese school of painting is dramatically special. It is a refracted Byzantine world of gold backgrounds; oriental, but craftily seeing, eyes; rapt fervour. Siena is mystically religious; Florence is definitely secular. The patron saint of Florence, as a male city, is St John; Siena is formally pledged to the Virgin Mary.

Florence is intellect; Siena is sentiment. If the streets of Florence seem to oppress, those of Siena, strangely, render people larger than life. Florence is sober and ordered; Siena is dressed to kill. Florence lies in a valley; Siena (population 65,000) graces three hills, small and compact. At night, Florence swelters; a cool breeze wafts around Siena.

Getting there

Via the free *superstrada*, Siena is 68 km south of Florence, on a plateau in the heart of Tuscany. The express Sita bus from Florence takes one hour; the infrequent train one and a half. From Rome by road, it is 224 km: take the A1 to the Valdichiana turn off, then left on the SS 326. By rail from Rome, change at Chiusi.

Tourist Offices

The handiest, municipal, one is the *Azienda di Turismo*, in the main square, 56 Piazza del Campo; tel. 280551. The main office is at 43 Via Città nearby; tel. 42209. The stuffier Siena Province office is at 92 Via Montanini; tel. 47051.

Getting around

If you are driving, head up to Piazza San Domenico, supervised by the Dominicans' severely Gothic great preaching church, and park. The buses from Florence also give up here. Then make straight down to the main square, Il Campo, where it all happened, and still does. Responding to its three hills, Siena is choppy with ups and downs, but the ridges of the hills form trunk and legs, and all merge and peter out in the hollowness of the Campo, the very essence of Siena's femininity. Elsewhere in Central Italy, the centre of life is usually the defendable highest point; here, it is at the most sensitive and lowest.

The city's three old parts, called *Terzi*, match her hills. Their main arteries, known as **Banchi di Sopra** (above), **Banchi di Sotto** (below) and **Via di Città**, run into each other behind the high rim of the Campo at the so-called **Croce di Travaglio**, Cross of Trouble. This was the nerve-centre of Siena; when factional fighting broke out, this junction was barricaded to stop it spreading.

The Via di Città climbs up from it towards the hypnotic Cathedral complex and the Picture Gallery – after the Campo, the two big attractions of Siena. The street itself is perhaps the most evocative in the city, a kind of canyon through the wealthy Gothic past. The stumps of rough medieval tower-houses go almost unnoticed among the high, stately *palazzi*, all outclassed by the curving and graceful fourteenth-century **Palazzo Chigi-Saracini** on the left, now a noted Academy of Music.

Its rows of pointed-arch windows enclosing trios of smaller arches are typical of Siena's elegant use of Gothic and of fancifully decorated windows all over the city. They are among her hallmarks; so are battlements underlined by tiny arches resting on shelves of upside-down 'pyramids'. Another superb example of Sienese Gothic is the nearby fourteenth-century **Palazzo Salimbeni**, the backdrop to the most perfect small square, of the same name, off Banchi di Sopra. On the right of this square is the Florentine-like Renaissance **Palazzo Spanocchi**. The contrast speaks tomes.

You are never left in any doubt at to what *Contrada*, or ward, you are in. Their names are embedded in the walls and their rival banners flap above the undulating streets in rivalry. It is a city of warm, red brick and grey stone which often seems to hem you in; then, through an alley, there is a sudden glimpse of horizon or of green valley beyond the walls. And strangely, wherever you are, you never see the hidden Campo until, drawn downwards, you stumble into it.

History

Montaigne thought the Campo 'the most beautiful square there is, not to be seen in any other city.' Some see a fan in its bold, descending symmetry; others a daring shell; for the Sienese, it is no less than a cloak of the Virgin spread out by the Virgin herself in magnificent recognition of their loyalty.

Holding centre stage, with its enormous needle of a tower, is the **Palazzo Pubblico**, the most elegant Gothic *palazzo* in all Tuscany, a difficult marriage of power and prettiness. The seat of the *Podestà*, and now the Town Hall, it was built at the turn of the thirteenth and fourteenth centuries, of brick over a first layer of travertine marble. The great copper disc below the battlements bears the monogram of Christ, the symbol of San Bernardino, one of Siena's two saints (the other is St Catherine).

The *palazzo* itself is also a symbol of Sienese Gothic. The ground floor's pointed arches enclosing rounded ones demonstrate the so-called 'Sienese arch'. Its delicate fretwork and decoration more or less set the trend for the whole city. Almost facing it with a stunted tower is the graceful, equally curving **Palazzo Sansedoni**. The similarity is striking.

A climb to the top of the nimble **Torre del Mangia**, 102 metres high, is the strenuous way to get the hang of Siena. Named after its first bell-ringer, it served as a watch-tower and alarm-sounder, but it was also an assertion of Siena's fierce civic pride, meant to impress the neighbours, a sort of medieval Eiffel Tower. Its great height was further meant by the city's fathers to play off that of the Cathedral, and balance the power of the Church with that of the politicians. The two brothers who built it were from Perugia and would have understood such things.

The Nine   Those particular city fathers are remembered in the very composition of the Campo, designed in nine bricked segments. They immortalise the so-called Government of Nine – wealthy commoners who ran Siena for sixty years, from 1292 onwards, the one little happy stretch of Siena's past. After decades of violence, fighting between the wards and, above all, conflict with Florence, the Nine ushered in peace at last and with it, Italian-style, wealth. To the Nine, we owe the Siena of today.

They achieved peace, though, only through a deal with the enemy. Florence was Guelf, and Siena had become the Ghibelline stronghold of all Tuscany, an ally of Pisa. She had wrung favours and privileges out of grateful Teutonic Emperors; as a result, Sienese merchants and bankers freely roamed Europe, selling and loaning, bringing back the interest long before the Florentines, and putting much of the money into embellishing their beloved city.

Even today the Sienese still relish the day in 1260 when, on a nearby hill at tiny Montaperti 12 km away, their troops trounced Florence in battle, killing 10,000 of the foe. The Florentine banner, tied to the tail of an ass, was triumphantly trailed through Siena's twisting streets.

That was before the Nine came to power. When they were finally overthrown in 1355 turnstile government and anarchy ensued, but the bloodiest scenes the Campo witnessed were in the sixteenth century when Florence had her revenge for Montaperti. Egged on by the Medici Duke Cosimo I, Charles V of Spain laid siege to Siena with 24,000 men.

The population held out for a year. Useless mouths were ejected; the defenders ate rats and grass. Around the city, trees creaked with the pendant corpses of would-be food smugglers hanged by the besiegers. When it was all over, only 8,000 Sienese were left alive. Their city, and the extensive Republic it ruled, passed to Florence.

Just outside the walls, Florence erected a watch-dog fortress to bully its new slave into submission. It throttled the Sienese sense of life, as it had earlier done to Pisa. Time stopped for Siena; its role was over.

The Palio

The Sienese re-live the roughness and tension of their lost freedom twice a year, through the famous three-lap bareback horse race around the Campo on 2 July and 16 August. It is the liveliest fiesta in Central Italy, a mix of medieval pomp, courage and subdued hooliganism dominated, say the Sienese, by destiny itself.

The Palio is Siena's life, its *raison d'être*. Even in mid-winter the talk is centering on the choice of jockeys and horses; the endless preparations are underpinned by lust for victory. The Palio is the only survivor of a string of violent contests staged in a medieval Siena especially given to inter-clan thuggery. It is war between the city's *Contrade*, or wards, and nothing angers a Sienese more than any supposition from outsiders that it must be a tourist gimmick.

The seventeen *Contrade* each have their own colours; an eagle, a panther, a giraffe and an owl figure among their emblems. They have their own elections, museums, fountains and churches where, on the day of the race, their horses are ceremonially blessed. It is taken as an excellent omen if the horse ignores etiquette in church. Only ten *Contrade* can run, and they are chosen by lot. So are the horses, but the jockeys are not Sienese at all. They are hired 'foreign' professionals, including 'cowboys' from the Maremma. They scheme and cheat, and are monitored with intense suspicion. 'He's a jockey,' means in Sienese, 'You can't trust him.'

The Palio run on 2 July is 'recent', begun in the seventeenth century. The August race was first held in 1147 to honour the Assumption of the Virgin, and is the more splendid and important. Tickets for seats around the square, or a place at a window, cost extravagantly 150–300,000 lire (£65–£130), and it is a tiresome rigmarole to obtain them. The form is to apply to an agency in touch with the thirty-three 'box-owners' *a year in advance*. One is Palio Viaggi, 7 Piazza Gramsci; tel. 280828, telex 573320.

But you can copy the Sienese and watch the race *free* from the centre of the Campo which can hold 40,000 people. Officials insist there is always room.

The Siena School

In a city dedicated to the Virgin, it is perhaps hardly surprising that its delicate painting was largely devotional. Sienese painting proper, with its bright colours, stiff groups, and intense spirituality, belongs to the thirteenth and fourteenth centuries. Here are Siena's foremost artists:

● **Duccio di Buoninsegna** (1255–1319), the master, elevated the stately Byzantine tradition to a new expressiveness and set Sienese painting on a new path. His many followers rarely strayed from it. His masterpiece is in the Cathedral museum.

● **Simone Martini** (1285–1344), wandered Italy and died in

Avignòn where he knew the poet Petrarch, who wrote of him (in Latin) that he was as popular as Giotto. He is Siena's Gothic painter – delicate, courtly, affected, and the first to work in fresco, in the Palazzo Pubblico.

● **Pietro** (1280–1348) and **Ambrogio Lorenzetti** (1285–1348) both echoed Giotto in a Sienese way. Pietro also reflected Duccio while Ambrogio developed a highly personal style and, as you can see in the Town Hall, was Italy's first political cartoonist. They superseded the mannered ways of Simone Martini with a strong sense of action. They died together in the plague.

● These four dictated the way; a cohort of Sienese artists marched behind them throughout the fourteenth century. In the fifteenth, **Il Sassetta** (1392–1451) introduced the elegance and gentleness of the so-called International Gothic style to Siena. One artist clearly influenced by him was the sculptor and painter **Il Vecchietta** ('Little Old Woman') (1412–80) who has left newly restored frescoes in the Baptistry.

● **Il Sodoma** (1477–1549) arrested the decline of the real Sienese school with his innovations. He was so called, we are told, because he lived with 'beardless boys' and a menagerie of dwarf donkeys, miniature horses and a talking crow that created a scandal.

● **Beccafumi** (1485–1551) is Siena's best-known sixteenth-century painter, influenced by Michelangelo and Raphael, and described as 'solitary beyond words'.

● **Jacopo della Quercia** (1371–1438), the maker of the girl's tomb in Lucca, is Siena's greatest sculptor. A plaque in a square named after him generously lauds him as 'a bridge of glory' between Giovanni Pisano and Michelangelo. He created the famous fountain in the Campo, known as the Joyful Fountain because of the festivities that greeted the arrival of water in the square in the fourteenth century. The bas-reliefs around it are poor copies of his damaged superb originals, now in the Loggia of the Palazzo Pubblico.

What to see

Museo Civico

The Civic Museum is on the first floor of the Palazzo Pubblico, where the walls of the so-called Room of Peace (*Sala della Pace*), are covered by the first political fresco cycle in the history of Italian art. They are by Ambrogio Lorenzetti and glorify the Nine. They form the biggest cycle dealing with a lay theme to have emerged from the Middle Ages in Italy. In essence, they are a serious lecture, in allegorical form, on the effects of Good and Bad Government, a heavy treatise on medieval political philosophy, packed with erudite references. In effect, they are a lively, amusing panorama of life in contemporary Siena.

The didactic preface facing the window teaches that illuminated government moves in the company of divine and human virtues including Justice, the lady alone on the left. The ruler in the centre symbolises the Nine. On the wall to the right are shown, vividly, the benefits: an industrious, happy Siena, with plants in the windows, houses going up, and well-dressed citizens. The countryside also gains; hunters and ploughmen prove it. The badly faded wall opposite illustrated the reverse, with justice meted out by a horned devil and a countryside ravaged. The reverse, alas, actually happened; the Nine were ejected when the cycle was only 20 years old.

On the same floor, in the *Sala Mappamondo*, is the vast masterpiece that brought Simone Martini fame, his *Maestà*, which he painted in 1315 and later restored himself because of damp. Its attraction was the originality of his tender scene of the enthroned Virgin under a canopy ruffled by a breeze, being offered flowers by kneeling angels. She is an unusually 'human', maternal Madonna; conventional remoteness has gone. The damp is winning again.

The contrast between the gentle Madonna and Martini's famous soldier-of-fortune going off to war on the wall opposite is complete. The mercenary, a certain Guidoriccio, Captain of the Sienese, is setting out on his quilted horse to smash a local siege, and this fresco of 1328, which seems to convey all the mannered courtliness of the Middle Ages, ranks as one of the most delightful the Sienese school produced. Afterwards, however, the captain fell into disgrace and his place was taken by a revolving map of the world; the scratches it left are quite visible.

In the same room, Il Vecchietta has portrayed St Catherine on a pillar, and there are two admired saints by Il Sodoma.

Cathedral

Siena's black-and-white Cathedral is one of the dumbfounding sights of Central Italy. It belongs to the thirteenth century; it is Italian Gothic at its most flamboyant. It is jewellery in stone; a medieval *Dama* dripping with diamonds; a thoroughly Italian show-off signifying wealth and delight in fine ornament. Its only rival is the Cathedral in Orvieto.

Had the Nine had their way, it would have been far, far bigger. The Cathedral as it is now would have been the mere transept of a colossal affair intended to outdo the Cathedral in detested Florence. Unfortunately, their haste was so great that the structure wobbled, and most was torn down. But the huge arches still standing, to the right of the façade, give some idea of what a mighty snub it would have been.

Giovanni Pisano and his helpers spent twelve years peopling the lower façade. But for once, outside appearance isn't all; inside, it's a low-ceilinged jungle of marble trees with an army of Popes – 172 of them – posted in their tops. They and the stripes deliberately stunt the upward thrust of North European Gothic; the Italians had, and have, no need to reach up for the sun.

A main feature of the Cathedral is its pictured **floor**. Forty Sienese graffiti and inlay artists pored over these scenes from the Old Testament for two centuries, until 1547. The most prolific was Domenico

Beccafumi. For one month a year only, from 15 August, the entire set is uncovered.

The **pulpit** by Nicola Pisano, helped by Giovanni, is Italian Gothic sculpture in full flower, superior and more ardent than the Pisa pulpit, fashioned in a period of prosperity and calm; when the pair came to Siena, times were more unsettled. A black, harshly bedraggled *John the Baptist* done by Donatello in his old age, presides over the Baptist's chapel.

For a contrast, do not miss the colourful **Piccolómini Library** next door, covered with bold frescoes by the fifteenth-century Umbrian master, Bernardino Pinturicchio. Piccolómini was the great Renaissance Pope and humanist, Pius II: a man of letters, archaeologist, patron of the arts, and one-time Archbishop of Siena. The storybook pictures narrate his life. The last shows him in Ancona urging a speedy crusade against the Turks who had seized Constantinople; it never came off, and he died in Ancona.

Cathedral Museum The centrepiece of the Cathedral was once the famed *Maestà* of Duccio Buoninsegna, displayed on the altar, but it is now in the Museo dell'Opera del Duomo, outside opposite the Cathedral's right flank. In Siena 9 June 1310 was a great day: Duccio had finally finished the commissioned masterpiece after three years of labour. A procession was formed, headed by the Archbishop; trumpets sounded, and the precious work was slowly borne through the streets from Duccio's workshop to the Duomo.

It inaugurated the great age of Sienese painting – a mingling of stately neo-Byzantine forms and Gothic refinement. Duccio painted this great altar-piece on both sides, but in the eighteenth century it was sawn up to make do for two altars. It is on the first floor of the Museum, and its front now faces the door. Its back is to the door's left, and the panels affixed to the left wall are from the picture's crown and predella.

Observed from the seating, the glinting host of rather aristocratic faces in perfect repose slowly registers. The Madonna is in the company of ten angels, seven apostles and four patron saints of Siena. They tell us the influence of the French miniaturists was strong in Siena at the time. On the step of the Madonna's throne, Duccio has written in Latin: 'O Holy Mother of God, bring about peace for Siena, and long life for the Duccio who painted you like this.'

The back of the *Maestà* narrates twenty episodes from the Passion of Christ.

On the Museum's ground floor you can get an unusually close look at ten august personages by masterful Giovanni Pisano, including a somewhat bewildered *Moses*, taken down from the Cathedral façade, one of the rarest groups of Gothic statuary in Europe.

Baptistry The Battistero, down the steps from the Museum behind the Cathedral, hides beneath its apse one of the treasures of Siena – a tall, graceful baptismal font, decorated by some of the biggest names in Tuscan art in the fourteenth century. Jacopo della Quercia fashioned it in 1417, as well as the figure of the Baptist who surmounts it. Donatello is very evident: Faith and Hope, two of the figures standing between the six panels around the font proper, are his, and so is the *Herod's Banquet* scene, agreed to be a *capolavoro*. Two other panels, including the *Baptism of Christ*, are by the famous Florentine Lorenzo Ghiberti, and this too is where Il Vecchietta came into his own, frescoing the lower apse and the vaults near the door.

Picture Gallery

Siena's large Pinacoteca Nazionale, in Via San Pietro (at the top of Via Città to the left), houses the entire gamut of Sienese painting, from the school's very first picture, an altar-piece of the Redeemer dated 1215, to the seventeenth century, the biggest such collection in the world. You can spend hours on its dramatic transitions because happily, strangely, it is no tourist draw at all. It contains one of the very rare paintings on canvas done in the Middle Ages by Guido da Siena in the late thirteenth century. There is a panel by Duccio in room 14 that is almost miniature work and, in the next room, a Madonna and Child by Simone Martini, one of his happiest creations.

The Lorenzetti brothers are particularly well represented and so is Il Sodoma. Others who stand out are Barna di Siena, a fourteenth-century disciple of Duccio and Simone, with a mind of his own; Bartolo di Fredi, and his follower Taddeo di Bartolo; Sassetta, that courtly exponent of the international Gothic school, the most prominent Sienese painter of the fourteenth century, and Il Vecchietta.

San Francesco

Other things to see if you have time include the Basilica in the Piazza San Francesco behind the Piazza Salimbeni. Though it has a modern façade, the huge, single-nave, Gothic interior was begun in the fourteenth century, and it has two chapels frescoed by the Lorenzetti brothers.

San Domenico

Up by the Florence bus terminus is this cavernous, severe, brick Gothic church begun in the thirteenth century. The head of St Catherine is kept in a chapel on the right past the second altar, where Il Sodoma movingly describes moments in her life.

Santa Maria dei Servi

Well behind the Campo in Piazza Manzoni, this lonely church with a rough, thirteenth-century façade, is warm with colour inside. In a chapel near the altar, Pietro Lorenzetti outshines them all.

Complementary to Siena, because of Il Sodoma, would be a trip to the Abbey of Monte Oliveto Maggiore, 20 km south.

What to do

Siena, being mood and art, conceals no Place Pigalle: extras are a bit limited. Most Sienese on the loose spend evenings in the former mutual-help clubs of their *Contrade*, playing billiards or cards, or plotting revenge at the next Palio. The places where others dally after dinner are obviously the cafés around the Campo: the Birreria Bavari; the Manganalli; the Bar Palio; the Jolly Bar or, perhaps the most pleasant, the Fonte Gaia, on the far right facing the Palazzo

Comunale. They are not exorbitant, given the stage. Otherwise, watch out for frequent concerts laid on in summer by the Chigiana Musical Academy, often by visiting ensembles.

Wine and food

Siena has the biggest State wine *Enoteca* in Central Italy, where the country's whole range can be studied at leisure. It is in the old Medici Fort, now called Piazza Libertà (!), close to the centre and open until midnight. Sometimes, they also organise a Gastronomic Fair, for the free sampling of Siena's delights.

Those delights are capped by Siena's specialities – its cakes, usually known as Sapori, after their maker. They include untranslatable varieties. The best-known is *Panforte*, made in Siena since the Middle Ages, a kind of honeycake spiced with cloves, cinnamon or peppers. *Ricciarelli* are diamond-shaped almond biscuits, enlivened by candied orange-peel, egg white and honey. *Cavallucci* are biscuits of monkey· nuts, aniseed and spices.

You will also find attractive pottery, but no straw hats: 'They belong to Florence.'

Where to stay

Top range

The four-star **Jolly Hotel Excelsior**, 1 Piazza Lizza, tel. 288 4480 is yards from the walls, and about as Italian as Christmas pudding. It offers international comfort, at a high price.

Hotel Continental, close to the Campo at 85 Via Banchi di Sopra, tel. 41451 is an old-style hostelry with wide marble staircases, great halls, winter draughts and stylish decay.

Mid range

Three-star hotels include **Castagneto**, 39 Via Cappuccini, tel. 45103; **Duomo**, 38 Via Stalloreggi, tel. 289088, and **La Toscana**, 12 Via Cecco Angiolieri, tel. 46097.

Bottom range

A modest two-star: **Piccolo Hotel Il Palio**, 19 Piazza Sale; tel. 281131.

Where to eat

Sienese wanting reasonable bills after eating well pack into the busy **Ristorante Papei** down behind the Palazzo Pubblico in the Piazza del Mercato; tel. 280894 (closed Mondays). A speciality is rabbit in white wine.

Of justified renown, near the Campo, is **Osteria Le Logge**, 33 Via del Porrione; tel. 48103 (closed Sundays). It offers books to while away the waits.

Less flamboyant and cosier is **Osteria da Cice**, 38 Via San Pietro, opposite the Picture Gallery (closed Sundays).

Western Tuscany

The countryside of western Tuscany is a thick, obtuse-angled wedge of hill country sticking out of Siena towards the west. The fielder on the north-west is tiny **Certaldo**; its opposite number on the south-west is weird **Larderello**, and by far the least interesting is poor

Poggibonsi, which was all but murdered in the Second World War and now makes furniture. Around its beds and cupboards, though, the hills are populated and alive; further west, they are on their own and almost bleak. **Volterra** is their hardy chief, still aloof, like the Etruscans who lived there.

Monte-riggioni

But the nearest dream to Siena, to the north-west, is half-way to Colle di Val d'Elsa, a quite irresistible page from a child's story book. It looms up from far off, an isolated fortress on a hill behind quite intact *circular* walls, punctuated by fourteen pugnacious towers. Siena put it there in the early thirteenth century, as a forward defence position against the Florentines. The seeing is over in fifteen minutes but two restaurants, bars and a shop selling the local wine await the endless cavalcade of visitors.

Down on the once malarial plain 3 km away lies the Abbadia Isola, a ruined Cistercian monastery founded in 1001 that wielded immense influence over the whole area between the twelfth and fourteenth centuries. Its simple eleventh-century Lombard-like church still stands, with a perishing Taddeo di Bartolo fresco to the right of the door. An old lady has the key.

Colle di Val d'Elsa

Seven km south of the furniture, Colle di Val d'Elsa is worth longer – it is a surprise. Its old town is a long raised finger pointed towards the River Elsa, a seemingly wall-to-wall Renaissance city isolated amid gentle hills. Its streets are lined with bold, swanky *palazzi* with pronounced eaves and rough-hewn assertiveness. The explanation, again, is money. The city was a major centre of the woollen trade in the Middle Ages, as well as one of the foremost paper-making centres in Italy.

That there was once money around is clear. Look, for instance, at the smart Palazzo Campana, the one blocking the bridge (once a drawbridge) leading to the Castello, as the old town is called. Built in the early sixteenth century, it is a vivid instance of what post-Renaissance 'Mannerism' did to architecture.

Here and there, toned down yet still soaring medieval tower-houses appear. The most medieval feature is Via delle Volte, even by day a night-time tunnel burrowing under the Castello. It comes to light in the central Piazza Duomo, with a fourteenth-century, badge-wearing, Palazzo Pretorio. At the bottom of Via Castello, beyond the square at number 53, is the tower-house where Arnolfo di Cambio was born, honoured by the plaque for snatching Florentine architecture from 'the decadence of letters and the fine arts in Italy.'

Where to stay and eat

The only hotel in the old town is the commodious three-star **Arnolfo**, 8 Via Campana; tel. 0577-922020. The adjacent restaurant, with the same name, is not the hotel's and, though the fare is reputedly excellent, the prices are not. Good Tuscan cuisine is just metres away at **Cantina della Fortuna**, Via Fontanelle. Try their light, homemade *pollo in gelatina*.

San Gimignano

All visitors in this area flock to the town with the most striking profile in Tuscany. It is another fable, sitting on a hill with tall, very tall, towers poking up into the sky, like a medieval picture – or a nightmare. Yet it is so used to visitors that it has the feel of a film-set waiting for the extras – you. But it is quiet, and without those motorbikes . . .

Getting there   San Gimignano is some 36 km north-west of Siena and 56 km south-west of Florence. By car, take the *superstrada* linking them and turn off at Poggibonsi. Cars are banned from the centre; you must park in the Viale dei Fossi, to left of the main gate of San Giovanni. Hotels issue access chits just for the time it takes you to unload your luggage. Three buses a day go from Siena; from Florence, catch a Sita bus.

What to see

The towers   The town today still conveys some idea of what many Tuscan townships must have looked like in the Middle Ages, although per square metre this *was* the most embattled place in Italy. Once it bristled with as many as seventy-two towers; someone noted in a travel diary that it was positively unsightly. Only fifteen are left.

They shot up in the twelfth and thirteenth centuries as warring families vied to outdo each other by building higher and higher. The mean slits in the pill-box towers spat out flaming oil, or supported planks uniting allies. There was money around: at the time, small San Gimignano traded as far afield as Syria; its chief commodity was saffron, used as a rare dye. Its *bête noire* was Volterra, since it came under the Bishop there. Resentment sparked off three wars between them.

The focus of local discord centred around the two adjoining main squares, the Piazza della Cisterna (The Well) and the Piazza del Duomo at the top of the main street, Via San Giovanni. The humble-looking twelfth-century cathedral faces the Tower of the *Podestà* (Governor), who always had to be an outsider the better to umpire the unending feuds. A thirteenth-century bye-law banned any towers higher than his (51 metres). The pro-Ghibelline Salvucci family got around this by raising their twin stumpy towers to the left of the square: on top of each other, they boasted, they pipped the Governor's. Their enemies were the Guelf Ardinghelli family. Between them, these two clans plunged the little republic into untold bloodshed for two centuries – until it chose vassalage to Florence in the fourteenth century.

Collegiata   Under the rule of Florence, prosperity continued. They had their Romanesque church turned into a huge picture-book by Sienese artists. On the left wall, the Old Testament story is told in an amazingly spirited way by **Bartolo di Fredi**. Surely he had his tongue in his cheek as he showed the ladies in modish hats turning their backs to the unpleasantness in the water as they cross the Red

Sea. As for the New Testament on the right, it is alleged that its author, **Barna di Siena**, crashed to his death from the scaffolding while working on the Crucifixion. The requisite horror-show is high up on the inside wall of the façade: **Taddeo di Bartolo**'s grotesque Hell is complete with hacksaws.

Palazzo del Popolo

In the Pinacoteca (open 9.30 a.m.–12.30 p.m.; 3.30–6.30 p.m.) **Taddeo di Bartolo** relates the life of the city's saint: in one scene, he is leaving the church for a bodily need, and is attacked by a waiting devil, duly vanquished by the sight of the Cross.

Sant' Agostino

At the far end of the town, further 'talking pictures' are to be seen behind the altar of the church of Sant' Agostino. The biographer this time, with more refined gusto, is **Benozzo Gozzoli**.

Where to stay and eat

Mid range

First choice must be the three-star **Hotel La Cisterna**, 23 Piazza della Cisterna; tel. 940328 (restaurant closed Tuesdays). This solid, traditional hotel has a panoramic restaurant, the best in town and an excuse in itself for over-nighting. It specialises in herbs from the surrounding woods and hills. Try, for instance, the *risotto* with field herbs (*erbe di campo*) or the breast of chicken with Tuscan herbs.

Opposite is the three-star **Hotel Leon Bianco**; tel. 941294.

The only other three-star in town is the **Hotel Bel Soggiorno**, Via San Giovanni; tel. 940375.

Bottom range

A cheaper recommended hostelry is the **Locanda Il Pino**, in the Via San Matteo which leads off the Piazza del Duomo away from the Palazzo del Popolo; tel. 940414.

Certaldo

On the SS 429, about 15 km north of San Gimignano, Certaldo has a large-ish population of 15,000 and is a messy, industrial place, but the old town, Certaldo Alto, crowns its steep hump, and repays a look. You will find a striking, walled, medieval village, alight with a reddish brick that leavens its austerity. Whether Boccaccio was born here, as they claim, may be unsure, but his father was, and the mischievous begetter of *The Decameron* certainly died here. He is buried in the church of Iacopo e Filippo, half-way up the main Via Boccaccio.

The rising street ends in the Palazzo Pretorio, a definite highlight, the centre of local politics since the thirteenth century. Coloured terracotta coats of arms belonging to the many Florentine 'Vicars' (Governors) who lived in it encrust both the façade and the interior. In the courtyard, fragments of frescoes by Benozzo Gozzoli have been recomposed. The rough *loggia* in front has heard many proclamations read out, and sheltered many a feast-day.

Where to stay

Almost adjacent is the **Osteria del Vicario**, with a hotel; tel. 0571-668228 (closed Wednesdays).

Volterra

Some 30 km south-west of San Gimignano, Volterra drips with dourness. Today still a medieval city, it was once a major Etruscan stronghold and you can see why. In a typically aloof Etruscan position, there is still something forbidding about it. It is perched on a sharp ridge 555 metres high, amid curious fossilised landslides of clay.

Getting there
Some 65 km south-east of Pisa, Volterra has a population of 16,000. It is at the head of a branch-line from coastal Cecina; but the station is down at Saline di Volterra, 9 km away, where salt has been mined since the ninth century.

What to see

Porta dell'Arco
Volterra's era of power began in the fourth century BC, to fade only in the first century AD. The left-over of those days is its heavy Etruscan gate, or at least the base of it – untidy slabs and outside jambs. The arch itself is Roman.

Priors' Palace
The city centre, all grey stone, is dominated by the oldest town hall in Tuscany, started in 1208, and emblazoned with the crests of Florentine governors. They took over the city in the fourteenth century and then had to put down three rebellions. Opposite stands the Palazzo Pretorio.

Cathedral
Curiously hidden away behind the Priors' Palace is the rich, twelfth-century Cathedral, stamped Pisa. You enter through the apse.

Galleria Pittorica
Names such as **Luca Signorelli** and **Rosso Fiorentino** exhibit in the small gallery in the Via dei Sarti (open 9.30 a.m.–1 p.m., 3–6.30 p.m.).

Etruscan Museum
Volterra's vaunted thirteenth-century tower-houses in the Via Buonparenti are puny compared to San Gimignano's, but its Museum, at 15 Via Don Minzoni (open 9 a.m.–1 p.m., 3–6 p.m.), is among the most important of Italy. You will find some six hundred funeral urns, some in the form of houses with roof lids; *sarcophagi* with reclining figures; illustrated tombs, some with war scenes; Etruscan coins and much else.

Many of the urns are made of Volterra's soft, translucent alabaster, still a major source of income in the town and quarried nearby. Forty alabaster workshops dot the streets, making everything from telephones to chess-sets.

Further along from the museum is one of the most massive Renaissance forts in Italy, built by the Florentines, and now a jail.

Where to stay
The smartest hotel is the four-star **San Lino**, Via Santo Lino; tel. 85250.

There are two three-stars: the **Nazionale**, Via dei Marchesi; tel. 86284; and the **Etruria**, Via G. Matteotti; tel. 87377.

Where to eat
Reasonable *trattorie* line the Via delle Prigioni, near the main square. The best known is **Il Porcellino**; tel. 86392 (closed Tuesdays). It specialises in rabbit (*alla cacciatora*) and *pappardelle alla lepre*.

Larderello | This whole area is a lost Tuscany, holding surprises. One of them, not particularly pleasant, is almost due south of Volterra in the middle of the highly agitated so-called Metaliferous Hills (*Colline Metallifere*), where the Etruscans extensively mined for metals.

Nasty shiny pipes snake all over the wooded landscape; power-lines are strung out above it, and modern concrete cauldrons belch out something off-white. Larderello is named after an ingenious nineteenth-century Frenchman who discovered how to harness the hot vapours bubbling up through local muddy ponds to heat huge vats, in which he somehow made boric acid. This was and is derived from the same ponds.

Since then Italy's Electricity Board has got into the act too, and the whole area puffs with vapours. This modern township pompously calls itself 'World Centre of Geo-Thermal Energy' and there is a museum to prove it. But they're a jumpy lot. Sitting in my car grappling with these technicalities, I suddenly found two men pointing a sub-machine-gun and a pistol at me.

'We're *carabinieri* and we're going to check you . . .'

I had parked opposite a bank, and some suspicious body had tipped them off.

Castelnuovo di Val di Cecina | The nearby tiny village affixed to a mountainside offers a fairer view of the Metaliferous Hills – which here are great plunging humps, blanketed with oak forest. The village itself is a winding upward alley, that halts in a porch under the church.

Southern Tuscany

Draw a line under Siena and everything below it could be called southern Tuscany; in fact, however, the lie of the land splits the vast region into two very distinct shires. One is the neglected wild southwest or the Maremma, once Tuscany's malarial belt. The other is and was far more civilised, since most of it belonged to the medieval Republic of Siena, to the south and south-east of its fair capital.

This is 'ridge country', where you will often find the hills laid out as high cat-walks snaking through quite an audience of river valleys. The land seems to be forever falling away from the road and often has lost its blanket of woods. Around San Quirico d'Orcia almost in the centre of this 'shire' it is unseemingly naked; far to the south, around tiny Radicofani, trees are lonely things, in empty, forsaken country.

The 'capital' of this south is Renaissance Montepulciano in the south-east, close to the Umbrian border; its little Renaissance gem is Pienza; famous vineyards flourish among the hills, which also hide two of the great abbeys of Central Italy, one of its finest Romanesque churches, Sant' Antimo, and stranded, fortified villages, abandoned by the Middle Ages.

Monte Oliveto Maggiore

The closest main objective to Siena is the great Abbey 33 km to the south-east. On the way down the *Cassia*, at the 16-km mark, tiny **Lucignano d'Arbia** warrants a glance. On the merest hump just off the highway, it is an oddity, a mini-mini fortified village with fourteenth-century mirror-image gates facing each other from either end of the main drag, all of 50 metres long. It feels somehow strange, then you realise why – it's *flat*. For the Abbey, turn off the *Cassia* at Buonconvento.

Hidden away from the world in a wood of cypress trees amid crumbling clay cliffs, the great lonely Abbey stands in forbidding surrounds once written off as a 'desert'; it is one of the best known, biggest and most awesome in Italy. It owes its existence to three wealthy gentlemen from Siena, led by a noted law professor, who chose this uninviting spot on Mount Olive as a spiritual retreat after renouncing the pleasures of life in the city. Other hermits joined them and the present Abbey dates back to 1320 when they slowly began placing stone upon stone. They named their congregation the 'Olivetan Order' after the hill, but are Benedictines.

The Abbey now owes its renown to a long, vivid fresco cycle by Luca Signorelli and Il Sodoma telling the life of St Benedict, one of the biggest and most astonishing of the early Renaissance and still in excellent shape. Between 1497 and 1508, though working separately and not continuously, the two used up all four walls of the handsome Chiostro Grande ('Big Cloister') for their biography, told in scenes often homely, racy, spicy and entertaining.

Il Sodoma's scenes begin on the far wall opposite the entrance, next to the church, showing St Benedict leaving his native Norcia for Rome. They continue for three walls. Signorelli, who began the cycle, frescoed only the wall to the right of the entrance. Winged devils flit around in plenty; Il Sodoma pictures an especially vicious one silencing the bell that should have alerted the saint in a cave to the arrival of his food-basket at the end of a rope. Il Sodoma can be charming, too, as when exposing the straying attention of peasants being preached to. There is wickedness when, for instance, in the third scene from the end of the 'first' wall, hermits beg St Benedict to be their abbot, but then chafe at the discipline and try to poison him with a glass of wine, which he smashes with a sign of the cross. Il Sodoma's delicate, almost Chinese, background landscapes delight people, but his triumph is the colourful scene of St Benedict greeting two children from Rome, especially the young dandy and the truly gnashing horse.

Then come the firmer, more stylised, episodes by Signorelli. His fascination with the workings of the human anatomy and its stances comes across strongly when St Benedict first sees through the disguise of the fake Totila and is shown in to the real general. (For more on Signorelli, see under Orveto, page 187.)

The draw of the Abbey's church is the incredible sixteenth-century wood-inlay work in the choir, among the rarest in Italy: it includes views of Siena. The solemn, church-like library can be admired; the high-vaulted, frescoed refectory peeped into. The monks sell honey, jams, herbal cures, soaps and ointments.

Montalcino

One of Tuscany's most exclusive wine towns is within half an hour of the Abbey, to the south-west, 40 km south of Siena (turn off the *Via Cassia* after Buonconvento). Draped over a 564-metre hill, overlooking two strangely desolate river valleys, it is synonymous with *Brunello di Montalcino*, one of the great red wines of Italy.

Wine

Brunello has a renowned talent for growing old, and is marketed only after six years. Sample it before you buy inside the massive fort overlooking the town. It was erected by the Sienese who seized Montalcino after thrashing the Florentines in 1260. They kept up a rear-guard action here long after the fall of Siena.

Far below, Sienese influence also shows in a fourteenth-century town hall and a handsome colonnade added a century later, which dominate the picturesque Piazza del Popolo.

Museum

Painting of the Sienese school, including Bartolo di Fredi and Il Sodoma, can be unearthed in the Museo Diocesano in the Via Ricasoli, near the fort (open 9 a.m.–12 noon, 4–6 p.m.).

Where to stay and eat

The old **Hotel Giglio**, one of only two in the town at 5 Via Soccorso Saloni; tel. 848167, has a serious restaurant. Book in summer.

Sant' Antimo

The Abbey church of Sant' Antimo is a car-stopper: it stands quite alone in a meadowy dell among olives below the road, and is the most perfect expression of Romanesque monastical architecture in Tuscany. This is worth an effort. The dell is beneath the village of **Castelnuovo dell'Abate** ('Abbot's New Castle'), about 14 km south of Montalcino. What is so captivating, even from the road, is the church's utter purity of line; and inside, a luminous simplicity that reduces you to whispers. But it is not 'Italian'. This is the model itself of the kind of design 'exported' to Italy by dissident Benedictines from Cluny in Central France, as well as by 'Benedictine' Cistercians from Dijon. Only the façade and bell-tower are 'Italian' – Lombard, that is.

The original church on this spot was part of a Benedictine monastery founded by no less a personage than Charlemagne. The plague was decimating his men as they trudged back to Teutonic mists, and he intended his contribution as a spray-gun. Much later, in the twelfth century, the monks came into money, perhaps a donation, and splashed it on what now stands.

Inside and out, the walls are in travertine marble, but the decorations are in locally quarried onyx, radiating the light with touches of gold. The decoration of the capitals is darkly medieval: look at *Daniel Among the Lions* atop the second column on the right. But the most striking feature of this limpid corner of heaven is the large, light-filled apse with an unusual semi-circular 'walk' behind the altar, one of the very few in Italy.

It has other oddities. In the fifteenth century, the Bishop of Montalcino actually set up house inside the church, moving into the lofty Loggia, known as the *Tribuna*, up on the right. The second door on the left leads up to the prelate's flat, and the third down to the crypt, which is what remains of Charlemagne's church. And in the tiny crypt under the main altar, the slab on the mini-altar is a Roman tombstone.

But then the local bishops came to prefer Montalcino as a residence; a fifteenth-century Pope suppressed the Abbey, and little of the original remained. But then restorers moved in, to prepare the way for a new Augustinian community, under orders to resume services in Gregorian chant.

Valley of the River Orcia

A sparrow's flight 8 km due east is the home town of Il Vecchietta, with a patterned square named after him clearly unchanged since his death, rustic and forgotten.

Castiglione d'Orcia

A medieval midget of utter charm, also learning oblivion, is the nearby village clinging to a sudden peak with flabbergasting visions of domains below. Towering still further above is a stern thirteenth-century fortress, and its fulcrum is a many-sided well. There is an heirloom even here: a Bartolo di Fredi in the church of San Simone.

Rocca d'Orcia

San Quirico d'Orcia

Certainly meriting a stop because of its thirteenth-century Collegiata (Collegiate Church) at its entrance is San Quirico. The bishops of Siena and Arezzo squabbled over it for six centuries. The sweeping Romanesque door in the façade, with knotted columns on lionesses and fighting monsters, is dated as early as 1080. An accomplished disciple of Giovanni Pisano is thought to have created the later, thirteenth-century Romanesque-cum-Gothic side door and its stalwart caryatids on their obliging lions.

Pienza

Follow the SS 146 for Pienza and Montepulciano, *the* places that embody the Renaissance in the countryside. A tiny village (population 3,000) some 50 km south-east of Siena and 491 metres high, Pienza today earns compliments such as 'the pearl of the Renaissance'. It was built from scratch by a Renaissance Pope who dreamt of translating into practice the contemporary obsession with urban utopias. As such, this is the modern world's first instance of town-planning. But it *is* minute, and an hour sees all.

It was never finished, because Pope Pius II, the same learned Pontiff whose life is told in Siena Cathedral, died two years after they had put up the centre. So did his architect. As his site, he had chosen Corsignano, his own tumbledown native village. He wanted it transformed, overnight, into the last word in graceful living. It was built in three years, from 1459. The scheme was to have ecclesiastical juniors move in and build their own dwellings to Papal specifications. A handful did.

The result sits on the hill, which commands strangely skinless country of unclothed breasts. It is essentially Pienza's toy main square. It is *the* Renaissance square, unrivalled anywhere, and perfectly proportioned.

The small Cathedral (the Pope promoted his village to a city!) suffers from subsidence in the apse. Flanking it on the right is the *palazzo* of the Pope himself. An authoritarian guide will whisk you around the dingy first floor in compulsory groups (he'll bawl you out if you step on the carpets). If you behave, he will allow you to see what he calls the first terraced garden since 'Antiquity'.

Cardinal Rodrigo Borgia, the future Pope Alexander VI, was responsible for the Archbishop's palace, to the right of the Cathedral.

Where to stay   The only hotel is the comfortable **Hotel Corsignano**, with a restaurant, at 11 Via della Madonnina; tel. 748501 (closed 10 January–10 March).

Monticchiello   For a total contrast, the medieval village 6 km east of Pienza is the answer: a flinty, superbly isolated comma overlooking an open landscape of gently dipping grass slopes from exactly 500 metres up. No wonder Siena and Florence fought over it obsessively. A little too well-kept to be true, it is time frozen nonetheless, with walls and towers as witness. In July, the villagers usually perform re-enactments of their past in a cinematic square. The apse of San Leonardo is emblazoned with fourteenth-century Sienese frescoes.

Montepulciano   Twelve hilly km east of Pienza, Montepulciano (population 14,000) marks the late Renaissance as it was lived outside Florence. Do not expect the drama of medieval Italy: this is the civilised sixteenth century, one of the most stately hill towers there is, yet in a spectacular setting of plunging hills and vast panoramas. At an altitude of 605 metres Montepulciano offers the best. From the top of the town hall tower (open 9 a.m.–1 p.m.), Siena and Perugia come into view on a willing day. But the town is best known in the rest of Italy for its fine, dry ruby-coloured wine, baptised *Vino Nobile* because it was the tipple of the local aristocrats. Its minimum alcohol content is 12.5 per cent, and it won the DOCG title in 1982. The cellars are fun.

Getting there   Some 70 km south-east of Siena, it is best reached directly from Florence or Rome via the A 1 motorway. Buses are frequent from Siena and meet the trains at Chiusi on the Rome–Florence line.

What to see   Like many hill towns, Montepulciano was founded by valley people (in this case from Chieti) fleeing uphill from the godless barbarians charging south. The town's axis is the Via nel Corso, which changes names as it climbs steeply up from the main gate to the crowning main square, Piazza Grande, passing Renaissance *palazzi* on its way. One of them, the curving Palazzo Bucelli at number 73, has Etruscan and Roman funeral urns embedded in its flank.

Much of the building was created by fashionable architects from Florence. The imposing fifteenth-century Palazzo Comunale in the

Piazza Grande, for instance, will, justly, remind you of the Palazzo Vecchio in Florence; experts see in it the hand of Cosimo de' Medici's favourite architect, Michelozzo Michelozzi. The *palazzi* facing the raw Cathedral and the Town Hall are believed to be the brain-childs of the famous later Florentine architect Antonio da Sangallo the Elder (1455–1534).

His masterpiece, Montepulciano's bonus, is 2 km outside the town at the foot of the hill, the jewel-like church of **San Biagio**. To get there, leave the town by the Porta de' Grassi or take the Pienza road. Eccentrically isolated on its own green, and built in the form of a Greek cross entirely in travertine, this geometrical prodigy is acclaimed a Renaissance marvel. Except for an unfinished spire, it was completed in 1545, and is unmissable.

Where to stay The best hotel is **Il Marzocco**, Piazza Savonarola, near the main gate; tel. 757262. It has a reasonable restaurant.

Close by is **Il Borghetto**, Via del Borgo Buio; tel. 757535.

The modest **Albergo Duomo** is far away, at the top of the town, at 14 Via San Donato; tel. 757473.

Where to eat **La Diva**, close to the main gate, is crowded but reliable; tel. 716951 (closed Tuesdays).

Il Cittino, up the Via del Corso at number 72; tel. 75355 (closed Wednesdays).

Rosticceria Voltaia, 86 Via del Corso; tel. 75782 (closed Tuesdays) has sought-after fare, despite its unprepossessing appearance.

At all costs **avoid** the Bacco Pulcino and the Cantuccio.

Montefollonico Around Montepulciano there is the picturesque, and the sad. The very essence of the former is the nearby imposing thirteenth-century fortified village to the north-east off the SS 327 on the way to Torrita di Siena. The low, smooth hills surge gently, and this former Etruscan settlement is at the top of a mast moving through them. It's a real lookout post, once seized by Montepulciano from Siena, which then retrieved it. Little has changed since then; scrubbed and remote, it still has its walls and gates. Its small stone church has tended local souls for seven centuries.

Sinalunga Sinalunga to the north, on the other hand, is not for gasping about. Siena obviously once agreed; after subduing it, she gave it away to Milan. The city looks out over the valley of the river Chiana from a great height, and a hulking Collegiata is lord of a big main square, while the pint-sized Palazzo Pretorio, with a high, graceful tower, guiltily hides in obscure Piazza IV Novembre. Over the altar in the left transept of the Collegiate Church Il Sodoma has a sensuous Madonna and Child, her femininity equalled by that of San Sebastian at her side.

Chianciano Terme Less titillating is the cheerless spa town half-way between Montepulciano and the A 1, a geriatrics' mecca. Modern hotels cram a magnificent, curving ridge and during the *passeggiata* older people are elbow-to-elbow in the jostle. The waters are claimed to do their livers good.

Sarteano

A younger spa resort with big swimming pools and hotels is further south, a red-tiled former feudal possession set out in a semi-circle at the foot of a castle, peppered with gentlemanly Renaissance *palazzi* (Palazzo Piccolomini, for instance).

Chiusi

But just beyond the A 1, Chiusi easily pips it for looks. Visitors take to this place, unusually pretty and smiling for a former Etruscan stronghold, with reason.

What to see

The odd-sock pillars in the nave of its small twelfth-century **Cathedral** are loot from local Roman homes. The **Museo del Duomo** offers a rare display of fifteenth-century hymnals and psalters; Chiusi's heyday was between the seventh and fifth centuries BC, and in its **Etruscan Museum** opposite, warriors do battle on vivacious funeral urns or dance and seduce on vases.

One km outside town, a guide is on hand in the late morning to explain the **Catacombs of Santa Mustiola,** a third-century martyr flailed to death by iron balls on chains. The passages were the hide-out for her little community as well as its burial ground, but one of the 202 graves is that of an unknown French pilgrim on his way to Rome along the *Cassia*. Etruscan tombs are scattered around Chiusi, which also has its own lake down in the valley, for boating and camping.

Where to stay

The sole hotel is the friendly **Albergo La Sfinge**, 2 Via Marconi; tel. 0578-20157.

Abbadia San Salvatore

It would be unwise to sit up over the bold type on the map for Abbadia San Salvatore in the far south, close to Lazio. The important type honours the modern town, a holiday resort with hotels named after an Abbey which was once the most powerful in Tuscany, but of which nothing now remains except a drastically restored church. Its crypt, a silent crowd of thirty-six columns, came into existence beforehand, probably in the eighth century when a Longobard king on the march had a vision of the Redeemer and built the Abbey to mark the spot. Once, the Abbey named the local town council and picked its *podestà*. The medieval quarter is still there.

Radicofani

For explorers, this remote and very medieval former fief of the Abbey is 18 km east, skirted by the 'old' *Cassia*. Atop it, an English Pope, Hadrian IV, alias Nicholas Breakspear, built a fort which is still a huge flagpole 804 metres high sticking out over the entire gaunt, bare countryside. He probably did so because the Papacy and the Abbey tussled over this strategic dot.

Austere, stony, and grey, it fits into its surroundings, a steeply sloping, mirthless place clinging to a volcanic eruption. The only concession its 1,500 souls have made to colour is up in the thirteenth-century church of San Marco, gleaming with terracotta figures and scenes of the Robbiano school, once widely popular. Andrea della Robbia himself did the dossals to the high altar's two satellites.

A stone plaque recalls bones close by of those killed while repelling a grim Medici siege in 1555, in defence of 'the communal freedom of Siena'. Radicofani caved in to Florence four years later, after the fall of the Sienese outpost of Montalcino.

The Maremma

Surprisingly, the artistic Etruscans were expert drainage engineers. Under their tutelage, the marshes of the Maremma, the hinterland of today's Grosseto, was prosperous, healthy, and peopled. The Romans had other priorities when they moved in, and when the barbarians flashed through, they were obviously flummoxed by the engineering and moved on. Since then, *Maremma* in Italian became a synonym for malaria and pestilence.

Only in the eighteenth century did Tuscany's Lorraine dynasty, successor to the Medicis, begin to reclaim the Maremma; Rome was still 'colonising' it (their word) in the 1950s. Loosely, *Maremma* can mean any once swampy coastal area, but properly it today coincides with the Province of Grosseto, and encompasses bits of the encircling mountain ranges, including a peak 1,107 metres high.

As you will notice from the place-names, the Maremma's big ruling feudal family before Siena took over were the Aldobrandeschis, though they were often opposed by the Orsinis from Rome; the saying was that they owned a castle or fort for every day of the year. The best-remembered of the family is the Countess Marguerita (1255–1313), a great beauty placed by Dante in Purgatory because of her passion for another great lady's husband.

The mosquitos naturally enticed few great artists to the Maremma, which is thus less well endowed than the rest of Tuscany, but it is now being 'discovered', especially its hill towns around Arcidosso, north-east of Grosseto. In Massa Marittima to the north, it has a hugely attractive medieval city, and the Roman spa resort of Saturnia to the south-west still is one, and popular. As for the charmer among the small townships, Pitigliano in the extreme south-east walks away with it, but the most startling must be Roccatederighi to the north.

The Maremma is cattle-country; many a Tuscan steak grew up here. Herds of semi-wild horses roam around, as well as some wild boar and, if you get lost in the remoteness, there is just a chance that a pair of the very last *butteri*, the cowboys of the Maremma, will put you right. They usually stage a 'tournament' on 15 August in Albarese, 10 km south of Grosseto, which is also the 'entrance' and ticket-window for the coastal Maremma Natural Park, in which you follow a signposted tramp of two hours or explore on horseback. Ask for *Centro Turismo Equestre*.

Grosseto

For many Italians, Grosseto merely stands for the busy place on the *Aurelia* where they got stuck behind a procession of flatulent lorries grinding through the centre, but in fact the small old town is surprisingly agreeable – ideal for an overnight stop or as a base-camp for investigation. The Tourist Office is at 5 Corso Carducci; tel. 488207.

What to see

The **Centro Storico** is encased by a big, intact hexagon of a black wall, begun by the Tuscan Grand Duke, Francis I, in the sixteenth century after the crushing of the Sienese Republic, of which Grosseto was part. You can walk around it.

In contrast, the main square, **Piazza del Duomo**, is an airy stage with arcades dominated by a fussy, fake-Gothic Palazzo Provincia, to which a squat, striped thirteenth-century Cathedral shows its apse. The delicate, 'storified' panels and embellishments around the side door, its main attraction, are by a Sienese sculptor.

Where to stay and eat

The elegant but not costly four-star **Bastiani Grand Hotel**, 64 Piazza Gioberti, tel. 20047, is by far the best of a little cluster. Book if you can.

Near the Piazza del Duomo, the professional **Ristorante Canapone**, 4 Piazza Dante, tel. 24546 (closed Sundays) specialises in fish and ember-grilled dishes and, unusually, has a full Tuscan wine-list.

Roselle

A dreamy hour or two can be spent among the ruins of a former Etruscan and then Roman settlement only fifteen minutes from Grosseto to the north-east. It is on the edge of Grosseto's plain on a stubby hill, enveloped in an atmosphere of remote tranquillity. Walls, gates, roads and the two people's forums are easily identifiable. One of the Etruscans' twelve confederated towns, it then sank to a second-class Roman one. Wasted by the barbarians, it was finally abandoned in the twelfth century when, after seven centuries of residence, the local bishop removed to minute Grosseto, re-populated by Roselle's refugees.

As this book went to press, the Etruscan tombs at Vetulonia, north-west of Grosseto, were closed for restoration.

Monte-pescali

The closest wholly medieval village to Grosseto is 12 km to the north, off the *Aurelia*. Here is a genuine survivor still bound up in chunks of defence wall, with gritty alleys, handkerchief squares, two frescoed Romanesque churches and, above all, a view. Hence they call it the 'Balcony of the Maremma' – though further off, there's a far finer one.

Massa Marittima

Twenty-three km north of Follonica is this little-known medieval hill town (population 10,000) – it is pure theatre. The stage is its original main square, Piazza Garibaldi. As if in a play, the main characters in the city's history could step out of the doors around it at any instant . . . The Bishop from his Cathedral, his neighbour the Proctor, the Count next door, then the Mayor who lived next to the Prince. No wonder they use the square for opera in the summer; and it is good to contemplate the spectacle from the café in the evening.

The characters played their roles for real in the thirteenth century when Massa, as a mini-republic, flourished as a centre for mining silver, quartz, pyrite, copper and iron. It is in a mineral basin, bounded by the so-called Metalliferous Hills to the north.

Cathedral

The cork-coloured Cathedral, facing the square at a distrustful oblique angle, marks the deepest penetration south of Pisan Romanesque architecture. The three uppermost pillars, the middle one resting on a kneeling man, are thought to be by a follower of Giovanni Pisano. The citizens' most valuable possession is behind the altar in the luminous, low-slung interior. This is the fourteenth-century Sienese marble tomb or 'ark' of their African-born patron saint, Cerbone. He proved his saintliness by miraculously escaping from the bears to whom he had been thrown by Totila for hiding Byzantine soldiers. Leaflets in English explain the rest.

The 'new' town

Massa is two towns: you reach the 'new' (i.e. fourteenth-century) one via the steep Via Moncini. At the top are the remains of a huge fort put up by the Sienese after capturing the old town in 1335.

Mining Museum

Speeded by malaria, the decline of Massa Marittima set in when the Florentines ousted the Sienese. Life – and mining – revived only a century ago with the draining of the marshes. A facsimile mine is now the Museo della Miniera (open 10 a.m.–12.30 p.m., 3.30–7 p.m.; closed Mondays).

Where to stay

The two-star **Duca del Mare**, 25 Via Massetana Sud; tel. 902284, and the **Girifalco**, 25 Via Massetana Nord; tel. 902177, are both on the skirting main road. The latter has a great view.

The one-star **Cris** is the only hotel within the walls, at 9 Via Roma; tel. 903830.

There are ten *trattorie* and *pizza* places.

**Rocca-
tederighi**

This could claim to be the most sensational fortified village in the Maremma. It lies 15 km east of Massa Marittima in a straight line, below Mount Sassoforte. Named after its first feudal lords, the little castle is a lonely light-house from a distance, and the village an icicle of rock in mid-air. Close up, you discover one of the toughest tiny places in Central Italy, literally hacked out of rock. Even the locals pant as they toil up their perpendicular alleys. The Salita dell'Incoronata leads up to the very tips of four quite dizzying needles of reddish-grey rock. From the top of the giddy one behind the church, 520 metres up, the entirety of the Maremma is at your feet, stretched out to the sea. If the Maremma has a balcony, this is it.

Its first mention in documents is dated 1110, but it 'lost its independence', as the locals put it, 120 years later. Rebellion against the new master, Siena, sputtered on for nearly another century until a local girl married into the ruling family in the 'capital'.

Two superb names cry out for company in the extreme south of the Maremma, west of Lake Bolsena near Lazio – Pitigliano and Sovana.

Pitigliano Easily one of the most strikingly placed villages in Central Italy. There is little to do or see there, but the setting is a wonder.

History It was – could not fail to be, given its position – an Etruscan stronghold. The Romans took it over, and in the Middle Ages it became a stronghold of the powerful Roman Orsini family, which was pro-Guelf. As the strength of the Popes grew, so did the importance of Pitigliano, and it became a Bishopric, depriving neighbouring Sovana of the title. Later, it came under the Medicis.

It is perched on a huge buttress jutting out between deep gorges with waterfalls like a sharp wedge. The city clings to the very brink of sheer cliff faces, resembling one huge rampart. Dominating all is the massive fourteenth-century, turreted Palazzo Orsini, remodelled in the sixteenth century. A peculiarity of Pitigliano is the contrast between its medieval lay-out and the number of its fine Renaissance *palazzi*.

It is known for its dry white wine.

Where to stay and eat The only hotel inside the town is the neat **Albergo Guastini**, 4 Piazza Petruccioli; tel. 616065. Its restaurant (no closing day) is reputedly good, but others do exist.

Sovana Pitigliano's poor twin is 8 km away and the two are worth seeing in conjunction. Sovana is a solitary, medieval village, picturesque, half abandoned. Part of it fell down thirty years ago and the rubble is still there. It, too, was Etruscan; it, too, occupies a platform between ravines. It, too, flourished under a powerful family, but then it was outshone by Pitigliano, attacked by Siena and laid low by malaria. This isolated spot was the birthplace of the great medieval Pope, Gregory VII.

Eastern Tuscany

Now, lastly, eastern Tuscany, which lies between Lake Trasimeno in Umbria and the Mugello. Its centre is now industrialised Arezzo; its most southerly, untouched township is pretty Cortona; but its real appeal is further north, in the upper valleys of both the Tiber and the Arno, known as Val Tiberina and the Casentino.

This is a land of forest, dark green, streams and often fragrant air dotted with medieval castles, hermitages and hamlets. The Casentino is soft, cultured hill country. The Val Tiberina, further into the Apennines, is rougher and mountainous; it is the home of Michelangelo, born at **Caprese Michelangelo**, a rugged hill township where his father was *Podestà*. His sturdy home is now a museum, and only a few kilometres away to the south another giant of the Renaissance was born, Piero della Francesca, at San Sepolcro, where they keep a few of his finest pictures.

San Sepolcro

The overriding excuse for a stop in Borgo San Sepolcro (population 16,000), the main town in the Valley of the Upper Tiber and almost on the borders of Umbria and the Marches, is that **Piero della Francesca** was born there, and his work can still be seen.

The town lies 32 km north-east of Arezzo. It is a quietly pleasant place, a rectangular, low-walled medieval village playing host to modestly elegant Renaissance dwellings. Neither showy nor splendid, it has quiet character. Its name comes from a small oratory erected as a safe for alleged relics from the Holy Sepulchre brought back from the Holy Land by two local pilgrims.

Piero della Francesca

Long neglected, the work of Piero della Francesca (1410?–1492) is now regarded as marking the culmination of the 'first' Renaissance. He was a geometrician as well as a painter, and as such made himself supreme in the art of perspective, the challenge that so obsessed the fifteenth century. His world is abstract, dominated by his use of light and geometrical spaces, exactly proportioned. It is a lucid, intellectual place, almost logical. His pictures are a search for perfection through geometry, a search that went on all his life since he was fascinated by the idea that all appearances could be reduced to five geometrical forms.

In his world, man has thrown off all traces of medieval humility. He is no longer cowed by an awesome God, but aware of his own role and importance in history. Piero asserts intellect.

His father was a shoemaker and hairdresser who apparently died before Piero was born. He was known as 'della Francesca' after his mother, who brought him up. As a youth, he plunged into mathematics; Euclid was his hero. Apprenticed to Domenico Veneziano, he followed him to Florence where he fell under the influence of Brunelleschi and Donatello, his early mentors in perspective and space.

In 1442, he became a town-councillor in San Sepolcro and continued taking part in local politics for the next thirty years. He worked at Ferrara and Rome, and spent fifteen years on the cycle of frescoes in Arezzo, but commuted mostly between his home town and the court of nearby Urbino, where the enlightened and wealthy Duke Federico da Montefeltro became his principal patron. There, he met Flemish painters whose influence is seen in his great attention to detail.

Vasari claims he was struck blind at 60 but lived to be 86. Some now doubt this, and surmise he spent the end of his life writing, including a well-known treatise on, of course, perspective. His main pupil was Luca Signorelli.

What to see

Piero's pieces are in the Museum at 65 Via Niccolò Aggiunti, near the Cathedral. He painted his *Resurrection* exactly where it is, for the

Museo Civico

building was formerly the town hall. Apparently he was still working on his great cycle in Arezzo at the time; Vasari judges this one the best he did anywhere. The Christ rising from his tomb amid perfect geometry personifies dignified vindication and, as the patterned guards sleep, the dead wintry landscape on the left comes back to life on the right in spring. The standard Christ bears is San Sepolcro's.

His polyptych *Madonna of Mercy*, who protects humanity with her ample cloak, is an early work commissioned by the local Fraternity of Mary for their church's high altar. They stipulated its general appearance – Piero had to produce a work 'gilded with fine gold and done with precious colours, principally ultra-marine blue' – and gave him three years. The full-faced figure with upturned eyes on the left of the serene Virgin is the artist's self-portrait.

His third piece, the damaged fresco of a curly-haired St Julian with a look of offended purity, was originally in a local church.

You can see Piero's home close by at 71 Via N. Aggiunti. He probably had a hand in its design himself.

Where to stay and eat

The **Albergo Fiorentino**, 60 Via Luca Pacioli; tel. 76033. An old, comfortable and quiet hostelry founded in 1807, this is only yards from the Museum. Its restaurant, obviously appreciated by the local bourgeoisie, is probably the best in town. It serves its own wines.

Otherwise, try **Dà Ventura**, a hotel and restaurant in Via San Puccio; tel. 76560.

Anghiari

Only 8 km south-west of San Sepolcro, Anghiari (population 6,000), is a totally intact medieval village, though you must climb to the top to find it. It is a silent maze of steep alleys, tunnels, squat houses, steps and sudden views. The centre is the sloping Piazza del Popolo, overlooked by a frescoed *palazzo*. It is well worth a look, especially just before lunch.

The **Ristorante Alighiero**, Via Garibaldi (near the lower piazza; closed Thursdays) is atmospheric.

Monterchi

The walled medieval village of Monterchi (population 2,000) is 20 km from San Sepolcro, a left turn off the SS 73 to Arezzo. A chapel outside the graveyard will reveal **Piero della Francesca**'s famous *Pregnant Virgin (Madonna del Parto)*.

Arezzo

A former Etruscan town and Roman military base, and birthplace of Petrarch, Arezzo is today a traffic-plagued industrial sprawl (population 90,000). The impelling reason for fighting your way through it once was the cycle of frescoes by Piero della Francesca in the Basilica of San Francesco, one of the most famous in the history of Italian art. But his *Legend of the Cross*, under attack by calcium sulphate, is in for restoration after two years of tests and the work is not expected to be completed until 1992, to coincide with the 500th anniversary of Piero's death. 'The frescoes are in very poor shape, but we'll find a way of saving them,' says the city's Director of Fine Arts.

What to see

Besides Piero, the attraction of Arezzo is the magnificent Romanesque church of **Santa Maria della Pieve**, at the top of Corso Italia, the climbing main street. Its thirteenth-century façade, three storeys of colonnades, is very like Pisa or Lucca, almost an entertainment. By contrast, the interior is loftily serious and unusual, with what must be the most elevated choir in Central Italy. Over the main altar is a prized polyptych by **Piero Lorenzetti**.

Behind the *Pieve* is the city's great sloping main square, the Piazza Grande. On the first Sunday of September this is the scene of a tense jousting tournament between eight wards: their lancers charge on horseback at the effigy of a fierce, swivelling Saracen who belts them with a lead-weighted whip if they're not fleet enough. It is worth seeing.

Cortona

Occupying a mighty spur at an altitude of nearly 600 metres, Cortona (population 22,500) is an understated medieval hill town with its own mind, still protected by large chunks of its original Etruscan walls. Overlooking the valley of the river Chiana, it commands perhaps the vastest panorama in Tuscany. One horizon is blocked in by the hills of far-away Siena. It is a rich little artistic centre, the birthplace of Luca Signorelli, and an ideal stop-over point, but do not arrive late because the restaurants close especially early, doubtless due to the habits of a resident British-American colony.

Getting there

Cortona is 30 km north-east of Montepulciano. Arezzo is 32 km, and Florence 102 km, to the north-west.

What to see

Though not strikingly handsome, Cortona has a market-town 'homely' feel to it, and wears its original uniform of local sandstone free of modern stains. Its scrubbed alleys are steep and present a closed aspect to visitors. Eight of them debouch into the tiny main square, the Piazza Repubblica.

Palazzo Pretorio

The piazza is dominated by the thirteenth-century Palazzo Pretorio. The façade is a face-lift but its flank in Via Casali hung with coats of arms, and its austere courtyard, hark back to the real thing. It is also a rewarding Etruscan museum, with an unusual array of small figures in bronze and a noted fifth-century BC candelabra. You may also fall upon an intriguing collection of Roman coins, from the Republic onwards.

Museo Diocesano

Cortona's highlight is its picture gallery, in the museum opposite the dull Cathedral. It boasts one of the best-known works of **Beato Angelico**, his *Annunciation* with predella, showing the angel pointing a finger at the Virgin in a setting of very Renaissance symmetry. The artist-monk lived in a Cortona monastery for a time.

There is a big, dramatic crucifix by the Sienese **Pietro Lorenzetti**, but otherwise Cortona's best-known son, **Luca Signorelli**, prevails. His *Flagellation* in a predella is an almost clinical study in sadism.

San Domenico

Another Signorelli is in the simple Gothic church of San Domenico just outside the walls, together with a widely admired altar-piece by Lorenzo di Niccolò, dated 1402. (For more on Signorelli, see Orvieto, page 187).

What to do

Shopping for Cortona pottery is a good idea: it is of local design, becoming and inexpensive.

Where to stay

The best hotel by far is the **Albergo San Michele**, 15 Via Guelfa (near the main piazza); tel. 604348. Set in a raftered Renaissance palazzo, it is superbly decorated. Booking is advised. Other hotels have faults.

Where to eat

La Loggetta, Piazza Pescheria, tel. 603777 (closed Wednesdays), is perhaps the most chic, but is expensive.

Il Cacciatore, 11 Via Roma, tel. 603252 (closed Wednesdays), is locally recommended but not cheap either.

Dardano, 24 Via Dardano, tel. 601944 (closed Tuesdays), is family, informal and reasonably priced.

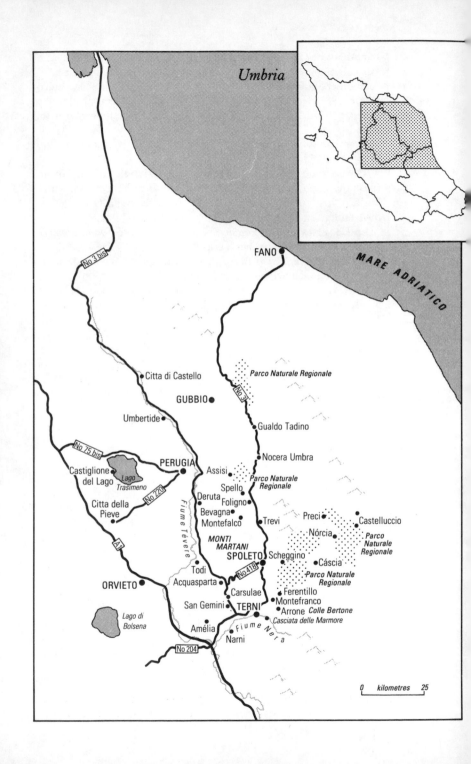

Umbria

Introduction

Umbria is the heart of Central Italy, its smallest and greenest part. It is also the least unspoilt. The film-directors, writers and fashion designers who now have second homes there – usually converted farmhouses – still find it as gentle and verdant as the patrician families of Imperial Rome who chose it for their repose in flashy villas.

Its undulating landscape of tortoise-like hills and thick black oak woods is oddly familiar – it is the same landscape that the Umbrian painters of the fifteenth century depicted. The slopes glinting from the green of the olives are still there as well, the squads of cypress trees, their background castles – and the silence. So is the source of the green. Water is everywhere – in lakes, rivers, underground streams, springs and waterfalls. Bears and wild boar are rare, but otters, badgers, squirrels and hare are in abundance everywhere.

The countryside is very much part of time off in Umbria, although it has not been left to itself. It is crocheted together by tiny medieval 'city-states', still as they were when they emerged from the local stone as go-ahead emblems of independence. They are everywhere, usually guarding something – a gorge, a road. Their nearness to each other has bred an Italian play-on-words: Umbria is 'a state of cities'.

You will also find forceful evidence of the Etruscans in Umbria, and of occupation by Rome. Main towns are Perugia, the capital; Spoleto, and industrial Terni. But the places to see are, above all, Gothic – the splendid cathedrals of Assisi and Orvieto, and rival lay exhibits in Gubbio, Todi and elsewhere.

Its moods, as visitors discover, are variable. Umbria was violence, but mysticism and religious fervour as well. It was the home of St Benedict, founder of Western monasticism, born in Norcia in AD 480; it was a crucible of hermits and heretics; the revolutionary St Francis of Assisi contemplated its vast forests. It is still dotted with monasteries; today some put up tourists in unmonastic comfort to make ends meet.

And, of course, Umbria means painting. Some masters left their greatest works in its churches, from Giotto in Assisi to Luca Signorelli in Orvieto.

Where to go
Umbria is the only region in Italy not exposed either to the sea or to a foreign country. It is shaped almost like a heart, dissected down the

middle for 210 km by the Tiber: the valley of the Tiber, the *Tiberina*, is one of its big communication routes. The other is the so-called Umbrian valley, or *Valle Umbra*, a huge, intensely farmed trench or basin, once a lake, running from Perugia south-east to Spoleto. The Apennines screen off Umbria to the east; their peaks accommodate to the scenery, looking like cathedral cupolas, not fierce at all.

These two valleys converge near Perugia, and then split away like an upturned 'V'. In themselves, they are not too thrilling, but the tranquil hill towns overlooking them, removed from the bustle down below, will surely please. Unspoiled, grandiose and empty hill country lies to the north-east of the capital, awkwardly called the *Eugubino*, after Gubbio, and the drive there from Perugia is superb.

Around Orvieto in the far south-east, it is a strange, slightly desolate picture that emerges, but the 'true' Umbria, with isolated hill towns and superb panoramas, begins to appear in the south, from Todi down along the valley of the river Naia, a tributary of the Tiber. For many, Umbria is at its most enchanting, with lush mountain scenery and impossibly picturesque villages, in the south-east below Spoleto, in the so-called *Valnerina*.

History   Before the Romans, the Tiber was the demarcation line between the Etruscans on the fertile west bank and the meeker Umbrians, an original Italic tribe, pushed up against the hills. Linguists say the split can still be heard in the dialects. You will doubtless use the key to Roman 'pacification' – the *Via Flaminia*, opened up in 220 BC – which still strikes across Umbria on its way from Rome to the Adriatic. Towns sprang up along it. Later it was the axis for the spread of Christianity.

Today's Umbrians blame their hapless past on their closeness to Rome. They were *too* close. The Romans, then the barbarians, and then the trembling Popes all saw Umbria as a potential bridgehead in the hands of enemies. They had to have control. Once the Romans had faded away, the story of Umbria was of how the Roman Church gained a right to it and then fought to assert it until its control was complete.

In Umbria the forces sent over from Byzantium smashed the Ostrogoths; Totila was slain north-east of Perugia. When the Longobards swarmed in, the Byzantines kept open a narrow corridor through Umbria linking Rome and Ravenna, the seat of their 'viceroy'; it more or less followed the River Tiber. When the Longobards were crushed by King Pippin, it was this corridor he made over to the Pope, as well as Spoleto. Eight towns bordered it, headed by Perugia; they formed the Umbrian nucleus of the temporal power of the Papacy, its legal title to territorial authority for centuries to come.

But it took the Papacy seven centuries to assert control. First, the towns of Umbria rebelled against their masters, often bishops, and declared independence. With a quarrelsome prosperity began their civic pride. The towns took violent sides in the tussle between the Church and the Empire. Frederick II attacked constantly: at one point all of Umbria was his except the Guelf town of Perugia. Perugia held out longest against subjugation by the Pope: no other city-state in Italy lasted so long. When it finally fell in the sixteenth century, all of Umbria was in the grip of the Roman Pontiff.

The result still shows. Church rule signified neglect. Roads crumbled; isolation followed; absentee feudal landlords stepped in; agriculture stagnated. Italian Unification made the situation worse by letting in damaging competition. The new State was as indifferent as the old, and Umbria slipped even further backwards. In 1911, 50 per cent of Umbrians were illiterate. The first wave of emigration began; a second followed the Second World War, together with a rural exodus. The population now stands at 800,000.

Today, Umbria is a stronghold of the Communists. Either alone or allied to the Socialist Party, they run most of the town councils; the Christian Democrats take a poor third place. Rome still sees Umbria as depressed; the Umbrians see Rome as uncaring. Roads are now good, but links with the rest of Italy are still poor; there are only 57 km of autostrada.

Umbria is Tuscany's poor cousin. Landlocked, of course, it cannot dream of Tuscany's economic power. But temperaments differ: if Tuscany is rational, Umbria is dreamier, its soul more diffuse. The Renaissance did not catch on there at all. Tuscans look to Florence, but Umbrians look to Rome. If they are less pretentious, it is perhaps because they have fewer great names to boast of. They are still simple, modest folk of peasant stock. Today, the important Umbrians are usually top officers in the Italian Armed Forces, a salute to the times before the Papal takeover when Umbria produced the ablest *condottieri*, soldiers of fortune, in Central Italy.

The two names Umbria does chalk up were contemporaries in Umbrian art, which blossomed only for a brief sixty years.

Perugino (1445–1523), an ambiguous character, was a pupil first of Piero della Francesca in Arezzo and then of Andrea del Verrocchio in Florence. From them, he is thought to have inherited his flair for perspective and his use of architecture. He is the Renaissance master of piety, a lyricist who saw a celestial world of worship and unworldly yearning peopled by inclined heads and upturned oval faces. His serene figures feel no pain; drained, they inhabit pure ecstasy.

His personal life, however, was not quite the same. He is alleged to have been a non-believer, to have refused a death-bed confession, and to have kept doubtful company, a murderer included. He once sued Michelangelo for calling him a fuddy-duddy. He ran a lucrative workshop in Perugia and was known to be money-mad. More importantly, he supervised the apprenticeship of Raphael.

Pinturicchio (1454–1531) is the only Umbrian to approach

Perugino. A narrator of charm and wit, he flings open a window on to contemporary style, dress and manners, especially those of foppish youths shown against demure Umbrian backgrounds. You can see his eye-opening work in Spello and Orvieto Cathedral.

Getting around, eating and drinking

Umbrian hotels are a shade more modest than Tuscany's. Except in the north, the roads and railways are efficient. In the many small places, the problem is evening boredom. The solution is to rove from bases, the best being Perugia and Spoleto.

Umbrian cuisine lacks commanding personality. Its pluses are simplicity and freshness, meat and game. Specialities include macaroni pie (*pasticcio di maccheroni*), with mixed, minced meats; spaghetti with truffles (*tartufo*); *porchetta*, piglet on the spit with aromatic herbs; *palombaccia*, wild pigeon first roasted and then sautéed in wine.

Umbria's only well-known wine is the light, white *Orvieto*, from the city of the same name.

Perugia

Umbria's capital is the most pugnacious medieval city in Central Italy, virtually unchanged for the last three centuries. Steely and arrogant, an old Etruscan stronghold, it sits astride a jagged hill and lords it over the valley of the Tiber from a height of 500 metres, with a cold eye on the seething lines of communication below.

It is also the centre of Umbrian painting, and a springboard for central Umbria. As such, it is good for three days.

Getting there

Perugia lies 50 km from Cortona by road and 120 km from Siena. From Rome, take the A 1 and turn off at Orte; the journey takes 3 hours. The train from Florence takes 3¼ hours.

The city's solution to traffic congestion lands you in the bowels of its past: drivers are meant to park down in the Piazza dei Partigiani and take an underground escalator (*scala mobile*) up to the centre. On the way, it disgorges you into the subterranean caverns of the Rock, a mighty fortress built by a sixteenth-century Pope to quell Perugia, described by an eye-witness as 'the most violent city in Italy'.

But the Perugians were not to be subdued. To make way for his giant bunker, the Pontiff tore down an entire quarter. 'It was worse than a major earthquake,' a chronicler remembered. They never forgave him. Twice during the Risorgimento, they tore into the hated Rock with picks and bare hands. You are amid what is left.

History

Perugia was one of twelve major cities in the Etruscan Federation. It was rubbished by Totila in 547, and formed part of the package Pippin handed over to the Papacy. Five Papal conclaves were held there while Rome was unsafe, but on three occasions the Papacy repressed its wayward son with unbridled force.

First it was excommunicated for smashing the Umbrian town of Foligno into debris; war broke out, and the Pope won. Next it led a revolt against a Papal tax on salt; Pope Paul III responded with 300 horsemen and 7,000 infantry . . . and the Rock. Then, hardly more than a century ago, in 1859, Perugia rose up again in the name of Italian independence; it was massacred by the Pope's Swiss troops before their surrender to the Risorgimento liberation fighters the following year.

What to see

Perugia is atmosphere. It is toiling up and down steep, ribbed alleys beneath oppressive vaults and arches, hemmed in by thick, mirthless walls that stare blankly. Every so often, there is the relief of a glimpse, between the chunky *palazzi*, of distant hills or the valley far below. In the cascading web of alleys behind the Cathedral, where dwellings are hunched up together as if in fear, one feels a trespasser, almost afraid to speak out loud. Perugia is forever either on the defensive or defiant. Distrust and threat pervade the city.

Piazza Quattro Novembre

The centre is the Piazza Quattro Novembre, at the end of the main Corso Vannucci. Carefully planned in the thirteenth century, this is the model square of Umbria, with civic and ecclesiastic authority symbolically played off against each other. The unusual, naked, Gothic Cathedral and the massive, overbearing Priors' Palace, begun at the same time, are squared up for conflict.

Church and State are separated by the **Fontana Maggiore** in the centre, one of the most beautiful in Italy. Easily the most elegant water-piece the thirteenth century produced, it is a masterpiece of bas relief by the father-and-son team of Nicola and Giovanni Pisano. They worked so closely together that experts do not really know who pictured what on the lower basin which, among other things, narrates two Aesop fables and depicts the months of the year. It is agreed that the twenty-four statuettes around the upper basin betray the hand of Giovanni; one shows a famous 'Traitor Cleric' who gave away Perugia's defences to Totila.

The square around the fountain has witnessed a degree of bloodletting chilling even by Italian standards. As in other cities, rival families battled for supremacy with sword and ambush, but in Perugia, the Baglioni and the Oddi families tore into each other with such ferocity that the Oddi were virtually exterminated. The victorious Baglioni then set to fighting among themselves and, in the year 1500, most were hacked to death in a conspiracy. After an especially murderous flare-up, priests set up thirty-five altars in this square and celebrated Mass for three days non-stop. After another explosion of violence, they swilled the square down with red wine.

Cathedral

Work stopped on the incomplete Cathedral only in 1490 after 145 years of labour. It disowns the Priors' Palace, rudely turning its flank to it. The vigorous sixteenth-century bronze figure waving in front of it is Pope Julius III, thus honoured by Perugia for restoring the city's judiciary, which had been suppressed by his hated predecessor, Paul III. The outside pulpit was specially affixed to the flank for St Bernardino of Siena, who blessed the people of Perugia from it in 1425.

The interior is a surprise: the three naves are all of the same height, though the central one is twice as broad as the others, giving the impression of a vast assembly hall. Indeed, the main idea was space in which to preach to maximum numbers. There were only two others like it in Umbria.

Palazzo dei Priori The curving Priors' Palace ranks as one of the most grandiose medieval public buildings in Italy, and only the grudging Gothic windows soften its flaunted haughtiness. In pace with Perugia's increasing might, it grew bigger down the centuries, gobbling up homes and churches as it progressed down the Corso. The fan staircase in the Piazza Quattro Novembre leads up to the magnificent **Hall of Notaries**, once known as the Hall of the People – a brilliant tunnel of eight sweeping arches, vividly frescoed with fables and biblical scenes in the thirteenth century, probably by the Roman primitive Pietro Cavallini.

Over the staircase, they vindictively hung from chains the keys to the gates of Siena, seized as a trophy after battle in 1358: they have dangled there ever since. In another show of good-neighbourliness, the massive **Archbishop's Palace** in the square's gloomiest corner is still devouring, as its façade shows, hefty chunks from the former Palazzo del Podestà, burnt to the ground in 1534.

National Gallery of Umbria Juxtaposed with this savagery and harshness is the gentle, spiritual world of Umbrian painting, to be seen in the National Gallery, the region's biggest, on the third floor of the Priors' Palace.

It follows Umbrian art from the thirteenth to the eighteenth centuries in date order, and discloses the other face of Umbria – a typical dichotomy you will find everywhere, between the outdoor nastiness and an almost unbelievable inward niceness. Whenever they lived, these Umbrian artists see softness and delicacy in the Umbrian landscape, which they dress as nicely as they do the young thugs who pose in their pictures as little gentlemen.

The wooded quietness of their countryside is also a natural background for what Italians term their 'mysticism', their world of abstracted rapture. Some see it as pure escapism from a contemporary Umbria too rough to bear, but you would almost expect this ethereal quality of a region with a tradition of religious contemplation going back to the arrival of Syrian monks in the sixth century. St Benedict, founder of the great monastic movement, was born in Norcia, Umbria, in 480.

In room 7, Beato Angelico and Piero della Francesca each offer a Madonna and Child. You will find a wealth of Peruginos, together with Pinturicchio, in rooms 12 to 15.

Collegio del Cambio | Perugino's greatest achievement is his cycle of frescoes in the intimate Audience Chamber of the fifteenth-century Money-Changers' College, on the ground floor of the Priors' Palace at number 25. Commissioned in 1496, he was instructed to demonstrate that 'harmony is reached through the fusion of the culture of antiquity with Christian sentiment'.

Hence the gods of mythology inhabit the vault. The experts argue over the cycle's internal logic, but agree that Perugino touched his peak on the right wall, where the grouping of the flowing figures beneath the Eternal Father contrasts so sharply with the pattern of composition used for the others.

It was long held that Perugino's pupil, Raphael, had a hand in these frescoes, but the current view is that the master would not have let the future genius attempt anything too crucial – he was only 17. The chubby-cheeked, placid face in the painting of a painting on the left is Perugino's self-portrait.

A few doors further up is the small hall, with a tiny wooden pulpit, where the Merchants' Guild met to pick from among themselves two of the city's ten priors. They still vote today, but simply on sums for charity.

San Pietro | Down by the south gate, San Costanzo, reached along Via Cavour, it is a hike to get to this church but worth it – it is the most spectacular in Perugia. Aim for its bullet-shaped spire. Originally tenth-century, it became the heart of a walled Benedictine monastery where the mighty of the church, including Popes, sought refuge when the going got flinty.

Inside, you are buried beneath an animated avalanche of colour, accumulated in the sixteenth and seventeenth centuries. The second column on the left is the 'Miraculous Column', so called because it was saved from collapse by a sign of the cross made by a local noble, later made a saint.

The secret is the sacristy, in the far right-hand corner. For a tip, the sacristan opens it up with an ingratiating grimace. Immediately to the left of the door are panels by Perugiono; above, a Caravaggio; and above the right-hand corner, two infants by Raphael.

A plaque in the cloister recalls how the monastery gave shelter to innocent Perugians fleeing from the assault on the city by Papal 'mercenaries' on 20 June 1859.

The Etruscan Gate | The Etruscans survive: their walls served Perugia until the Middle Ages. The great slabs still enclose the city's heights; and the most famous Etruscan gate in Italy, the very emblem of Perugia, frowningly guards the bottom of the steep Via Baldeschi, facing the University for Foreigners. The Etruscan kernel is the thick arch; the Romans built up the gate above it, giving it its name of Arco d'Augusto. Then it was topped by a charming Renaissance *loggia* – palimpsest manifest!

Archaeological Museum	Etruscan urns and the like are in the mournful museum next to the dead whale of San Domenico in Corso Cavour, on the way to San Pietro. They are belittled by those in Rome.
Tomb of the Volumni	This deep underground Etruscan family tomb is still 'fresh', with the dead in the same comfortable positions they were found in, by accident, in 1840. There is nothing like it in Central Italy. It is a sensation, and alone justifies a visit to Perugia.

It is tricky to find, being some 7 km south-east of Perugia. You take the Viale Roma to Porta San Costanza, passing San Pietro on your left. Then take the SS 75B and at the edge of the valley suburb of Ponte San Giovanni ask for the Ipogeo dei Volumni. You descend past a slab – the seal – into the cool netherworld of Arunte Velimnas, son of Aules, magistrate and head of a noble family buried in the late Hellenic period.

The tomb is shaped like a Roman house and there Arunte reclines in cushioned splendour amid his family, above two young winged guardians in whom Italians see an eerie premonition of the Renaissance. His daughter, Velia, is finely seated on his right. The profusion of urns above, adorned with winged horses, battle scenes and mythology, come from a nearby Etruscan cemetery.

What to do

As the seat of two universities, Perugia is a mecca of the cosmopolitan young. In summer, especially during the July Jazz Festival, the thronged Corso Vannucci throbs to the strong pulse of African drums, musicians, singers, clowns, vendors and good spirits.

From July to September you will find the evenings quite varied – with concerts, theatre, exhibitions, opera, a band contest and a fair.

Where to stay

Top range

The smartest hotel in the centre is the four-star **Brufani**, at 12 Piazza Italia; tel. 62541.

Mid range

Central and nicely old-fashioned is the three-star **Hotel della Posta**, 97 Corso Vannucci; tel. 61345.

Nearby is the three-star **Fortuna**, 19 Via Bonazzi; tel. 22845.

And near the main 'valley' car park there is the three-star **Excelsior Lilli**, 9 Via L. Masi; tel. 20241.

Bottom range

The two-star **Aurora**, 21 Viale Indipendenza, tel. 24819, is on the upper 'ring road'.

The one-star **Rosalba**, 10 Corso Vanucci, tel. 26265, is very central.

The one-star **Anna**, 48 Via dei Priori, tel. 66304, is just behind the Palazzo dei Priori.

Where to eat

Flanking the Cathedral and upmarket is the **Trattoria Ricciotto**, 19 Piazza Danti; tel. 21956. The speciality is *Cartocci Kaiser*, veal in silver paper.

The **Lanterna**, in a cellar behind the Cathedral, at 6 Via Ulisse Rocchi, tel. 66064, is friendly and immaculate. Its speciality is macaroni with ricotta.

Assisi

Strung out along a spur overlooking a plain, glinting under the sun or looming through the haze, Assisi (population 24,000) is one of Italy's great sights – as well as a modern symbol of world peace and the ecumenical movement.

Unfortunately, 2 million other people are drawn to Assisi too, and in September and October it is a scrum. The churches become Towers of Babel, the guides bookies shouting the odds, and mums from Madrid moaners about feet. It is quietest in May and June – and after lunch.

Getting there

Easily reached by road from almost anywhere, Assisi is 20 km south-east of Perugia, 82 km from Orvieto, 135 km from Siena and 175 km from Rome. The station, 5 km from the centre, lays on direct trains to Rome and Florence.

Regular buses go to Assisi from Rome and Florence.

History

Assisi is where two quiet revolutions began. St Francis, born in 1181, began a meek revolt against the corrupt and power-hungry Church. Giotto learned revolution from his tutor Cimabue (see page 103), and followed his path until he had snapped the stranglehold of Byzantine art, heralding the painting of today.

St Francis

St Francis, patron saint of Italy, never became a priest.

Down behind the Tourist Office in the Piazza del Comune (the main square), a small church now occupies the probable site of his home. Further down the alley, there is a former ox-stable, now the tiniest church in Europe, where his mother was allegedly ordered by a voice to give birth. His real name was Giovanni, but his father nick-named him *Francesco*, the French one, after his French mother. As a wealthy draper, his father did much business in France.

His son frittered his time away as an indolent *fils de papa*, revelling and chasing girls. His conversion began in jail, where he ended up after fighting the Perugians and being taken prisoner. A painted cruci-fix in the derelict church of San Damiano outside Assisi spoke to him: 'Francesco! Go and repair my House which is falling down!' At the time, he took it simply to mean San Damiano. The greater import sank in only later.

He returned his fine raiment to a furious father, taking to a rough habit belted with a thrice-knotted cord like an Umbrian peasant – it has been the symbol of the Franciscan order ever since. At the time, they dubbed him the local fool.

On a later trip to Rome, he wrung approval for his new order and rule from a reluctant Pope. Those who had preached poverty before him had all been branded as heretics.

What to see

A shrine to both the saint and the artists, made of one church on top of another, the Basilica is the focal point of Assisi. It marks the first

Basilica of
St Francis

appearance in Italy of Gothic architecture from northern Europe, and was commissioned by Pope Gregory IX in 1228.

Wait for a friar to guide you around. The claustrophobic lower church was hacked out of sheer rock; in the sepulchral gloom, among the low arches and pillars, try not to miss a restored fresco by Cimabue. It is a Madonna with angels, in the right-hand transept on the bottom right, and is held to include a portrait of St Francis, on the right. The figure certainly tallies with a contemporary pen-portrait, detailing the saint's small, flappy ears and long nails.

The other frescoes in the transept are Giotto's. He was only 25 years younger than Cimabue, but the difference spans light years.

The frescoes emblazoned over the first chapel on the left of the entrance tell the life of St Martin, and are agreed to show Simone Martini of Siena at his pinnacle.

St Francis was buried in bare rock beneath the main altar for fear of a body-snatch by the Perugians. It was only in 1818 that he was found, after fifty-two nights of excavation. The body now lies in the crypt.

Giotto's famous biography of St Francis surrounds the walls of the more luminous, loftier Upper Church, intended to convey 'liberation' from the oppressiveness of death below. The story begins at the far right of the nave, showing a simpleton laying down his cloak for the young Francis, predicting his greatness. With incisive simplicity, the story of his life is told clockwise, with the best-known episodes on either side of the main door, where he is shown calling forth a spring for a thirsty traveller, and then preaching to the birds.

Local experts testily reject any doubts about the authorship of the cycle. For one thing, they argue, a solicitor's letter just discovered, certifying that Giotto had re-paid a certain debt, proves beyond doubt that he was physically present in Assisi when he was meant to be.

The apse, in bad shape, is almost entirely Cimabue's creation – the biggest exhibition of his art there is. The crucifixion in the right transept, daringly showing a Christ contorted in agony, is deemed to be his masterwork.

Rocca
Maggiore

But there is more to Assisi than St Francis and Giotto. After all, it began as a flourishing Roman <i>municipium</i> and later the Longobards incorporated it into the Duchy of Spoleto. As a newly thriving town in the Middle Ages, Assisi always acted as a wedge between Spoleto and the Guelf Perugia. The birthplace of St Francis was fiercely Ghibelline, and came under the personal control of the Emperor Frederick II, who was brought up under a German tutor in the fortress overlooking the north of the city. Not the impressive present one, though; the people of Assisi rebelled against the tutor and tore down the imperial fort. It was rebuilt by a Spanish cardinal, Gil Alvarez Carrillo de Albornoz, sent to Italy while the Popes were in Avignon to retrieve lost Papal lands, which he did by building terrifying fortresses everywhere.

Piazza del Comune

Though dwarfed by the enormous thirteenth-century so-called **People's Tower**, what seizes the eye in the elongated piazza is the astonishing Corinthian **Temple of Minerva**. It is so intact that you think it must be a fake, but it is just as it was when two officials, brothers, had it erected on the edge of the Roman forum, probably under the Republic. Goethe, strange man, thought it the most perfect object he had seen.

The inevitable confrontation of the classes is symbolised by the thirteenth-century Palace of the People's Captain, next to the Tower. Opposite, a century older, is the Priors' Palace, a slightly unhappy fusion of four earlier buildings.

Santa Chiara

Beyond the piazza is the Church of St Clare, the façade of which mirrors the Upper Church of St Francis. It is dedicated to the daughter of a noble family from Assisi who ran away to join St Francis as a disciple; she later founded the Second Franciscan Order, the Poor Clares. In a chapel on the right you will see a crucifix said to have spoken to her. If you ask, the veiled nun behind the iron grille will list the relics she guards, including the tunic of St Francis. The nuns have agreed to a proposal to submit all of these relics to dating by carbon testing.

Cathedral

The patron saint of Assisi is in fact St Rufino, a third-century bishop drowned by his persecutors in a river. The Cathedral dedicated to him, up the Via Rufino from the Piazza del Comune, is well worth a look: its stern façade, packed with heavy early medieval symbolism, is a triumph of Umbrian Romanesque art. Begun in 1140, it marks a flux in the art world: the stylish, animated 'modern' trend is already ousting the rough old art of the Dark Ages. The main door – all geometry, tracery and gesturing little figures and animals – is the astounding evidence. One recurrent message is put across by fighting beasts, which represent Christianity's struggle on earth: the lion starting on a head is Christ abolishing pagan rites. Inside, the church is a boring re-jig.

Around the Cathedral you will find escape from the tumult below, in the quiet alleys and small squares of upper Assisi, all built in the red and white stone from towering Mount Subasio above.

The Hermitage

It takes peace for the beauty of Assisi to come through, and it is to be found at the Hermitage, the *Eremo delle Carceri*, a monastery built around a mountain cave – the retreat of St Francis.

It is a steep, ten-minute drive south-east of the town, an eagle's-nest on the lip of a cliff in thick forest almost 800 metres up, below the crest of Mount Subasio. The quiet is profound. A friar will show you around, into the saint's minute cave with its stone bed, and point out the vista he beheld. Nowhere else in Umbria touches the spirit in the same way.

Even Italians are thrown by the name and ask to see the prisons, the meaning of *carceri*. There are none: the sense of the untranslatable name is, roughly, Retreat of the Self-Incarcerated. In the surrounding wood are the satellite caves where the saint's followers imprisoned themselves in meditation.

San Damiano

A fifteen-minute walk downhill from the main gate, the Porta Nuova, through quiet olive groves towards the plain, the peaceful little monastery of San Damiano still seems to suggest something of the seclusion that St Francis sought. By car, follow the Viale V. Emanuele ring road up to a signposted left turn, before a sharp bend; the drive is 2 km.

This was the tumbledown chapel where the saint heard the voice from the crucifix. To carry out the instruction to repair it, he sold silks filched from his father's stock in Foligno, but the priest was too frightened to take the money, whereupon the angry young man hurled the stuff out of the window. Later he rebuilt the church by hand. He made room for Santa Chiara and her first followers; she died here.

The crypt-like refectory, candle-blackened, is just as it was. Here, St Francis as a dying man wrote his *Canticle of the Creatures*, one of the first attempts at religious poetry in Italy.

Santa Maria degli Angeli

St Francis died, in 1226, on bare earth in a borrowed habit in a microscopic 'infirmary', a few steps from the tiny, kennel-like church known as the **Porziuncola** where he founded his order. You will find it inside the massive sixteenth-century basilica 4 km away, which dominates the plain with its great cupola. No visit to Assisi is complete without a pause to look inside. It was after this church that Franciscan missionaries later named a certain city in California, iberianising the Italian, of course.

Where to stay

Closest to the Basilica is the three-star **San Francesco**, 48 Via San Francesco; tel. 812281. It is comfortable, but noisy.

Near the Piazza del Comune is the three-star **Dei Priori**, 15 Corso Mazzini; tel. 812237.

On the access road outside the walls is another three-star, **Windsor Savoia**, 1 Viale Marconi; tel. 81220.

Where to eat

Despite the name, the **Medioevo**, at 4 Via Arco dei Priori, tel. 813068, is an elegant and quiet local middle-class favourite.

Pallotta, 4 Via San Rufino, tel. 812649, is less pricey, but serious.

Spello

Still using Perugia as a base, it is easy to see in a day four neighbouring townships that sing out Umbria in four rival voices – Spello, Bevagna, Montefalco and Trevi, all in the Umbrian valley, to the south-east.

Some 35 km from Perugia, Spello takes after the capital like a small brother. It looks down from its foothill on to the SS 75 with the same kind of scorn. Made of Mount Subasio's limestone, it is hard, not convivial. Its impact is powerful. It has remained as it was – steep alleys, chill shadows, and walls that turn their backs. Perhaps you will find the people (population 7,000) a fraction sharp, too. They seem indifferent to the present.

Typical of many Umbrian places, Spello has thrived continuously since Roman times, changing from a Roman *municipium* into a mini-Ghibelline medieval republic. As times got worse, it simply climbed further uphill, away from its original Roman site. One of Pippin's theoretical presents to the Church, Spello rebelled to be independent, sought the rude protection of Perugia, but thankfully returned to Rome's embrace in the sixteenth century.

What to see

The fine consular **Roman Gate** stands at the bottom of town; the affixed statues, found near the amphitheatre, are Republican. Further up (take Via Torri di Preperzio), twin towers guard the restored **Gate of Venus**, built under Augustus, while the tiny twelfth-century church of **San Severino** is perched at the top. Nearby is a **belvedere** commanding a brilliant mock-up of still forest and smarmed-down hills.

Some way up the main street, Via Cavour, is **Santa Maria Maggiore**; inside, on the left, below the sickly rococo, is the most famous fresco serial Pinturicchio ever did. You can see why he was judged such a sharp observer of fifteenth-century manners. In his Adoration, the bored, well-dressed youths around the groomed horse are the same *vitelloni* of post-war Italian films. Perugino, in the same church, is a different universe, despite there being only ten years between them.

Where to eat

Pinturicchio is the speciality of the **Molino**, next to Santa Maria Maggiore, tel. 651 5500 (closed Tuesdays). This is a pie on a cushion of mushrooms, cream, cognac and spices.

Bevagna

Twelve km away on the other side of the SS 75, Bevagna (population 5,000) is also a Roman town turned medieval. It is placid, down on the plain, and boasts the most enchanting, and the most intact, central square in Umbria.

Near the Cassia, amid fertile land, the town flourished under the Empire. The dressing-rooms in the local amphitheatre are now private cellars. Like Spello, it was sacked by Frederick II, and commended itself to the Church in the fifteenth century, but its temper was, and remains, sweeter.

What to see

The **Piazza Silvestri**, the uncluttered little square, is, for once, spared of cars. Here, the temporal and the spiritual state their positions at close quarters, yet diplomatically, at angles that avoid confrontation.

The tiny Romanesque church of **San Silvestro**, so modest it is almost a manor house, took shape in 1195, about the same time as the square-faced San Michele – note him in flight atop a jamb. The oblong, Gothic **Palazzo dei Consoli**, equally simple, came to life nearly a century later, but refused the obvious chance to impose itself Perugia-style. On the contrary, the broad outside steps signal accessibility; bulkiness hides behind. Italians claim that they planned their squares as carefully as they design *pasta* today, and that the real architect was always local temperament.

Where to eat

In the Palazzo's rough and nice old ox-stables is the **Taverna dei Consoli**, Via del Gonfalone; tel. 360555 (closed Mondays). The speciality is *stingozzi*, tagliatelle made without eggs.

Montefalco

From Bevagna, the road for 7 km south is a climbing tightrope over precipitous nature, tied at the top to the walled township of Montefalco, known as the Ringhiera dell'Umbria, the Balcony of Umbria. From its magnificent position 472 metres high, it looks out over a well-known landscape of plains and horizons. Montefalco is also an Umbrian home-from-home for painting. In Roman times a village, it suddenly discovered repute when a fourteenth-century Pope based his rector to the Duchy of Spoleto on its hill, complete with walls. Church patronage then drew the artists.

What to see

Frescoes by Umbrian painters from the fourteenth to the sixteenth centuries blanket the Gothic church of **Sant' Agostino**, half-way up Corso Mameli, the mounting high street. The real show, however, is in the run-down former church of **San Francesco**, beyond the main square, a forlorn circle where dogs play, opposite 19 Via Ringhiera Umbria.

The star, among lesser names, is Benozzo Gozzoli (1420–97), the pupil of Fra Angelico who made his name in the Palazzo Medici in Florence. In the apse, the man who so delighted in fine clothes, delicate people and pageantry, the narrator of St Augustine's life in San Gimignano, tackled a biography of St Francis, some 150 years after Giotto's in Assisi. This was the first major cycle he took on after venturing forth from under the wing of the good friar, but he tells his tale with typical gusto and eye for detail in twelve clear panels, starting bottom left and to be read in ascending fours from extreme left to extreme right.

Number 3, where the saint returns his fine clothes to his father, could be a page out of a fifteenth-century *Vogue*. The sermon to the birds is number 7, where the mastery of perspective marks the advent of the Renaissance in Umbria. Later, he vividly frescoed what was a chapel to the right of the entrance, his subject this time being the doings of St Jerome.

Montefalco is known for *Sacrantino*, a heavy, sweet red wine with the kick of an ass.

Trevi

On the other side of the valley, 14 km away, the 7,000 people of Trevi sit on a conical hill overlooking the highway and try to compete, but they don't quite make it. They too are in a fine position, with good air, distant views, and no present. But Trevi has stayed unpretentious.

This is another Umbria – low-key, family, strangely intimate, with higgledy-piggledy alleys, jumbled houses, junior-size arches, and a Tower in vicarage ivy. Aggression is unknown. This was one of the few places wiped out by Hungarian invaders in the tenth century.

Foligno

Down in the plain, now with a population of 50,000, Foligno was a

Roman town of some importance, being on the *Flaminia*. It was the most loyal Ghibelline city in Umbria. But it is impossible to find your way either into or out of the place. It does have, however, a stately main square and a curious, originally twelfth-century, Cathedral, opening up on to two different squares.

The friendly three-star hotel, the **Italia**, Piazza Matteotti, tel. 50412, has a pleasant restaurant.

Deruta   Worth a trip south from Perugia, some 20 km away on the SS 3 bis in the Tiber Valley, Deruta is a contradiction in terms: an Italian hill town that is a bore – dull and prosaic. But it also happens to be the biggest pottery centre in Central Italy. The Deruta style is not everyone's definition of beauty, but dedicated potters should certainly pause.

The pottery tradition began in the fourteenth century, but won real fame for the town in the sixteenth, when fifty workshops were busy. There seem to be as many today. They reproduce the sixteenth-century lines – historical scenes and mythological themes, portraits, heraldic arms. The colours are 'child-like' bright: dark blue and orange prevail. Deruta's special objects are pine-cone-shaped vases and chemists' jars with bulb-shaped bellies.

Spoleto

A snug hill town tucked into thick woods, Spoleto is now synonymous with one of the first artistic festivals in post-war Europe. Today it's a tourists' sugar-lump. Its setting is spectacular, dominated by the most massive fortress ever erected by Albornoz. Its political importance rivalled Perugia's, and it can claim to have more strata of its past on show than anywhere else in Umbria.

Getting there   It is 212 km from Florence, 47 from Assisi, and only 126 km from Rome or 90 minutes by train. The station is right on the doorstep of the town.

What to see   Spoleto's convenience was one reason why the Italian composer-conductor-impresario Gian Carlo Menotti picked it as the site for his Festival of Two Worlds, conceived in 1958 as a cultural bridge between Italy and the USA. Every August, it draws prestigious orchestras, artists and devoted audiences, even though the last note now fades out in the red.

Roman theatre   One of the twenty stages and forecourts pressed into use during the Festival is a concrete-restored Roman theatre built in the first years of the Empire. It flanks the anodyne main square, Piazza della Libertà, and was completely unearthed only in the 1950s as Menotti's experiment began.

Roman bridge   Another Roman construction still underground, believe it or not, is a complete bridge. It is at the foot of Spoleto, in Piazza della Vittoria. The entrance resembles a sunken public toilet and, as if it were, you obtain the key from the nearby Bar Lilly, or by phoning 6811 – ask for *Ufficio Cultura*.

Built under Augustus, its name – 'the bloody bridge' – was passed on through the generations. It was earned, so they say, because the bodies of early Christians killed in the nearby second-century Roman amphitheatre were flung from it into the river Tessino below. The river later switched its course so, with the bridge pointless, they covered it up.

San Gregorio

The big inscription over the church of St Gregory the Great in the adjoining Piazza Garibaldi claims that 10,000 Christian martyrs are buried beneath. This is reliably presumed to be a misreading of a lost text, but graves and remains do show that the *Flaminia* was the axis for the advance of Christianity into Umbria, and that around Spoleto, where Christians gathered, Roman persecution was probably severe. Many of the early Christians reached Umbria from the Middle East; Spoleto's first bishop was Syrian.

The unusual church, begun in 1079, echoes the then new monastic theory that a church, as a prelude to heaven, should aid ascent towards the invisible via the pleasantly visible. As you see, the surprise is the raised altar area, very high: this is apparently the oldest example of this style of church, which was later widely copied. The altar area, it is believed, was intended to seat the clergy and to symbolise the reforms of Pope Gregory VII, who strove to transform the priesthood into a model of perfection, to be placed on high, like a light, and followed. Scholars further see in this concept of the altar the origin of the Italian stage, which had its remote beginnings in Umbria.

With one exception, there is no other church of such an age in Umbria where so much of the original, if flaking, fresco work has survived. The oldest fragments, on the interior façade, are twelfth-century. And it would be a job to find a more disarming example of the wholesale use of Roman remains in the fabric of a church – from columns in the naves to the blocks supporting the bell-tower.

Porta Fuga

Spoleto had been thoroughly pro-Roman, and its lasting hold on glory is to have sent Hannibal packing. He attacked just after decimating the Roman army at Lake Trasimeno. As you climb up Corso Garibaldi, you will come to the whiteish gate where the fearsome Carthaginian supposedly turned tail. It is aptly called the Gate of Flight.

Cathedral

After the Romans and Totila, Spoleto became a powerful dukedom under the Longobards. The man who destroyed her was Frederick Barbarossa, incensed at the city for siding with the Church against him. But today's Spoleto owes its main draw to him: the Romanesque Cathedral, consecrated in 1198, was built to replace one the angry Teuton tore down. Once more, outside appearance provides its impact. The façade is unique, above all because of the Renaissance porch added to the medieval face. The Byzantine-like mosaic it wears is dated 1207.

As so often, the interior, a seventeenth-century re-hash, would be a let-down were it not for the cycle of frescoes in the apse by Filippo Lippi and two helpers. They took two years; in one group, he is believed to have painted himself and his son.

Consecration coincided with Spoleto coming under the Church for good, but in contrast to what often happened elsewhere, that did not spell stagnation. The cash, and building, continued so that as you stroll around you will meet styles from every epoch. This eclectic look – very un-Italian outside Rome – makes Spoleto special.

Rocca and Ponte delle Torri

So does the immense rectangular fortress with which Cardinal Albornoz crowned the town in the fourteenth century, with the idea of providing the Popes with an ultra-powerful stronghold when they returned from Avignon. He too ordered the stupendous bridge behind it, the Bridge of the Towers, spanning a steep little valley set in a telling landscape. An aqueduct and an escape route, it is the best, and the best-kept, example of medieval military engineering in Central Italy.

San Pietro

It would be a pity to miss the extraordinary 'lesson about life' preached by the 'talking' façade of the solitary Romanesque church of San Pietro, just outside Spoleto at the foot of Monteluco, the city's 'Holy Mountain', where refugees from the East set up a hermitage in the fifth century. The original St Peter's was built at about the same time, as a reliquary for a bit of the saint's chains brought from Rome, but the façade belongs to a twelfth-century reconstruction. Geometrically divided into frames, it is a strip cartoon peopled by humans and animals, full of admonitory tales based on the New Testament, on fables and on medieval treatises. The work of unknown hands, this is an agreed masterpiece of Umbrian Romanesque sculpture.

It also offers a fascinating insight into the workings of the medieval mind, even if some panels are a trifle obscure. The third panel down to the left of the central door, for instance, shows that there must have been some cautionary story about a cunning fox playing dead before stupid ravens. Within the door's framework, hinds feed their young while devouring snakes; above, peacocks peck at grapes. The most terrible lesson is 'Death of a Sinner', second down on the left. Someone is boiling upside-down in a cauldron, and a second unfortunate seems to be under torture.

Other sights

If you have time, try also to see the tiny, intimate eleventh-century church of Sant' Eufemia, hard by the Cathedral; the so-called 'Roman House', the probable home of Emperor Vespasian's mother (apply to the police in the town hall on top of it for entry). Inside the town hall, Spoleto's picture gallery is less than gripping.

Where to stay

Of 17 hotels, the most central is the two-star **Hotel Aurora**, 3 Via Apollinare, tel. 28115, comfortable and welcoming.

Close by are the three-star **Charleston**, 10 Piazza Collicola, tel. 38135; and **Hotel Dei Duchi**, 4 Viale Matteotti, tel. 44541.

The three-star **Clarici Commercio**, 32 Piazza della Vittoria, tel. 46706, is at the bottom of Spoleto.

Where to eat

Restaurants formicate, but two good, sanely priced ones are the **Trattoria del Festival**, in Via Brignone, tel. 54119 (closed Fridays), and the **Trattoria Del Quarto**, 1 Via C. Cattaneo, tel. 21107 (closed Thursdays), with a garden.

Gubbio

Cut off from the rest of Umbria beyond a majestic swell of hills, a sinuous 40 km north-east of Perugia, Gubbio involves spending time. It pays back by lodging in the mind. Gubbio is a medieval mirage, like something out of a childish nightmare, distant and terrible; this one hangs off a mountain. No *city* in Umbria is so exclusively medieval.

Getting there

Gubbio has no railway station, but lies only 13 km from the *Via Flaminia* and could therefore be a stage on the way to Urbino. Buses from Rome filter through. They and cars park in the lowland square flanked by the large church of San Francesco, standing on the spot where the saint first stripped off his finery to don his rough habit, in 1206. Frescoes record it.

History

Like Spello, Gubbio began life Roman. But after being occupied by the Longobards, sacked by the Hungarians, threatened by Perugia, then backed by Frederick I, it climbed uphill to escape further trouble. It was attacked by Ghibellines, turned Guelf, and then witnessed two *coups d'état* as well as a popular rebellion. Worn out, it begged to be taken under the wing of the house of Montefeltro in nearby Urbino, in 1384. Protection lasted until Gubbio was ceded to the Church as part of the Urbino realm two centuries later.

During the Second World War, it was a mountain partisan base. In the worst of the Nazi reprisals, forty townsfolk were executed by machine-gun.

What to see

Daringly, Gubbio is five hillside balconies, each higher than the last. Bare perpendicular streets of pinkish limestone, blackened by the centuries, hang down from them like vines. Many homes have an Umbrian 'dead man's door', a small spare door with a higher threshold than the big door. Some say it was reserved for exiting corpses; but it may just have been the main access to the upper floors, cut out above street level for security.

Piazza della Signoria

The main spectacle, after a stiff climb up through this arrested time, is the most daring balcony, the Piazza della Signoria, visualised as a giant proscenium that would dominate the entire city as a symbol of centralised people's power. It grew from a challenge thrown down by the city fathers in 1322. They wanted a new city centre; it had to be the physical centre and the psychological one, but it was not to be part of any one of Gubbio's existing four districts.

Who took the project on is still not known but, as you can see, his bold answer was to throw out a platform from a sheer cliff into space. From Via Baldassini just below you can see its formidable stays.

Palazzo dei Consoli

Partly because of political troubles, the piazza was never finished; the Proctor's Palace, now the Town Hall, fails to match up to the proudly elegant *palazzo*, with its make-believe embattlements and aloof, paired, windows. Now one of the classic images of noble panache in medieval Italy, it took only five years to build, in the same square-hewn local limestone as the rest of the city.

When Gubbio's eight consuls first mounted its fan staircase, all citizens who had passed a means test had political rights, but that did not mean they were trusted. In the roof of the cavernous big hall, you can make out the holes through which the suspicious Consuls spied upon meetings of the 500-strong General Council. No wood was used in any part of the *palazzo*'s construction, to guard against incendiary attack.

The *palazzo* includes a museum possessing the valuable so-called Gubbio Tables, seven bronze plates which add up to the most important linguistic text of pre-Roman Italy. Four plates dating from the third century BC are written in ancient Umbrian with dashes of Etruscan; the others in Umbrianised Latin. A religious rule-book, it lays down, for instance, the protocol for annual processions to two nearby sacred woods.

Ducal Palace

Known in Gubbio as the Court, the 'country' residence of the Montefeltros occupies the highest 'balcony', and is a small-scale fifteenth-century version of its parent *palazzo* in Urbino, especially its courtyard. Its garden offers a princely view of the Gubbio fiefdom, and a welcome bar. Its unprepossessing front faces the entrance to the small Gothic cathedral from a mere five metres away – the closest confrontation between city-state and Church in Umbria.

San Francesco

On the way back down, in the Via XX Settembre, is the tiny church of St Francis of Peace and in it, a stone. St Francis is said to have performed his best-known miracle standing on it: he tamed a wolf that was terrorising the people. The beast is purported to have given the saint a paw in return for a pledge it would be fed by the town.

What to do

Shopping

Decoration of pottery in Gubbio goes back to the fourteenth century, and the art reached its peak in the sixteenth with the creations of Central Italy's best-known potter, Mastro Giorgio, the first to heighten his effects with gold, ruby and pearl. When his sons died, the secret of his iridescent glazing died with them.

The tradition was revived in the 1920s with the use of Etruscan designs and a fragrant clay, *bucchero*. The *università* (guild) of potters still exists; the craft is dying out, but Gubbio pottery is still a good buy, as well as wrought-iron ware.

The big day	On 15 May every year members of the stone-masons' guild race three pole-like contraptions weighing 1,000 lb each to the city's summit.
Where to stay	Near the Piazza della Signoria is the distinctive three-star **Bosone**, 22 Via XX Settembre; tel. 927 2008.
	San Marco, Via Perugina; tel. 927 2349. Three stars.
	Oderisi, 2 Via Mazzatinti; tel. 927 3747. Two stars.
Where to eat	The smartest place is **Alla Fornace di Mastro Giorgio** in the street of the same name; tel. 927 5740.
	Also recommended is a **Taverna del Lupo** (Wolf Tavern), at the top of Via della Repubblica, tel. 927 1269 (closed Mondays in winter).
	More 'family', chaotic and cheaper is **Da Fiorella** (ask for directions; it is known to all).
Gualdo Tadino	You could return to Perugia from Gubbio via the SS 219 southeast. After 25 km, it meets the *Flaminia* (SS 3). Now you are close to the border of the Marches, where the road snakes around the edge of a plain, lurching through the feet of mountains. Gualdo Tadino (population 12,000) is one of Umbria's better known pottery centres. It is also where the awesome Totila finally met his end, to be beaten and slain by Narsete. A mountain is the backdrop to the scenic main square, **Piazza Martiri**, which retains more than a whiff of a medieval Comune, which Gualdo was before becoming an adjunct of Perugia and then of the Church. The twelfth-century **Cathedral** shows off a splendid rose window and faces the flank of its contemporary, the stately, now empty, **San Francesco**. The **Palazzo del Podestà** still attempts to dominate the little square from behind a café. San Francesco was once host to Gualdo's valuable picture collection, before its removal for security reasons to Frederick II's stolid **fort** at the top of the town.
	Curiously, Gualdo runs to not one pottery shop. Workshops down on the *Via Flaminia* sell their wares directly.
Nocera Umbra	Some 14 km further down the *Flaminia* brings you to this medieval town known for its mineral water. It is on tap from fountains near the main gate, and is claimed by a poet (quoted on a plaque) to be far better for many people than Chianti. The steep, bare, main street ends in a modest **Cathedral**, dwarfed by a giant turreted tower, the remains of a fortress in which, one night in 1421, the local squire murdered his elder brother and his unfaithful spouse.
Umbertide	Back in the Tiber valley, on the SS 3 bis to the west of Gubbio, Umbertide hardly merits a detour since bombs and shells dismembered its 800-year-old body during the Second World War. Now, it is a pleasant, modern little town (population 14,000) in the 'V' of the confluence of the meandering upper Tiber and an unwilling tributary, overlooked by lush hills.
Città di Castello	Half-way between Umbertide and San Sepolcro in Tuscany, this former Roman town (population 35,000) is a pleasant, if not striking,

medieval town amid green hills. It is worth a stop on the strength of its well signposted picture gallery, superseded in Umbria only by Perugia's.

Pinacoteca

Sited in a sixteenth-century princely *palazzo* with original furnishings, the gallery holds the only one of four works done for the city by Raphael as a young man. If his two-sided *Processional Standard* (1500–04) seems in poor shape, that is presumably because it was regularly paraded through the streets until 1627. It was painted to mark the town's deliverance from the plague.

Luca Signorelli was also active here; his dynamic, buttocky *Martydom of St Sebastian*, showing the saint being attacked by cross-bows, is held to have taught Raphael something, as you can see from the copy of his sketch on the right.

The gallery also has a Domenico Ghirlandaio; works by the Mannerist Pomarancio who was in Città from 1570 to 1577; and a valuable collection of fourteenth-century panels on gold background, the most prized being the black-robed Virgin flanked by six angels, the work of the city's unknown, so-called *Maestro*.

Piazza Matteotti

The centre is the piazza with its two-faced **Palazzo del Podestà**, Baroque facing the square and powerfully Gothic in Via del Corso. It leads to a big, sloping square and a fusion between Church and State, with the handsome Gothic **Palazzo Comunale** (you should peep inside) and the **Cathedral** almost embracing.

Where to eat

An unusual place with local dishes and wines consumed in former stables is **Enoteca Altotiberina**, half-hidden hard by the Cathedral.

Todi

The impressive city of Todi (population 17,000) dominates south-west Umbria, a lush, hilly, triangular wedge, hemmed in by the Tiber and Nera rivers which join forces at Orte on the Autostrada del Sole. This is sometimes a remote area, abounding in water; it was inhabited by the original Umbrians.

Todi is walled medieval Italy in brief – aloof, splendid, compact, private. Its walls, breached through hefty gates, are Roman, Etruscan and medieval. It is a place of brown houses, twisting alleys, sudden glimpses of the outside world below, medieval wells and photographic musts.

Getting there

From Rome, Todi is a 2¼-hour bus ride via the A 1 and Orte. It is 41 km south of Perugia by road and 43 km by train; in theory, a minibus should be in waiting at the station.

What to see

Looking down into the broad valley of the Tiber from 400 metres, Todi's hardy inhabitants enjoy such a strategic advantage that they have been spared the attentions of the barbarians. Theirs is a frontier

GAZETTEER

town, sitting on the old demarcation line between Umbrian Umbria and Etruscan Umbria. The name Todi itself is a corruption of the Etruscan word for boundary.

The city's enemies were Orvieto to the west and Spoleto to the east and, by the time the People's Palace was standing in the main square, Frederick II. Thereafter, Todi spent life as a ward of the Roman Church; controlling such a key position, what else could it expect?

Piazza del Popolo

The Pontiff's Governors ruled from the towered **Palazzo dei Priori**, the last creation to be finished, in 1337, in the astonishing main square. It is a nearly all-round exhibition, including the Cathedral, of how ingeniously the Italians could mould alien, northern Gothic to their own taste for flamboyant severity – with a splash of the unusual. In this case, the unusual feature is the outside staircase that serves both the Palazzo dei Priori *and* the Palazzo del Capitano.

The forcefully simple Gothic façade of the elevated **Cathedral**, with its sweeping prelude of steps, completes the enclosure of the square, one of the most pleasing in Umbria. The Duomo was begun in the twelfth century, apparently on the site of a Roman building; inside, the capitals above the columns dividing the naves, some depicting saints, fascinate the connoisseurs who see in them an unusual mingling between late Romanesque and emergent French-style Gothic.

The walls

Go down Via del Monte, on the café side of the square, and lean over. You will appreciate the seriousness of the Etruscan-Roman walls, and why the barbarians thought better of it.

San Fortunato

Sampling of Italian Gothic in Todi must include the *finale* to another sweeping overture of steps in Piazza della Repubblica, behind the Priors' Palace. The patiently sculpted central door is a garbled echo of Orvieto Cathedral, but the barn-like interior, designed solely for packing them in, is one of only three like it in Umbria (the other two are the Cathedral and St Domenico's in Perugia).

Santa Maria della Consolazione

Take a little commuter bus to switch to the sixteenth century, and go down to gaze upon the solitary Renaissance creation of the church of Santa Maria. Outside the walls and against the background of Umbrian nature, this elegant essay in geometrical balance is brilliantly out of place, like something from a Fellini film, but it takes no specialist to see why it is ranked as one of the happiest ideas of the Renaissance in Umbria. Scholars now seem sure that its design is by no less a man than Lazzari Bramante, the first architect of St Peter's in Rome. The satellite cupola, for instance, was characteristic of him; he 'invented' it!

Where to stay

The only hotel in the centre is the small, adequate two-star **Cavour**, 12 Via Cavour; tel. 882417. Outside the walls is the four-star **Bramante**, Via Orvietana; tel. 884 8381.

Where to eat

Another reason why *le tout Rome* seems to know Todi is the **Umbria**, judged by some to be among Umbria's best restaurants. It

178

has a panoramic terrace and specialises in charcoal grills; a candid red wine on offer is Ciliegliolo from Narni. It is at 13 Via S. Bonaventura, off the main square; tel. 882737 (closed Tuesdays).

Acquasparta

Rearing up from the winding, narrow valley of the river Naia, about 18 km south-east of Todi, is this small, walled, spa town (population 4,000), known for its waters which have been good for gout and dyspepsia since Roman times. It earns a quick look on the strength of a fine Renaissance **Ducal Palace** in the little main square. Built by a member of the township's ruling family, the Cesi, in the sixteenth century, it vaunts a courtyard with an unusual double *loggia* and, inside, frescoes and superbly carved wooden ceilings.

In the seventeenth century, the *palazzo* was the seat of one of Europe's first scientific academies, the *Accademia dei Lincei*, where Galileo spent a month in 1624. In July and August, the rooms no longer echo to lofty discourse but, oddly, to the lusty voices of German *lieder* singers going in for contests.

Carsulae

Not to be missed are the evocative nearby Roman ruins, about 5 km south of Acquasparta. At San Gemini Fonte, a signposted rough track leads up to the ruins; at the top, where it joins a road, turn left. Tacitus wrote of the great natural beauty of the place, and his words amazingly still stand. But the importance of Carsulae, founded in the third century BC, was as a major staging point on the *Via Flaminia*; a long stretch of that original *Flaminia* is still there, rutted by chariot wheels. It ends at an arch and a sturdy circular funeral monument, before vanishing beneath the vegetation. (The Roman *Flaminia* forked at Narni, near the present-day motorway. One *Flaminia* led to Terni and Spoleto, while the other ran through Carsulae to Bevagna and beyond.) Time stopped at Carsulae when an earth tremor brought down its main buildings in the first century AD.

San Damiano

The tiny early medieval church, at the entrance to the 'city', with winged figures and animals over the door, stands on top of some Roman building and incorporates pieces from the forum. The tallest of the ruins opposite were two temples (the old layout is displayed on a board).

Cesi

The country road running south from the ruins leads past San Gemini Fonte to Cesi which, at 437 metres, justifiably claims to be a balcony over the vast plain of Terni. A settlement of the original Umbrians, it clings to Mount Eolo just below its no-nonsense peak, and the vista alone is worth a stop. It is an attractive medieval microcosm, run for centuries by the same Cesi family from Acquasparta. Bits of Roman tombs stick out of the disused Romanesque church of **Sant' Andrea** in the square at the top, and the vicar of **Santa Maria**, lower down, keeps the town treasure locked up: an expressive altar-piece by the so-called Maestro of Cesi, dated 1308. He willingly opens up.

Mount Erasmus

On their day off, the locals like to grind up to the top of the next-door peak, named after a tiny, locked, twelfth-century church presiding over a sea of green at the top, amid a litter of mysterious pre-Roman chunks. The scene could cause movement of breath. The vertical track up to it is off the country road just north of Cesi.

San Gemini

On the other side of the Terni plain is this nationally known spa with a mineral water named after it. The placid medieval hill township is perhaps over-rated, but its mini main street, **Via Casventino**, copies the route of the Romans' *Via Flaminia*, a much choppier mode of transport than schoolboys are led to expect, and its most original church is at the end of it, **San Giovanni Battista**. This was built as a diocesan baptistry by the very first bishop of shattered Carsulae. After being gutted by the barbarians, it was rebuilt in the sixth century in hexagonal font form to recall its original purpose; it received another side during its third edition in the twelfth century. In the 1950s, restorers discovered fifteenth- to seventeenth-century frescoes in the niches of **San Francesco**, in the French-looking main square outside the main gate.

Amelia

Less well-known, but worth a detour if you are unhurried, is the pleasant town of Amelia to the south-west, poured over a hill between the valleys of the Tiber and the Nera. It is remarkable because its 3-metre thick **walls**, made up of massive, nicely interlocking slabs, have been there since the fifth century BC, when the town was a stronghold of the Umbrians. They are amazingly well preserved. Beyond the gate through them Amelia is quiet medieval, with touches of late Renaissance. In the main square, **Piazza Marconi**, elegant sixteenth-century *palazzi* co-exist with an outside staircase and dais, from which edicts were read out in the Middle Ages. A rough, imposing eleventh-century **bell-tower** tops the town, and marks a great vantage point.

Lugnano

Eleven km to the north-west, Lugnano (population 1,500) sits on a solitary hill above the valley of the Tiber. It also deserves a look because of **Santa Maria Assunta**, hailed as one of the most striking Romanesque churches in Umbria. The proud façade and picturesque porch belong to the twelfth century; its admirers rave about its sculpted, scurrying animals, as well as about the choir and crypt, which are restored.

The Valnerina

Valnerina means 'valley of the river Nera', the fast stream that tumbles down from the Sibillini mountains in the south-east, races through industrial Terni and then plunges through a deep gorge into the Tiber at Orte, on the A 1 motorway. The Valnerina proper, though, is that part of the valley above Terni, where the river flows through some of the most overwhelming scenery in Umbria.

It is a thinly populated region, as it always has been, but a problem for some time has been desertion and neglect; here and there, cranes and cement-mixers now attempt to stem the decline. The valley was the invasion route for Imperial and foreign armies tramping south towards the Kingdom of Naples, but in the Middle Ages the movement of traders and raiders was *across* the valley, not along it. They used roads that have now vanished, and the valley-bottom road was some 300 metres higher than it is today, which helps to explain the precarious location of its settlements.

These were fortified 'borgs', built to control crucial points such as valley junctions; to squeeze tolls and duties out of travellers; and, above all, for defence in an area of constant trouble, since the strategic valley rather appealed to both Emperors and Popes. The town which most exploited the unsettled times and acted as the local villain was Spoleto, an expansionist borg-swallower.

Terni

You won't want to tarry in communist Terni itself (population 110,000). Thanks to the last war, it is a modern city. It was, and remains, the core of the biggest industrial complex in Central Italy, and was therefore bombed out of existence; for one thing, it made munitions. The part of the 'old' city left standing is depressing, relieved only by a modest art gallery in a seventeenth-century *palazzo* in Via Fratini, which has a Benozzo Gozzoli.

Within its shell of overlooking mountains, Terni is leafy and not unpleasant, neither smelly nor smoky, and it serves as a handy base for local meandering, or as a fall-back for sleeping if inns in other towns are roomless.

Where to stay

The best hotel is the four-star **Valentino**, Via Plinio Giovane (off the main Piazza Tacito, with a fountain); tel. 0744-55246.

De Paris, 52 Viale Stazione, tel. 58047, is much cheaper with three stars, and quite adequate.

Where to eat

The reasonable **Ristorante Tacitus**, Piazza Tacito, tel. 425147 (closed Fridays) serves local specialities.

The cheaper **Da Vicenzo**, 11 Via Biblioteca, tel. 53951 (closed Wednesdays), specialises in casual, family style.

Cascata delle Marmore

Only 6 km from Terni along the Valnerina (also the name of the SS 209), just before a tunnel, the famous Waterfall of the Marmore Mountains suddenly appears. It is, *occasionally*, one of the sights of Europe.

The waterfall thunders down from the lip of a plateau 165 metres up with impressive violence, taking three spectacular leaps to crash into the river Nera, amid mighty roaring, spray and mist. It is artificial, though the artifice is respectably ancient. The Fall was a trick to drain the swampy plateau thought up in 271 BC by the Roman Consul Manilus Curius Dentatus, more famed in his day for crushing the tiresome Samnites. The stagnation of the river Velino caused the marshes, so the Consul scooped out a great channel to offer it the compelling escape route you see.

If you see. A sluice usually diverts the Velino to feed a big, nearby hydro-electrical plant; it is only opened at certain times, and the timetable varies. From 15 July to 31 August, for instance, the sight is turned on 5–6.30 p.m. and on Sunday afternoons; enquire at the Terni Tourist Office, 5 Viale Battisti; tel. 43047. A siren sounds before it all starts.

Arrone

Perched on a rocky needle, Arrone comes into view 13 km northeast of Terni on the right of the Nera, surmounted by a romantic-looking tower. It must have looked less so in the Middle Ages. Lording it over the junction of two valleys, Arrone was in a strong position to exact its tolls, but it was also a desirable acquisition in the eyes of any power wishing to boost its authority, such as Spoleto. Naturally, it fell . . .

Today, the sense of trespass is acute in the tiny alleys beneath the tower. But the borg proves more interesting from afar than in close-up, except for the small church of **Santa Maria Assunta** in Piazza Garibaldi. Highly rated sixteenth-century Umbrian frescoes fill its niches, discovered not long ago. The Emperor Frederick II stayed here in 1240.

Montefranco

Across the valley, on the other side of the Nera, the higher Montefranco, 375 metres, beats Arrone for startling bird's-eye views of the lush surrounds. But its medieval quarter is partially collapsed, and they're a glum lot, unable even to produce a sandwich. It was first settled by refugees fleeing Arrone when the dreaded Spoleto moved in.

Polino

Occupying a still more strategic position is this charming borg, a 12-km, twisting, uphill drive 'inland' from Arrone through almost claustrophobic forest. Lodged just below mountain crests, it is a pugnacious wedge guarding the head of a profound, deep green valley. It has 350 souls, a nameless *trattoria*, a mini-fortress, old men who mutter comments and, apart from these, silence.

Colle Bertone

The road climbs higher, to peter out 8 km further on, on the very roof of these Umbrian uplands, at 1,241 metres. Here, a pine forest hides a hotel with a restaurant and a tennis court, called **La Baita** ('The Hut'); tel. 0744-789132 (open all year).

Ferentillo

Back down in the Valnerina, 5 km north of Arrone, your foot could slip off the accelerator when two facing towers high up on either side of a gorge loom into view, each a king-pin for cascading defence walls. This is a picture-postcard, stoutly fortified stronghold that once totally blocked the Valnerina. It controlled a bridge across the river, once much fuller than it is, as well as two roads toiling up the valley on either side.

Probably dating from the eighth century, its location obviously inspired envy. It was constantly at war with greedy Spoleto and Montefranco. It is still, itself, split into two rival quarters: Precetto on the Nera's east, and Matterella opposite.

The Mummies

Outside Precetto, signs announce 'Mummie' – which means what it seems to. They are macabre company, kept in the gloomy crypt of the disused church of San Stefano. For a tip, a watchman will open it up and introduce you to a hanged murderer, bandits, priests, children and others. They were all simply left on the ground of the crypt, without coffins or burial, in the sixteenth century, and were apparently mummified by the properties of their bed of sandy soil, which includes nitrates and salts. One poor man is as unshaven as on the day of his demise.

San Pietro in Valle

Medieval Ferentillo depended heavily on the great Abbey 4 km further on, up a sudden, but signposted, track to the left.

This is an experience hard to forget. Quite hidden from view from below, it nonetheless overlooks the whole valley from a discreet position on a wooded mountain slope. Furthermore, the Abbey boasts vast, rare frescoes documenting the very infancy of Italian art, showing how lively it could be.

The Abbey was founded in the eighth century, on a spot where two hermits once lived, by a Duke of Spoleto who needed a monastic retreat. He allegedly died in the Abbey but, far from remaining an isolated spiritual Benedictine refuge, it grew into the capital of a virtual state, commanding townships, castles and vast estates throughout the Valnerina and beyond. The Bishop of Spoleto, the *Comune* there, and then the Pope, all tried to lay hands on it, until it was privatised under lay lords. It was deserted by the monks in 1910.

The Abbey church

The eleventh-century church, with a pretty Lombardian bell-tower echoing many in Rome, is a true historical anthology. It is utterly dominated by the frescoes covering its walls. In very bad shape and being restored (the goal is 1994), they are still visible through the scaffolding. The unknown hand behind them, thought to be a late eleventh-century precursor of Cimabue, is shown here in merry mutiny against strangulation by the stiff Byzantines. He belonged to the so-called 'Roman school' and so he scoffs at the rigid, Eastern trendsetters. High up at the start of the left wall, facing the altar, he brazenly depicts God Almighty himself as a beardless young man, busy separating Light from Darkness. 'Noah called to Eternity' is taking off in windswept robes with eyes closed in ecstasy, while in the middle Adam goes about naming the animals with un-Byzantine gusto. On the right wall, now almost a ruin, was the New Testament. In the rest of Central Italy, such expressiveness, on such a scale, so early on, seems virtually unknown.

Bits of two Roman sarcophagi help make up the altar to the left of the apse; the designs on the high altar are rare examples of the art of the Longobards; the left apse was frescoed by a disciple of the Sienese school; the one on the right by followers of Giotto; and the style of Christ Redeemer in the apse was favoured in Umbria and the Marches in the fifteenth century.

It is open until about 6 p.m. every day.

Scheggino

After the Abbey, it is the lot of Scheggino, 7 km further north on the valley floor, to be an anti-climax. It, too, guarded a vital gorge, and is topped by a crumbling defence tower, but it is touristy and tarted up. It has two restaurants, a hotel, and the narrow Nera obligingly gurgles by. So on to Norcia, about forty minutes away to the north-east, through scenes that live up to the Valnerina.

Norcia

At an altitude of 604 metres, Norcia sits exposed on the edge of a vast plateau rimmed in by mountains. With a population of 5,500, it is a much smaller place than its fame in Italy might suggest: a main, flat street, a pleasing square and *basta*! The buildings are low, by law, as the town is prone to earthquakes. It is 48 km from Spoleto and 99 km from Perugia. For most Italians, Norcia stands not for St Benedict, who was born here, but for black truffles and pork products. The town has contributed to the Italian language: *norceria* means pork butcher, as the bursting local shops attest.

History

In pre-Roman times, bland Norcia was the most northerly settlement of the hardy Sabines. Devastated by the Goths, then invaded by Longobards and Saracens, it flourished like so many other Italian cities as a free *comune* until, after long bouts of strife, the Church took over. During the Second World War partisan groups operated in the area.

What to see

St Benedict, founder of Western monasticism, and his twin sister St Scolastica, were born here in the year 480 in a first-century Roman building, now part of the crypt of the curiously soulless church of **St Benedict** in the main square, to the right of the elegant little **Palazzo Comunale** with its fourteenth-century porch. The twins' birthplace was converted into an oratory in the sixth century, and enlarged into a church in the late fourteenth, but only the simple façade remains, with the two saints in niches above the door. The **Cathedral**, revamped in the sixteenth century, occupies a corner of the square, but the nearby fourteenth-century church of **Sant' Agostino** is of more interest. Its frescoes, especially the Madonna with Child near the first altar on the right, dated 1502, are probably by Ansovino da Camerino, a Marches man.

What to do

Norcia is a gourmets' paradise, full of shops specialising in sometimes very unusual delicacies, such as suckling piglet, mountain ram, Norcia *capocollo* (pig's neck) and mules' testicles. Hams abound, some with grated truffles, as well as salamis, cottage cheese made from sheep's milk (claimed to last two years), salted sheep's milk ricotta, pluck of mountain lamb, sausages galore, and famous local lentils.

There is a digestive made of truffles (*Amaro di Tartufo*) as well as truffle Grappa and truffle ice-cream. Norcia's own ham comes from small black pigs brought up on acorns, and it owes its charcuterie tradition to the packs of pig and boar that roamed the local oak forests for centuries. But one local expert has another reason: pigs were raised in Norcia, he argues, to supply a once famous school of surgeons in nearby Preci, who used the beasts for experiment and practice. Most of the pigs treated in Norcia today hail from the environs of saintly Assisi.

Where to eat

Oddly, there are few places to sample all these delights! The only one real shrine to them is the excellent **Dal Francese**, 16 Via Riguardati; tel. 816290 (closed Fridays October–June). This is a 'serious' place, hung with pictures mainly dedicated to truffles, specialising in spaghetti with caviare and truffles, truffled *Saltimbocca* and grilled sausage.

Where to stay

La Posta, 10 Via C. Battisti (near the main square); tel. 816274. More conveniently, outside the main gate, is the **Hotel Garden**, 2 Viale XX Settembre; tel. 816726.

In summer, the hotels are packed with subsidised pensioners, despatched to Norcia by local councils 'for the air'.

Castelluccio

A stunning excursion from Norcia is up to the highest Apennine village in Umbria or the Marches, at 1,453 metres. It is inhabited by sturdy shepherds and overlooks the magnificent **Piano Grande**, a solitary plain 8 km long beneath the grey peaks of the Sibilline mountains, given over in summer to grazing, the home of wild horses and giant rooks.

Campi Vecchio

For mellower mountain scenery, the road north to Preci passes beneath this semi-abandoned village hit by an earthquake in 1971 with two closed churches ('we've no priest'). One, **Sant' Andrea**, has a frescoed façade under a fetching late-Gothic porch, while a fifteenth-century artist from Norcia called Sparapane painted the vault of the other, **Madonna di Piazza**. A lady has the key.

Preci

Seventeen km from Norcia, Preci thrives – a huddled, flinty, introspective hill townlette, boasting a modern hotel with a swimming pool, **Agli Scacchi**, tel. 743-99224. It is hard to believe that this is where thirty families kept medical secrets to themselves for two centuries, producing widely known surgeons celebrated for their removal of stones and their eye operations.

Cascia

Cascia nestles, at 700 metres, among green hills 18 km south-west of Norcia, and is often thronged by pilgrims venerating Saint Rita, born here in the fourteenth century. At prayer one night, she suddenly found her forehead pierced by a thorn from the crown of Jesus. The church named after her was built under Mussolini.

Orvieto

Orvieto is an enormous whale just surfaced – with a striped cathedral on its back, the apex of Italian Gothic. It is the most curious town in Umbria – a solitary hulk of rock sticking out of flatness for no reason at all. Apparently it sprang up out of what was once a gulf on the Tyrrhenian Sea during a volcanic eruption. Its cliffs stare down upon the *Autostrada del Sole* from a slight distance, and bemused motorists look twice.

Getting there

Orvieto is the most accessible town in Umbria. Via the A 1 motorway, Florence is about 150 km away and Rome 100; it is a 75-km trip to Perugia. The station, beneath the cliff, sits on the busiest line in Italy; buses take you up to the town every 20 minutes or so.

History

High, alone, strategic, Orvieto was just the feature to figure in Etruscan dreams; they made it a stronghold. Twice the Goths tried to seize it but were thrown back. As a 'free comune', it fought Papal rule, as well as Siena and Viterbo over an outlet to the sea. Like other cities, it was then torn asunder by family feuds before being ruled by a succession of soldiers of fortune, all outsiders. It returned to the Church for good in 1450.

What to see

Orvieto (population 23,000) is the gentler side of Umbria, the antithesis of Perugia. Its buildings don't tower, its streets are man-size and its charm seeps out at night when the day-trippers have gone. Then people sit on the stone benches in front of the Cathedral and, under the illumination, watch its stupendous façade like a television.

Cathedral

Typically Italian, the façade is a screen in its own right, on its own plinth, as if the Cathedral itself were irrelevant. For many, the façade *is* the Cathedral. Comparison with the face of the Siena Duomo is inevitable; purists award a points victory to Orvieto on grounds of clarity and balance. They prefer its restraint to the riot of the Siena frontispiece, in which they even find design faults.

The Sienese architect Lorenzo Maitani conceived it in 1305 as a giant triptych, and he himself carved some of the lively biblical scenes at the bottom of the four pillars, as well as the evangelists above. But, for all its appearance of unity, the façade is the creation of a tacit team, of fifteen artists who worked on it for three centuries. The fifty-two small heads around the big rose window stand for the weeks of the year. The mosaics setting off the lines of the façade are not the originals, however: *they* were packed off to Rome as a present for a Pope.

The **interior** has to be a let-down, and is. Its style is divided. The lofty nave is Romanesque, as per the original plans: the progressive shortening of the granite columns aims at an illusion of length. Yet the apse area, as rebuilt by Maitani, is Gothic.

This incredible Cathedral was ordered by Pope Urban IV who stipulated that he needed something of unheard-of splendour to commemorate a miracle: during Mass in a church near Lake Bolsena, not far from Orvieto, blood had dropped from the host on to the altar linen. The novelty was convenient, since it helped to discredit a troublesome local sect that rejected the sacraments. The **altar-cloth** is now in the reliquary above the altar, in the left-hand chapel.

Another miracle is in the **New Chapel** on the right. Luca Signorelli's overpowering fresco cycle is one of the highlights of the Renaissance. Signorelli has been called 'the morning star of Michelangelo', and his boldness and sweeping vision are a foretaste of the Sistine Chapel in Rome.

Profoundly influenced by Dante's philosophy of life, Signorelli began these frescoes when Michelangelo was 25 and he was 35 years older, at the peak of his form. You can see his self-portrait to the left of the door, the stern figure in black staring from the left foreground in the picture of the anti-Christ.

Signorelli's passion as an artist was the human nude, as you may notice. He examined it carefully in mortuaries and at executions. When his beautiful 17-year-old son was killed in a duel, he had him stripped and spent the day painting from his corpse without shedding a tear. He had no patience with anything else. In his famous Resurrection, for instance, all the usual Renaissance trappings – background and hangers-on – have been eliminated. The athletic, buttocky figures struggling out of the clay are all the more naked for being quite alone. He has also desisted from making them too handsome, for fear that that would have detracted from a study of pure form. The subject of Hell, for him, was a chance to master the form of contortion.

Rocca

Few visitors venture into the silent, intact, medieval quarter, beyond the Piazza della Repubblica, but for a vivid idea of Orvieto's commanding position it is worth peering down from the balustrades of the fort, another construction by the indefatigable Cardinal Albornoz, and a fair walk down Via Postiera.

Well of St Patrick

Close by is Orvieto's curiosity, a well sunk by Pope Clement VII, a fugitive in Orvieto from the sack of Rome in 1527. He wanted to make sure of water in case his refuge, too, was ravaged (it wasn't). Ingeniously, the well is lined with interweaving, but separated, spiral staircases, so that pack-animals going down to draw water would not meet those coming up. Today, lovers tread the 248 steps.

What to do

A pottery centre since the twelfth century, Orvieto is still highly active. The prevalent colours are white, green and yellow; favourite designs include medieval heads, sculpted leaves and deer. Experts judge the craftsmen not as skilful as Deruta's and only average copiers of Faenza and Tuscan themes.

Another speciality is woodwork, especially wooden horses and pinocchio dolls. Orvieto's semi-sweet (*abboccato*) and dry white wines, among Italy's best known and fermented in caves riddling the cliffs, are the surest buys.

Where to stay

The best hotel, tucked away in the medieval quarter, is the four-star **Aquila Bianca**, 13 Via Garibaldi; tel. 41246.

The four-star **Maitani**, 5 Via Lorenzo Maitani, tel. 42011, is opposite the Cathedral.

To one side is the snug three-star **Virgilio**, 5 Piazza Duomo; tel. 41882 (no credit cards).

Those touched by noble decay will delight in the three-star **Grand Hotel Reale**, 25 Piazza del Popolo; tel. 41247. A former *palazzo* facing the Gothic Town Hall, it has frescoed ceilings and large rooms.

Where to eat

Yards from the **Grand Hotel Reale** is **Dal Moro**, 1 Via San Leonardo; tel. 42763 (closed Fridays). A modest, family establishment.

Classier is the **Trattoria dell'Orso**, 18 Via della Misericordia; tel. 41642 (closed Tuesdays). **Etrusca**, 10 Via L. Maitani; tel. 44016 (closed Mondays). **Giglio d'Oro**, Piazza Duomo, tel. 41903, is the expensive best in town.

Città della Pieve

Some 47 km north of Orvieto, on a ridge looking out over the valley of the river Chiani, the impact of Città della Pieve, the birthplace of Perugino, is instant. It is different – a graceful, medieval town in red brick, which lends it a remarkable harmony. It also claims to have the narrowest alley in Italy.

Its main buildings, the fourteenth-century **Fort**, the sixteenth-century **Cathedral** and the tall 'Public Tower' growing out of it begun about the year 1000, cluster around the dome of the town in no obvious order. Uniform, red medieval streets gently curve their way down its slopes.

Perugino has two works in the Cathedral, but his reputedly best work in his home town, a frescoed Epiphany of 1504, is in **Santa Maria dei Bianchi**, in the sloping Via Vannucci (Perugino's real surname), near the Cathedral. At the *gelateria* near the bottom, ask for the famous narrow alley, called **Baciadonne** ('Kiss ladies').

Where to stay

The local hotel, sought out in summer, is the **Vannucci**, 1 Viale Icilio Vanni; tel. 298063.

Lake Trasimeno

Placid Lake Trasimeno, the largest in peninsular Italy and a half-hour drive west of Perugia, would be a yawn if it weren't where Hannibal inflicted his crippling defeat on the Roman army. Now, after more than 2,000 years of mystery, we know pretty well exactly where the action was fought. The findings are recent.

Your observation point is the tripper township of Tuoro on the north bank, which was almost lapped by the now receded lake when Hannibal struck. Only a narrow strip of marshy land, that is, separated the high ground from the lake. He saw an ambush site. Scholars now recognise Hannibal was the first to use scouts and fifth columnists with brilliance. Forewarned of the movements of the Consul Flaminius, hunting for him with a huge host, he chose the battlefield and posted his men. At dawn on 24 June 217 BC, thick mist hid them. Unsuspecting, Flaminius entered the trap from the east. His men were caught in marching order as the horsemen, then the infantry, swooped down. The attack was so sudden that many hadn't time to draw their swords. The massacre lasted three hours: some 15,000 Romans died out of a force of 20,000, including Flaminius, transfixed by a lance. Hannibal lost perhaps 1,500 troops.

The battle scenario is now almost certain thanks to Hannibal's tidiness: his sapper/grave-diggers had orders to bury the fallen on the spot. All 113 of the cremation sites they dug for the Romans – deep stone wells with lids – have now been found. Carbon tests have verified that the ash is of the right date, so the sites are taken as reliable markers, finally, of the exact battle area. Place-names recall the battle, too: Sanguineto means 'bloodbath' and Ossaia, over the border, 'bone dump'. A local red wine is called 'Roman Blood'.

Castiglione del Lago

A balmier view of the lake and its 45 km of shoreline is had from this trendy medieval village with a walled castle on a limestone headland.

Of the five hotels, try the oaky two-star **Miralago**, 5 Piazza Mazzini; tel. 951157.

Narni

If you are off to Rome, Narni is the exit from Umbria, or, in the other direction, a rather dramatic introduction. Perched high upon steep limestone cliffs near Orte, with the river Nera far below battling through a profound gorge, Narni (population 20,000) is palpably aloof.

Once it was a vital Roman military base: it guarded a crucial river confluence; it was a staging point on the (old) *Via Flaminia*, and it served as the Romans' jump-off base for the 'pacification' of restive Umbria. Because of its commanding position, tireless Frederick II laid siege to it, but in vain. In the thirteenth century it ganged up against the Empire, in league with Perugia and, of course, with Rome.

That blunder was not forgotten. Much later, the same Imperial, Spanish-Germanic riff-raff who had sacked Rome in the sixteenth century, rampaged through Narni in turn on their staggering way home. The place recovered only later, when the railway materialised deep down in the valley. Until then, Narni rotted.

The sense of neglect lingers on. The view from the top may be sweeping, but Piazza Garibaldi, the medieval centre, remains broody and heavy. The **Duomo** was consecrated in 1145, though the frescoed apse is Gothic and some of the painting is Renaissance; the **Palazzo del Podestà** is a cocktail of three thirteenth-century tower-houses. From the pulpit in front of the Priors' **Loggia**, they used to read out the proclamations.

Where to stay and eat

The best hotels are the four-star **Dei Priori**, 4 Vicolo Comune, tel. 726843; and the two-star **Fina**, 419 Via Tuderte, tel. 733648.

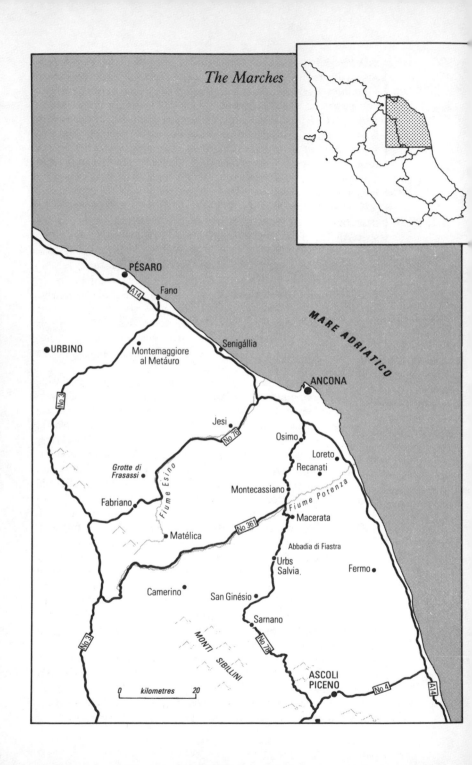

The Marches

PÉSARO
Fano
A14

URBINO
Montemaggiore
al Metáuro
Senigállia

MARE ADRIATICO

No 3

ANCONA

Jesi
No 76
Osimo

Grotte di
Frasassi
Loreto
Recanati

Montecassiano
Fiume Potenza

Fabriano
Fiume Esino
Macerata

No 361

Matélica

Abbadia di Fiastra

Urbs
Salvia
Fermo

Camerino
San Ginésio

Sarnano
No 78

No 3

MONTI
SIBILLINI

ASCOLI
PICENO
No 4
A14

0   kilometres   20

The Marches

Introduction

The Marches belong to off-beat Italy. Sandwiched between the Apennines and the shallow Adriatic in the north-east of Central Italy, it is a region off the tourist caravan routes. The millions who seed the unending beaches every summer usually stay there, leaving the unusual hinterland unexplored.

The Marches is hardly Italian; neither is the name, which comes from the German *Marka*, a term introduced by Charlemagne. It means a frontier region, usually administered by a Marquis. In the Marches, there were three *Marka*. The people of the Marches still feel they are frontiersmen, forgotten and neglected by distant Rome. Until recently, it was an impoverished region populated by peasants, and witnessed mass emigration to the United States. It is classic Italy, domesticated.

Getting there

By car

The logical approach is from Perugia to Urbino via Gubbio, which is 111 km. The quickest direct route from Florence and Rome to the northern Marches is via the A 1 to Arezzo and then to San Sepolcro, 70 km from Urbino. For the southern Marches, many prefer to take the A 24 (Rome–L'Aquila), to Teramo and then branch north.

By train

The Rome–Ancona inter-city, thrice daily, takes 3 hours and 20 minutes. From Florence, nothing doing.

By air

There are daily flights from Rome and Milan that land at Falconara airport, just to the north of Ancona.

What to see

It is a convenient region; from anywhere on the coast, you can be up in the Apennines within an hour. But the characteristic of the Marches is what lies between, which is spare hill country. The hills are naked, stripped by man and nature. They are incredibly smooth, and march towards the heights in open order. It is weekend country, good for Sundays.

The south, at one with the Abruzzi mountains, is almost alpine. Monte Vettore, the tallest peak, touches 2,476 metres, and there are well-equipped ski resorts. Ascoli Piceno, cramped and noisy, still bursts with its past – from Roman to Nazi eras. The 'must' of the Marches is Urbino in the north, tucked up in the hills behind Pesaro. The Ducal Palace there, magnificently restored, is the Renaissance in stone; it was twin to Florence, though of a more rarefied disposition.

In between, thousands flock to a new natural spectacular, a gigantic cave complex known as Frasassi. Even those usually bored by nature will find it mind-bending.

History

The Marches have always offered the main invasion route into Italy. They all used it – Hannibal, the barbarians, the Holy Roman Emperors, bent on benediction or benefit. This is where Italian history falls into place: you may have wondered how all those northern hordes did their streaming down into Italy. There was no way through on the western coast: even today, the train from Genoa to La Spezia clings to the cliffs like a lizard. Italy's backbone was irksomely mountainous. No, they took the easiest route on the east – with flat coastal strip, screening hills, hilltops for holding and valleys for moving.

This is where the school-book horrors took place. Near Macerata, for instance, you can stand amid the smoking ruins of a Roman town left behind by rampaging Alaric in 410 – a rare sight indeed. The Marches were also put to the sword during the fighting between Goths and the avenging army sent over from Byzantium. The Goths actually held on to some of the towns you will pass through, which they rarely did elsewhere in Italy.

The Marches also saw the origin of the temporal power of the Papacy, when Pippin and Charlemagne drove out the Lombards and handed over the land to Rome. The Church, though, was initially too weak to wield power on its own and leaned on local strongmen and mercenaries. The most brilliant was Duke Federico da Montefeltro, a soldier of fortune who, in Urbino, became the single most powerful personality of the Renaissance. His forebears had won land and fortune fighting on the side of the Pope's German foes.

The Church slowly asserted itself through deals with single townships which then came directly under Rome. This is the crucial clue to the character of the Marches, because these deals deprived the region of an identity which, in the rest of Italy, was the stamp of a dominant town. It leaves the Marches of today the most atomised part of Italy. Nobody really feels, for instance, that Ancona is the capital. Local rivalries remain real, if on a microscopic scale. Dialects abound: in the small coastal town of Fano, they speak three. The people of the Marches enjoy a terrible reputation. A proverb goes: 'Better a death in the house than a man from the Marches at the door.' That is because such men were often Papal tax-collectors.

The Marches now form a buffer-zone between the industrialised North of Italy and the backward, subsidised South. Official figures show that the average family income is the highest in the country. The north is a political spill-over from industrial, neighbouring Reggio Emilio, and since the end of the Second World War has been firmly Communist; in the south they tend to be Christian Democrats.

Food and wine

Cuisine in the Marches mirrors its make-up: regional dishes hardly exist. The seafood is what to go for, since it is fresh and rich in flavour.

Along the coast, a speciality is the *brodetto*, an assorted fish soup that comes with tomato, parsley, garlic or celery, depending on where you stop. Around Pesaro, try a baked mille feuilles (*millefoglie*), puff-pastry interlarded with béchamel sauce, Perugino cheese and meat sauce. Another speciality is stuffed, grilled squill (*canocchie*). Around Ancona, stockfish with anchovies in wine is popular; while a traditional dish in Ascoli Piceno is stuffed green olives with meat, egg and cheese. Also along the coast, try spaghetti with clams (*vongole*).

The best known wine from the Marches is *Verdicchio*, grown in the Esino valley inland from Ancona. It is a brilliantly clear, dry white with a slightly bitter aftertaste. You may well also like *Bianchello del Metauro*, named after the river which dribbles into the sea near Fano: a dry, slightly acidy white of varying shades that goes well with the fish. The best red is *Conero Rosso*, from around Ancona. The reds from the Colli Piceni in the south are roughish.

The arts   As you might expect from a frontier zone, prominent artists in the Marches were transients and the influences external, especially Venetian. Raphael is the only giant from the region, but it has hardly anything to show for it. Only in the past fifteen years have the Marches cast off an inferiority complex and begun to 'discover' a regional heritage. The platoons of minors now packing local galleries lack anything but punch. The most noted are:

Carlo Crivelli A Venetian, jailed for six months in 1475 for adultery with a sailor's wife. After wandering around Yugoslavia, he settled in Ascoli Piceno for twenty years and was involved in several court cases; he was buried there in a common grave in 1495. British and German critics recently re-appraised him as one of the foremost artists of his century. While he lived he was renowned for his so-called 'ambiguous' style. A follower was **Vittorio Crivelli**, his brother.

Lorenzo Lotto (1480–1556). A very different Venetian, a pious painter whose work seems suffused with the colours of his native lagoon. He ended his life in retreat at the then pilgrim town of Loreto.

Urbino

Undoubtedly the show-piece of the Marches, Urbino is perched high up in the foothills of the Apennines, windswept and isolated. Its Ducal Palace is a huge monument to the Renaissance ideal of life. But this small town (population 8,000), run by the Communists, has been so much admired that it risks being a let-down for the over-expectant. It requires a few hours, but is not the ideal place to spend a night. It is a university town, and during term time the population doubles.

Getting there

Urbino is 67 km almost directly north of Gubbio, 35 km inland from Pesaro and 180 km from Florence via Arezzo. The nearest station is at Pesaro. A morning bus from Rome (from the Piazza della Repubblica) takes six hours.

What to see

The Ducal Palace

Begun in the second half of the fifteenth century and left unfinished, the palace is considered one of the great triumphs of Renaissance architecture. It is open 9 a.m.–7 p.m. every day from June to October, and 9 a.m.–2 p.m. in winter.

Its very design was intended to embody the philosophy of the epoch. It was commissioned by Duke Federico da Montefeltro (1448–82) to perpetuate his 'glory', as an inscription puts it. He was a highly successful mercenary commander; as one of the first experts in psychological warfare, he developed the battlefield pep talk into an art; he was a scholar and a superman of the Renaissance. Today, he would be a far-fetched figure: the equivalent of a Montgomery turned Bertrand Russell, with the income of a Getty, playing host to everyone from Graham Greene to W. H. Auden in a castle in a remote Scottish glen.

The Duke was the genius of the Montefeltros, a family of soldiers of fortune in the service of the German Emperors. They were given Urbino to reward their loyalty, and Federico extended the family domain until it stretched from Rimini and Pesaro on the coast to the borders of Tuscany. That ensured recruits for his main business, hiring out mini-armies to warring clients.

The fortune he thus amassed went into the Palace and its works of art. He intended it to reflect the Renaissance notion of life as ideally rational, harmonious, enjoyable and at one with nature.

After his death, Urbino became the most civilised princely court of the Renaissance, ruled over by Elizabetta Gonzaga, wife of the Duke's ailing son. The greatest minds of the Renaissance gathered under her roof; one of her guests for ten years was Baldassare Castiglione, whose book *The Courtier* (1516), based on what he saw, was the first modern manual of etiquette.

The Palazzo was a tremendous innovation. The Middle Ages were forgotten; for the first time, a warlord did not build a fortress to exclude a hostile world, but preferred a place designed to please. The best view of it is from the car park, from where a hidden lift in a corner will whisk you up to town level. Those two slender cylindrical towers, for instance, were obviously not meant to frighten anybody; they are grace notes. And more unusually, the Dalmatian architect had the Palace melding into the hill rather than dominating it. It is a deliberate, didactic statement of the Renaissance view of the ideal relationship between man and nature.

Further, the experts tell you, the Palace enshrined advanced contemporary ideas about equality. Its main entrance, up in town, is modest, and the square outside it unintimidating. The Courtyard of Honour beyond the door was a democratic invitation, too; in its implacable geometry, one scholar sees the hand of Piero della Francesca from nearby San Sepolcro.

The bare ground-floor rooms once housed a library of 10,000 volumes, built up by Federico. It was taken off by Cesare Borgia and today forms the most valuable part of the Vatican Library in Rome. The worst plunderer was the niece of the last Montefeltro duke who, to make up for her plainness, took carriage-fulls of treasure as a dowry to Florence, where she married a Medici.

To the right of the wilfully simple **Throne Room**, you move into the **Hall of the Late Nights** (*Sala delle Veglie*), where Elizabetta conducted her salon with aplomb and tact. The rooms progress with inevitability towards the 'sanctum', the private world of the Duke. His **Study** (*studiolo*) looks over the countryside from between the two Hans Anderson towers. The utter disproportion between where he read and prayed and the vast horizons he espied through the small window was the Duke's permanent reminder of man's stature.

The 'Famous Men' above the panelling (once there were twenty-eight) represent his belief that guidance was to be sought from both the luminaries of antiquity and of the Church. The intarsia inside the make-believe shelves below, perhaps designed by Botticelli, reiterate the theme. And the Duke reiterated his (very Renaissance) conviction that the sacred and the profane are complementary by putting his den above two tiny places of worship. If you descend the spiral staircase in the spindly tower, you will find, side by side, his so-called **Chapel of Pardon** and a **Temple of the Muses**.

The Duke walked around Urbino unarmed, a ready listener to complaints. He ran the Palace with the strictness of a housemaster. He let nothing go to waste, turned management into an art and had Livy read to him during his frugal meals. Down in the cellars you will find evidence of his gusto for efficiency and the novel, including his fridge. Known as the 'snowery', it trapped snow from the roof-garden above and kept produce fresh between layers of straw.

But the Palace has not always been appreciated. In the last century, it served as a prison and a salt deposit.

The National Gallery

Although Raphael was born in Urbino, the Gallery (in the top floor of the Palace) has only one of his pictures, the *Portrait of a Gentlewoman*, known as 'The Dumb One', painted in Florence. It is a good example of Raphael's 'essentialised' style, with all encumbrances cut out.

Controversy still swirls round Piero della Francesca's 'problem' picture, the *Flagellation*, a study in mathematical perspective. Once the critics read it as a risqué parallel between the Passion of Christ and the death of the Duke's brother, on the right between the counsellors who murdered him. Now they think it symbolises the misfortunes of the contemporary Church, flailed by heresy.

Do not miss Piero's *View of an Ideal City*, a ghost town of immaculate proportions, all ready for the first arrivals, with doors ajar and plants on the balconies. It is one of the most noted instances of the Renaissance fascination with utopias.

Perspective, as ever, is the language of Paolo Uccello's strip cartoon, the *Profanation of the Host*, telling a probably true story of how a woman and a baker came to violent ends for dealing in a consecrated host.

Raphael's birthplace Outside the Palace, the signs point to the artist's birthplace, and you are in an almost intact Renaissance township. Nearly everything dates from the fifteenth and sixteenth centuries, not because of nagging conservationists, but because of decay. Funds for change faded away with the Dukes.

Raphael's father Giovanni Santi was also a painter, often in the Duke's employ; his home is an insight into the standing the profession had by then achieved. It was Giovanni who taught his son the rudiments, and then sent him to Perugia as an apprentice to Perugino. In the alleged room of his birth is his first picture, a Madonna with Child, which the experts say he completed at the tender age of 13.

San Giovanni Battista Sixty-seven years before Raphael's birth, the brothers Iacopo and Lorenzo Salimbeni smothered the walls of the tiny nearby Oratory of St John with a racy cycle of frescoes on the Baptist's life, packed with blunt detail and happy touches. They were finished in 1416. The brothers now rate high up on the list of exponents of the International Gothic school.

Where to stay and eat Reputedly the best hotel is the **Bonconte**, 28 Via della Mura; tel. 2463.

It is followed by the **Montefeltro**, 2 Via Piansevero; tel. 328324.

The **Vecchia Urbino**, 3 Via di Vasari, tel. 447 (closed Tuesdays), is expensive and offers raftered smartness.

Downstream is **Da Bruno**, 45 Via Veneto; tel. 2598.

Studenty, family style but good value is the **Trattoria di Leone**, 5 Via Battisti; tel. 329894.

Pesaro After Urbino, a convenient place to spend the night is sedate Pesaro (population 90,000), usually explored by bathers only when rain stops play on the beaches, unless they are interested in pottery.

The city has been fiercely Communist since the Second World War when furniture making, now its main industry, brought together its two clans, the fishermen and the peasants, who up till then had been separated by dialect and inclination.

A former Roman fortress, later occupied by the Goths for eight years, it was part of the packet handed over to the Papacy by Pippin, but only became really part of the Papal States in the seventeenth century. It was the birthplace of Rossini, in 1792.

What to see The **Ceramics Museum** in the Palazzo Toschi-Mosca, is claimed locally to be 'unique in the world for the number of pieces and the variety of workshops' on view. The pottery of the Pesaro–Urbino area derives from particularly fine local clay and minerals capable of producing unusual colours. The craft reached its zenith in the sixteenth century and dictated taste throughout Italy.

Plates were either 'storified', to illustrate historical or biblical events, or 'Raphaelistic' – as a local boy, Raphael's influence on local, and hence national, pottery was enormous. His designs echoed the so-called 'grotesque' decorations found in Nero's 'Golden House' in Rome.

Pesaro's artists rediscovered the technique for adding lustre to pottery which had been pioneered by the great sixteenth-century potter Mastro Giorgio from Gubbio. It involved adding iridescent metals, including gold, to plates already glazed normally. His 'secret' ingredients apparently included horse hooves and gorse. A case on its own in room IX displays three of the Mastro's precious creations.

The emblem of a revived pottery scene in the eighteenth century is the so-called 'Rose of Pesaro', shown sprouting another flower, often a tulip. Today, few real potters remain in Pesaro.

The fifteenth-century **Ducal Palace** in the main square was based on the one in Urbino; Lucrezia Borgia once lived here, and her small bathroom is Raphaelistic, too. Today, the *palazzo* is the Prefecture, and can be seen only once a week through arrangement with the Tourist Office, 164 Viale Trieste; tel. 69341.

What to do

For opera lovers, Pesaro is known for its seventeenth-century Rossini Theatre, hub of a Rossini Festival straddling August and September. This is now at risk of becoming only a bi-yearly event, because of lack of funding.

Where to stay

Pesaro's huge procession of modern, anonymous hotels, mainly wearing three stars, takes place in the beach-side Viale Trieste. Towards the town end are the **Atlantic**, 365 Viale Trieste, tel. 61911; the **Caravelle**, 269 Viale Trieste, tel. 64078, and the **Nettuno**, 367 Viale Trieste, tel. 64434.

At the other, quieter, end are the 'see-through', functional **Nautilus**, 26 Viale Trieste, tel. 67125; and the **Embassy**, 64 Viale Trieste, tel. 68158.

In the two-star class are the **Aurora**, 147 Viale Trieste, 61912; and the **Due Palme**, 52 Viale Trieste, tel. 31355.

Where to eat

In the resort area, the smartest restaurant is **Ristorante degli Sfingi**, 219 Viale Trieste; tel. 69194 (closed Tuesdays).

Inside the old town, a pleasant atmosphere reigns in the **Taverna dei Giordani**, once the stables of a fifteenth-century *palazzo*, Via Barignani; tel. 35641 (closed Mondays).

More casual and younger is **Cigno Bianco** (White Swan), 6 Via Castelfidardo; tel. 34364 (closed Mondays).

Fano

Some 11 km south of Pesaro, Fano is a compact, pleasant town (population 50,000). It is one of the three main fishing harbours on the Adriatic.

This is where the great *Flaminia* highway from Rome, opened in 222 BC, still reaches the coast; it was first mentioned by Julius Caesar, who reported stationing a cohort in Fano after crossing the Rubicon.

What to see

The street plan is still Roman and Fano's trophy is its Roman Gate, or **Arch of Augustus**, at the end of the Via Arco d'Augusto, built before the year 9 BC by a town grateful to the Emperor for its walls. What it looked like then is shown by a stone drawing on the façade of the tiny church to the right of the outside of the gate.

Its superstructure was blasted away by the artillery of Duke Federico who brought Fano to its knees in 1463, ending two centuries of tyrannical rule by the Malatesta family from Rimini. The rubble built the church.

In August, they run chariot races around the gate: only townsfolk duly garbed as Romans may watch.

The local court of the Malatesta, part of it now a bank, suffers from re-modelling, but the **Palace**, over the four arches in the courtyard, is genuine latter-day Gothic, dating from the early fifteenth century. A *Guardian Angel* by Giovanni Guercino from Ferrara (1591–1666) in the upstairs picture gallery is idolised in a poem by Robert Browning, while a *Resurrection of Lazarus* by two locals renders the miracle positively odiferous.

Two Peruginos lurk in the gloom of **Santa Maria Nuova**, otherwise noted for a striking Renaissance façade. Beneath the Madonna and Child, over the third altar on the right, the scenes from the Virgin's life are held to be the work of his pupil Raphael.

Where to stay and eat

One of the best among the army of hotels is said to be the **Elisabeth Due**, 2 Piazzale Amendola; tel. 866146.

An interesting oddity is a self-service, paper-plate fish canteen run by local seamen at sea-bottom prices to promote second-league fish such as mackerel; **Al Pesce Azzuro** is in the port area.

Montemaggiore

The military minded might like to see the vantage point from which Winston Churchill watched the Eighth Army spring the final offensive against the Germans' Gothic Line on 25 August 1944. This was the last big battle of the Second World War fought on Italian soil. A plaque marks the spot in this medieval hill village, about 15 km inland from Fano along the *superstrada* to Fossombrone. It was a symbolic choice. More than 2,000 years earlier Rome had finally beaten the Carthaginians under Hannibal's brother nearby.

The kick-off to the more recent battle was the Canadians' big moment in Italy. While battered Polish units moved on Pesaro along the coast, the Canadians launched the attack under a monumental artillery barrage. They forded the river Metauro and seized their objectives beyond it, Saltara and Serrungarina. They took amazingly few prisoners; the Germans, apparently tipped off, had pulled back.

Where to eat

A good, expensive, frenchified restaurant guards the plaque: the **Argantua**, Piazza Bramante; tel. 894958 (closed Mondays).

Senigallia

Some 14 km south of Fano, Senigallia was the first Roman colony on the Adriatic. Destroyed first by Alaric, and later by Manfred for infidelity, twice conquered by the Montefeltros of Urbino, today's lively little walled township (population 40,000) is still dominated by the massive fifteenth-century fort built by a Pope's nephew, Giovanni della Rovere, who was assigned the town. He married into the Montefeltro family and Senigallia then came under Urbino; it later came under the Pope when the Montefeltro line died out. The **Fort** was designed to parry Turkish pirates, and as an emergency dwelling in case of attack by Italians.

From the fifteenth to the eighteenth centuries Senigallia, as a free port, was the site of a famous trade fair. In bumper years it drew 50,000 visitors and 500 ships from Europe and the Levant.

It is the birthplace, open for inspection, of Pope Pius IX, the controversial nineteenth-century Pontiff who declared war on modernity and proclaimed the doctrine of Papal infallibility.

A way out

This could be your first exit from the Marches, via the caves of Frasassi and Fabriano. This is the track the text now takes, before back-tracking to begin a big sweep inland via Macerata, the peak country and Ascoli Piceno. Then it follows the coast northwards to Ancona. For the Frasassi Caves, turn off the A 14 *after* the exit for Chiaravalle to join the SS 76 super-highway.

Jesi

On the way, to your right, you will see atop a big rounded hill the town of Jesi (population 40,000), about 30 km inland from Ancona. It once won for itself a permanent footnote in history, by a fluke.

In 1194, it chanced to be the birthplace of that formidable man Frederick II, the German Emperor who challenged the power of the Church of Rome, and lost. The only evidence left of the birth is a square named after him, the hub of a dark medieval warren hemmed in by ponderous fourteenth-century walls and towers, built on top of Roman walls.

The modern centre is Piazza della Repubblica, flanked by the Teatro Pergolesi, named after Jesi's second most illustrious son.

What to see

A compelling reason for a stop could be Lorenzo Lotto, who occupies two rooms in the eighteenth-century sugar-cake **Palazzo Pianetti**, a splendid extravaganza of 'Italianised Bavarian Rococo' (open 9.30 a.m.–12.30 p.m., 4–7 p.m.; closed Mondays).

In room 6 is Lotto's famed and powerful *St Lucia before the Judge*, with its graphic panels of the saint being dragged away by oxen. Commissioned in 1523, it was not finished for nine years, long after Lotto had pocketed his fee.

What to do

Good buys are trinkets in gold (goldsmiths are active in Jesi) and *Verdicchio* wine, for which this is the main production centre.

Caves of Frasassi

About 30 km past Jesi, turn right off the SS 76 for Genga. The train from Ancona stops at nearby Santa Vittore del Chiusi. The unreal world of the Frasassi Caves is the wonder of the Marches.

It is the biggest cave complex in Italy, and the part opened to the public is called the Great Cave of the Wind. It is open all the year round, including holidays, 9 a.m.–12.30 p.m. and 3.30–6.30 p.m. The guided visit, over a route 1,500 metres long, takes about 70 minutes; guides speak English. The temperature is kept constant at 14°C and a light pullover is advisable. In summer, 6,000 people a day gingerly tread the route.

The caves were discovered by pure chance in 1971 by three young potholers. They became curious when they saw vegetation around a hole no bigger than a football being wafted about by a strange air current on a still day. They investigated, and broke into the skylight in the dome of the enormous first cavern.

It is called the Abyss of Ancona after the three boys' home town. As the guide will doubtless tell you, it is 240 metres high and huge enough to accommodate Milan Cathedral. Later, 150 other caves were found.

The caves induce a strange loss of proportion. Stalagmites 20 metres tall look small from not far away. Distances shrink. It is a glittery, fairy-like world, and all around you the Italians will be exclaiming: 'Che bello! Che bello!'

Naturally, the weird shapes all have rather corny names such as the Witches' Castle, the Two Camels and the Organ Pipes. One is even called Dante Alighieri.

Fabriano

The mountains around the caves regally fade away to the west and, after 11 km, Fabriano (population 29,000) emerges. It is well worth a quick look because it is such an arresting variation on the theme of a square.

It started as a refugee centre for those fleeing the barbarian invasions. In the fourteenth century it was run by a Ghibelline family of Germanic extraction. The 60 years of their reign marked the zenith of Fabriano's power and wealth. The town was known throughout Europe as a paper-making centre; this is where the water-mark was invented, and fine paper is made still. But prosperity came to a bloody end when all the male members of the ruling family were murdered in the Cathedral in 1435. The town was then annexed to the Church.

What to see

The **Piazza del Comune**, arguably the most singular in the Marches, is pure theatre. It is oneness created out of disparity: the backdrop, the bridge-like Palazzo del Podestà, is Gothic-Romanesque and goes back to the thirteenth century; the *palazzo* on the left went up two centuries later to serve as the murdered family's 'court'; while the nineteen arches of the elegant raised arcade belong to the seventeenth century, and were once the prelude to a church, now destroyed.

Look into the **Picture Gallery** opposite. The first frescoes to confront you are considered the finest known examples of thirteenth-century painting in the Marches; by unknown artists, they once adorned a monastery refectory. Fabriano had a school of painting of its own but there is nothing in the gallery of famed Gentile da

Fabbriano (1370–1427). There is a fair sampling of Allegretto Nuzi (1320–73), regarded as a leader of the school since, although he absorbed influences from Florence and Siena, he had his own personality.

Where to stay   Not far from the centre is the **Aristos Hotel**, 103 Via Cavour; tel. 22308.

Osimo   To make another sweep inland, you need to desert the A 14 south of Ancona and head for Osimo, 19 km away on the SS 361. It is poured over the top of a formidable hill, 265 metres high, and still looks as impregnable as it did to the Goths who made it one of the main strongholds in their defensive war against Byzantium.

Except for an elegant Palazzo Municipale flanked by a medieval watch-tower, Osimo today (population 25,000) has few other draws. It is a picture of sixteenth- and seventeenth-century prosperity and order, this time under the wing of the Church. It is also a cameo of Italians 'at home', unmolested by tourists.

Osimo is known for its manufacture of musical instruments, especially accordions.

Macerata   In July or August, opera is Macerata's great draw, when its enormous open-air theatre becomes one of the operatic centres of Italy, attracting top singers and staging lavish super-productions.

Getting there   The town (population 44,000) caps a hill dominating a backbone between two river valleys and is 27 km from the A 14 along the SS 571. From Rome, leave the A 1 at Orte and travel via Foligno.

A single railway line links the town to Civitanova Marche on the coast.

What to do   The theatre is just outside a main gate (open 8–11 a.m. and 3–8 p.m.). Known as the Sferisterio, which means a stadium for 'arm-ball', it was built as such. The game, which entails hitting a ball with an armlet and bouncing it off a wall, was once highly popular in the Marches, Emilio Romagna and Tuscany. Such stadiums were once numerous; Macerata's, opened in 1829, is the finest surviving. A neo-Classical concept, it was paid for by a hundred rich fans of the game, and consists of the massive regulation wall, faced by a gently curving gallery of boxes topped by 'gods'.

Circuses, buffalo jousting and other rude entertainments were also staged in the stadium, until somebody realised how uncannily perfect its acoustics were. The first opera, *Aida*, was put on in 1921. At an altitude of 314 metres, it does not suffer from the drawback of the Baths of Caracalla in Rome, where summer opera-singers are plagued by night-time damp.

Since 1967, summer opera has been a regular fixture, attended by demanding audiences. The stadium's shape ensures that nobody is behind a pillar. It seats 7,000. Same-day tickets are usually available from the Box Office, Arena Sferisterio, 18 Piazza della Libertà; tel. 44903.

What to see

The town itself is not the most alluring of the Marches. From the Middle Ages onwards, with gaps, it was a stronghold of the Papacy, but was the first town to rebel against Rome during the Risorgimento. The centre, built between the sixteenth and the nineteenth centuries, is the spacious Piazza della Libertà. One oddity is a horse-carriage museum.

Where to stay and eat

One hotel in town is the **Centrale**, 96 Via Amaroli; tel. 47276.

But the most pleasant and unusual hostelry is the isolated **Villa Quiete**, down in the valley on the way to the village of Montecassiano, Vallecascia di Montecassiano; tel. 599559. It is a former manor house in its own grounds with an oddly 'British' atmosphere. Its restaurant is good.

If you then have an after-dinner drink in the main square of **Montecassiano** itself, you will not be disappointed.

Abbadia di Fiastra

Along the SS 78, some 10 km south-west of Macerata, is a fine twelfth-century Cistercian abbey (open May–September 3–6 p.m.). It was founded by monks from Milan who took up a donation of land in 1142; apparently they were led by St Bernard himself. For three centuries, the Abbey made its influence felt throughout the Marches and beyond both as a religious and as an economic force. The brothers drained swampland, processed produce, came into estates far and wide, and made lesser abbeys mend their ways. It is now restored, the industrious atmosphere included.

Urbs Salvia

To build their grandiose church, the brothers looted stone from the roadside ruins of the Roman town some 3 km further on. This is one of the few remaining traces in Italy of destruction wrought by the hordes of Alaric. The town was built in the first century BC, and gutted in AD 410. But, as you can see, the barbarians did leave remarkably intact the small amphitheatre, now sprouting oaks from its stands. It is an islet of peace.

San Ginesio

The SS 78 continues to snake towards the Apennines, overlooked by towering ranges. For a superb view of terrain now in a major key, drive up to this walled medieval village (population 4,500) at 680 metres high, even though they prefer to be left in peace. They are still resting after a past of exceeding violence; constant rebellion only ended in 1443 when they threw themselves, exhausted, into the arms of the Church.

Because of its view, San Ginesio is dubbed 'the balcony of the Sibilline mountains'. It is also the scene of an unsolved mystery: nobody can account for the bizarre façade of its Cathedral, reminiscent of a florid Gothic style usually found in Flanders.

Sarnano

Sarnano (population 3,500), the ante-chamber to the alpine south of the Marches. It is a triad: a medieval village, a ski-resort and a spa town. It is 539 metres up, 38 km from Macerata, and overlooked by the peaks of the Sibilline mountains. The nearest, the Sasso Tetto (1,625 metres) is equipped with ski-lifts and hotels.

What to see   The medieval village is a curious spiral of narrow streets, a cork-screw designed for defence. The main square at its summit, the **High Square**, is curious, too. Rising above the usual symbols of civic power – the *palazzi* of the People, the Priors and the Police Chief – is the commanding bell-tower of a frescoed **Church** built by the Benedictines at a time when religious orders, as competitors of the 'official' Church, were usually banned from town centres. But the monks won this position as compensation for the seizure by Sarnano of abbey land in the valley.

The **Picture Gallery**, at the base of the hill, is on the site of a Franciscan monastery.

St Francis, once in Sarnano in person, settled a dispute between the town's five rival wards over a municipal coat-of-arms by designing one himself, showing the face of a seraph. It is still used. If you could make out the local dialect, you would hear them still using words once spoken by their Longobard occupiers. They call a wood, for instance, *gualdo*, from the Longobard *waldrum*. Old rivalries still sting like salt. A Sarnano policeman claims: 'The difference between Sarnano and San Ginesio is that between night and day.' He poured scorn on San Ginesio's snow since it was 'of no use'. In Sarnano, he said, they made it work.

Where to stay   In town, the 'traditional' place is the two-star **Hotel Terme**; tel. 667166.

Near the ski-lifts are the **Hotel Hermitage**, tel. 665121; and the **Albergo la Sibilla**, tel. 665102.

Ascoli Piceno

From Sarnano, it is a twisting, often spectacular drive of 55 km over a mountain pass, the Croce di Casale, down into Ascoli Piceno (population 56,000) – Roman, medieval and Renaissance, and the most interesting fully fledged city in the Marches. The position is a 'natural' for a city: in the neck of a valley, torrents cut out a stage in an amphitheatre of hills, and Ascoli now occupies it. The Adriatic is 25 km away. The Ascolani are held to be distrustful and slippery, and they mind their own business. 'They throw the stone and hide the hand,' as the saying goes. Today, their city is as politically rebellious as it has always been; in 1987 they got through nine mayors.

It was in Ascoli that the spark flew that set off the Social War against Rome – the murder of Roman emissaries. The town paid by being burnt to the ground. The Longobards, who occupied the area for two centuries, razed it a second time. After their ejection, the city went to the Papacy and, as you might guess from all the churches (ninety-four), it remained a Papal fief (more or less) from then on.

What to see

Piazza del Popolo

Ascoli is best known for the most striking main square in the Marches. Known as the *Salotto*, the Drawing Room, it is the city's resplendent meeting place. Before dinner people swarm on to its polished floor of travertine in droves and the Room echoes to the drone of local gossip. It is a perfect rectangle and, although its façades contrast, they compose by some miracle a balanced whole. Even so, the arches of the elegant Renaissance arcade are unequal: that is because a Papal legate let each shopkeeper pick the arch he could afford.

Another legate was responsible for the present appearance of the **Palazzo of the People's Captain**. He set fire to the original medieval *palazzo* to smoke out rebel nobles holed up there in 1535; he then disembowelled it to make way for its geometric Renaissance courtyard. The backdrop to this strangely 'private' square is a flank of the church of **San Francesco**, part Romanesque, part Gothic, the finest Franciscan church in the Marches.

Santi Vicenzo ed Anastasio

The Via del Trivio alongside San Francesco points you towards the nearby medieval quarter. If you are directed towards the Porta Solestà, you should pass one of the most unusual churches in the Marches, dedicated to Saints Vincent and Anastasius, begun in the eleventh century. The sixty-four stone panels making up its fourteenth-century façade were once all frescoed; only two other such façades exist in Italy.

Climb down into its tiny crypt. Some scholars believe it was a fourth-century semi-underground church used by the first Christians. The well you will see was probably used for baptisms; in the fourteenth century, its water was used to treat leprosy.

Several tower-houses sprout up from the medieval quarter, but ninety-two are missing. They were demolished during the third sack of the city, the work of Frederick II, angry with Ascoli for being Guelf.

Ponte di Solestà

Some Roman vestiges survive: alleys in the medieval quarter, for instance, are called *Rua* instead of *Vicolo*. A more solid vestige is the nearby imposing Roman bridge, a daring arch 62 metres long thrown over the deeply bedded Tronto river. Built under Augustus in the first years of the Roman Empire, it is one of the biggest Roman bridges in Europe.

If you ask at the Tourist Office (1 Via del Trivio, tel. 63288, or Piazza del Popolo, tel. 55250), you may actually be allowed to worm through its innards.

Duomo

The Cathedral, back behind the Drawing Room, dates originally from the fourth century and is dedicated to St Egidius, a German, the city's first bishop. He is still vividly recalled: he was beheaded, but picked up his head, strode to the present site of the Cathedral and there, intentionally, dropped dead. During the Second World War, Italian Jews were hidden from the Nazis in the Cathedral's tunnels.

Today, most people visit the Cathedral to see Carlo Crivelli's masterpiece. His Madonna and Child altar-piece, done in 1473, is in the gloom of the Chapel of the Sacrament. The foppish young man above the Virgin is St George, as we are supposed to realise from the brooch in the form of a dragon on his chest. Precious, courtly refinement is Crivelli's hallmark. He produced a very similar young man, this time playing a sensitive St Sebastian, in a triptych in the municipal gallery, in the nearby Palazzo del Comune.

Where to stay

The most modern hotel, four-star, is a 15-minute walk from the centre, the **Hotel Marche**, 34 Viale Kennedy; tel. 45575. Avoid the restaurant.

Inside town are the two-star **Piceno**, 10 Via Minuccia, tel. 52553; and the one-star **Nuovo Picchio**, 11 Via C. Battista, tel. 25851.

Where to eat

The **Cantina d'Arte**, 5 Via della Lupa, tel. 65135 (closed Thursdays), is informal, rustic, reliable.

The 'in' place is the **Gallo d'Oro**, Corso V. Emanuele; tel. 53520.

Fermo

Back up the coast, Fermo (population 34,000) is one of the most ancient cities on the Adriatic, reached from the coast at a giddy angle of 45 degrees, which presumably is one reason why Imperial Rome picked it as a major stronghold.

What to see

The main point of interest is a huge, underground, **Roman reservoir**, only steps from the sloping central square. Enquire at the Tourist Office, 5 Piazza del Popolo, tel. 23205, for the compulsory guide, who is free. Built under Augustus, the reservoir's purpose was to water both a Roman legion garrisoned in the town and a Roman fleet of some 200 vessels down at what is now Porto San Giorgio. The name *Piscina*, Baths, is quite misleading.

The reservoir is utterly intact; its thirty linked vaults stored 15,000 cubic metres, and tapped a curious feature of Fermo. Despite being 319 metres up, it sits on strata of water, and cellars still get flooded.

Fermo was so loyal to Rome in the Second Punic and the Social Wars that its civic plaque still recalls its fidelity: *Firmum firma fides romanorum colonia.*

The Pope imparting his blessing from the sixteenth-century **Palazzo Comunale**, shaped like an altar-piece, is Sixtus V, once Fermo's bishop. They put him there for elevating them to an archbishopric. The **Picture Gallery** inside (open 9 a.m.–2 p.m.) has a fine collection of local faces, including Cesare Borgia's, and, surprisingly, a *Nativity* by a youthful Rubens. The **Library** next door has letters written by Christopher Columbus.

Inside the **Cathedral**, which lords it over town and country from the flattened tip of Fermo's peak, is kept a silk and gold chasuble of St Thomas à Becket, made in 1116 in Almeria, Spain.

Loreto

Loreto, 30 km north of Fermo, 27 km south of Ancona and 4 km inland, is the Lourdes of Italy. A village of 10,000, it revolves entirely around the so-called 'Sacred House'. Pilgrims from around the globe trek there; the handicapped and infirm often arrive by special trains. Stretcher-bearers mill about. Incense mingles with surgical spirit.

The Church calls Loreto 'the new Nazareth' since, according to a tradition still officially honoured, the Sacred House is the very one in which the Virgin Mary was born and where Jesus lived until he was 30. It was allegedly transported from Palestine to Italy by angels in 1291 after the Moslem invasion. They lowered the House on to a hill not far from the present spot covered with laurel, from which the name Loreto derives. But criminals lived there, whereupon the angels made a brief diversionary flight with the House, only to find themselves on land owned by two brothers who quarrelled over ownership. After a final hop, the House landed where it is today.

In 1920, the Madonna of Loreto was proclaimed the patron saint of airmen.

What to see

The **Santa Casa** is inside an immense sanctuary built around it on the orders of Pope Paul II in 1468 after he was cured of plague by a visit to the House. But the **Sanctuary of the Sacred House** took three centuries to fashion and, since so many had a hand in it, the result lacks an overall style.

At first it was Gothic; Tuscan architects then turned it into a church-cum-fortress; successors finally superimposed the Renaissance façade, one of the latest in Italy. Nine apses make the Sanctuary all the more unusual. The Sacred House itself is luxuriously padded on the outside by marble bas reliefs designed by the Renaissance architect Bramante, the first architect of St Peter's in Rome. One section narrates the aerial peregrinations; a groove has been worn into the marble by the knees of penitents. The smoke-blackened interior is the only part of the original house visible.

The chapels clustering around the House, some in doubtful taste, were funded by Catholics from abroad. The American chapel traces the history of human flight, from Icarus to space travel. The only frescoes worth attention are by Luca Signorelli, in **St John's Vestry**. Those who have seen his *Resurrection* in Orvieto will find those writhing anatomies in the *Conversion of St Paul* very familiar.

Outside, graceful **Renaissance arcades**, like those on the left by Bramante, were meant to have bracketed the entire square, but the money ran out. Above them, in the **Apostolic Palace**, is the Picture Gallery, best known for the last works of Lorenzo Lotto. Tired of wandering, he spent his last years at the Sanctuary as an oblate, and died in 1556. He bequeathed the paintings to the town.

Where to stay

Small Loreto boasts nineteen hotels. The biggest are the **Bellevue e Marchigiano**, 14 Piazza Squarcia, tel. 97165; and the **Giardinetto**, 10 Corso Boccalini, tel. 977135.

Recanati

Pilgrims of another kind flock to Recanati, 9 km inland from Loreto, a shrine to its most famous son, Giacomo Leopardi (1798–1837), Italy's greatest romantic poet. The tenor Beniamino Gigli was also born here.

Today's Italians place Leopardi on a pedestal not much lower than

Dante. He is that very rare figure in Italy, a tortured soul; a convinced pessimist, dogged by sickness, he wrote of solitude and nature.

What to see Such is the veneration for Leopardi in Recanati that the citizens built a huge new **Town Hall** in his honour, leaving only a twelfth-century bell-tower in the main square, because it figures in a Leopardi poem. The museum on the second floor, by the lift, exhibits memorabilia of both Leopardi and Gigli. Heart-rending arias are played on a cassette while you browse. The **Picture Gallery** in room 5 has three Lorenzo Lottos, including his greatly popular *Annunciation*.

Once a fortified early medieval castle, all Recanati is now a museum, with the home of Leopardi's unloving parents as the focal point, and you can tarry in the library where their son ruined his health learning Latin, Greek, Hebrew, French and English between the ages of 10 and 17.

Where to stay The main hotel is **La Ginestra**, 2 Via Calcagni; tel. 980355.

Ancona Sixteenth-century pictures in its municipal art gallery show Ancona, founded by the Greeks, as a lively and comely harbour town in the lee of a promontory shaped like an elbow, the Greek for which supplied its name. Today, the capital of the Marches is also its wreck. To blame: heavy bombing in the Second World War, a severe earthquake in 1972, industrialisation and choking traffic.

What to see The symbol of its desecrated past is an elegant **Roman triumphal arch** in the middle of the docklands, hemmed in by cranes. It was put there in AD 115 to thank the Emperor Trajan for a new jetty.

With a population of 110,000, Ancona (291 km from Rome) is the biggest town in the Marches, busy with ship-building, metal and chemical industries, and ferries which usually leave at night for Yugoslavia, Greece, Turkey and Cyprus.

Dominating Ancona from atop the promontory is its exceptional **Cathedral**, built over three centuries from the eleventh, a rare blend of Romanesque and Byzantine. Saint Ciriaco, to whom it is dedicated, suffered martyrdom in the Holy Land by being immersed in boiling water and forced to swallow molten lead. His corpse was transferred to Ancona in the fifth century.

The pride of Ancona's three-storey **Art Gallery** (17 Via Pizzecolli, near the port) is a large restored altar-piece by Titian, a Virgin and Child. Laden with symbolism, its theme is stated to be how the human and divine worlds encounter each other. The key symbol is the fig tree.

The centre of the modern part of Ancona is the anonymous Piazza Cavour. There is no beach.

Where to stay Reputedly the best hotel is the four-star **Passetto**, 1 Via T. De Revel, tel. 31307, outside the town near the cliffs.

Inside town is the traditional, three-star **Roma e Pace**, just off the main Corso Garibaldi at 1 Via G. Leopardi; tel. 202007.

Where to eat A convenient restaurant nearby is **La Moretta**, 52 Piazza del Plebiscito; tel. 202317 (closed Sundays).

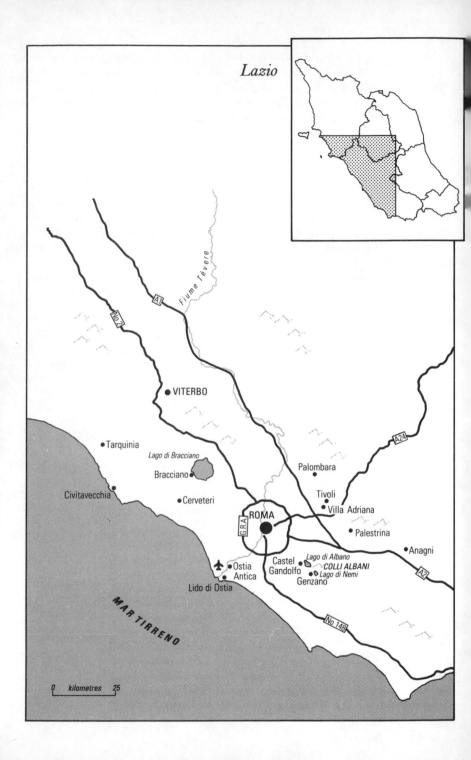

Lazio

Fiume Tevere

A1

No 2

VITERBO

Tarquinia

Lago di Bracciano

Bracciano

Cerveteri

Civitavecchia

Palombara

Tivoli

Villa Adriana

A24

G.R.A.

ROMA

Palestrina

Anagni

Lago di Albano

Castel
Gandolfo

COLLI ALBANI

Lago di Nemi

Genzano

A2

Ostia
Antica

Lido di Ostia

No 148

MAR TIRRENO

0   *kilometres*   25

Lazio

Introduction

Lazio is an artificial hotch-potch of a region which only took on its present shape in 1934; Rome is its most important province. The name Lazio itself had been officially resurrected a mere seven years earlier, after nearly two thousand years in limbo. It is Italian for Latium, the land of the Latins – originally a tiny rectangle of territory south of Rome, stretching from the Alban Hills to the sea. The ascendancy of Rome over Lazio began with the first kings, but under a defence agreement in 493 BC, Rome and the Latin cities remained equals; only in the fourth century did Rome become master. And Latium never included the former Etruscan land north of the Tiber.

Under Emperor Augustus, Latium officially evaporated to become part of the First Region and, as the Empire crumbled, it dropped out of common usage. After Italian Unification, Lazio simply meant the province of Rome. The other provinces now included are, from north to south: Viterbo, Rieti, Latina and Frosinone.

It is amazingly varied. In the north-east, Mount Terminillo, at 2,216 metres, is one of the highest peaks in the Apennines. The south-west of Lazio, around modern Latina, has the flat monotony of former marshland. To the south of Rome there are volcanic lakes, and to the north undulating vistas.

Lazio has 300 km of coastline yet, excluding Rome, it is a desert – one of the most sparsely peopled areas of Italy, with a population of only 2 million, or 123 people per sq km. Industrial productivity is not its strong point. It turns out only 6 per cent of the national output, but is surprisingly strong on wine, being the biggest producer in Central Italy, ahead of Tuscany. The best known is *Frascati*, the white wine from the Alban Hills. People work mainly in the civil service and service industries and they mostly vote Christian Democrat, with 5 per cent fewer supporting the Communist Party.

The most interesting places to see after Rome are Tivoli, Ostia Antica, the Etruscan sites and Viterbo.

Rome

Rome is a beautiful, rather secretive, old lady; she has been through it all, including dishonour, and now lives amid a stupefying jumble of family treasure, not caring whether you like her or not. It is a shock, probably unpleasant at first, to find a parking lot instead of a city, to be assailed by the din, the shoals of motorbikes, the constant honking, the wails of sirens, and to cough over blue fog in clogged alleys. The heat unscrews the knees; there is nowhere to sit down; and when you get there, the bank is shut, or on strike.

The second shock is usually more of the kind expected – one of bemused bewilderment at the abundance of the lady's riches and their stunning variety. Rome is a scene-change every few paces. The switches follow no sequence, but chop and change like cocktail talk. The lady abhors rationality; she is a riot.

Rome is no museum. It is as they left it – emperors, barbarians, prelates, plunderers, planners, fascists. None of them cleaned up before moving in; they simply added to what was there, or incorporated what they found into what they founded. A lot of Rome is grafting; one noble medieval family ensconced themselves in a Roman theatre, another in the Colosseum itself.

That is part of Rome's fascination. In no other capital are so many strands of Western civilisation exposed and intertwined. Rome means the Roman Empire and the succeeding Papacy; wandering through the streets is a zig-zag back and forth through their centuries. Rome is a strange experience in time. Eventually, after you have shuttled between Imperial bath-houses and Baroque extravaganza long enough, a kind of seamless continuity emerges. For some residents, the frontier between past and present can become blurred – it is one of the bonuses of the city. So are its luminous skies, the freshness of its changing colours, the mild climate, the greenery, the summer breeze from the sea 25 km away – and the constant, constant surprise.

Rome cannot be known. The lady is always hiding something – a little square with painted walls, a church with a gloom-shrouded masterpiece, a 2,000-year-old cellar near the Pantheon where a man just as old sells firewood in summer. You can live a lifetime and never possess her secrets. Much of your pleasure will be in simply strolling about without a map, baiting the surprises your way. Rome is far more than its 'sights', which is its greatest pleasure.

It is anything but modest. It is panache, the grand gesture – from the massive, grandiose structures of Imperial Rome to the highly theatrical squares and the gushing fountains, all designed with unashamed bravado for operatic effect.

Rome survives continuing vandalisation, and five eras still show through:

● Chunks of ancient Rome are embedded in the centre, but Imperial splendour mainly stands aloof, centred on the Colosseum.

● The second Rome is the more scattered domain of the early Christian era – 'mystical' churches with Byzantine mosaics, chilling catacombs.

● The third is today's centre, designed by Popes between the sixteenth and eighteenth centuries, solidly Renaissance, exuberantly Baroque. This is the Rome of narrow streets and cobbles, dank passageways, churches caked in adornment, princely dwellings, inventive fountains and tiny squares, some of them wells of silence and others obliterated by cars.

● Then comes the overwhelming Renaissance world of the Vatican, of Michelangelo and Raphael.

● The fifth is all-enveloping modern Rome, symbolised by the horrendous Victor Emmanuel Monument in Piazza Venezia, erected to celebrate Italian Unification and known to Romans as 'the Typewriter'. There are periodic campaigns for its disappearance, but it is cheaper to stay execution.

Satellite attractions, rarely more than 40 minutes away, cluster around Rome – a Roman town, an Imperial villa, lakes and heights. You will need five very full days to get to know the lady just a little.

Getting there

Fiumicino airport (also known as Leonardo da Vinci) is on the coast some 25 km from Rome. Taxis into town are expensive at, officially, 47,000 lire. Buses take about an hour and cost 5,000 lire. A train service into town was scheduled to be inaugurated in 1990.

By air

Ciampino airport, 14 km to the south, handles charter traffic.

By train

The main trains from Paris are the nightly, smart *Palatino* taking fifteen hours, and the slower, less smart *Naples Express*.

By car

A ring road surrounds Rome, called the GRA, for *Grande Raccordo Anulare*, the hub of all trunk roads. If you arrive on the A 1 from Florence, take exit (*Uscita*) 6, marked *Flaminia*. If on the A 12 from Civitavecchia, wait for *Roma Centro* before turning off; afterwards, it is not easy. Keep asking for Piazza Venezia.

Tourist Offices

The main enquiry office is at 5 Via Parigi (near the station, next to the Grand Hotel); tel. 463748. Another is inside the station, opposite platform 3 (hotels are bookable there); tel. 465461 and 475 0078. There is also one at Fiumicino airport, in the customs area; tel. 601 1255 and 601 2447.

For printed material to be sent by post, write to: EPT, Via Parigi 11, 001855 Rome; tel. 461851.

Getting around

Rome is best seen on foot. With few exceptions, its sights are within not too strenuous walking distance, and you may not need to savour public transport.

Tubes and buses

The city has two busy underground lines which intersect at Termini. The older 'B' line stops at the Colosseum on its way to Mussolini's new town, EUR. The 'A' line station Ottaviano is close to

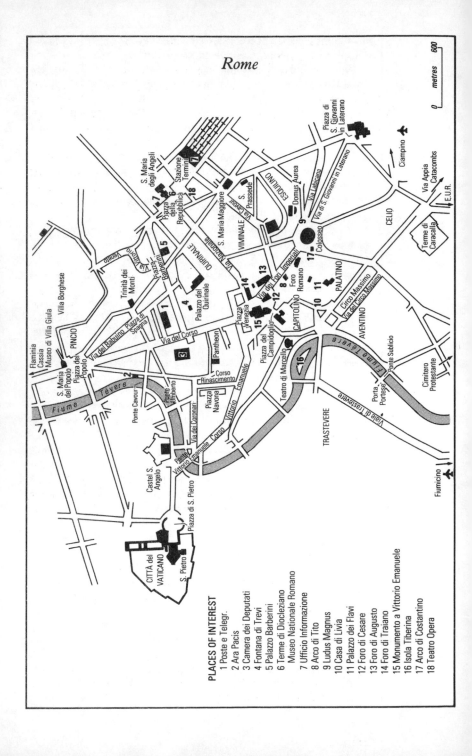

Rome

PLACES OF INTEREST

1 Poste e Telegr.
2 Ara Pacis
3 Camera dei Deputati
4 Fontana di Trevi
5 Palazzo Barberini
6 Terme di Diocleziano
  Museo Nationale Romano
7 Ufficio Informazione
8 Arco di Tito
9 Ludus Magnus
10 Casa di Livia
11 Palazzo dei Flavi
12 Foro di Cesare
13 Foro di Augusto
14 Foro di Traiano
15 Monumento a Vittorio Emanuele
16 Isola Tiberina
17 Arco di Costantino
18 Teatro Opera

0 metres 600

the Vatican, the alternative being bus 64, from Termini to St Peter's Square, via Corso Vittorio Emanuele.

Buses and tubes are cheap, at a flat rate of 700 lire a ride, with tickets on sale at tobacconists or from little sheds at the terminus. Buses start out from around the station for most of Rome and Italy.

Taxis   Official taxi rates are moderate, but drivers cheat on routes. At night, radio taxis, tel. 4995 and 8433, answer summonses with alacrity.

Main areas   The key to the essence of Rome is a wobbly 'Y', with busy Piazza Venezia at the joint. Close by is the rock of the Campidoglio or Capitol, the political hub of Rome since the twelfth century. The stub of the 'Y' is Mussolini's Via dei Fori Imperiali, leading to the Forum and the Colosseum.

Rome's main street is the right-hand fork, the Corso, a mile-long stretch linking the Typewriter at Piazza Venezia to the Piazza del Popolo. Piazza Colonna is a third of the way along; nearby, on the right, is the famed Trevi Fountain. On the left, in the square behind the offices of *Il Tempo*, Rome's conservative newspaper, you will find the Chamber of Deputies. This is the heart of Rome, centred on the Pantheon – a well-heeled labyrinth of twisting back-streets and small shops. It echoes to voices and shuffling feet. Further along the Corso, centred around Via Condotti, Rome's Bond Street, and the famous Piazza di Spagna, are the most elegant parts of central Rome and the most exclusive shops.

The left arm of the 'Y' is the Corso Vittorio Emanuele, which starts off from Piazza Venezia as the brief Via del Plebiscito, and cuts a swathe through old Rome, to end at the bridge over the Tiber for the Vatican. A third of the way down, off to the right, is the city's most animated square, the elliptical Piazza Navona. Opposite, over the road, is the bustling Campo de' Fiori (Flower Field): in the mornings a lively market, a huge splash of colour in a popular neighbourhood of dark alleys, washing, chaos and clamour; at night the focus of a sprinkled galaxy of enjoyable, crowded *trattorie*. Restaurants dot the centre fairly consistently, but the heaviest concentration is in Trastevere, 'Across the Tiber'.

Eating places fairly jostle with each other in this overrated, 'Cockney', part of Rome, supposed to be the preserve of descendants of the few 'real' Romans and also inhabited by Rome's more arty foreign residents. Young Romans flock into Trastevere in search of a rowdy night out, and buses pour tourists into its narrow, car-choked alleys to have *Arrivederci, Roma* sung to them in hangars of restaurants offering simulated jollity and fake parchment menus.

Watch out for child pickpockets, and syringes underfoot. The plus of Trastevere is the overlooking Janiculum and its sweeping view of Rome. This is where Garibaldi so valiantly stood up to the French in defence of the brief Roman Republic.

213

A part of Rome usually written off as commercial lies roughly between Piazza Venezia and the station, called Stazione Termini. It is sleazy, a prostitution area and best avoided at night. But the din and anonymity hide an imposing Roman bath complex (Diocletian's), and a trio of Rome's oldest churches. If, from the Via dei Fori Imperiali, you amble up Via Madonna del Monti towards Via Urbana, you will not see one other tourist, and you will get an excellent idea of how Romans must have lived in everyday, unsung Rome some three centuries ago.

The Seven Hills

'Where *are* the hills?' people always ask.

The Seven have been eroded into hummocks, but they do provide unexpected vistas, help with the hang of Rome, and coax along summer breezes.

The highest is the Quirinale, five minutes from the Trevi Fountain and topped by the massive Presidential Palace, once the residence of the Popes (closed to visitors). Santa Maria Maggiore, the biggest church in the world devoted to the Virgin, surmounts the next biggest, the Esquilino. Between them is the punier Viminale, now occupied by the Interior Ministry.

The Campidoglio is now the most central hill; the Palatino perhaps the 'oldest'. Facing it, across the Circo Massimo, is the Aventino, the hill chosen for Rome by Remus and now a discreet, almost rural, residential area. The least well-known is the Celio (Coelian Hill), the grassy high ground overlooking the Colosseum into which trams disappear. It was a chic area until the rampaging Saracen troops of the Norman Robert Guiscard, urged up to Rome to rescue the Papacy, wiped it out in 1084.

The action

Piazza Venezia might be Rome's physical centre, but the human centres are elsewhere. On summer nights, Romans and tourists pack into Piazza Navona, the capital's biggest spectacle; or they crowd the tables in the small Piazza del Pantheon around the fountain; or they while the night away on the Spanish Steps, balmy and bizarre.

Popular among Americans is the animated Via Vittorio Veneto, home of the vast American Embassy and set of Fellini's film *La Dolce Vita*, his gentle exposure of night-life among the languid rich in the 1950s. Today they have fled, and it is tout, night-club and rip-off country. But this short street is the only Gallic parade strip for the non-poor that Rome has, and nightly they sit under the pavement awnings outside the Café de Paris or the rival Doney's, enjoying attentive service and the least Italian scene in Rome.

The artists

No two men did more to fashion the features of today's Rome than Michelangelo and Bernini. Rome is also the city of Raphael and the murderer Caravaggio.

● Michelangelo, the young protégé of Lorenzo the Magnificent in Florence, first arrived in Rome in 1496 as the guest of a cardinal, and spent most of his long life in the city. In his first few years he was immersed in sculpture, which he always insisted was his true domain. To this period belongs his *Pietà*. Then, after a spell in Florence, he was recalled to Rome in 1503 by Pope Julius II, his first Papal patron, the man who ordered the re-building of St Peter's – impatient, authoritarian. For him and for other Popes, Michelangelo was 'impossible', a bit rough, intolerant of niceties. One Pontiff said of him: 'You know, I always ask him to sit down, in case he sits down without asking.'

Michelangelo was a loner, intransigent, superior and touchy. His hatred of Leonardo da Vinci is documented; he would stand no rivals. It is typical that while Raphael was all the rage in Rome, the older man was away in Florence. He had left Rome in 1516, and did not return until 1532, well after the Sack of 1527, but this time for good. His father, whom he loved, had just died.

He was introspective; creation was torture. He wrote to his brother: 'I'm deeply worried and tremendously tired in my body. I've no friends of any sort and don't want any and I've no time to eat what I should.' His masterpieces are in the Sistine Chapel. He spent much of his late life on architecture, and his imprint on Rome is still there, above all in the shape of the cupola of St Peter's. He died in Rome when he was nearly 90.

● Gian Lorenzo Bernini (1598–1680), the inventor and master-extraordinary of Baroque, left a more evident seal on the city. Born in Naples of a Neapolitan mother and a Florentine sculptor father, he owed his start in life to a cardinal who admired his skill as a carver. A man of seductive charm and sunny disposition, he once said that setting about a new creation was like 'entering a pleasure garden'. He was devout, a practical joker, had eleven children, and was hugely popular. His influence was felt throughout Europe, except in France; his greatest achievement was St Peter's Square.

● Raphael (1483–1520) was born in Urbino in the Marches where his father was a court painter. An apprentice of Perugino, he spent four years in Florence before being called to Rome by Michelangelo's patron, Pope Julius II. No love ever existed between the two artists, though the older man's influence on the younger Raphael was marked. They were opposites: Raphael was handsome, sociable, cheerful, a ladies' man, and was worshipped as a young god in his short lifetime. His work is a celebration of beauty and the sublime, of clarity and tenderness, though his portraits are subtle psychological studies. His triumphs are the *Stanze* in the Vatican. He worked as an architect, too, and was the one who finally had a stop put to the pillaging of Rome's ancient remains by writing to Pope Leo X.

● Caravaggio (1573–1610) was a quick-tempered, swaggering thug from near Naples who first came to Rome when he was 15 and owed his keep and first commissions to a powerful cardinal. He roamed Rome with a big sword and evil companions looking for fights, which he invariably found. His highly dramatic paintings were not always appreciated; he showed saints with dirty feet. Some see his work as a violent reaction to a world of hypocrisy. He fled Rome in 1606 after killing a man in a brawl, escaped from jail in Malta, but was arrested in the then Spanish Porto Ercole, near Grosseto, where he died of fever.

History

Foundation

Rome's yellow buses sally forth from their garages on 21 April every year sporting the capital's yellow-and-red plastic pennants to mark its legendary birthday – on exactly that day in the year 753 BC. The precision, and the legend, have always been accepted with good humour, but a recent archaeological dig has actually produced a potential confirmation of the tradition. An Italian professor has unearthed what he identifies as part of a 'boundary wall', precisely where Romulus was supposed to have built one, around the Palatine Hill. He dates it back to the eighth century BC, which would also fit.

Everywhere you will find Rome's emblem, the kindly she-wolf that suckled Romulus and Remus after finding them near the Tiber at the foot of the Palatine. Twins born of an alleged virgin raped by Mars, the God of War, they had been flung into the flooded river in a basket, which got caught in a tree. When the waters receded, the wolf appeared. When of age (as schoolboys are told) they resolved to found a city in memory of their salvation, but quarrelled over the name and the location. Angered Remus leapt over his brother's unfinished wall and was slain . . .

It was Romulus who engineered Rome's survival, through rape. His men being womanless, he lured tribes down to Rome with the promise of feasting, among them Sabine ladies from the hills to the north-east. His men paid them a lusty compliment, as their families fled in terror.

Culturally, these first Romans came under the influence of the more sensitive Etruscans to the north, and through them were introduced to the art of Greece. Their leaders copied Etruscan dress and regalia; others learned how to drain land.

At the bottom of Via Nazionale, the piled stone blocks are the remains of what are commonly known as the Servian Walls, after Servius Tullius, one of the six kings, probably Etruscan, who followed Romulus. But archaeologists now believe they belong to the Republican era, which began in 509 BC after the monarchy had tottered (after another case of rape).

The initials SPQR you see everywhere, even on drain covers and park benches, still stand for *Senatus Populusque Romanus*, the Senate and the Roman People, the Republic's motto. They were not always in tandem. The 300-strong Senate was run by powerful bosses with vested interests, and it was only after a protracted struggle that the plebians won a theoretical equality before the law.

Expansion

By the fourth century BC, Rome had seized Lazio. Sixteen km north, off the *Cassia*, you can explore Etruscan tombs at Veio, a forward Etruscan stronghold and the first Etruscan place to fall to the Romans in 396 BC. It took a ten-year siege, which ended when the attackers tunnelled under the town and sneaked in.

Other Etruscan towns further and further north then caved in. Italic peoples were also subdued: the Umbrians and to the south the Latins. The last to give in were the warlike Samnites who held vast hilly tracts to the south-east. At a remote place in the Molise, Pietrabbondante, is a silent Samnite theatre and temple complex, the centre of their resistance (see page 273).

By about 270 BC, all of peninsular Italy was Rome's. By the time 80,000 troops had razed Carthage to the ground in 146 BC, the entire Mediterranean area and far beyond was hers; Greece was a mere province under another name.

But Greek influence in Rome became total. The wealthy procured Greek tutors for their sons. Their homes – as you will see at Ostia Antica – were of Greek design, with rooms around an inner courtyard; they took over Greek gods, including Bacchus; and today's museums are crammed with copies of Greek originals churned out in Rome by platoons of hack Greek sculptors. Temples followed the Greek model, too; at the centre of a whirlpool of Roman traffic some delicately survive in a sunken 'Sacred Area' in the so-called Largo Argentina, near Piazza Venezia.

Julius Caesar

By the time Julius Caesar took power in 48 BC, with the title of 'Dictator for Life', Rome was literally *Caput Mundi*. In a certain *trattoria* in the Campo de' Fiori area, you will be very close to where they stabbed him twenty-three times, within the walls of Rome's first stone theatre; the cook will show you its foundations down in the cellar. Shakespeare got it wrong when he staged the killing 'in the Capitol'.

Imperial Rome

The remains of massive Imperial Rome on view today took shape under the Emperors. The first, Augustus, made the famous boast that he had found Rome brick and left it marble. Architecture, in fact, was the Romans' medium – grandiose, majestic, huge, daring. The Colosseum belongs to this long era of might and unpunctured confidence, as well as the Pantheon, the Baths of Caracalla and Diocletian in Rome and, at the foot of Tivoli, Hadrian's Villa.

The Greeks may have been more idealistic, but the Romans also excelled in realistic sculptured portraits and often chillingly candid bas relief work, especially spiralling around their triumphal columns, now free of scaffolding. When the confident Empire faded away, it was another thousand years before such secrets were rediscovered.

The first Emperors included:

Augustus	31 BC–AD 14	Titus	79–81
Tiberius	AD 14–37	Domitian	81–96
Caligula	37–41	Trajan	98–117
Claudius	41–54	Hadrian	117–138
Nero	54–68	and	82 others …
Vespasian	69–79		

In the second century AD, Rome was at its most splendid, the gleaming marble reflecting wealth built on conquest, booty, plunder, tributes and taxes. More than a million people thronged its streets, many living in the first-ever high-rise flats. The Palatine had turned into one vast Imperial Palace; the single forum had become a series. The city was dotted with the massive bath-houses still standing, theatres, temples and gardens.

The first crack in the confidence appeared when Emperor Aurelian (270–275) heard the barbarians shouting on the frontiers; he ringed Rome with its thick Aurelian Walls, 18 km long. Because they are far from the centre, few visitors realise what long stretches remain intact. One of the finest, on the south, runs from the bizarre Pyramid, a tomb a praetor called Cestius had built against his death in 12 BC, to the Cristoforo Colombo highway. Contrary to the general belief, the barbarians seem to have done relatively little damage when they finally did storm the city. Rome really crumbled through abandonment and *Italian* pillage.

Medieval Rome

Its leaders left, and the capital moved to Constantinople. During the Gothic wars, Rome lay deserted for days at a time. The Popes had become its virtual rulers, but then they went absent too – at first, morally. They sank deepest in the tenth and eleventh centuries. One was executed for murdering his predecessor; another exhumed the body of a forerunner and put the corpse on trial before flinging it into the Tiber; a third was killed by the jealous husband of his mistress.

There were then usually two Popes at a time, nominated either by the German Emperors or by the big families who presumed to run Rome (the same names are still in the telephone directory). Their resistance to the Germans' denial of their rights, as they saw it, led to brutal punitive attacks and constant street fighting between rival clans. Once the families elected a mere boy as Pope.

The Republic

As in the rest of Central Italy about this time, the new classes – artisans, guild-members, notaries – lunged for independence. They proclaimed a republic, restored the Senate, and demanded an end to the temporal power of the Papacy. A Pope who tried to put down the revolt was killed by a stone. But the rebellion failed. Elsewhere the successful mini-republics raised fine medieval *palazzi* to honour their civic pride; in Rome, you'll find little. Through diplomacy and German help, the Papacy won.

The fall

When the Popes went absent physically, betaking themselves to Avignon from 1305 to 1377, Rome all but went under. A wooded hill close to Piazza Venezia is still called Monte Caprino because goats grazed there. At the time when cities such as Florence and Perugia were rich and resplendent, Rome had dwindled to a village, with a population of about 20,000. At night, the cries of wolves could be heard from the Forum.

ROME

The Renaissance

Rome's revival had to await the return of the Popes and the Renaissance, which was when today's Rome began to emerge. The Pontiffs gained unprecedented authority and Rome's transformation was due entirely to their wealth, their love of posterity and their patronage.

As the Renaissance in Florence faded away, two of the greatest patrons, Popes Julius II and the Medici Pontiff Leo X, brought it to a new climax in Rome by pressing Tuscans into their service. Palazzo Venezia was the first of the grand Renaissance *palazzi* to go up. Palazzo Farnese, now the French Embassy, has been called the finest Renaissance princely palace in the world.

A gigantic vision was broached – an entirely new St Peter's. To guide the vision and embellish the new Rome in other ways, a super-human trio was summoned to the city: Michelangelo; the beautiful young man he hated, Raphael; and the architect Bramante. The big families were building, too, and they, along with the Popes, quarried the monuments of Imperial Rome for marble, materials and decorations, on the pretext that because they were pagan they didn't count.

Sack of Rome

The ferocious Sack of Rome in 1527 lasted a week; after the first night 6,000 corpses littered the streets. The city was systematically ransacked, the Spanish and German troops breaking into homes and tombs for treasure. They stabled their horses in churches and held orgies on altars. The Pope fled to Orvieto. Overnight, it is reported, the population of 90,000 shrank by two-thirds. The artists in the city scattered.

But, as you can tell today, not for long. In the rest of Central Italy the Sack ushered in a long sleep, but in Rome it marked only a pause, and the beautification soon resumed. Michelangelo finished the *Last Judgement* in the Sistine Chapel, and designed the square of the Campidoglio. Caravaggio was revolutionary, and rejected.

Baroque

In the seventeenth century, the era of Baroque dawned, totally dominated by the powerful personality of Gian Lorenzo Bernini, best known as the creator of St Peter's Square, but whose work and style dictated the overall look of Rome today.

The Piazza del Popolo is the happiest example of later eighteenth-century neo-Classicism in Rome, meant to stun travellers then arriving from the north.

Imagine what it must have been like: in 1870, when Rome became the capital of the newly unified Italy, only 200,000 fortunates lived in the city.

Rome today

Old Rome still glimmers through, but if its present crisis continues it is doomed to dim. Rome today lives permanently on the brink of collapse. A city meant for a few is now a metropolis of nearly three million, most of them unhappy with where and how they live. The visibly main problem is the traffic, and the wild parking that impedes its flow. The cause is the absence of car parks and the absence of alternative public transport, wholly due to a town hall that can only defer deci-

219

sions eternally because the quarrelling parties, as in the rest of Italy, can never agree on the need to decide to decide. Access to the city centre is, in theory, limited to permit-holders, but this has starved shops of customers and worsened the chaos beyond the centre. To lessen congestion, a project called *Roma Capitale* wants government ministries transplanted to a disused airfield on the eastern outskirts. Ministerial enthusiasm is not catching.

Far worse a problem is the concrete jungle outside the Aurelian Walls which mocks the pride of the Italians in their taste. These vast post-war slums were erected with political connivance; it is an imposed wilderness, first denounced by the murdered film director and poet Pier Paolo Pasolini.

In 1989, to the face of Rome's mayor, an angry Pope John Paul II decried Rome as a two-tone, schizophrenic city: 'Side by side with immense treasures', he scolded, 'there are corners of the Third World.' For the same reason, some indignant foreigners dub Rome 'Cairo North'.

Three tips

● Visitors worry about crossing roads. Cross by zebras, and walk deliberately looking at the windscreens. *It is risky to run*: they won't stop if they can help it, and will swerve around you, but it does work.

● Beware of child bag-snatchers near the Forums and in Trastevere. They are identifiable by bits of cardboard they use to hide their hand movements.

● To fool bag-snatchers, carry bags and cameras etc. in plastic carrier bags.

The Romans

Real Romans, those who have lived in Rome for generations, are today very few, yet the false majority somehow manage to live up to the reputation of the ancient populace with uncanny flare. Today's Romans are mainly immigrants who flocked into the capital after the Second World War, chiefly from the impoverished south. By second nature, they soon picked up all the attributes of the old fickle and demanding population of Imperial Rome, who were used to being spoilt with free grain from Egypt and lavish entertainment at the Colosseum or the Circo Massimo.

The Florentines and Milanese write off Romans as indolent – expert only at going to great lengths to go nowhere, or to get somebody else to go there. The Roman dialect, *Romanesco*, is quickly ceding ground to television Italian, but the refrain of a dialect ditty is an open confession: 'We like to eat and drink/Of work we care not to think!'

Like their forerunners, Romans greatly enjoy company and lifting the elbow around groaning tables, preferably in the presence of *Mamma*, their Queen. Cheerfulness sets them apart from Italians further north; you'll often hear them joking or quipping and, up to a decade ago, in the more popular quarters you would have caught renderings of love songs or opera. Like Caesar's Romans they tend not to be over-extended. Inside the walls, Rome remains an unproductive place. Many citizens are still happily parasitical, living off a lax State. It is a city of civil servants, State employees, clerks and clerics – with not a hammer or a spade in sight.

For today's Romans, doubtless yesterday's too, the art of living consists of being *dritto*. Untranslatable, that means gain for nothing, the trick of having the better of things or getting out of them, an eye for milking the less gifted. 'When the fools sleep/The *dritti* don't eat,' goes the Roman proverb. That's in the old tradition, of course: from the early Middle Ages Romans lived off fleecing pilgrims, above all during the popular Holy Years. In a way, they are still at it, though their luckless victims nowadays tend to be fellow-Romans.

Treatment of foreigners

No city in the west has been more trampled upon by foreigners, in the guise of penitents in sandals, warriors with swords, or tourists with maps. One consequence is that the Romans have, or soon acquire, a philosophical, weary attitude to life; overburdened with experience and a collective memory of horrors seen, they are resigned to the lot. 'Nothing surprises!' they sigh, and the most typical Roman gesture features eyes rolled up to heaven, shoulders in a shrug, palms face upwards and cherry-spitting lips exclaiming, 'Boh!'

But they have a special relationship with foreigners which, on the whole, stands you, the traveller, in good stead. With 2,000 years of outsiders behind them, Romans will find neither you nor your behaviour an exception, and they will leave you alone. Certainly they will treat you as green cousins in the former capital of the world for the first time, but since you have shown the wisdom of paying it homage, and because you are often their livelihood, they will reward you with a display of skill at respect and service, acquired through centuries of apprenticeship in the art of pleasing for survival. They see you as an asset to be cossetted, and fleeced only in the most felted possible way.

Habits

Tuscans cruelly put down this willingness to serve to an inherited 'slave mentality' among Romans. Some doubtless do descend from imported slaves, but the faces of Romans are many, mirrors of an Empire that was history's first multi-racial society. All are quietly proud of being Romans and secretly in love with the place. The young dream of getting away because it's dull. But then they return and join in with the old *'Ma Roma! Quanto sei bella!'* The real Romans are grandly proud of their background, and make their superiority over the recent interlopers very clear.

But the past equalises everybody in the end; it is part of everyday life. A tube station is called Kings of Rome, a residential area Nero's Tomb, a street the Alley of Divine Love. They still baptise their sons Caesar or Pompey, and the Records Office is next to a Roman theatre.

New Romans are as litigious as the old: watch them after a car accident. They insist on rights and are volubly touchy if those are infringed; they can be the same sticklers for form as their predecessors were over pagan ritual; etiquette is strict; they tend to the formal.

Because the ancients refused to budge from where they lived one Emperor resorted to town-planning by fire. Nothing has changed. Everybody calls Rome a village; in fact, it's many. If they can, Romans stick to their self-sufficient districts or *rioni*, and often avoid the centre. The favourite meeting-place of older men is the barber's, just as it was under the Empire.

Today, many Romans live beyond the Aurelian Walls in the squalid tenements they bitterly call *casermoli*, 'bumper barracks'. You can see examples of this runaway post-war speculation from the Roma-L'Aquila motorway. The only escape-valve for the young trapped there is a massive invasion of Rome on Saturday nights.

The Church

Romans judge the Papacy on merit; they have been too close to it for too long to accord it automatic respect. They know too many stories; they smell scandal at once; and they believe, rightly or wrongly, that their opinion can still help or harm a Pope, as in the past it made or broke him. They are possessive over the Roman Pontiff; they miss the veto right they once had. Faced by the Roman mob and the big warring Roman families, the Orsini or the Colonna for instance, Popes once trembled. After street violence in 897, Pope Stephen VI was dragged through the alleys to jail and strangled. A century later, the populace mutilated the murdered body of Pope John XIV and flung it in a common grave.

They rarely venerated St Peter's successor with pilgrim fervour; Rome was the only major city of Christendom that forgot to take part in the Crusades. Familiarity braked and still brakes ardour. Today in Rome, the churches number 610, priests 5,000 and nuns 20,000. Parents forget to baptise some 20 per cent of babies; 40 per cent of the baptised drop out before confirmation; and 75 per cent boycott Mass on Sundays.

What to see

The places to see are set out here by area, not by era. This makes for convenience, of course, but does involve some violent to- and froing across the time-zones. We begin with Rome's landmark and then backtrack to the centre.

Colosseum

The Colosseum is the biggest monument to Imperial Rome in existence. Its girth measured almost a third of a mile; it could seat 45,000 excited spectators, with standing room for 10,000 more. It was the most challenging engineering feat the Romans ever tackled. It was, and is, a symbol of might. It is also a sizeable piece of evidence as to the power of the troublesome Roman people, and the huge importance attached to keeping them happy.

The Emperor Vespasian who started it in AD 72 in fact had a reputation for penny-pinching. Earlier, he had made a name for himself by falling asleep while Nero was singing in Greece. He deliberately sited his theatre over an artificial lake at the bottom of Nero's garden, belonging to the sprawling *Domus Aurea*, 'Golden House', Nero had built for himself after 'his' Fire in 64. Vespasian's idea, it is now thought, was to liquidate Nero's image, and thus win acclaim for his demolition. It was the first theatre in Rome all in stone, three tiered colonnades of arches completed by a windowed wall. Inaugurated only eight years after the work was begun by Vespasian's son Titus, it was known as the Flavian Amphitheatre, after the name of their dynasty. The title 'Colosseum' first cropped up only in the Middle Ages.

The opening launched a hundred days of celebration, during which professional 'hunters' slew 5,000 animals, including elephants, tigers, giraffes, hyaenas, hippopotami and deer. Tamer numbers were crocodile races with young boys as jockeys. Later, sentenced criminals were put in among the animals, but under exactly what terms Christians were included is still debated.

Emperors entered the Colosseum through the north entrance and sat near today's wooden cross, out of the glare of the sun. The rest were seated by class; women were kept segregated in the 'gods'. Scholars argue over whether the shows were free for everybody. Virtual 'season tickets' did exist, in the shape of metal tokens – many have been found showing the number of one of the seventy-six entrances.

Below the rim of the intact outer shell, you will see a row of small buttresses. These were 'shoes' for poles supporting cables that could quickly haul an enormous slatted awning over sections of the audience, to spare them sun or storm. Sailors worked the rigging, and the stone bases for their winches are now in the dungeons.

The maze beneath the oval 79-metre long arena was a pen for the beasts. You can make out their cages, as well as thirty-two vaulted openings in the surrounding wall: these were shafts for lifts which suddenly sprang the confused animals before the public. By then, the scenic department, in the central rectangle of the maze, would have hoisted up their props – hills, boulders and trees – to set the stage for the bloody 'hunt' about to begin.

To celebrate the thousandth anniversary of the founding of Rome in AD 249, a thousand pairs of gladiators fought it out. If, starting from the main west entrance, you walk around the arena to the right, you will soon be peering down into the sinister passageway now unearthed that linked the killing zone to a gladiators' school across today's road. Many, of course, did not return, but the 'free' gladiators (as opposed to the conscripted slaves) were in it for the glory: some were like soccer stars, commanding outrageous fees. The fights were stopped only in AD 409, when a monk who dashed into the arena to stop a contest was torn to pieces by the mob.

From the outside, the Colosseum appears to have been machinegunned: the holes once housed invisible bronze pins which held the theatre's marble cloak in place. This was stripped off by Popes and princes from the Middle Ages onwards – St Peter's and Piazza Venezia were among the results. It also suffered from four earthquakes, and by the nineteenth century it had become a filled-in wilderness, celebrated for its plant varieties. It was scooped out only after Italian Unification.

Arch of Constantine

Hard by the Colosseum is the biggest and best preserved of all Roman arches. It was erected in AD 315 to commemorate the first Christian Emperor's victory over his predecessor at the Milvan Bridge, near today's Olympic Stadium. A former military commander in York, Constantine claimed to have seen a cross of light before the battle. Retrospectively, the fight was taken as the first step towards the Christianisation of the Empire, although Constantine himself was baptised only when close to death.

Despite the scope of his victory, his Arch was done on the cheap. Most of the statuary was 'borrowed' from existing monuments, including the eight dignified 'Barbarians' around the top. One of the few custom-made reliefs, over the small left-hand arch facing the Colosseum, shows the triumphant Emperor addressing the people. Art historians choose it to demonstrate that by the fourth century Roman art was decaying. Constantine was apparently quick-tempered, but obviously a diplomat, too. The Latin inscription ascribes his victory to 'divine help and intelligence': the Christians' protector was in no hurry to commit himself.

Gladiators' Barracks

Now to the right of the Colosseum and across the road towards the bars, you will find sunken remains of the barracks, called the *Ludus Magnus* at the start of Via San Giovanni in Laterano. The biggest in Rome, they rose to three storeys around a big inner courtyard. In the centre, as you can infer, they worked out in a small training ring.

Golden House

Under the hillocky gardens and umbrella pines opposite, across the Via Labicana, lie the buried halls, corridors and painted rooms of Nero's extravagant house, surrounded by gardens that extended almost to today's station. For many Renaissance artists, including Raphael, their decoration was a revelation that inspired a new style, called 'grotesque' because it derived from Nero's 'grottos' (now unfortunately closed).

It would now right the balance to enter the world of the early Christians.

San Clemente

Two hundred and fifty paces further along Via Labicana is the basilica named after the fourth Pope, and now run by helpful Irish Dominicans (booklets are on sale). It is one of the most dramatic examples in Rome of time in layers.

San Clemente consists of a surface church atop an underground one, beneath which there is a 'cave' dedicated to the pagan god Mithras, the whole structure built on rubble used to fill in the Rome gutted in Nero's fire. You can climb down to the cool penumbra of the third level, which remained buried and unknown for seven centuries until its discovery by an Irish father.

The interior of the twelfth-century upper church is in itself among the most intact in the city, singular because of the marble-walled choir precinct in the centre of the nave. From the commanding medieval pulpit, the officiating priest would unroll a long scroll of pictures to ensure the congregation vision as well as a voice.

The marble and granite columns are imports from Imperial Rome, but the climax to the church is *The Triumph of the Cross*, the glittering mosaic on a gold background in the apse. The Cross is shown as the Tree of Life, and its harmony of colour and composition have led it to be judged a *chef d'œuvre* of a 'Roman school' in the late twelfth century.

From the sacristy, steep steps lead down to the murky lower church, built in the fourth century above the first floor of a first-century *palazzo*. Bright, fading frescoes painted in the ninth and eleventh centuries puncture the gloom, three of them about St Clement, a first-century Pope who may have been a freed slave banished to the Crimea and executed by being drowned at sea because of his many converts. The waters parted and two Slav saints brought his body back to Rome. One of them, St Cyril – inventor of the cyrillic alphabet – is believed to be buried in the left aisle.

Against the sound of rushing water, descend deeper to find a tunnel-shaped chamber with stone benches along the sides. This is the required make-believe 'grotto' in which worshippers of the eastern god Mithras, in the block of apartments next door to the *palazzo*, had ritual dinners to commemorate a victory banquet shared by their own god and Apollo. The victory was the slaying by Mithras of a bull – which is the remarkably clear scene on the hewn chunk of altar picked out by the spotlight. The victor, conceived from rock, then ascended to an after-life. Mithraism was banned in AD 395, as a possible threat to Christianity. The present underground church was destroyed by the same Norman hordes who razed the Coelian Hill to the ground in the eleventh century and then, like Nero's work of destruction, it was filled in and forgotten.

San Pietro in Vincoli

Not far away is one of the great masterpieces of Michelangelo. Turn back towards the Colosseum for the climbing Via Nicola Salvi on the right, and follow the yellow signs for the Basilica of St Peter in Chains. The testy sculptor's *Moses* is behind the scaffolding in the right-hand corner, doubtless glaring at a chattering busload on a culture stop. *Moses* was one of the very few sculptures Michelangelo ever finished. Usually, explained his admiring biographer, he was dissatisfied with his efforts, but in *Moses* he saw the very work of God, who through the sculptor prepared the body of the prophet for resurrection.

The prophet is shown as majestic and dignified, yet full of wrath, scorn and sadness, having just descended from Mount Sinai tightly clasping the Ten Commandments to find the Israelites still bent on idolatry and worshipping the Golden Calf. This is the work of a man of about 40, already embittered himself, and no other figure better conveys what the Italians call Michelangelo's 'terribility' – the almost awesome force of his super-beings, driven by violent emotion and grand visions.

Grasping his long, biblical beard, his fierce stare fixed upon the wrong-doers, Moses' muscles, veins and tendons seem to bulge with an anger almost real. Only in a few cases did Michelangelo lavish such care on 'finish', and it says something of his indifference to things that in a country like Italy he could equip the great man with a pair of horns, instead of having him struck by two beams of light, as was more usual. But once horns symbolised divinity. At one point, Michelangelo is alleged to have hurled his chisel at the statue, shouting out, 'Speak!'

Why is this renowned work hidden in an almost hidden church? Originally, *Moses* was destined for the centre of St Peter's, as part of a colossal forty-statue tomb for Pope Julius II, commissioned from Michelangelo by the Pontiff himself. For many reasons, it was never finished. The so-called 'tragedy of the tomb' dragged on for forty years, and what you see in this small basilica is all that became of the grand scheme.

The two figures on either side of Moses, enraptured Rachel on the left and Leah, are by the master himself, but the other eight figures were farmed out, including the proud, good Julius himself, who is the effete weed slumped on the couch above Moses. The work had been stored in Michelangelo's Rome workshop for a full twenty years when one day a new Pope, Paul III, called upon him with a stool of cardinals, anxious for his services. When he saw *Moses*, this powerful, choleric character exclaimed, 'That's enough for one Pope!' Whereupon he had the heirs of Julius settle for what you see. He gave Michelangelo other commissions, including the *Last Judgement* in the Sistine Chapel and the re-modelling of St Peter's. Why *this* basilica? Because, before becoming Pope, Julius had been its titular pastor.

The first basilica, built in the fifth century, was paid for by a Western emperor's wife as a shrine for chains alleged to have been borne by St Peter during his captivity in Jerusalem. She had come into them through her mother, wife of the Eastern Emperor Theodosius. Miraculously, they joined the chains used on the saint in Rome, and the amalgamation is what is displayed in the case.

The Forums

In an incredibly brief space, the Forums and the Palatine Hill sum up the rise, fall and neglect of ancient Rome, and wandering among these sad remnants of glory can be overwhelming – as well as confusing. They need a whole morning and one evening at least. At the end of it, the present returns rather slowly.

With your back to the Colosseum, the initial 'Roman' Forum is on your left, while the later 'Imperial' Forums are on the other side of Mussolini's freeway behind the greenery. But in Roman times the Forum area was all one. The Via dei Fori Imperiali swept away a medieval and a sixteenth-century quarter, but the archaeologists say that the rest of the Imperial Forums beneath it are intact; modest new digs to make sure began in 1988.

Major excavation of the Forums began only a century ago; until then, buried by time, the whole area was known as the Cow Field and used for grazing. During the Renaissance, as the Popes re-did the face of Rome, it served as a huge marble quarry. Earlier, the big families had grafted fortresses on to the ruins; churchmen made them into churches.

Roman
Forum

From the entrance in Via dei Fori Imperiali, the Forum may strike you as impossibly cluttered, an odd kind of city centre, an archaeologist's fantasy. Surprise is justified. In its heyday, when it was the religious and political centre of Rome, a complex of temples and lawcourts dominated by the Senate, the Forum was far smaller, less crowded. That was under the Republic. When the Emperors took over, the judiciary and the administration moved into *their* forums, and they turned the Roman Forum into a monument centre, constantly adding to the original nucleus. These commemorative accretions went on for six centuries. The last monument was squeezed in as late as AD 608.

Rome's initial political centre was to the extreme right of the entrance, in the shadow of the **Triumphal Arch** of Septimus Severus (AD 193–211), put up to hail the Emperor's victories over the Parthians. His prisoners support the four columns, and the Arch owes its good shape to having been cocooned by a medieval building. This is the most copied model of triumphal arches – versions are scattered all around the world.

In the small open space front of the Arch was the **Comitium**, where delegates from the city's thirty *curiæ* met to debate bills. There is little left of the small circular structure, but nearby under a cover, sheltering steps, is the oldest and once most sacred point of the Forum, the so-called **Niger Lapis**, the Black Stone. The stone covers remains, and includes an altar bearing the first Latin inscription known, possibly scratched out in the sixth century BC. Some scholars claim this is no less than the tomb of Romulus, co-founder of Rome.

The incongruously preserved tool-shed shape looking down on the Stone is the **Curia**, where the Senate used to meet – a single great hall with a floor inlaid with multi-coloured marble, closed to the public. This owed its survival to its conversion into a church. Founded in 80 BC and often revamped, the present version was ordered by the Emperor Diocletian in the third century AD. On the day of the murder of Julius Caesar, an earlier Senate building was under repair after a fire, which is why he was killed in an alternative venue – a temple attached to the Theatre of Pompey, in today's Campo de' Fiori.

It was Caesar who began to re-model the Republican Forum, and his doing is the 'new' curving **Rostrum**, from which the orators addressed the populace, immediately to the left of the Arch of Severus.

One was Mark Antony; and it was from here that he delivered his famous speech after the assassination.

The old Forum proper of Republican Rome was the oblong of rather forlorn emptiness right in front of the Rostrum, flanked on the right by stumpy pillars. This was the *piazza*, where Romans met to deal, gossip and execute the equivalent of the *passeggiata*. Under the Republic, it was also where judges meted out sentences in public, where the news was read out, and religious rites observed.

To be chronological, immediately beyond it is where they cremated Caesar – the stone blocks, in a recess let into low brown remains on two steps, were an altar to him. His will had been read out: he had left all his possessions to the Roman people and they were incensed at the assassins. Rich women flung their jewellery into the flames to honour him. The assassins fled . . . This is the **Tempio del Divo Giulio**, a temple dedicated to the first Roman to be proclaimed a god.

The three magnificent corinthian columns soaring over the ruins on your right, for long a favourite symbol of the Forum, belonged to the **Temple of Castor and Pollux**, two legendary brothers who helped the Romans win a decisive battle over the Latins and the Etruscans in 496 BC, and who then sped into Rome on white horses to bring the tidings of victory. You will next meet them dominating the steps to the Capitol.

Roughly between these last two temples is the small circular **Temple of Vesta**, Goddess of the Hearth, where white-robed Vestal Virgins tended the Sacred Flame, symbol of Rome's eternity. Chosen by the High Priest from among the patrician families of Rome when they were between 6 and 10 years old, they numbered six and were bound by a vow to remain chaste for thirty years. The punishment for transgression was burial alive; the guilty man was whipped to death.

The Vestal Virgins were lodged in great style, as you can gather from the large courtyard of their two-storey residence hard by. Here, around the three pools, perhaps amid flowers and roses, they spent their days. The rooms you see were perhaps store-rooms and kitchens; their rooms would have been on the first floor. The statues in the garden honour Virgins who had put in distinguished service, but probably include the shamed Claudia, who turned Christian. Their residence marks the boundary of the original Forum.

The Virgins were disbanded only in AD 394 by the fair-haired Christian Emperor Theodosius I: they had kept the flame alight for a thousand years.

You should backtrack now to the remains of the once grandiose **Basilica Emilia**, the scene of devastation immediately to the right of the entrance. First built in 179 BC, this was to typify the Roman basilicas – great, cool barns of places with three 100-metre-long naves held up by granite pillars marching abreast. This particular one was devoted to business. Money-changers occupied the front colonnade, and what brings it all back are the brownish stains you will see here and there on the floor. Rome's top archaeologist has confirmed that they are copper coins, fused into the marble by the intense heat when barbaric Goths under Alaric set the Basilica on fire during their sack of Rome in AD 410.

The last basilica to be raised in the Forum was the huge brick hulk glowering over Mussolini's road, built in memory of a son who died in infancy in AD 308 by the Emperor Maxentius, slain in the Milvan Bridge battle. What remains is just one of its three naves; it housed law courts.

The exit from the Forum, at the top of the Sacred Way, is the **Arch of Tito**, built to celebrate the capture of Jerusalem by Titus in AD 80. On the inside, a relief shows loot being carted off after the destruction of the Temple, including a candlestick. This became a medieval family fortress, hence its health.

The excavations just behind you mark the spot where a professor from Pisa University identified the boundary wall.

Palatine Hill

The climb to your right leads up to the Palatine. If the Forum conjures up something of Republican Rome, the Palatine is where to mull over the fate of Imperial Rome. The city's oldest hill, only 50 metres high, was the hub of the Empire. It is more bewildering than the Forum – one colossal palace, a word itself derived from the name of the hill, *Palatium*. Its complications nag the scholars still and, frankly, it is pointless to try and make sense of it: there is no need. The spectacle has fascinated painters unversed in history for centuries; the grand scale of it all still overawes, and the associations tumble in.

Romulus was not the first to take possession, as Iron Age huts unearthed prove. Under the Republic, the Hill was the chic part of town, and Cicero was among the prominent men who moved in. It was where Augustus was born and he continued to live in a villa he bought on the Hill after he became Emperor. The ruins on view today were produced by his successors.

The winding path to the right of the climb, if you keep left, will get you to the **House of Livia**, the strong-willed wife of Augustus; some maintain the Emperor himself also lived here. It is a must, chiefly for its delightful frescoes, but also as an insight into how a pre-Christian aristocratic family lived.

After Augustus, Emperors erected 'palaces' more fitting to their station and that of Rome. The first was Tiberius, but the frame of the Imperial Palace proper, later added to, was laid out by Domitian in the first century.

About 60 metres from Livia's house you will stumble upon a spacious peristyle, or garden courtyard: this is the middle of the official palace, known as the **Flavian Palace**. The surrounding halls included the audience chamber and, towards the brow of the Hill, the massive banqueting hall.

Two more peristyles close by amid the jungle of masonry signify the private residence of the emperors, called the **Dwelling of the August**. Further over still is the **Palatine Stadium**: whether it was private or sometimes thrown open to the *plebs* is not known.

Beyond the Stadium, make for the **Belvedere Terrace**, built by Septimus Severus (193–211) over enormous, plunging, supporting arches. Overlooking the Circo Massimo, it commands a stupendous view.

If it feels all jumble, try to see it illuminated at night from the rising road opposite. Then it makes matchless sense.

Imperial Forums

The Imperial Forums as seen today expose only a fraction of the majestic, vast, original layout. They convey hardly any idea of their former splendour, so they provide the main battleground for an endless fight between those who want to turn Rome into a great open-air museum and those who argue for the needs of a modern city. The Communists belong to the former party; the ancient Romans themselves would certainly have sided with the latter. They built the new Forums – all within a century – precisely to accommodate the expanding business of Empire which the old Forum, hemmed in by crowded housing, could no longer handle. They knocked down the housing to make way for their plans, just as another dictator in the twentieth century did. The only difference, of course, was that his was a dream of grandeur, and theirs was a fact. The new Forums were meant as a dazzling, overpowering display reflecting the Empire at the apex of its power.

It was also Roman artistry at its best – an ensemble of squares, colonnades, basilicas and graceful temples, intended for the administration of justice, ceremonial occasions, public assemblies and business. The immense project was begun by Julius Caesar. Its fate is to be seen along Via Alessandrina where gypsy child pickpockets lie in wait for you.

The most completely uncovered fraction is the **Forum of Augustus**, near the start of the street. It was constructed in a spirit of vengeance, to celebrate the killing of the assassins Brutus and Cassius in the battle of Philippi in AD 42. The steep flight of marble steps leads up to the podium of the Temple of Mars Ultor, Mars the Avenger. It served as an Imperial shrine and housed precious relics, including the sword of Julius Caesar. On either side are clear traces of two basilicas with giant lateral apses. In the niches stood Augustus's selection of Great Romans, wisely including his army commanders.

To the right of his Forum are the scanty remains of a **Temple of Minerva**, which stood at the head of the adjacent **Forum of the Emperor Nerva**, once stretching across the road to the edge of the Roman Forum. The temple was demolished by a seventeenth-century Pope to build a fountain. Note the delicacy of the freshly cleaned scenes over the two odd columns in the near corner. They show a regal

Minerva presiding over women going about their household chores, which was her role. As for the columns, they are a visual trick meant to suggest a gate and so widen this narrow forum.

Trajan's Forum is harder to visualise, though it was by far the largest and most impressive. It was a huge rectangle stretching from the twin churches at the end of the street down to the wall of the Forum of Augustus, which was much longer than they now let on.

The massive, treble-tiered semi-circle you next come to, **Trajan's Markets**, overlooked a side of the immense oblong. Few seem to know that these incredibly well preserved Roman shops are open to the public. The way in – straight on for the moment – takes you past a restaurant named after the Emperor's sister and the once huge **Basilica Ulpia** which completely transversed the Forum. The two rows of sunken pillars over the road are all that is left.

After years of restoration, **Trajan's Column**, on the other hand, is almost just as it was, and among the finest examples of classical art to survive. Originally coloured, its spiralling scenes feature some 2,500 figures, sculpted with an astonishing lightness of touch by an unknown artist. They illustrate Trajan's expeditions to subdue Romania, ancient Rome's last major conquest, at the start of the second century. It is a comment on how dark the Dark Ages were that after the Empire's fall it was to take more than 500 years for such art to re-emerge.

If you climb the steps in Via Magnanapoli, you will hit upon the back door to the Markets on the right. Little of Roman Rome is so enormously intact, including the street, *Via Biberatica*, encircling the 150 shops, but surprisingly they are no big draw. Perhaps they are *too* intact: perhaps the imagination has to have ruins.

The vaulted entrance hall with six shops or offices on either side was unique in the second century. Experts suppose it was a bazaar or a kind of stock exchange. In some of the shops in the first circle are central gutters, to drain off splashings from poured wine or oil; their absence elsewhere suggests that a wide variety of different goods was sold. Trajan's Markets were obviously the first Harrods. But the curving open space in front of the markets was no pedestrian mall; except for Via Biberatica, it was an apse on the flank of the Forum.

Capitol or Campidoglio

Hidden behind the Victor Emanuel Monument in Piazza Venezia, you will find the heart of Rome. It seems superbly fitting that the spiritual centre of ancient Rome should have been passed on to posterity by the greatest artist the city has ever known. Michelangelo's graceful and grandiose **staircase** leads up to the most perfect square in Rome, and the first planned one since Imperial times. It is Capitol Square, or Piazza del Campidoglio.

Its patterned symmetry is almost unreal in the city of jumble, its silence quite unreal. The two flanking *palazzi*, identical in each detail and now museums, were also designed by the master, as well as the façade of the main one, the so-called **Senator's Palace**. See the square from the balcony. The regal staircase and the pedestal in the raised centre of the circular basin is all Michelangelo lived to see finished. For four centuries, until 1981, it bore the magnificent gilded statue of bearded Marcus Aurelius on horseback, one of the most famous bronzes of classical times. Then he was dismounted and the steed led away for restoration, but the experts warn that they can stand the Roman air no longer. If they were put back, it would kill them.

Michelangelo sketched out the square to honour a man who had done more to dishonour Rome than any other. He worked under the orders of a Pope who wanted a suitable setting in which to greet the Holy Roman Emperor Charles V, whose wild soldiery had subjected the city to the most brutal sack in its history in 1527. It was not ready on time.

But the Florentine's façade *is* a front, a thin cover-up for the medieval mass behind it which was intended as a new senate by Romans who rebelled against Papal rule in the twelfth century and set up a new Roman Republic, in tune with other Italian cities. The hero of the moment was Cola di Rienzo, a self-styled 'Tribune' with somewhat crazed notions of grandeur, who canvassed the dream of a new Rome as capital of all Italy, 600 years before it happened.

Finally, the Roman mob turned on him. His statue is down on the left of the staircase. Other Italian cities grabbed independence, but the Papacy obviously could not brook any such challenge in Rome itself. After much haggling, the senate was whittled down to one Papal appointee – which is why the apostrophe in Senator's Palace is where it is.

If you go down to the right of it, you begin another wrenching time trip. Looking up at its walls, you have left the Renaissance for the rough Middle Ages – there are few medieval vestiges in central Rome – and if you mount the six steps at number 3 Via del Campidoglio and peer in, you will make out a plaque reading *'Tabularium'*. You are looking into what was the Public Records Office of Imperial Rome. In medieval times, they used it as a salt depot and a prison.

To travel further back in time, turn right into the Via del Monte Tarpeo and climb up Via del Tempio di Giove. On the left, embedded into the modern wall, is blackish rubble belonging to the foundations of the **Temple of Jupiter**, the most venerated, sacred site in Rome and the spiritual centre of the entire Empire. The first such temple, in more or less the same place, is attributed to Tarquinius, allegedly the first Etruscan king of Rome, in the sixth century BC.

As you will realise, the Campidoglio, as the entire Town Hall summit is called today, is in fact not one hill but two. The traces of Jupiter's Temple are on the original Capitol Hill. On the next-door hill, now dominated by the church of Aracoeli, the Romans had their mint.

The Senator's Palace was in a dip between the two.

Down behind it to the left is a shattering view over the Forum, the most moving scrapyard anywhere. At night, the masterful illumination almost brings back the crack of whips and the rumble of chariot wheels as a Triumphal Procession slowly makes its way up to the holy temple.

As for the museums, entered with a single ticket, they can be skipped if time is short, but the Capitoline Museum on the left has something unique: an Imperial snapshot album. Its lined-up busts of sixty-five emperors, including Nero, and some of their wives, are startlingly realistic. In the courtyard opposite, next to the chicest registry office in Rome, lies the head of a colossal statue of the Emperor Constantine, once in the Forum; assorted parts of his anatomy accompany it. The museum possesses the charming, famous, first-century BC bronze statue of *The Boy with a Thorn in his Foot*, thought to be the legendary young Messenger of the Romans, who bravely went on running despite his impediment.

Church of Aracoeli

This is at the top of the 122 steep fourteenth-century steps competing with Michelangelo's right next to them, but there is an easier side-entrance behind the museum which takes you into one of the oldest, most typical, legendary and loved churches in Rome. It is typical because of the fusion of eras. Dedicated to the Virgin, it stands on the same site as a temple devoted to the pagan goddess Juno Moneta, after whom the nearby mint was named, and hence the word 'money'. Its twenty-two pillars are all pillaged from the ruins of the Empire. The church is legendary since this is held to be the spot where the Emperor Augustus raised an altar, after being told by a summoned sibyl of the coming of Christ. The church's name means Altar of Heaven.

Franciscans gave it its present Romanesque appearance in the fourteenth century when Rome's elders all but turned it into another forum, meeting inside to decide on public issues. Today, ordinary Romans worship the church as the home of the hugely popular and deeply venerated Santo Bambino, a fifteenth-century wooden figure in a side chapel smothered with jewels. They are offerings from people confident of special favours from the Bambino in return for a sacrifice. He is also known to have miraculous healing powers and, until recently, used to be rushed off to desperate sick-beds by taxi. People in need write to him from throughout the world; you can see the letters.

The church's other prize is the chapel frescoed with sharply observed scenes from the life of San Bernardino of Siena by that enjoyable Umbrian painter, Bernardino Pinturicchio, here at his very best.

Palazzo Doria-Pamphili

One drawback of Rome is the inaccessibility of the enormous Renaissance *palazzi* that, psychologically anyway, seem to dominate the centre – hulking, near-blackened affairs with inner courtyards and watchful caretakers (*portieri*) in pressed uniforms. The short-cut to this world is the picture gallery and apartments inside the Palazzo Doria-Pamphili.

The obscure entrance is in a corner (number 1a, marked NBC) of Piazza Collegio Romano, 200 metres up the Corso, reached via a stubby alley on the left, Via Lata. In it, on the right, you can slake your thirst at the most jovial small fountain in Rome – a man holding a leaking barrel. He actually existed, as a real porter in the fifteenth century, and your author knows from observation that he is the most drunk-en man in Rome.

The Palazzo (open Sundays, Tuesdays, Fridays and Saturdays) was first built by a cardinal for himself in the late fifteenth century, before passing through the hands of four powerful families. The fourth still lives there, letting out the hundreds of rooms at fair rents, and the gallery, a quadrangle of sumptuous corridors overlooking two courtyards, gives an exact idea of the rational splendour of the late Renaissance. The Italian highlights of this 'family' collection are three Caravaggios, including the very early work, *Magdalene*, a cameo of despair and abdication.

Column of Marcus Aurelius The column rising up from Piazza Colonna, a few metres further up the Corso, is a horror-comic; I saw it in close-up during restoration. It is entwined by a strip cartoon 200 metres long in twenty-one spirals – a report in marble on laborious victories won by the philosopher-Emperor Marcus Aurelius over tough Germanic tribes in the Danube frontier zones from about AD 170 onwards.

Although the Emperor found time to pen high-minded reflections on life in Greek, he spent most of his 14-year reign commanding the Danube fighting in person, so he must have seen some of the 'atrocities' the Column celebrates. It dwells particularly on the execution of prisoners-of-war, one scene showing them bound hand and foot being clubbed to death. In another, troops in plumed helmets charging into a mass of prostrate barbarians skewer them with spears . . .

The Column is also a documentary on contemporary dress and military techniques. Pontoon bridges, for instance, were already common. Officers wore daggers in their belts, as today's carry pistols. There are dignified senators in togas or on horseback.

The Emperor himself once chaired the Column, until he was replaced by a bronze St Paul in the sixteenth century.

Trevi Fountain The Fontana di Trevi is the essence of central Rome – its sense of surprise. It is a surprise no matter how often you stumble upon it, which is what you virtually do. The most famous fountain in Italy, the star of a Hollywood smash hit, it is tucked away in an unlikely pocket-handkerchief square off the Corso, at the abrupt end of Via Sabini.

That was precisely the idea, of course: to astonish through disproportion. Were it in a bigger square, the theatricality would be gone. Instead, brazenly out of place, people stare and stare at the extravagance and smile at the cheek of it, and try to fathom the gushing vitality of it all.

At the centre is a triumphal arch called the Kingdom of Ocean; mighty Ocean himself has just passed under it in a shell-carriage drawn by two sea-horses, the left one wild and the other placid, representing states of the sea. They are being led towards a perilous reef by two Tritons, half-men, half-fish.

The fountain is not old. The designer was a certain Nicola Salvi, winner of a competition set by a Pope, but it was finished only in 1762, after Salvi's death. The origin of the site *is* old: the upper bas-reliefs on either side of the arch laconically explain it. On the left is the Consul Agrippa who, in the year 19 BC, had a 20-km aqueduct built to feed a bath-house complex on the same spot as the fountain. The right one has a young girl showing parched Roman soldiers back from battle the spring that was to feed the aqueduct. Its water was named after her the Virgin Water, preferred by Romans above all their other choices. Fourteen aqueducts served Imperial Rome; three are still in use.

It was once said that those who drank the Trevi's water would return to Rome. When the custom started of throwing coins into it to induce the same consequence has always baffled the pundits.

Piazza di
Spagna

This ravishing piazza is and always has been the very heart of the Rome of 'foreigners'. It is the visitors' forum, their point of reference. Tourists feel strangely at home here at last, as if the superbly romantic setting spoke a familiar language. For young Italians, it is the only setting for long spells of looking and smiling at these strange foreigners, just as it was a century ago when young country lads would pose on the steps in the hope of being chosen as models by transient weekend painters. Only the coldest days in winter clear its travertine balconies. Usually cosmopolitan youth packs them, except in May when the steps are decked out as dazzling cascades of azaleas.

The Spanish Steps must be the most sat-upon steps in the world, as well as composing the world's most famous, and mis-named, outside staircase. The 138 steps and the square became 'Spanish' merely because the Spanish Embassy to the Holy See happened to be there. The steps were first planned and partly paid for by the French, as a fitting approach to the French community's church at the top, **Trinità dei Monti**, ordered by a French king in 1502.

The stairway was designed by an Italian with the approval of an Italian Pope and built in the early eighteenth century. The three sweeping flights of steps correspond to the dedication of the Gallic church. From the curving top balustrade, you can gaze out over much of Rome and, at the bottom, contemplate the ingenuity of the so-called Rotten Boat, sinking in its own basin, leaking from bow and stern. The idea turned to good account the low water pressure in the Virgin Water pipeline, which would never have raised a more traditional fountain. It is not sure whether the great Bernini himself or his father hit on the ploy, thought to be based on some memory that in ancient Rome they played at naval battles on the spot.

The Piazza di Spagna was one of the highlights of the Grand Tour. Poets and artists of Europe thronged the quarter, including Keats who died in digs half-way up the steps on the right, occupied now by the fascinating **Keats-Shelley Memorial**. Keats is buried in the Protestant Cemetery.

The square perpetuates its name as a haven for foreigners in the shape of **Babington's Tea-Rooms**, at the foot of the steps on the left, opened by an English spinster at the turn of the century. No corner of Italy could be less Italian, and it is still tea and scones – at a price.

Piazza del Popolo

Once in Piazza del Popolo at the top of the Corso, one of the biggest, you will have sampled the gamut of the physical city, having passed from Classical into Neo-Classical Rome (which you may find majestic but bloodless, as emulation often is). This Piazza is no part of the jumbled Rome of surprises: its marks for being just right – symmetrical and pleasing – are too high. It is called People's Square, after the early Renaissance church to the right of Bernini's Gate, but it isn't. It is where Italy's neo-fascists like to stage their rallies and where, on Sunday afternoons, Rome's *fils de papà* gather, sitting on their motorbikes licking ice-creams in casual white shirts and frayed jeans, carefully starched.

The Piazza is a creation of Popes who wished travellers from the north, the majority, to be suitably impressed by their first sight of the Eternal City. If you stand with your back close to the gate, you will see how the twin churches channel your vision down the princely Corso like pillars on a stage by subordinating the streets on either side.

Their debut was in the seventeenth century but it was not until the nineteenth that an Italian with a French name conceived the actual square, in which many detect a Parisian air.

The extreme left-hand chapel of the dark **Santa Maria del Popolo**, built over the rumoured site of Nero's grave, hides two of Caravaggio's most startling pieces, the *Conversion of St Paul* and the *Crucifixion of St Peter*.

But for lovers of Rome, including Sunday Romans, the square means the overlooking parapet of the **Pincio**, gardens first laid out under the Roman Emperors. They offer one of the most splendidly embracing views of Rome there is.

Ara Pacis

Re-threading your way down the Corso, on your right, after the headquarters of the PSI, is a strangely empty square built around a giant mound of earth, thick with cypresses. It is the Etruscan-style tomb the Emperor Augustus had built for himself and fourteen of his family, once surmounted by the Emperor's statue. It had a varied career, ending up under Mussolini as a concert hall. In the Middle Ages, it served as a fortress for the Ghibelline Colonna family, before being seized by the offended Papacy. It is closed to the public, but behind it, and often open, is a big glass coffin containing an almost miraculous reconstruction of the *Ara Pacis Augustae* (Altar of Augustan Peace), fashioned between the years 13 and 9 BC to celebrate the long period of peace the first Emperor ushered in.

One of the finest specimens of Roman art in existence, the altar is, above all, a picture of the times. It depicts with telling detail an Imperial procession in Rome that actually took place in 13 BC. One of the ladies is the Emperor's wife Livia.

The first fragments of the altar were discovered in the fifteenth century, but it was finally put together only in the 1930s, when widely scattered pieces were re-assembled in Rome, a rare instance of pre-war co-operation.

Pantheon   The Pantheon is the king of Roman architecture, casually left hidden in a warren of back streets to the right of the Corso in the Piazza Rotonda. As a feat of engineering, it remained a mystery until the Renaissance. Until the present century, its massive dome was the biggest in the world; even St Peter's is smaller. It is also the best-preserved Roman edifice there is, owing its salvation to early consecration as a church, and the most admired.

The Pantheon, above all, stands for satisfying proportion but Romans who pass under its dwarfing walls are also known to feel reassured, buoyed up by its robust example of survival.

The boastful inscription over the granite columns – 'M Agrippa L.F. Third-time Consul. Did This' – is a fib. Marcus Agrippa, the son-in-law of Augustus, did indeed build a pantheon for the gods on the same spot, but it was pulled down because of damage and totally rebuilt by the architect-Emperor Hadrian. An understanding man, he let the conceit stand.

Hadrian is believed to have designed the Pantheon himself, as he also planned his magnificent Villa at Tivoli, which you should try to see (pages 257–8). His passion for things Greek is reflected in the Greek-style porch with its triangular pediment, but when he decided upon the gigantic circular hall he obviously had great, roomy, Roman-style basilicas in mind.

It takes no expert to see how bold he was and what imagination must have gone into working out how to put up, and keep up, the huge cupola, once tiled with gilded bronze until an Eastern Emperor made off with it. The secret of the proportion is that the Pantheon's height and the diameter of the dome are exactly the same.

Spying down from its centre is the disturbing, bronze-rimmed 'eye', open to the sky, exposing those below, it seems, to distant scrutiny. It also lights the whole building and, incredibly, is 9 metres across. Statues of the deities stood in the recesses. A Latin epitaph on the best-known of the tombs now in the hall, a marble sarcophagus, reads: 'Here lies Raphael, held in awe by Nature, the great mother of all things, for fear of being overshadowed while he was alive and of dying when he died.' Modern Italy's first two kings are also entombed within.

Piazza Navona

Among Romans, this is *the* square – the most handsome, striking and democratic of them all – on the other side of the Corso Rinascimento from the Pantheon. It is the heart of Baroque Rome at its liveliest, and a ban on traffic helps. It wears different faces for the time of day or year. At Christmas, it becomes a bazaar; on a summer evening, a milling stage of fire-eaters, fortune-tellers, guitar-players, portrait-painters, card-sharpers, coffee-drinkers, wallet-pinchers, art-lovers and strollers.

They all tread on an ancient Roman athletics stadium, built by the Emperor Domitian, the size and shape of which the square copies exactly. Its name is a corruption of the Latin for 'athletics'. Pageants, races, jousting contests and fairs have been held in the square since the Emperor's time, as well as aquatic entertainments: when the square was concave, they could flood it, and the carriages of princes and prelates would plough into the water for matches, egged on by the roaring populace.

Now the square is dominated by the **Fountain of the Rivers**, the most flamboyant fantasy that ever came to Bernini (and he was never dull). For many, this is the very symbol of Baroque art, and often provokes strong reactions. A lion and other weird beasts have emerged from caves in an exotic reef to drink; above them, the personifications of the Nile, the Ganges, the Danube and the River Plate lord it over the rocks. . .

But the fountain is also a below-the-belt round in the scrapping between Bernini and his rival and enemy Francesco Borromini, author of the church overlooking the fountain, **St Agnese in Agone**. The church, which is all cupola, was a technical challenge, so the South American river is mockingly holding up his hand to prevent its collapse. The Nile, too, has covered its face, not only to indicate the river's then unknown source, but in horror at Borromini's alleged blunders in construction. Dickens found Bernini too much, calling his works 'the most detestable class of productions in the wide world . . . intolerable abortions.'

That is the end of Rome-by-lightning. Whether or not time is shouting, the next logical step is really across the Tiber to the Vatican and the Sistine Chapel. If there is still time left, these are the further places to see, arranged in a very subjective order of importance.

The Catacombs

The underground cemeteries and meeting places of the early Christians consist of literally hundreds of miles of tunnelling outside Rome. They can prove a disturbing experience. The thousands of dead were placed just as they were on shelves cut into the soft tufa rock. Compulsory guides lead you through these cool mazes, some in storeys, and may try to dispel notions that Christianity was once a secret society.

A score of catacomb areas have been discovered, but the vastest, and easiest to reach, are the **Catacombe di Santo Callisto**, named after a third-century supervisor and later Pope. On the Via Appia to the south, the 118 bus from the Colosseum drops you at the entrance. The exit from Rome by car is the Porta San Sebastiano.

The tombs of Popes put to death in the third century are there, as well as precious fragments of frescoes, Greek inscriptions and the crude code-signs of the young fraternity, including the symbolic fish.

The Appian Way

If you have a car, a drive along the Regina Viarum, Queen of Roads, as the Romans called the Appia, complements a visit to the flanking Catacombs, and is certainly one of the most solemn and moving sights of Rome. Patches of the original road, inaugurated in 312 BC by Appius Claudius, have been left bumpily uncovered. Perfectly straight, it makes towards the Alban Hills, lined by great tombs of the wealthy of Republican Rome, cypresses, umbrella pines, statues and inscriptions.

The most famous tomb, 3 km out and at a 118 bus-stop, is the massive cylindrical mausoleum built for **Cecilia Metella**, daughter of the general who had conquered Crete, and wife of Crassus, one of Caesar's generals in Gaul. It was later incorporated into a medieval castle.

The Appia struck across Italy to Brindisi and thus was the gateway to Rome's Eastern Empire. The many parked cars suggest that today's Romans find the tombs romantic.

The Jewish Quarter

Still known officially as the Ghetto, this is off the tourist trail, but repays a visit because it is a muffled play-back of the times when ruins were a part of life. The Ghetto lies behind the sturdy shell of the **Theatre of Marcellus**, two minutes down the road from the Capitol. This was named by the Emperor Augustus after his sister's son, who died when barely 20. It could seat 15,000, and in the Middle Ages served as a formidable fortress in the urban warfare between the big families. Then it graduated into a Renaissance dwelling, before demotion to an exclusive warren of flats.

Circle around the back of the theatre into Via del Portico d'Ottavia, the name of a big cloister-like **colonnade** Augustus dedicated to his sister. More than 100 metres long, it was a public place adorned with Greek statues and paintings. Down on the right, there is a bright glimmer of what it must have looked like.

Pillars and pediments of an arcade now serve as an elegant forecourt for an initially eighth-century church called **Sant' Angelo in Pescheria**, St Angel in the Fish-Market, since that is just what part of the Emperor's art gallery became.

Pillars stick out of the street itself like sore thumbs. This is about the only 'popular' quarter in truly classical Rome left, and on the right are some of the few remaining medieval houses in the city. Peep into the dark courtyard of number 13.

Scattered remains of the Portico and its hundreds of pillars are kneaded into the quarter, especially evident if you wheel around the left of the church towards the quiet **Piazza Campitelli**, which has a special angle on the theatre.

The Ghetto was the site chosen by a sixteenth-century Pope as a laager for Rome's Jews. They were restricted to it, subject to curfews and, until Italian Unification, forbidden to own property. Gates sealed it off from the rest of Rome. In a gesture of conciliation, the current Pope made the first Papal visit to the nearby Synagogue, but some Roman Jews quietly resent what they view as an attempt to paint out centuries of discrimination in one afternoon.

Fountain of the Tortoises

Only steps away in the Piazza Mattei stands what is for many the most delightful fountain of all, though this sixteenth-century joy is easy to miss.

Santa Maria in Cosmedin

Commonly known as the *Bocca della Verità* and under constant assault by battalions of Japanese, this church is 100 metres further down from the Theatre of Marcellus. The familiar name belongs to an ancient stone drain-cover in the porch in the likeness of a river-god. This was the lie-detector of medieval Rome, mainly in infidelity cases. Anyone whose hand dared enter the god's mouth would, in case of deceit, have it snapped off. It is Rome's toy. First built in the sixth century, the rigorously simple church was frequented by Greek residents and exiles. The chill crypt burrows beneath a temple to Hercules.

Opposite are two republican **temples** of the second century BC; the circular one, wrongly assigned to the Vestal Virgins, is the oldest example of a pagan temple in marble.

Etruscan Museum

Out of the way but quite simply the best museum in the world, this is housed in a Renaissance Pope's summer villa. Now called the **National Museum of Villa Giulia**, it is in Viale delle Belle Arti, 15 minutes north of Piazza del Popolo along *Via Flaminia*. It covers all of pre-Roman art and is dominated by the Etruscans. The intricate delicacy, the sheer artistry of the pottery they fashioned between the eighth and first centuries BC can be a revelation to supercilious twentieth-century eyes. There is also an underground reconstruction of a dwelling-tomb from Cerveteri, north of Rome; exquisite eighth-century BC jewellery in gold, and finds from tombs in southern Etruria somehow missed by the looters. A recent section, backed up by new evidence, traces the Etruscans' Mediterranean trading routes.

Santa Maria Maggiore

Near the top of Via Cavour but before the station is the world's largest church dedicated to the Virgin Mary. It was built by a fifth-century Pope to celebrate the findings of the Council of Ephesus (in present-day Turkey) that Mary was indeed the Mother of God.

The main reason for a visit (unfortunately also discovered by travel agencies) is that St Mary Major is the only one of the seven chief basilicas of Rome that has survived *inside* more or less intact, a great hall of a place with forty columns in strict marching order, decked out in rare, stupendous, fifth-century mosaics.

In panels, they line both sides of the upper nave, telling of the doings of Old Testament prophets, while on the triumphal arch over the altar they portray the Mary exalted by the Council. In the top left-hand corner, she is portrayed as a bejewelled princess of the Eastern Empire.

The great, glowing, later mosaic of the apse, executed by a Franciscan friar in the thirteenth century, brings the theme to its climax: here, the Virgin occupies a position of far greater glory, side by side with a Jesus who is crowning her.

Four Popes are buried in this basilica; the coffered ceiling is gilded with the first gold ever to come from America; and every 5 August a snow storm is simulated outside to commemorate a miraculous one sent down to show an early Pope where the church should be built (pedants say it must have been another church).

Santa Prassede

Hidden behind the caffè Cottini in the square outside and entered by a side-door, is a church which also boasts a blaze of mosaics, but in a far more intimate atmosphere; it possesses the most perfect example of Byzantine art in Rome. This is the tiny, square chapel of Santa Zenone, to your left, erected by a ninth-century Pope as a tomb for his mother. People once called it the Garden of Paradise, understandably. Now they simply draw a breath at the symmetry and warm brilliance of it, at the spare figures and bold colours bathed in gold. In the vault, four angels hold up a medallion in which Christ is depicted.

The other mosaics were all done in the same century. The setting for the figures over the nave's triumphal arch is Celestial Jerusalem, while in the large apse a kindly Paul places a reassuring arm around Santa Prassede's shoulder, shy in the presence of Jesus. Peter similarly comforts her sister Prudenziana on the right . . . Prassede used to hide wanted Christians in her house. If they were caught and killed, she would keep their sponged-up blood in a well; the circular stone at the start of the nave is said to cover it. Both sisters were martyred in turn.

Santa Maria degli Angeli

Only 15 minutes away in Piazza Repubblicà near the station, the point here is to see not a church but a Roman bath complex. This was the biggest *terme* in Rome, built by the Emperor Diocletian between 298 and 306, but later redesigned as a church by Michelangelo.

At once the church conveys the immensity of the original complex. The bare, concave, façade was part of the portico of the hot baths; the vast transept was the tepid bath (*tepidarium*), and beyond the apse was the immense *frigidarium*. Some 3,000 bathers could disport themselves at once. Like others in Rome, the complex included gardens, pavilions, exercise areas, perhaps a library, and a perimeter wall.

The massive granite columns in the *tepidarium* are the original ones: leave through the Sacristy for an abrupt change from church to tubhouse. On a plaque, a sixteenth-century Pope denounces Diocletian as an 'impious tyrant' and 'extremely cruel enemy of the Church', while the Emperor listens as a bust. Chunky remains litter the surrounds.

San Luigi dei Francesi

The national French church, in a piazza of the same name near Piazza Navona, is the home of three masterpieces by Caravaggio. His *St Matthew and the Angel*, *Vocation of St Matthew* and *Martyrdom of St Matthew*, all in the saint's chapel, the fifth on the left, are the works of a man at the height of his powers, his highly dramatic style perfected. They were his first religious paintings. Every image is subordinated to the violent play of luminosity and shadow. Caravaggio is spotlights, realism and anger. An untrained natural, he broke off from contemporary 'mannerism'. These pictures created scandal and controversy, and were seen by some as irreverent and harsh. He reacted to criticism with challenges to duels, slander and symptoms of nervous crisis, foreshadowing his end as a hunted murderer.

Palazzo Barberini

Seventy metres up the steepest hill from Piazza Barberini at the bottom of Via Veneto, this is not only a spectacular Baroque *palazzo*, with a façade by Bernini, but the home of the misleadingly named **Gallery of Ancient Art**, which has little trace of classical times. Caravaggio dominates room 13. You'll also find Filippo Lippi, Perugino and Il Sodoma, and in room 6 there is a seductive portrait by Raphael of his muse and mistress, *The Baker's Girl*, painted in the year of his death. Henry VIII, dressed as for his fourth wedding, is also in attendance, portrayed by Holbein.

Galleria Borghese

Occupying what was once a cardinal's summer villa in the extensive Villa Borghese park near Via Veneto, his art collection is perhaps the richest in Rome, excluding the Vatican. As well as startling third-century mosaics showing gladiators in violent action, note a famed marble statue by the neo-classical sculptor Antonio Canova of Napoleon's sister Pauline naked on her couch, as well as canvases by Raphael and Caravaggio. The Gallery is an unbeatable pretext for a pleasant stroll in this huge, ordered park.

Castel Sant' Angelo

Across the Tiber near the Vatican, the castle still retains the cylindrical shape of the original Etruscan-style mausoleum designed by the architect-Emperor Hadrian for himself; Emperor Septimus Severus is also buried there. Hadrian's broad spiral staircase leading up to the funeral urns is still in place.

The castle is associated with the very grimmest bits of Rome's past, yet it takes its name from a vision of an angel sheathing a sword to signify the end of a terrible plague. The angel was seen above the mausoleum by a Pope during a solemn procession held to beseech deliverance.

It was a river bastion during the Empire, and then a stronghold and refuge of the Papacy. A raised corridor links it to the Vatican; Pope Clement VII hid within its thick walls during the Sack of Rome. Eminent prisoners languished in its dungeons, while unwanted ones, including a Pope or two, were murdered, poisoned or starved to death.

There is an armoury to see, furnished Papal apartments hung with paintings, and a terrace bar with a superb view.

San Paolo fuori le Mura

Though out of the way south of the centre, the biggest church in Rome after St Peter's is easy to reach on the 'B' Metro line. It conveys what must have been the 'feel' of Ulpia's Basilica in the Imperial Forums, since its dimensions (it is 132 metres long) and design are almost identical. Erected by the Emperor Constantine on the site of a memorial to the Apostle Paul, it was gutted by fire in the nineteenth century and what you see is a faithful reconstruction, except for the apse, with a huge mosaic of Christ imparting a blessing in the Greek fashion, which is the thirteenth-century original.

E.U.R.

A bit further out on the same Metro line (20 minutes from centre) is Mussolini's new town. The acronym stands for the 'Roman Universal Exhibition', meant to be staged in the 1930s as a salute to Fascism, but never held because of the war. This is Italy's futuristic Brasilia, all geometry, open spaces and frigid rhetoric.

Museo Nazionale Romano

Sited amid the Baths of Diocletian near the station, and soon to be re-housed across the road, this is one of the world's richest collections of Roman remains, especially statuary. It was mostly brought to light during excavations to make way for new building after Unification in 1870, and is a must for classicists.

What to do

Rome isn't Paris or New York. There's no hectic night life to plunge into as a chaser to tramping around. Few bars or pubs exist where you would care to spend an evening, partly because it is usually too hot. The main part of any evening will be consumed by a leisurely dinner, which Romans begin at 8.30–9 p.m. as a rule, preferably outside. For them, eating *is* the main activity, and it sees them through until after 11 p.m. They might then stroll to Piazza Navona or Piazza del Pantheon for a slow night-cap in the open, waiting for a breeze.

But in summer especially, pleasant alternatives to sedentary pleasures do exist. A high priority should go to seeing two special spectacles at night: the illuminated Forum, seen from behind the Capitol, and the Palatine Hill, best surveyed from the top of Via del Circo Massimo.

● In July and August, the island in the middle of the Tiber, Isola Tiberina, turns into a multi-track pleasure island offering theatre, ballet, concerts, films, dancing and drinks in an enchanting setting.

● Italy's regions exhibit their products, wines and food on both banks of the Tiber around the Ponte Umberto bridge throughout July. Called Tevere Expo, it is an instructive whiler-awayer.

● A favourite fixture is a night at the opera in the dwarfing ruins of the Baths of Caracalla built in AD 211–17. Performances, as a rule on alternate nights during July and the first two weeks of August, can make up what they sometimes lack in quality with lavish spectacle. The most lavish is always *Aida*, with elephants as extras. Top artists, however, are reluctant to appear for fear of the damp night air. Book at the Opera House, Piazza Beniamino Gigli; tel. 461755.

● In July, the orchestra of Rome's Accademia di Santa Cecilia gives a series of concerts in the magnificent Piazza Campidoglio which is one of the year's social events. Traffic is diverted to enhance the enjoyment. Tel. 654 1044.

● Watch out for operas and plays staged in the Roman amphitheatre among the shadowy ruins of Ostia Antica. Theatre-goers can usually take a boat which leaves from Ponte Marconi (not every year). Enquire at the Tourist Office.

● A boat called *Tiber II* makes four-hour cruises with a buffet lunch down the Tiber and along the coast most months of the year. Information at Tourvisa; tel. 493481.

Shopping   The main good buys are designer- or low-priced **clothes**, as well as gloves, umbrellas, handbags, belts, luggage, silk scarves and ties, textiles, prints and engravings.

The axis of the main shopping tour is the Corso. Much of the street is lined with cheap 'jeanseries', as the Romans call them, blaring out pop. But among them you can dig out old, well-established silversmiths, large leather emporiums, and bargain shoe-shops.

But hard by is another world, of quiet elegance. Via dei Condotti is the heart of the fashionable shopping district. Many of the big fashion names are there – French and Swiss as well as Italian. The clothes are as expensive as they are luxurious.

The streets on either side and the intersecting ones each have their own character. Via Borgognona is quieter, with benches and shrubs in pots; it is the headquarters of Fendi, who have five shops in the area. Via Frattina is younger, more colourful, less expensive and a good place for cheap, pure silk ties. Along Via della Croce, the fashion in clothes is more extreme. Smart groceries jostle with clothing and leather shops. The shops selling gloves, handbags, belts and scarves for tourists offer reasonable quality but high prices.

For browsing among **antiques**, the two main streets are Via del Babuino between Piazza di Spagna and Piazza del Popolo, and Via dei Coronari near Piazza Navona. Bargains are few, but they can sometimes be found by early risers at the Sunday morning flea market, Porta Portese, over in Trastevere. Haggling is the order of the day; it can be done without any Italian, but don't look wealthy. It is awash with cheap clothing and household goods, but the more interesting items are right at the end, near Viale Trastevere. There you'll discover silver, china, pottery and sometimes painted enamel boxes sold by Soviet emigrés.

Textile shops dominate the area around Largo Argentina and the nearby old Jewish Ghetto, with a wide range of silks and other fabrics.

Clothing that is cheap, cheerful and fashionable can be found in the big department stores. La Rinascente is the smartest, with a branch in the Corso, but Coen, Upim and Standa are also worth a look.

Where to stay

The big 'American' hotels, the Hilton, Holiday Inn and Sheraton are far from the centre and not practicable.

Hotels abound around the station, including solid, decent, turn-of-the-century establishments. But the zone is also seeded with scores of more dubious hotels and, besides, it is a bit out of the way. The Vatican has also attracted hoteliers, but for convenience you should winkle out somewhere in the centre (*Centro Storico*).

Top range

The most central and best known four-star is the **Hassler**, 6 Piazza Trinità dei Monti; tel. 678 2651. At the top of the Spanish Steps.

Near the Corso is the elegant **Hotel D'Inghilterra**, 14 Via Bocca di Leone; tel. 672161. A gem of British stylishness and hush.

Visiting politicians, including Mrs Thatcher, often stay at **Le Grand Hotel** near the station, 3 Via Vittorio Orlando; tel. 4709.

Visiting journalists like the **Albergo Nazionale**, 131 Piazza Montecitorio; tel. 678 9251, tlx. 621427.

Many Americans prefer **Excelsior**, 125 Via Veneto; tel. 4708.

Best-known in the Corso is the conservative **Plaza**, 126 Via del Corso; tel. 672101.

Middle-rank diplomats admire the **Forum**, 25 Via Tor de' Conti; tel. 679 2446. Its roof-top restaurant overlooks the Roman Forums, but, trapped in traffic, the hotel is a nightmare to reach by car.

Mid range

In the **Spanish Steps** area: the **Gregoriana**, 18 Via Gregoriana, tel. 679 4269, is in a sleepy, unused street with large bedrooms.

The **Sistina**, 136 Via Sistina, tel. 475 8804, is discreet.

In the same street at number 79 is the **Internazionale**, tel. 679 3047; the front bedrooms are noisy.

Down the Steps, the **Carriage**, 36 Via delle Carrozze, tel. 679 3152, is smart and peaceful.

The **Condotti**, 37 Via Mario Fiori, tel. 679 4661, is rarified.

Nearby but noisier is the **Firenze**, 106 Via Due Macelli; tel. 679 7240.

Near the **Trevi fountain** are two small but surprisingly inexpensive hotels. Behind it is the **Trevi**, 21 Vicolo Babuccio; tel. 678 9563.

Opposite, among the din, **Fontana**, 96 Piazza Trevi, tel. 678 6113, with a roof garden.

Near the **Piazza Venezia** is a strangely secluded hotel, the **Bolivar**, 6 Via Cordonata (near a British news-agency); tel. 679 1614.

Near the **Pantheon** is the solidly respectable **Santa Chiara**, 21 Via Santa Chiara; tel. 654 1700.

Very old, facing the monument is the **Sole al Pantheon**, 63 Via del Pantheon; tel. 678 0441. Booking is essential because of its superb position.

A rival is **Del Senato**, 73 Piazza Rotonda; tel. 799 3231.

In a quieter position is the calm and tasteful **Bologna**, 4a Via Santa Chiara; tel. 656 8951. It has a private atmosphere.

Near the **station**: the **Esperia**, 22 Via Nazionale, tel. 474 4245;

and the **Nizza**, 16 Via M. D'Azeglio, tel. 461061, are both businessy and serious.

In a tranquil back street between the station and Colosseum is the useful **Colosseum**, 10 Via Sforza; tel. 475 1312.

Near **Via Veneto**: try the **Oxford**, 89 Via Boncompagni, tel. 475 6852; or the **Sicilia**, 24 Via Sicilia, tel. 493841.

The **Villa Borghese**, 31 Via Pinciana, tel. 859648, is a fading residence of Englishy charm, overlooking the park.

Near **St Peter's**: the **Columbus**, 33 Via Conciliazione, tel. 686 5435, was once a cardinal's fifteenth-century *palazzo*; it retains the air.

Also the **Della Conciliazione**, 164 Via Borgo Po; tel. 686 7910.

Bottom range
In the **Spanish Steps** area: nowhere could be more central and reasonable than **Scalinata di Spagna**, 17 Piazza Trinità dei Monti; tel. 679 3006. It is homely, with big bedrooms.

Nearby is **Trinità dei Monti**, 91 Via Sistina; tel. 679 7206.

Down the Steps is **San Carlo**, 93 Via Carrozze; tel. 678 4548.

Or you can try the slightly dowdy **Hotel Piazza di Spagna**, 61 Via Mario de' Fiori, tel. 679 3061, opposite the **Condotti**.

The **Croce di Malta**, 28 Via Borgognona, tel. 679 5482, is cosy.

Also reliable are the **Homs**, 71 Via della Vite, tel. 679 2976, and the **Hotel Brotzky**, in the Corso at number 509, a long-established *pensione* of the old, solid stamp.

You will appreciate the modest **Portoghesi**, 1 Via dei Portoghesi; tel. 656 4231. In an alley near Piazza Navona, it is central, quiet, cheap and homely.

Where to eat
A mention in this list is a recommendation in itself. The criteria for selection are good food, better prices, outside tables and a Roman atmosphere. Several of the more prestigious restaurants are also included, for birthdays and bits of luck.

The **Campo de' Fiori** quarter is perhaps the most picturesque for eating-out. **Grappolo d'Oro**, 80 Piazza della Cancelleria, tel. 686 4118 (closed Sundays), is the most welcoming and one of the best. Clients of the two affable brothers sit at bench tables and read the menu off a blackboard. The *hors d'oeuvres* buffet is excellent. There are tables outside.

La Pollarola, 26 Piazza Pollarola, tel. 654 1654 (closed Sundays), is 50 metres away, slightly more formal but more suited to conversation. Reasonably priced, with outside tables.

Grotte del Teatro di Pompeo, across the road at 73 Via Biscione, tel. 654 3686 (closed Mondays), is a shade glummer, but always busy. A speciality is green *fettuccine* with gorgonzola. It is built over the remains of the theatre where Julius Caesar was murdered; they will show you downstairs into part of the theatre's foundations. Al fresco seating.

Costanza, next door at 63 Piazza Paradiso, tel. 654 1002 (closed Sundays), is claimed to be among Rome's best restaurants, but it has prices to match and its outside passageway is cramped.

La Carbonara dominates the Campo de' Fiori; tel. 686 4783 (closed Tuesdays). This old institution is the best-known in the area. Its food may no longer be superb, and it is slightly pricey, but sitting outside in summer watching the action is a joy.

Ai Balestrari, 41 Via Balestrari, tel. 686 5377 (closed Mondays), is in an alley off the square and is a *pizzeria* too, with good, inexpensive food and in-house musicians. Cheery.

Polese, 40 Piazza Sforza Cesarini, tel. 686 1709, is 300 metres further down Corso V. Emanuele. It is a favourite among foreigners because its many outside tables are in a garden-like tiny square, away from the traffic. Good marks for fare.

The **Piazza Navona** area: the **Campana** claims to be the oldest restaurant in Rome, and its mention in a tax ledger for 1518 backs this up. It is at 18 Vicolo della Campana, a tiny alley off Via Scrofa, near Ponte Cavour; tel. 656 7820 (closed Mondays). It is for serious eaters, with few frills and its walls are half-panelled in dark wood. Specialities include *olive ascolane*, large green olives stuffed with ground meat, breaded and fried.

La Maiella, close to Piazza Navona at 46 Piazza Sant' Apollinare, tel. 686 4174 (closed Sundays), is for an expensive night out in the restrained surroundings of one of the best-known restaurants in Rome. Outside tables.

Trattoria Romana, 27 Vicolo Monte Vecchio, an alley off Via della Pace, is the other extreme: rather cramped, with slow one-man service, but good family fare at family prices.

Da Francesco, 29 Piazza del Fico, no telephone (closed Tuesdays), is on the same lines but bigger, bustling, crowded, cheap and very good. No place for peace and elegance.

In **Piazza Spagna** area: **Ristorante 34**, 34 Via Mario Fiori, tel. 679 5091 (closed Mondays), is a novelty: modern cuisine Italian-style, unusual dishes typified by lightness. Sword-fish rissoles are a speciality.

Otello, 81 Via della Croce, tel. 679 1178 (closed Sundays) has a small, inside garden and, though central and popular with generations of visitors, its prices remain remarkably reasonable. You are not rushed.

Hostaria al 31, 31 Via delle Carrozze, tel. 678 6127 (closed Sundays), is a tiny Sardinian place, useful in cases of liquidity irritation.

La Capricciosa, on the other side of the Corso in Largo Lombardi, tel. 679 4027 (closed Tuesdays), is a large, several-roomed *trattoria* frequented by the Italian middle class and some Japanese. It is staid, utterly reliable and not expensive. Named after its own patented *pizza*. In summer, it takes to the outside.

Trattoria all'Arancio, nearby at 51 Via dell'Arancio, tel. 687 6119 (closed Sundays), is crowded, youngish, generous and 'in'.

Other areas: Pasquale, 66 Via Santi Quattro, tel. 735903 (closed Mondays) is behind the Colosseum, popular with seminarists and knowing adults for its combination of fairness and quality. Atmosphere is often lively.

Taverna Cestia, 65 Via Piramide Cestia, tel. 574 3754 (closed Mondays) is not central, at the Porta San Paolo (Metro stop: Piramide), but some consider this the most attractive proposition of all. The fare is fresh, the choice large, the prices contained, and it boasts an outside terrace. It is heavily sprinkled with foreigners because of the nearby UN Food and Agriculture Organisation (FAO). Across the road is the Protestant Cemetery where Keats is buried and where Shelley, drowned in the Gulf of Spezia in 1822 and cremated by Byron, has his tombstone.

Da Valentino, 293 Via Cavour, tel. 461303 (closed Fridays), close to the entrance to the Forum. For the non-exigent, this is one of the best deals in Rome. Very family, busy, amiable, brisk, cheap, and very fair fare.

The 'in' cafés

The smartest café of all is **Rosati** in Piazza del Popolo. This is where anybody-who-is-anybody will spend afternoons watching and waiting to be watched. It is also a restaurant.

Opposite is the rival **Canova**, still fashionable but more crowded and younger.

The last of the 'old' cafés is the celebrated **Caffè Greco**, 86 Via Condotti, near the Piazza di Spagna. Founded in the eighteenth century by an unspecified Levantine, its marble-topped tables have hosted most European literary giants at some time or other. You still spot well-known faces in the narrow rooms which, of course, facilitate recognition.

Rome's most noted and 'in' ice-cream place is **Giolitti** in the narrow Via Uffici del Vicario at number 40, behind the Albergo Nazionale in the Piazza Colonna area. The variety will astound you. No outside tables.

The Vatican

The Vatican City is the tiniest state in the world, with influence over more people than any other. It covers just 108 acres, but its spiritual subjects are estimated at 800 million, about 18 per cent of the world's population.

Within the Vatican, any Pope is among the least democratic of world leaders. His rule is absolute; his decisions are without appeal. The present Polish pontiff was elected in the Sistine Chapel in October 1978, the first non-Italian Pope to be chosen in 450 years. He lives in the Apostolic Palace to the right of St Peter's.

He recites the *Angelus* from the window of his top-floor study overlooking St Peter's Square every Sunday at noon. Except in the height of summer, he holds 'general audiences' in the square on Wednesdays. But since the Turkish right-wing terrorist Ali Agca (now in jail) wounded him in the square in 1981, security is tight and to be anywhere near him tickets are needed. They are obtainable at the *Prefettura*, through the bronze door on the right of the square.

The Pope's 'subjects' within the Vatican include about 750 residents and some 4,000 employees. Swiss guards in their colourful striped uniforms, designed by Michelangelo, clang the Vatican's three gates shut at 11 p.m. Entertainment is provided by a Vatican football league.

The Vatican mints its own money; prints its own stamps; publishes a newspaper, with articles often in Latin; runs a powerful, Jesuit-managed radio station which broadcasts worldwide, and boasts a minute railway station. It has a helipad, duty-free shops, and gardens take up a third of its space

History

The Vatican became the seat of the Papacy only at the end of the fourteenth century after its return to Rome from a lengthy sojourn in Avignon. Earlier, the Popes' official residence had always been the Lateran Palace on the Rome side of the Tiber, now known as San Giovanni in Laterano.

Pope Nicholas V began to shape today's Vatican in 1450, by starting off the present Apostolic Palace around the so-called 'Parrot's Courtyard'. Virtually every Pope after him turned builder, adding to and beautifying the complex. The Sistine Chapel, for instance, is named after Sixtus IV, who built it twenty-three years later. Papal elections are held there. The most feverish constructor was the tireless Julius II, the towering task-master of Michelangelo. He had St Peter's itself redone. (The present incumbent has put in a swimming pool.)

When royal troops punched through the walls of Papal Rome in 1870 to complete Italian Unification, the Pope refused to surrender the Vatican, and his successors lived as virtual prisoners in its walls until 1929, when the Papacy and Mussolini came to terms under which Italy recognised the Vatican as a sovereign state.

What to see

St Peter's

St Peter's is the biggest church in Christendom, yet not without its critics – partly because Michelangelo did not get his way.

In a country where even the biggest churches are hemmed in by their towns, this is the spectacular exception. The elliptical **square** is the happiest of all the inventions of Bernini. His grandly curving colonnades surmounted by 140 saints form the embrace of Mother Church and invite the slightly intimidated faithful forward. Voices do drop during the approach.

There was nothing Christian about the man behind the obelisk in the centre. It was dragged to Rome from Egypt by blood-crazed Caligula to adorn Nero's nearby circus where many Christians met their end, including, it is believed, St Peter himself in AD 67 or 64.

Once inside, St Peter's is mesmerising, if only for its immensity. Its proportions were clearly intended to daze you; you can read the measurements of lesser places on the floor. St Peter's is 211 metres long whereas, for example, St Paul's in London reaches only 158 metres. Its rich adornments and repleteness bewilder. It is held up by 800 columns and has 44 altars.

Yet many somehow fail to feel what they think they should, and would rather agree with Dickens, who said, 'I felt no very strong emotion.' He was there during the lead-up to some *festa* and found it all like 'one of the opening scenes in a very lavish pantomime.'

The enforced focus of the church is the heavily ornate, blackish **canopy** over the altar, an unhappier Bernini creation which took him ten years. It was made from bronze plundered from the porchway of the Pantheon, for a Pope with the family name of Barberini, hence a pithy Roman saying that tells much of their history: 'What the barbarians didn't do, the Barberini did.'

The natural focus of course is Michelangelo's soaring **cupola**, the wonder, symbol and soul of St Peter's. He himself raised it up to the drum. It was not for twenty-six years after his death that somebody dared take his plan right to the top – which, including the cross, is 136 metres above ground. You can get there by taking a lift to the drum and then climbing on a slant to the lantern – to have all Rome beneath you.

Michelangelo, who served under seven Popes, was Chief Architect to St Peter's from 1547 until his death seventeen years later, one of a dozen employed on the scheme since Julius II laid the first stone of his new church in 1506, to its consecration 120 years later. The old genius grumbled. 'I'm working for free, unwillingly and to my very great cost. I do it for the glory of God, the love of St Peter, and the salvation of my soul.' But he also wrote to his friend Vasari when he was 81: 'If I left here, it would be the utter ruin of St Peter's . . .' Many think his judgement was vindicated. Pictures of his own show St Peter's as a magnificent, almost circular, edifice in Greek cross fashion, utterly dominated by a dome reaching for heaven and ringed by walk-around arcades.

A later, lesser, architect, Carlo Maderno, erected the present Baroque façade. It is an uninspired screen that, from the square, almost totally hides Michelangelo's cupola.

The other wonder Michelangelo left in St Peter's he did as a young man of merely 25. His **Pietà** is behind bullet-proof glass in the first chapel to the right of the entrance. One of the very few sculptures he finished, it is the only one he signed (on the sash of the Virgin), and some critics think he never surpassed it; it crowns the work of all his predecessors, and is the summit of fifteenth-century Italian sculpture.

It is also taken as a deeply moving statement of Michelangelo's faith, expressed above all in the utter serenity of the face of the

Mother, despite the murder of her Son. The sculptor apparently dismayed the public at the time by his portrait of Mary as almost a girl, holding a full-grown adult across her lap. 'But Death *is* old,' explained a priest to catechists peering through the glass.

That you are at the central point of Christianity is more palpable in the **Crypt**, to the left of the high altar, for here Popes are buried. The most recent tomb is that of John Paul I, 'the smiling Pope', whose death in 1978 after a reign of only 33 days led to refuted allegations of murder. St Peter's Chapel, beneath the high altar, has long been accepted as marking the grave of the first Pope, more as a tradition than as a certifiable fact. After excavations below the Crypt, Pius XII in 1950 announced with a fanfare the discovery of the actual tomb; and in 1968, Paul VI declared the remains of St Peter himself had been 'convincingly identified'.

On the way out, you will see the foundations of the original St Peter's erected by the Emperor Constantine in 324 on a Roman burial ground. Diggings have strongly suggested that he did indeed site it deliberately over some kind of memorial to the Apostle. Constantine's church weathered barbarians and the centuries, until Julius II had it pulled down to bring the Renaissance to Rome.

Vatican Museums — The pinnacle of any visit to the Vatican is the Sistine Chapel, which is inside Catholicism's enormous treasure house. The Museums involve a hike from St Peter's around the Vatican walls. Alternatively, a shuttle bus from the Information Office on the left of the piazza gets you there.

They are daunting. The Museums proper, including an Etruscan one, total ten – as well as galleries, apartments and the Chapel. To tackle more than a fraction at a time would tax the liveliest mind. The Vatican has signposted four optional routes, taking from ninety minutes to five hours, and hires out useful cassette commentaries for the short Tour 'A'. This is the advisable one, but switch to 'C' for Raphael's masterpieces in his four 'Rooms', **Stanze di Raffaello**, and, near the exit, see the Picture Gallery, **Pinacoteca**.

The Rooms were the private apartments of the same Julius II who commissioned Michelangelo to do the Sistine ceiling. The older hermit of a man came to loathe Raphael. His handsome rival swept about Rome surrounded by a cheerful band of assistants and admirers. He first came to Rome when he was about 25, specially summoned down from Florence by a Pope who had heard of his growing fame.

He set him a test, which was the ceiling of the Signature (*Segnatura*) Room. The Pontiff was so impressed that he dismissed the other talent he had hired and set his new young protégé to work on the rest of the Rooms. The *School of Athens* in it is often judged Raphael's masterpiece. The last Room, of Constantine, was painted by others after his death, although the vast battle-scene at the Milvan Bridge follows a Raphael sketch.

A famous trio of canvases by Raphael in room 8 crown the Pinacoteca, where there is also a superbly preserved triptych by Giotto to be discovered. But that is after the great highlight.

Sistine Chapel   In the vast Sistine Chapel, the greatest artistic event of the twentieth century is under way, according to many; for an angry few, the greatest disaster in the history of art is being perpetrated. When you enter you may not care a bit. It can be like being caught up in a revolution, or in the Friday rush-hour. While you are star-gazing, as you must, you can be jostled right off-balance. It must be some commentary on life that what many see as the greatest masterpiece ever can only be seen in extreme discomfort . . .

The Vatican began the restoration of the only frescoes done by Michelangelo in 1980; the enormous task is due to be over in 1994. But the 'new', startling, some say shocking, Michelangelo has emerged already. The Vatican calmly asserts that this is *the* Michelangelo, and that we are seeing the frescoes as he painted them for the first time. The difference between 'new' and 'old' is stunning. You get an idea of it in the contrast between the cleaned great barrel vault of a ceiling, now brilliant and luminous, and the sombre brownishness of the *Final Judgement* on the altar wall. The comparison may not be completely fair, since Michelangelo painted the *Judgement* in his sixties, twenty-two years after the ceiling, but the colouring did look roughly similar on both.

As a Vatican expert saw it, the 'old' ceiling resembled 'mottled old leather'; its tone was 'dull'; it was webbed with spidery cracks; and Michelangelo's famous *chiaroscuro* effect, revered by generations of critics, was not his at all, but partly the result of blackish strokes painted in later by restorers to arrest the fading definition.

The frescoes also absorbed grime and soot issuing from candles, oil lamps and braziers used during the long ceremonies in the chapel. But their greatest enemy was animal glue, usually made from rabbits, which was smeared over the whole surface by earlier restorers as a varnish to revive dying colours.

This glue was the main reason for the present restoration: it was contracting and tearing away the pigments. Rescue was imperative. The glue also masked dangerous salts deposited by seeping rainwater; it deteriorated in itself, flattening outlines, eliminating shadows, and above all helping to produce the darkish brown colours so long admired by so many. But until now, nobody could unglue the glue.

The colours caused by the glue, the Vatican firmly states, were 'totally opposite' to Michelangelo's original scheme. Unless the day is dull, you will notice the lights are off, whereas they used always to be on. The colours are so brilliant, they now light themselves. 'That's obviously what he intended,' they say. 'The frescoes are a long way up. People had to be able to see them.'

The curators ascribe the violence of some of the reaction to cultural

shock. The rediscovered Michelangelo demolishes libraries of conviction. Lecturers believed, for instance, that as a sculptor he actually
abhorred colours and glued the frescoes himself to tone them down.
Instead, he turns out to have been a dazzling colourist.

For the Vatican, Michelangelo's genius emerges enhanced from the
restoration. They compare the ceiling to easel painting, even though
he worked rapidly, with a decisive brush. The dispute between the
Vatican and its enemies is over Michelangelo's methods, and whether
the layers now being taken away include some of his.

Backed up by lengthy research and delicate instruments, the Vatican is confident that, as a good Florentine, Michelangelo abided scru-
pulously by his home town's rigid rules for 'true fresco' and painted
only with the plaster still wet, except for later corrections. The critics
argue that he used 'true fresco' only as an underpainting, and then
patiently built up the painting, even for weeks at a time. Their charge
is that the Vatican cleaners are demolishing his entire super-structure.

The restorers work on 25-cm squares, using a mobile computer.
Each square is first sponged with distilled water before a gooey mixture of four chemicals, called AB-57, is applied. It does not penetrate
the pigment. After three minutes, the cleaners remove it and wash
away the loosened glue and dirt. After a twenty-four-hour pause, they
repeat the process. They add no colour and they use no brighteners.
The Last Judgement poses trickier problems than the ceiling, because
more 'restorers' have been at it.

The work is being funded by a Japanese television company, in
return for the exclusive rights to all pictures.

Michelangelo, solitary, moody, full of pet hates, agreed to paint the
ceiling reluctantly, protesting to his patron that he knew nothing of
fresco work, which was true. But when he did start, in 1508, he locked
himself up alone in the chapel, and would have no snooping. When he
once refused to let in the Pope himself, threatening to drop a plank on
his holiness, he took fright at what he had done and fled Rome until
Papal ire calmed.

For four years, he worked on his back on patent scaffolding, often
with a candle strapped to his forehead. He so hurt himself, we are told,
that for months afterwards he could read only with his head thrown
back. But at one point, the impatient Julius struck him for not working
fast enough.

The painter fled again. This time the Pontiff sent a messenger after
him with money to make it up. They were both impossible characters,
and they understood each other. Later, fearing the approach of death,
Julius threatened to have his protégé flung down from the scaffolding
unless he finished soon. He did, and when the chapel was finally
thrown open to the public, Rome gasped.

Nothing had been seen like it before. The theme of the central band
is the *Creation*; the two most famous panels are the *Creation of Man*,

through the outstretched fingers, and the abject scene of naked *Adam and Eve* fleeing the Garden of Eden. The titanic scale of it is overwhelming, as is also the tremendous force of Michelangelo's medium, the human body. Through it, muscular, comely, god-like, he trumpets out his belief in the nobility of man and in a free mind.

When he started upon *The Last Judgement*, in 1536, Michelangelo was a very changed, almost broken, man; it took him eight years, and he finished it fifteen years after the shattering Sack of Rome. A world had come apart; under the humiliation, Renaissance confidence had sizzled and gone. Foreigners were in control; Rome, leader and symbol of a new civilisation, was in chains once more. Michelangelo is bitterness, rage and the disorientation of the day. *The Last Judgement* is a spiritual self-portrait. Christ, in the centre of the swirling multitude, is no passive sufferer, but an enraged, naked young man in his prime, damning the sinners to his left with a raised arm almost about to strike out. He does not, or will not, see the chosen on his right being hauled to heaven by angels.

In the far bottom right, in deepest Hell, you can make out a naked old man girdled with a snake. He was the Vatican's prim Master-of-Ceremonies who came to inspect the fresco with Pope Paul III one day, only to be profoundly offended by all the scandalous nudes: 'More fit for a tavern!' he snapped. He was punished in paint, in the same way as Dante had rewarded his enemies in print (Dante was Michelangelo's hero).

The Sistine Chapel is the finale to the incredible spectacle of the Italian Renaissance. In *The Last Judgement*, Michelangelo painted the word 'End'.

The environs of Rome

Cerveteri

The Etruscans are forty minutes north-west of Rome. For many, the vast, silent burial ground has an eerie immediacy matched nowhere else. Turn right off the SS 1, the *Via Aurelia*, after 31 km; climb up through the developers' effluvia, and Cerveteri is at the point where the long incline ends in typically Etruscan cliffs. To find the tombs, follow the narrow road dipping down to the left at the entrance to the village, flanked by pines, cypresses and odd mounds, until you reach a shaded car park.

Today's Cerveteri occupies only a small part of the old Etruscan city which, in the seventh century BC, was one of the most crowded in the Mediterranean, hard though it is to imagine. It was a large independent state, probably run by a king; in the sixth century BC its fleet fought on the side of Carthage to drive the Greeks from Corsica. To judge by the finds, its citizens were rich, cosmopolitan and refined.

The tombs, *tumuli*, look like great shaggy beehives on stone plinths. Inside, they are replicas of the homes of the well-to-do, spanning six centuries. Yet they feel as if they have just been vacated, and the sense of trespass is strong. Tarquinia is best known for its paintings; Cerveteri for the 'intimacy' of its rooms.

Some of these sunken cupolas are 30 metres in diameter. The two tiny rooms on either side of the entrance halls are thought to have accommodated the ashes of the servants. The main tomb is further in; heads of family were left in the intimate alcoves. Other dead were either placed in sarcophagi, cremated or simply laid out on the 'couches'. Don't miss the **Tomb of the Capitals** (*Capitelli*) near the entrance, modelled upon a sixth-century BC wooden house, complete with coffered ceiling and beams.

One of the best-known funeral homes is the so-called **Tomb of the Reliefs** (*dei Rilievi*), number 6, to the left before the path forks. Down the steep steps, you will find the walls of the large room hung with domestic utensils and the headman's favourite objects – helmets, swords, tongs, a foot-stool and dice. This is the most striking record of Etruscan domestic life there is.

There are hundreds of tombs in this virtual city of the dead, and you will need hours to clamber around. The biggest, made up of ten rooms around a vast central chamber, is called the **Tomba Giuseppe Moretti**, but it is a hike and you need a guide.

Ceri   On the way back to Rome, a dramatic setting for dinner is the isolated medieval village of Ceri (population 130), off the road left to Bracciano, 9 km down the *Aurelia*. It is a fort, with a steep entrance hacked out of the rock. The fare isn't Michelin, but the location is starry.

Ostia Antica   Ostia Antica fills in the big gaps between the craggy monuments of Imperial Rome. It puts Rome under a microscope, bringing out the lost detail of everyday life, what streets and houses must have looked like. If in Rome it takes an effort to imagine life under the Caesars, in Ostia Antica it takes none. It is the natural follow-up to Rome, yet you can find yourself almost on your own. Curious.

The vast place is usually open from 9 a.m. to one hour before sunset, and is closed on Mondays. Maps and books are for sale at the amphitheatre. Set aside at least half a day. Some find it an ideal picnic spot.

Getting there   It is quick to reach, only 20 km from Rome. By car, take the Via del Mare to modern Ostia (from *Ostium*, 'mouth of the river'). A frequent train service from Stazione San Paolo or Piramide whisks you there in thirty minutes; from Fiumicino airport, the ride takes only ten minutes.

History   Ostia Antica is sometimes called a 'poor man's Pompeii'. But while the eruption of Vesuvius in AD 79 crystallised just one moment, Ostia Antica betrays the whole cycle, from growth till decay, from the fourth century BC until the descent of the barbarians. Its heyday was under Trajan (AD 98–114), when its population was some 100,000.

Under the Republic, it was a crucial naval base, defending the Tiber mouth and Rome. It was then a river port, but in AD 54 Nero opened a new sea port just to the north to handle the increase in traffic, which was later linked to the Tiber by a canal or *fiumicino* ('little river'), hence the name of today's airport. By then Ostia was trading with the entire Latin world and provisioning voracious Rome, especially with grain.

Lapped by the now greatly receded sea, it was a prosperous place, regularly embellished by its wealthy citizens and attentive emperors, especially Hadrian who re-planned the town. It is 'his' Ostia.

The city has yielded up so much evidence of the daily life of the Romans because, rather unlike Rome, it was never re-occupied after the fall of the Empire, so its ruins and objects were left alone. Through literature, Rome became an idea; in Ostia, Rome is a fact.

What to see

Children's money-boxes have been found; bone spoons and knives with gladiators carved on their handles (but no forks; they were not used). Paintings show cages of rabbits on a shop counter, and two monkeys sitting there to attract customers. Snails were sold, and suckling pig, and there were public toilets . . .

There is so much to see in the great rectangular maze that if you are on foot it is wise to hurry past the Republican tombs by the entrance, and to begin exploring from around the horse-shoe **theatre** with its well-preserved stage and masks. If you are mobile, drive through the gate to the car park and walk back to the theatre, which was built by Agrippa and restored by Caracalla (AD 211–17). There is a (real) bar in one of the shop-niches in the outside wall.

Behind the theatre in the **Square of the Corporations**, inscriptions show that rope and tow merchants, boatmen, shippers, tanners and grain-weighers from Ostia, Rome, Carthage, Narbonne and Alexandria worked from seventy different offices. It was a business city, but obviously with a taste for luxury refinement and leisure, too. There is a well-appointed bath house every few metres. Courtyards and floors are decorated in pictured mosaics, some still in excellent shape. Ceilings and walls are painted. You will find patrician villas, homes with balconies, and blocks of apartments two and three storeys high. Near the old course of the Tiber (it switched in the sixteenth century), solid warehouses line the streets. The town is dotted with pagan temples, some dedicated to Mithras, whose sect was strong in Ostia. There is a laundry and, near the Forum, a **bar** (*Thermopolium*) with a marble-topped counter, shelves and big stone barrels.

The Forum is the focus of Ostia, and is still dominated by the city's imposing great temple, *Capitolium*, on a dais at the top of a steep flight of marble steps, built under Hadrian and still, remarkably, almost as it was. Opposite, at the far end, are the ruins of the Temple of Rome and

Augustus, and behind it to the left are the Forum Baths, with hot and cold water and vapour rooms, constructed in the second century. If you strike towards Via Guido Calza, the modern boundary road, you will fall upon another imposing bath complex, the **Terme della Marciana**, which was on the old beach.

The most elegant patrician dwelling is the fourth-century **House of Cupid and Psyche** (*Domus di Amore e Psiche*), so called after the kissing figures on a patterned floor of coloured marble. Facing the Capitolium, it is roughly at ten o'clock, off the Via del Foce to the right.

For a typical second-century middle-class home, see the tastefully decorated **Apartment of the Painted Ceilings** (*Insula dalle Volte Dipinte*), off the Decumano Massimo.

Tivoli

The powerful reason for getting out to Tivoli, a hill town 35 km east of Rome where the wealthy of ancient Rome had their summer villas, is the biggest and most spectacular Imperial villa in Italy, regarded as the flower of Greek-inspired Roman art.

Hadrian's Villa

The *Villa Adriana* is not in fact a villa, but a large estate once actually thought to have been a town. It lies at the foot of Tivoli, a turn-off from the *Via Tiburtina*, the SS 5, after 27 km. Alternatively, take the A 24 motorway to L'Aquila and then the Tivoli exit. You will need three or four hours to browse around, and there are no crowds.

More than a luxury residence, the Villa is a mental world. The Spanish-born Emperor Hadrian spent 12 of his 21 years in power travelling around Rome's possessions. He had a passion for architecture, and the Villa, designed by himself, is a re-creation of the sights that had most struck him on his journeys, especially in Egypt and, his other passion, Greece.

A scale-model on the right before the entrance conveys its spacious splendour, and the Romans' talent for domesticating nature to grace their building with a happy setting. It all went up between 118 and 134. Hadrian had much other building to his credit, including a certain construction in Britain, but he enjoyed this, his favourite composition, only briefly. He died four years after it was finished, aged 62.

It is an album, romantically framed. Through the thick outer wall, for instance, you enter into what is taken to be a reconstruction of a once painted portico in Athens, the *Stoa Poikile*. There is a Lyceum, an Academy, temples to Apollo and Venus, a Greek theatre and a library. And the site of the colossal Imperial palace, built around three great peristyles on the far left, overlooks Hadrian's idea of the Vale of Tempe in Eastern Greece.

A recurring theme is water. Perhaps the most touching sight, on the far right, is Hadrian's rendering of the **Valley of Canopus**, a canal named after a venerated temple near Alexandria in Egypt. This was where the melancholic, tormented Emperor had experienced his greatest grief: in AD 130 his favourite, the curly-haired Hellenic youth

Antinous, drowned in the Nile in mysterious circumstances. Hadrian had a town named after him, special coins minted, and he is remembered here in several of the figures lining the water's edge.

The Villa's most singular feature, over on the left, is the so-called **Maritime Theatre**: a delicate flight of Imperial fancy. Circular walls enclose a ring of ionic pillars, encircling a round moat encompassing an island, once a small villa. Scholars now believe it was Hadrian's retreat, his own version of the secret apartments used by his predecessors. They imagine him pulling up a drawbridge and cutting himself off to read or follow his hobby, painting.

Close by are the admired guest quarters, **Hospitalia**, a large hall flanked on either side by five rooms, with recesses for three beds and finely decorated mosaic floors.

The immense treasure Hadrian accumulated in his Villa is now scattered around the world's museums.

Villa d'Este

Up in Tivoli itself, the goal of the tourist buses from Rome is the famed 'Italian' garden, one of the finest in existence, just off the panoramic main square, Piazza Garibaldi. The Villa d'Este is named after a Renaissance prelate, Cardinal Ippolito II d'Este, a governor of Tivoli, who spent his life turning the former confiscated Benedictine monastery into a place of exuberant magnificence, partly by dipping into the marble and statuary at Hadrian's Villa.

The theme here is water, too, only there's rather more of it. Set out in a descending order of terraces, the cardinal's gardens are rationalised fun – a kind of sixteenth-century Disneyland, a world of fantasy complete with figures from legend and myth, gargoyles, mock-ups and novel ideas . . . in water.

It roars, tinkles, gurgles, gushes, flows, falls and flies everywhere. There are the fountains of the **Owl**, of **Bacchus**, of the **Dragons**. You can walk behind the cascading wall of the biggest, the **Fontana dell'Ovato**, the climax to the 'Avenue of the 100 Fountains'. You can peer into make-believe caves or watch great jets play games; then come waterfalls, streams and manicured lakes.

It is a rare spectacle, but really a coda to Hadrian's Villa; alone it possibly does not warrant a special trip. It is no longer illuminated at night, and usually closes around 7 p.m.

Hills and lakes

You may find it a relief in summer to escape from Rome to the south-east up into the nearby Alban Hills, usually known as the **Castelli Romani**, where temperatures can be much cooler, especially at night, and where the views may cause a gasp or two. They are called *Castelli* because that was the name for medieval fortified villages.

Getting there

Take the *Via Appia Nuova*, SS 7, and after Ciampino airport turn left along the *Via dei Laghi* (Lakes), SS 217, for Rocca di Papa and Nemi. For Velletri follow the signs. For Castel Gandolfo, Albano and Genzano, continue along the *Via Appia*.

Buses for the Castelli leave from near the Subaugusta Metro station on 'A' line.

Trains leave from Stazione Termini for Frascati, Marino, Castel Gandolfo and Albano.

Nemi   Though a mere village of 1,300 souls, Nemi, 34 km and 40 minutes from Rome, is the most striking of these hill townships. On the way, climbing up to it, the sight of Lake Albano, a navel in the earth, is so arresting that everybody brakes.

Perched on a promontory, Nemi looks down into its own lake as if into a deep well; the water filled in two coalesced volcanic craters. Down on its shores among the shadows are the remains, including a primitive altar, of a temple dedicated to Diana, the Goddess of Hunting. Stories are still whispered of blood-curdling rituals performed in her name, and of orgies held aboard a ship the Emperor Caligula had built in the lake, on the pretext it would be used for the worship of the goddess. The wreck was raised from the bottom in the 1930s, but destroyed when the Nazis burnt down the museum.

Nemi is famed for its succulent strawberries, grown all year round. Give the Strawberry Feast, 1–10 June, a miss: it's a crush.

A large restaurant overlooking the lake, reached through back alleys, is **Sirena del Lago**, tel. 936 8020 (closed Mondays). The speciality is lake trout (*Coregone*).

In the main street, try the more expensive **La Pergola** for game, tel. 936 8021 (closed Tuesdays).

Rocca di Papa   At 750 metres, Rocca di Papa is the highest of the Castelli. Thirty km from Rome, it clings to the drastic slopes of Mount Cavo, 949 metres high, the religious centre of the Latin League. The town is a precipitous experience, modern-ish at the bottom, medieval at the top where it is a private labyrinth of child-size alleys and nearly vertical homes.

It owes its name to the 168th Pope, Eugene III: he built and lived in a fortress (*Rocca*) here in the twelfth century, doubtless to deny his skin to the warring aristocrats down in Rome. Make for the topmost 'platform' road, where you will be greeted by surly hill-folk in indifferent *trattorie*, but also by magnificent long-shots of the country south of Rome.

At one minute before sunset, you are warm in the skimpiest wear. A minute after, you will wish you hadn't left that sweater down in Rome.

Castel Gandolfo   Thirty km from Rome and 426 metres high, the summer residence of the Popes lords it over Lake Albano. The palace, dominating the small main square, is a seventeenth-century structure built on the ruins of the castle of one of the warring Roman families. In the garden, the Pontiff can contemplate the hulky remains of a luxury villa inhabited by the pagan emperor Domitian (AD 81–96). This was the site of the legendary *Alba Longa*, the conquest of which set Rome on her way to greatness.

The domed Vatican Observatory is nearby and, pilgrims permitting, it is a summer pleasure to sample lake fish in two modest *trattorie* overlooking the lake, so profound that after nightfall it turns into a sinister abyss.

Genzano   Thirty-four km from Rome beyond snarled Albano, and 345 metres up, Genzano overlooks the crater of Lake Nemi opposite the village of Nemi. It is a picturesque seventeenth-century township (population 15,000) in a splendid position, with a good choice of restaurants for a leisurely evening. The Sunday in June after the feast of *Corpus Christi* is the day of the *Infiorita*, when the stepped main street climbing up to the rotting castle of the former duke, is carpeted with story-telling panels of flowers.

Anagni

Off the A 2 to Naples, 45 km south-east of the Rome ring road, this small, medieval hill town (population 8,000), with its ruined Roman walls, commands splendid vistas from an altitude of 424 metres over the valley of the River Sacco. It also possesses the finest cycle of thirteenth-century frescoes in Lazio.

The design of its imposing twelfth-century Palazzo Comunale is held to be unique in Italy and the main street is flanked by fourteenth-century houses. By ringing at the door, you can roam through the frescoed rooms of the *palazzo* of Pope Bonifacio VIII where, in an incident known to every Italian schoolboy, a Roman noble slapped him in the face in 1303, after he had excommunicated the King of France, Philip the Fair. He was one of three Popes born in this ancient township, which often served as a Papal seat when Rome was risky. The famous slap was the immediate prelude to the removal of the Papal court to Avignon where it was to remain until 1377. The next Pope, a Frenchman, didn't even set foot in Italy.

Cathedral   The eleventh-century Cathedral is rated as one of the finest Romanesque churches of Lazio. The famous frescoes, the work of three different Benedictine artists, are in the astonishing crypt, and are well preserved. Experts consider them of supreme interest because they document the change from Byzantine to 'Italian' art. The expressiveness about the first frescoes on the left, near the entrance, foreshadows Giotto, who started frescoing the Lower Church at Assisi sixty years later.

Palombara   Few people visit Palombara, 26 km from the Rome ring road to the north-east, on the SS 636. It is a typical Lazio hill town with a view and an agricultural centre (population 7,000), with memories of the eleventh century. It is not at all spectacular, but very Italian – a peep at everyday, rural Italy.

One good reason for going, on a circuitous and scenic way back to Rome from Tivoli, for instance, is a good restaurant, **Il Fontanone**, tel. 0774-66110 (closed Tuesdays). A speciality is *pappardelle* (broad, flat *pasta*) with artichokes and mushrooms.

There is even a spartan, panoramic, unfindable hotel, **Albergo Irene**, Via Forti, tel. 66121.

Viterbo

Viterbo (population 54,000) is the most impressive medieval city of Lazio. An easy excursion 82 km north of Rome, it keeps its past wrapped up in high defence walls and bears all the marks of having been a very bloody place. It is worth half a day, especially if you want to fit in the Middle Ages quickly, or a night as well if you want to see the painted Etruscan tombs at Tarquinia.

A Papal stronghold down the centuries, the city witnessed – in bizarre circumstances – the first Conclave ever. Once it bristled with 240 defence towers. The truncated ones you will see are tales of family defeats in fourteenth-century civic warfare between the 'Cats' and the 'Ringwormed'. Typical of Viterbo, apart from fountains, are its pretty outside staircases. In fact, they were defensive: they forced attacking swordsmen to fight with their backs to a void. The tiny, cramped Piazza Pellegrino is held to be the most faithful example in Italy of what an early thirteenth-century square really looked like.

History

Viterbo owes its scarred past to its command from high ground of the Cassia's last downward lap to Rome. It could cut Rome off from the north, or serve as a springboard for attack. The Longobard King Desiderius was one to see that, but after turning the town into a base, he thought better of it. Barbarossa press-ganged its males into his service and did attack Rome. When the Romans began turning upon the Papacy, the Pontiffs took to hiding in Viterbo. The first Papal refugee arrived in 1145.

Then the city became a key pawn in the struggle between the Papacy and the Empire. The citizens took unkindly to Teutonic soldiery left among them by Frederick II, hounding them out; they remained loyal-ish to the Popes from then on.

Italian scholars reckon Frederick probably saw Viterbo as a possible capital for a dream empire – stretching from the mists of Germany to the mosques of Sicily. All that remains of it now is a fenced mess of stones at the foot of the walls, opposite two petrol stations. They belonged to the fortress he built, which was torn down by energetic Cardinal Albornoz, fort-builder to the Popes in the fourteenth century.

What to see

The emblem of Viterbo was built as a Papal residence between 1255

Palazzo | and 1266, by a city hoping to be able to entice the Papacy away from
Papale | Rome. Now the seat of the archbishopric, it can be seen only from the outside. Viewed from down in the car park, it seems a forbidding fortress, yet from close up in the Piazza San Lorenzo it strikes you as gently elegant. The famous **loggia**, held aloft by slender twin columns, does the trick. The graceful structure is as fragile as it looks: one side tumbled into the valley in the fourteenth century.

From under its stone finery the French Pope Clement IV thundered out his excommunication of the young Conradin as the boy passed Viterbo down on the Cassia at the head of a small imperial army on its way to defeat. 'A lamb on its way to slaughter!' he shouted. Conradin came under an executioner's axe in a Naples square on the direct orders of Charles d'Anjou.

It was also in this *palazzo* that the Conclave was invented. When Clement died in 1268, eighteen cardinals spent three years inside it trying to pick a successor, canvassed by supporters of Charles d'Anjou who wanted another French Pope, and 'imperialists' who favoured an Italian. Unable to stand the suspense, the Viterbese locked the prelates up in the turreted hall to force them into a decision. They were, as the record has it, *clausi cum clave*, a phrase that begat 'conclave' and the Papal election procedure which is still in use. That first time, however, keys failed: the cardinals still could not agree. So the citizens removed the roof. Agreement was then reached.

Altogether, four Popes have been elected in the *palazzo*, including history's only Portuguese Pope, who dabbled in chemistry and probably blew himself up in his room. His tomb is in the twelfth-century Cathedral in the same square.

Chiesa del | Turning back along the Via San Lorenzo, beyond Piazza della
Gesù | Morte (the Square of Death), you arrive in the Piazza del Gesù, the former city centre. In the small church of the same name, Prince Richard of Cornwall, a son of Henry III, was stabbed to death at the altar during Mass by Guy and Simon de Montfort. They were avenging the death of their father, allegedly murdered on orders of the English crown. The Prince and his killers were all lobbying in Viterbo during the *cum clave*.

Santa Maria | A plaque clearly approves of Dante, who landed the Montfort
Nuova | brothers deep in Hell. Dante's mentor, St Thomas Aquinas, once preached from the outside pulpit of the nearby homely little Romanesque church of Santa Maria Nuova, amazingly still intact. The text says that he enjoined 'goodness and prayer' upon the populace from it.

Saint Rosa's | The big event is on 3 September, when in a punishing show of
Contraption | prowess a hundred costumed porters bear a dangerously swaying 30-metre high 'walking bell-tower' through the streets to honour their patron saint. Her corpse is displayed in a glass coffin in the modern church of St Rosa.

Where to stay

The most central three-star hotel is the **Leon d'Oro**, 36 Via della Cava, near Porta Fiorentina (one of Viterbo's main gates); tel. 344444. Cheaper and nearby are the **Tuscia**, 41 Via Cairoli, tel. 223377, and the **Milano**, 54 Via della Cava, tel. 30705.

Where to eat

Excellent and not expensive is **Il Grottino**, 7 Via della Cava (closed Tuesdays). Don't be put off by the frenchified interior. Specialities include *ravioli al Grottino*, ravioli with a sauce of whipped cream, tomato and sage, and *Viterbo Cotolette*, breadcrumbed veal slices with mushroom, ham and cheese.

For Viterbo 'peasant' dishes, try **Il Richiastro**, 18 Via della Marrocca (closed Mondays–Wednesdays and all of July and August). It has a garden.

Also recommended is **I Due I** (The Two 'I's), Via Cairoli; tel. 235921 (closed Sundays).

Villa Lante

Two spectacles very near Viterbo cry out for a look. One is the stupendous Villa Lante at Bagnaia, 5 km to the east on the SS 204. A former Papal hunting estate, successive cardinals transformed it into one of the most delightful creations of the late Renaissance in Italy, with the help of the Lombard architect Barozzi Vignola. Finished in only 1612, it's a vast, geometrical park and 'Italian garden', enlivened by fountains, caves, allegorical figures and a winged horse, whose hoof strikes a rock which, miraculously, spouts water. The best known fountain belongs to the boldly handsome 'Four Moors'.

Castel d'Asso

The other sight almost startles: it's of unusual Etruscan cliff tombs at Castel d'Asso, 8 km to the south-west of Viterbo, a bit hard to find. Leave town by Porta Faul, and keep asking. The narrow road is soon slicing through virtual gorges in the soft tufa rock and when it fizzles out, you've arrived. Rows of tombs are set into the sheer walls of gullies encircling the Etruscan township of **Axia**, on a wedge between the confluence of two streams. The site is untended, wild, and rather creepy. The heyday of Axia was in the fourth century BC.

Tarquinia

From Viterbo, follow the signs for Civitavecchia and the coast. Turn right off the *Via Cassia* at Vetralla for the vast Etruscan burial ground of Tarquinia, 30 km further on. The entrance is unobtrusive: on the right, 4 km before modern Tarquinia.

What to see

Tombs

Etruscan Tarquinia was one of Etruria's most powerful cities. It held sway over just about all the land between the coast and the Lakes of Bracciano and Bolsena. Aerial surveys show that the Necropolis might comprise some 35,000 tombs; about 7,000 have been identified. Of those, about 60 are painted. But be ready for severe disappointment: in compulsory groups, mute guides will show you only 4, and those very briefly. Visitors the next day will glimpse 4 others.

The purpose, of course, is to spare the paintings exposure to variations in temperature and humidity, which damage them. At one point, experts thought a solution would be to strip the frescoes from the tombs and display them in a controlled museum climate. Happily, they soon gave up the idea of such brutal surgery.

The pictures reflect a dramatic change in the local attitude towards death. When Tarquinia was at its most powerful in the sixth century BC, an after-life was regarded as an utter certainty, and the painting is exuberant, assertive. It records funeral games, dances and banquets, sometimes in the presence of the departed himself. You may be shown the **Tomb of the Jugglers**, where the dead man, holding a staff, is sitting on a folding chair, while to the sound of a double flute a young man throws rings at a kind of candelabra balanced on a woman's head. The date is about 530 BC. One of the most famous and delightful scenes, from the same era, is in the **Hunting and Fishing Tomb** (*Caccia e Pesca*). Jumping fish and soaring birds swirl around fishermen in a boat, while above they get on with a feast.

But in 307 BC the city fell to Rome after holding out for three years, and the paintings betray a people less certain about their spiritual future, tortured by visions of beasts and demons. Greek influence was then at its strongest. Archaeologists claim that the discovery in the 1960s of a big Greek warehouse complex at a nearby harbour, Porto Clementino, showed that links between the Hellenic world and Tarquinia were much closer than had previously been suspected. But what sets the Etruscans apart is their liking for realism, and the almost child-like gusto of their universe, not to mention their leopards with blue manes and their green horses. On the walls, the Etruscan artists painted on lightly whitewashed plaster, but on the ceilings they worked directly on to the calcareous rock, without any drafting.

Museum   Your ticket is also valid for the fine Etruscan museum in the town. The original Etruscan city, to the north of the Necropolis beyond a river, was abandoned because of malaria. The stupendous winged stallions on the left of the stairs were discovered in 1938 at the foot of a large temple in the old town. They were pulling a (lost) chariot and are judged to be the masterpiece of fourth- to third-century BC Etruscan sculpture.

The first floor is crammed with treasure from the tombs from the ninth century BC onwards. Many vases were straight imports from Greece; Tarquinia has yielded up the biggest collection of Greek ceramics in the world. Many themes are mythological, but some are outspokenly erotic.

As from 1989, four 'removed' tombs were to have been displayed permanently on the second floor.

Civitavecchia   Unless bound for Sardinia by boat, few rush to admire this city, half blown up in the Second World War and now an industrial complex where the choking inhabitants rightly complain of pollution. It grew around a major port built by Trajan in AD 106; the Saracens later used it as a base to attack Rome. It then became a Papal stronghold.

Sulphur baths

Five km from the town, at a place called Ficonella, the adventurous will find a small, crude, open-air thermal bath that has run throughout time. The few Romans in the know go there even at dead of winter to soak in the warm flow of sulphur-alkaline earth waters. Both sexes are admitted, now supervised by guardians of public morality. It is impossible to describe where it is, but everybody knows the way!

Beyond it and the motorway lie the remains of a rather larger bath-house complex, thought to have been part of an Imperial villa, perhaps Trajan's, put up so that he could watch his port develop.

The Sardinia ferries sail twice nightly, if they are not immobilised by frequent summer wildcat strikes. Booking is vital.

Where to stay

On the front, the two-star **Miramare** is passable and handy; tel. 26167.

With a garage 1 km from the centre towards Rome is the four-star **Sunbay Park Hotel**; tel. 22801.

Where to eat

A reliable, if chaotic, *trattoria* on the front is **Da Vitale**, 26 Viale Garibaldi (closed Mondays).

Further along is **La Lupa**, Viale Repubblica, tel. 25703 (closed Tuesdays). Entrance is at 5 Via Formino.

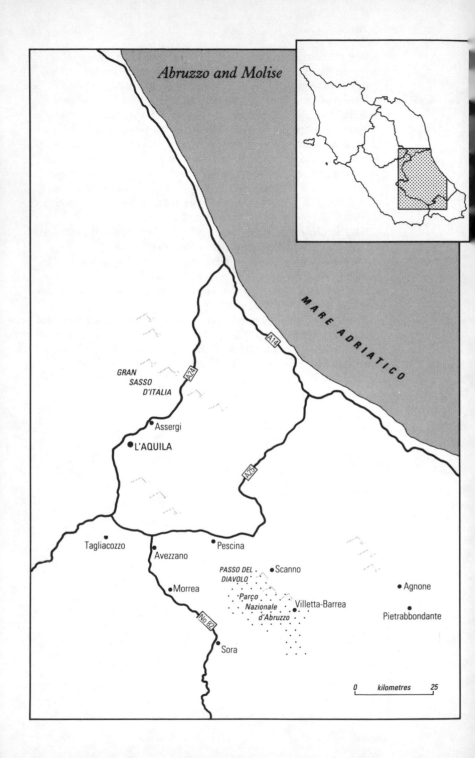

Abruzzo and Molise

MARE ADRIATICO

GRAN SASSO D'ITALIA

A14

A24

Assergi

● L'AQUILA

A25

● Tagliacozzo

● Avezzano

● Pescina

PASSO DEL DIAVOLO

● Scanno

● Morrea

Parco Nazionale d'Abruzzo

Villetta-Barrea

● Agnone

● Pietrabbondante

No. 82

● Sora

0   kilometres   25

Abruzzo and Molise

Introduction

This is the wildest, emptiest, least developed and most peaceful part of Central Italy. It is a land of great Apennine peaks and deep valleys, one of the most thinly populated in Italy. In the south the terrain is rolling and open. Mass tourism is not even on the horizon. It is the least known part of Central Italy, too, but it would be misleading to suggest that its neglect is undeserved. It can boast of few great cathedrals or picture galleries. Artistically speaking, it will be low on your list compared to the rest.

It could be far higher if you need a day or two 'off' amid splendid mountain scenery, or an untaxing drive around another Italy. The main attraction is the Abruzzo National Park. This is a world of braying asses, accordion and bagpipe music, of heady 75 per cent proof spirits (ask for *Cento-erbi*) and often poor roads, where straight-backed women in black still carry loads on their heads. The now autonomous Molise region, the small, drearier, southern part, was detached from Abruzzo only in 1963.

Abruzzo

History Though physically part of Central Italy, Abruzzo is historically a thorough foreigner. For centuries it came under Naples and had no link with Papal Italy. Initially, it was chiefly known as the redoubt of the fierce Samnites, the last of the Italic peoples to be subdued by the Romans. They held all Molise, and then expanded towards both coasts, forming a troublesome barrier against Roman penetration southwards.

When the Romans tried to encircle them near Benevento in 321 BC, they were badly thrashed. The Samnites then joined forces against Rome with the Etruscans and Umbrians; when these allies were beaten, they fought on alone until they were savagely repressed. The final revolt was in 90 BC when the Samnites fielded 100,000 men; they were defeated only four years later after losing three times that number.

The Abruzzo came under the Kingdom of Naples and Sicily after the defeat of Frederick II's 15-year-old grandson Conradin at Tagliacozzo, just south of the fork between the A 24 and A 25 motorways, about 30 km south of L'Aquila. The victor was Charles d'Anjou, who had been given the crown of Sicily by the Papacy in return for his help against the Empire. As the Kingdom changed hands, Abruzzo then fell under Aragonese, Spanish, French and Austrians.

Germans today claim that Abruzzo was its forward bastion, and that Frederick II actually founded L'Aquila ('The Eagle') as a potential mountain base for an offensive against Papal Rome. They argue that the city was 'the Mecca of the anti-clerical cause'. The Italians are not so sure.

The people

The people of the Abruzzo are reserved, untalkative, suspicious folk of hardy peasant stock, with long experience of extreme poverty and hardship behind them. Until recently, the illiteracy rate was high. The present sparse population of only 1½ million is largely the result of quite massive emigration to escape unemployment and hunger. The destinations of the first great wave, in the two decades before the First World War, were the United States and South America. The second reached its peak in 1960, when they mainly set out for Australia and Canada.

Getting there

Until recently, getting there was arduous. Now, Italy's latest motorway, the A 24, gets you from Rome to L'Aquila, the fulcrum for any touring, in an easy two hours. There is no train from Rome, but buses (from Piazza della Repubblica) are frequent.

The best time to go is in the late spring or early autumn.

L'Aquila

This is the capital of the Abruzzo, a sober and agreeable market town (population 65,000) with plenty of its medieval past to show, yet now dominated by numerous churches (about sixty) and, unusually, by florid *palazzi* from the eighteenth century. Just 101 km from Rome, it slopes down a valley, dwarfed by the *Gran Sasso*, or 'Big Stone', a mass of mountain more than 50 km long spiked with the very highest peaks of the Apennines.

What to see

Tourist Offices are the Provincial, 5 Piazza Maria Paganica, tel. 67100, and the readier Municipal, 8 Via XX Settembre, tel. 22306.

'Ninety nine'

The figure 99 dominates L'Aquila. It is traditionally the number of the scattered village-castles in the area that decided to agglomerate into one big place in the mid-thirteenth century, apparently under a licence issued by Frederick II. Serious scholars tut-tut, but every evening the bell in the Civic Tower rings out 99 times, for the ears of the original 99 wards, which each established 99 churches, 99 squares and 99 fountains. Its most novel draw is a medieval fountain with 99 spouts.

L'Aquila was destroyed a first time in the thirteenth century by Frederick's son Manfred as a punishment for treacherously siding with the Papacy. Charles d'Anjou rebuilt it and, for beating off the attacking Aragonese Spaniards in the fifteenth century, the Anjou family rewarded L'Aquila with privileges that bred prosperity and trade with Europe, especially in wool.

Castello During the struggle between the French and the Spanish for the Kingdom of Naples in the next century, it switched again and fell in with Charles V of Spain. His men behaved atrociously enough to spark off mass rebellion. As part of their brutal punishment this time, the people had to pay for the massive fort, still splendidly intact, an intimidating watchdog designed by a Spaniard, now in a park five minutes from the sloping main square, *Piazza del Duomo*, a big morning market.

Palazzi The city's troubles were not over. In 1703, an apocalyptic earthquake almost wiped it out, killing 6,000 people. This explains all the eighteenth-century *palazzi*, the result of rebuilding, although a few graceful fifteenth-century *palazzi* survived, such as the **Palazzo Camponeschi** in Piazza Paganica (site of the Provincial Tourist Office) and the **Palazzo Pasquali**, 171 Via Roma. Houses with the monogram of Christ, 'IHS', above the doors are also fifteenth-century, a compliment to the preaching of St Bernardino of Siena, who died here.

Santa Maria The most riveting spectacle is the cube-like façade of the thirteenth-*in Collemaggio* century basilica of **Santa Maria in Collemaggio**, just outside the city at the end of Viale Collemaggio. It is the masterpiece and model of Romanesque-Gothic art as interpreted in the Abruzzo. It is the Abruzzo's little Orvieto, a geometric theatre in pink and white local stone. The central Gothic rose window, a double 'wheel' of spiral spokes, hogs the spot. It was here that the only Pope ever to resign, an Abruzzese hermit, was crowned in 1249 by Charles d'Anjou as Celestine V. He gave up, confused, after only five months; you can inspect his corpse.

an Bernardino The corpse of the Sienese saint is two minutes from the market in the Renaissance church named after him. Built especially in his honour, it is the second most admired in the city, largely because of its stately, three-tiered façade. The carved, gilded ceiling of the post-earthquake, Baroque interior is a dazzling complement.

Fontana delle The symbol of L'Aquila is its weird and singular fountain, thought *99 Cannelle* up in 1272 as a portrait-gallery of the squires who ruled the city's ninety-nine component *Castelli*. Each spout is a different, startling face, and nobody seems to know where the water comes from. It is outside the town, at the bottom of Via XX Settembre.

Abruzzo National Museum

The Abruzzo's main museum is in the Castello, and is a disclosure of medieval art of the region. The main medium is wood – there are wooden Madonnas, and carved doors, for instance. A highlight is a big, damaged, wooden crucifix from the early thirteenth century, showing a 'live' Christ, 'triumphant' over death – the only such Christ found in the Abruzzo. The Museum also provides an ample run-down on Abruzzese contemporary art.

Where to stay

The best hotel is the central, four-star **Grand Hotel del Parco**, 11 Corso Federico; tel. 20248.

Facing the Castle is the utilitarian three-star **Castello**, Piazza Battaglione Alpini; tel. 29147.

In the main thoroughfare is the old-fashioned two-star **Italia**, 79 Corso Vittorio Emanuele; tel. 20566.

Where to eat

Restaurants abound, but especially sound is the **Remo**, 9 Via Flaviano, off Piazza Duomo; tel. 22010 (closed Saturdays).

Gran Sasso

The topmost peak, called the Corno Grande, reaches 2,912 metres. You can drive up to admire this majestic spectacle, flecked with snow even in summer, by taking the SS 17 bis from the centre of town, or the quicker A 24 towards Teramo. You then turn right up to a vast, grassy, treeless plateau, the 'Emperor's Field', where in summer horses gallop about amid multitudes of grazing sheep and cattle.

Beneath one peak, Monte Aquila (2,494 metres), the lonely **Campo Imperatore** hotel is under restoration.

Abruzzo National Park

The Park covers 400 sq km in the extreme south of Abruzzo. It is a nature reserve of beech forest, spectacular gorges, lakes, torrents and mountains, more than 1,000 species of flowers and above all, bears. Some 70 to 100 of them roam the Park, and it is not unusual now for them to be sighted far beyond it.

Chamois are protected there, as well as wolves, foxes, badgers, otters and weasels. Originally declared a reserve in 1923, the Park is not fenced in, although signs signal its confines. It includes eighteen villages, where tree-felling, grazing, building, hunting and fishing are banned. But there are only a handful of wardens to keep out the guns. Each village in the Park, especially **Pescassaroli**, the administrative headquarters, and **Alfadena**, is a jump-off point for signposted exploration on foot or horseback, the routes lasting from 30 minutes to 4 hours, ranging from 'easy' to 'demanding'. Ask for the local **Ufficio di Zona**.

A suggested route is to take the A 24 from Rome, fork right on to the A 25 towards Avezzano, then take the SS 17 towards Pescina. The Park begins at the Passo del Diavolo, the 'Devil's Pass', 1,400 metres high amid great magnificence. At Villetta-Barrea, turn north on the SS 479.

Scanno

This medieval township has a puzzlingly Oriental air to it. It is near Abruzzo's biggest lake, and could easily qualify as the most picturesque town in Abruzzo, partly because of the striking traditional costumes, including un-Italian turbans, worn by the women.

Where to stay and eat

Two of its eighteen hotels are the **Del Lago**, tel. 0864-74343; and the cheaper **Centrale**, tel. 745332 (street names unnecessary).

Further on, the road passes through the eye of a needle in the dramatic Gorge of Sagittarius.

Morrea

For a real taste of the Abruzzo, try finding this totally unknown, unsung, tiny village, 780 metres high, unmarked on most maps (!) To get there, take the road leading south from Avezzano to Sora, the SS 82. After about 30 km, past the village of Civitella Roveto, look out for a steep, left turn off the road – if you get to Balsorano, you've gone a few km too far.

Known to me for thirty years, it perfectly conveys the silent remoteness of an Abruzzo mountain settlement that has survived the centuries amid goats, cheese, mules ridden out to work before dawn, the fumes of wine, roof-high snow, misery and sheer beauty. In 1960, today's road did not exist, neither did electricity nor telephone. Ascent was by mule, the place was unpaved, and the young had fled. Their grandparents, given the healthy air, will doubtless still be there when you read this. They will be astonished to see you. There's a bar.

Molise

The infant Molise region to the south is the poor cousin of Central Italy, its most backward, least travelled, and least populated area. Tens of thousands have abandoned it in search of kindlier climes. Around the turn of the century, they fled to South America; and from the 1950s onwards, to West Germany. Only about 320,000 are left – in a vast remoteness.

The air of dereliction about Molise is an early-warning of run-down Southern Italy, and in places even Third World overtones come through. Communications are poor, resources few, and attractions limited, but it has an appeal, that of a world far away, forgotten and forlorn – and unspoilt. This is a certain Italy as she once was . . . sad, depressed, peasanty, timeless, gently attractive.

The Southern Apennines begin in Molise, but it's less operatically mountainous than Abruzzo and as the terrain dips towards the west the landscapes turn stark, rocky and desolate. The harshness then gives way to openness and undulating grassy vistas, but there's hardly anyone about. It's like travelling in the days when nobody had a car. Another mountain range shuts off Molise from Campania.

Two features set Molise aside from the rest of Central Italy. Firstly, its borders enclose more obvious traces than anywhere else of Italy's pre-Roman, 'Italic' (non-Etruscan) immigrants, obscure Indo-European peoples. Molise was the 'base camp' of the Samnites, for instance.

Poorly-funded excavations are still underway. One is near the strangely-named **Schiavi d'Abruzzo** ('Slaves of Abruzzo'), about halfway along the Molise–Abruzzo frontier, near isolated **Poggio Sannita** ('Samnite'). Schiavi, a granity, slatey place on a high, lonely ridge overlooking desolation, is utterly spooky. Arrive there at 8 p.m., (dinner-time), and you will find not a single being in its streets. Clearly, this was the original ghost-town.

Secondly, you could well end up in a few villages where you'll understand not even a split syllable. They're inhabited entirely by Albanese who fled invading Turks to settle in Molise in the sixteenth century. They're still getting ready to accommodate to the Italian tongue.

Campobasso The 'capital' is a modern sprawl down in the plain, with a small medieval quarter whose stepped streets spill over a hill. All is dominated by a sixteenth-century turreted castle, the Castello Monforte, 749 metres up.

Samnite Museum The town also has an unusual Museo Sannitico at 21 Via Vittorio Veneto, with Samnite weaponry as well as Samnite objects in gold and silver.

The Tourist Office is at 14 Piazza della Vittoria; tel. 0874-95662.

Where to stay The two main hotels are **Roxy**, 7 Piazza Savoia; tel. 91741; and **Kappa**, 21 Via S. Antonio Lazzari; tel. 67441.

Saepinum South of Campobasso, just off the main road to Benevento, are the plentiful ruins of this sacked Roman town which flourished under the Empire. There are private homes, a theatre and long stretches of wall, and the place is still inhabited – by local peasants and their beasts. Here, time has merged.

Isernia The main blemish of Molise is Isernia in the west, a very ancient town badly hit in the Second World War – to be skirted.

Agnone At a height of 833 metres, Agnone (population 7,000) is a 120-km crow's-flight south-east of L'Aquila, and 83 km south-west of the coastal town of Vasto on the SS 24. The bell-foundry there, which welcomes visitors, claims to be one of the oldest in Italy. They call it the 'Athens of the Samnites' and, pretty-ish rather than striking, the town is a draw for local tourists, where everything that copper and brass can be made into is on display in shops lining the sleepy main street.

The foundry, at the entrance to the township, is the *Fonderia Marinelli*; founded in 1300, it has served many Popes and prelates. The medieval recipe is still followed, meaning that the 'voice' of each bell is somehow built into it *before* casting. They'll also show you their replica of a two-sided text on a bronze slab dating from the third century BC written in the language of the Oscans, one of the four main invading Italic tribes. Here, they've set down liturgical instructions for rites to honour agricultural deities. The last two lines read: 'On the holiday, the garden is open to those who've paid the up-keep rates.' The original text, found near Agnone in the last century, is in the British Museum.

Where to stay and eat

Agnone's best, modern, hotel, with a panavision restaurant, is the relaxed four-star **Sammartino**, 44 Via Pietro Micca; tel. 0865-78239. Creakier is the **Hotel Italia**, 11 Piazza XX Settembre; tel. 78589.

Pietrab-bondante

Some 25 twisting km south of Agnone, at the foot of the township of the 'Abandoned Stones', is a recently excavated Samnite religious centre, on a slope dominating a handsome sweep of terrain. The temple goes back to the early second century BC, while the semicircular theatre, with its 'modern' anatomical backrests, was probably built in the last decades of the first century AD, shortly before the final showdown with Rome. This was the 'spiritual' headquarters of the Samnite resistance movement.

This is a worthwhile trip: very out of the way, but acutely evocative.

Further Reading

Books on Italy would fill the Colosseum; here is a minute, arbitrary sampling.

General

History of the Italian People, Giuliano Procacci (Pelican). A succinct, comprehensive, clear history of Italy is curiously hard to find in English. This tries to stop the gap, starting in the year 1000.

The Italians, Luigi Barzini (Hamish Hamilton). This mischievous classic ranks as a set book.

Italia, Italia, Peter Nichols (Macmillan). The author was *The Times* correspondent in Rome from the end of the Second World War until his recent death. Naturally, he is superbly informed.

The Woman of Rome and other books by Alberto Moravia and his wife Elsa Morante. Italian *letterati* wrinkle their noses at the 'popular' Moravia, but he has a robust insight into Italians.

Pictures from Italy, Charles Dickens (Granville). An eye-opener on changing tastes: he finds the Appian Way outside Rome a 'desert of decay, sombre and desolate beyond all expression.'

Etruscan Places, D. H. Lawrence (Penguin). This ecstatic classic written in 1932, Lawrence's 'discovery' of the mysterious burial grounds of Tuscany and Lazio, must still be about the best introduction to the Etruscans. It is included in *D. H. Lawrence and Italy* (Penguin).

The Etruscans, Prof. M. Pallottino (Penguin). The standard, readable, work by Italy's foremost expert.

Private Angelo, Eric Linklater (Buchan & Enright). A gentle, hilarious, wise novel about an Italian soldier in Second World War Italy.

Abba Abba, Anthony Burgess (Hutchinson).

A Short History of Italian Literature, J. H. Whitfield (Penguin). By a former lecturer in Italian at Oxford University.

Florence

The Civilisation of the Renaissance in Italy, Jacob Burckhardt (Phaidon). First published in 1860, this is the monumental basic text on the Renaissance as a period of civilisation; Burckhardt, a lecturer at Basel, was the 'inventor' of this, now challenged, concept. A slow, smooth, essential read.

Renaissance in Italy: the Fine Arts, John Addington Symonds (Smith, Elder). It is now fashionable to spurn poor Symonds, who wrote this study in 1898, but he is captivating, passionate, helpful, if you can find him.

Early Renaissance and High Renaissance, Michael Levey (Penguin). Reverential, reliable, with theories as well.

The Art of the Renaissance, Peter and Linda Murray (Thames and Hudson). If slightly humourless, this is a modern, useful, detailed guide to the early Renaissance; nicely illustrated.

Lives of the Artists (2 vols.), Giorgio Vasari (Penguin). First fully published in 1568 by the Florentine court painter, these biographies of the Renaissance artists are the basic crib for everything written later. Hugely readable.

The Stones of Florence and Venice Observed, Mary McCarthy (Penguin). Try not to miss this American novelist's gem; she has caught the 'feel' of Florence perfectly, with wit and a very sharp eye.

A Room with a View, E. M. Forster (Penguin). The 'other' Florence, the one owned by the English, in which the Florentines play 'Italians'.

The Rise and Fall of the House of Medici, Christopher Hibbert (Penguin). The definitive story.

Rome

The Companion Guide to Rome, Georgina Masson (Collins). This is the bible of Rome guide-books, an exhaustive, 541-page, authoritative, engrossing, chatty narrative pinning down that elusive detail. Not for digesting between two planes.

Rome – the Biography of a City, Christopher Hibbert (Penguin). The detailed tale of Rome's 3,000 years, including a few slips.

The Early History of Rome, Livy (Penguin). From the beginnings to the fourth century BC. An excellent translation of a fundamental text, packed with detail and anecdote.

The Roman Emperors, Michael Grant (Weidenfeld and Nicolson). A handy reference book, with pen-portraits of them all.

The Decline and Fall of the Roman Empire, Edward Gibbon (Penguin). Here in a digestible format.

Rome '44, Raleigh Trevelyan (Coronet). Based on fresh research, this is the gripping, maddening saga of the Allies' painful 'advance' on Rome via Anzio and Monte Cassino in the Second World War.

The Pope's Divisions: the Roman Catholic Church Today, Peter Nichols (Faber). The secret workings of the Vatican by a colleague who observed them for a lifetime.

A Thief in the Night, John Cornwell (Viking). A quoted, tortuous Vatican as it emerged during an exclusive probe into the death of Pope John Paul I.

Index

Abbadia di Fiastra 202
Abbadia San Salvatore 147
Abruzzo 71, 72, 267–71
Abruzzo National Park 267,
    270–1
Acquasparta 179
Agnelli, Gianni 21
Agnone 272–3
air travel 41
Alba Longa 259
Alban Hills (Castelli Romani)
    258–9
Alfadena 271
Amelia 180
Anagni 260–1
Ancona 207
Andrea di Firenze 115
Angelico, Fra 116
Anghiari 153
Ansedonia 76
Apennines 209, 271
Aouan Alps 83
Aquinas, Thomas 262
Arbia, Luciagnono d' *see*
    Lucignano d'Arbia
Arezzo 153–4
    history of 82
    jousting tournament 55
Arnolfo di Cambio 109, 137
Arrone 182
art galleries
    Ancona 207
    Città di Catello 177
    Cortona 154
    Fabriano 200–1
    Florence 106–9, 110–11, 114
    Perugia 162
    Rome 242
    Siena 135
    Urbino 195–6

arts 55
Ascoli Piceno 191, 203–5
    Cathedral 204–5
    history of 13
    hotels in 205
    Piazza del Popolo 204
    Santi Vicenzo ed Anastasio
        204
Assisi 165–8
    Cathedral 167
    churches
        Basilica of St Francis 166
        Santa Damiano 168
        Hermitage 167–8
    history of 165
    hotels in 168
    Rocca Maggiore 166
Augustus, Roman Emperor 217,
    229, 236, 239
Axia 263

Bagnaia 263
Bagni di Lucca 93
Balduccio, Giovanni 127
Barberino di Mugello 122
Barbischio 126
Barna di Siena 135, 139
Baroque architecture 219, 238
bars 49–50
Bartolo di Fredi 135, 138, 144
Bartolo, Taddeo di *see* Taddeo di
    Bartolo
beaches
    east coast 77–9
    west coast 75–6
Beccafumi 132
bella figura 31–2
Benedict, Saint 157, 184
Bernini, Gian Lorenzo 215, 238
Bevagna 169–70
birth control 27
Boccaccio, Giovanni 139
Bonifacio VIII, Pope 260
Borgia, Lucrezia 197
Botticelli, Sandro 14, 83, 100,
    104, 107–8

Bramange, Lazzari 178, 206
Brunelleschi, Filippo 83, 94, 103, 113, 113, 115, 116
 Florence Cathedral 109
Buoninsegna, Duccio di *see* Duccio di Buoninsegna
bureaucracy 20-1
bus services 43
butteri (cowboys) 148
Byron, Lord George 90, 93
Byzantine art 207, 241
Byzantines 11, 158

Caesar, Julius 217, 227, 230
Calvi, Roberto 27
Cambio, Arnolfo di *see* Arnolfo di Cambio
campanilismo 30-1
Campi Vecchio 185
campidoglio 55
camping 47
Campobasso 272
Caprese Michelangelo 151
car, travel by 38-41
car hire 41
Caravaggio 76, 108, 163, 215-16, 234, 236, 242
Carsulae 179
Cascata delle Marmore 181
Cascia 185
Casentino, The 151
Castel d'Asso 263
Castel Gandolfo 2259
Castellina in Chianti 127
Castelluccio 185
Castelnuovo dell'Abate 143
Castelnuovo di Val di Cecina 141
Castiglioncello 75
Castiglione del Lago 189
Castiglione d'Orcia 144
Castiglione della Pescaia 76
castles
 Chianti 124-5
 Fortezza di San Martino 122
 L'Aquila 269

Lucca 92-3
Monforte 272
Monteriggioni 137
Prato 95
Rocca Maggiore, Assisi 166
Rocca di Papa 259
Rocca delle Torri, Spoleto 172
Roccatederighi 150
Rome 242
Trebbio 123
Catacombs of Santa Mustiola 147
cathedrals (principal)
 Anagni 260
 Ancona 207
 Ascoli Piceno 204-5
 Assisi 167
 Florence 109-10
 Grosseto 149
 Gualdo Tadino 176
 Lucca 92
 Massa Marittima 150
 Orvieto 186-7
 Perugia 161-2
 Pienza 145
 Pisa 86, 88
 Pistoia 94
 Prato 95
 St Peter's 249-51
 Siena 133-4
 Spoleto 172-3
 Todi 178
 Volterra 140
caves, at Frasassi 199-200
Cavour, Camillo Benso di 15
Cellini, Benvenuto 113
Ceri 255
Cerreto Guidi 97
Certaldo 136, 139
Cerveteri 9, 154-5
Cesi 179-80
Charlemagne 11, 82, 143
Charles V, Holy Roman Emperor 14, 101
Charles VIII, King of France 14
Charles I (of Anjou), King of

Naples and Sicily 13, 267, 269
Chianciano 146–7
Chianti (region) 84, 124–7
history of 124–5
Chianti (wine) 84, 125–6
Chiusi 147
Christian Democrat Party 21, 23
churches (principal)
Arezzo
Santa Maria della Pieve 154
Ascoli Piceno
Santi Vicenzo ed Anastasio 204
Assisi
Basilica of St Francis 166
Santa Chiara 167
Santa Maria degli Angeli 168
Fano
Santa Maria Nuova 198
Florence
San Lorenzo 112
Santa Croce 115–16
Santa Maria Novella 114–15
Gubbio
San Francesco 175
Impruneta
Santa Maria 127
L'Aquila
Santa Maria in Collemaggio 269
Lugnano
Santa Maria Assunta 180
Montepulciano
San Biagio 146
Norcia
Sant'Agostino 184
Orcia
San Quirico 144
Rome
Aracoeli 233
St Agnese in Agone 238
San Clemente 224–5
San Paolofuori le Mura 243
San Pietro in Vincoli 225–6
Santa Maria degli Angeli 241
Santa Maria in Cosmedin 240
Santa Maria Maggiore 240–1
Santa Pras[illegible]d 241
San Casciano
Chiesa della Misericordia 127
San Gemini
San Giovanni Battista 180
San Miniato
San Francesco 96
Spoleto
San Gregorio 172
San Pietro 172
Todi
San Fortunato 178
Santa Maria della Consolazione 178
Cimabue, Giovanni 103, 106, 116, 166
cinemas 57
Città di Castello 176–7
Città della Pieve 188
city-states 12
Civitanova Marche 79
Civitavecchia 264
Clement IV, Pope 262
Clement VII, Pope 187, 242
climate 36
clothing 57
coffee 49
Colle Bertone 182
Colle di Val d'Elsa 137
Communist Party (PCI) 21, 22, 23, 83, 90
in Umbria 159
comunes 12
Conradin, Emperor 13, 262, 268
Contantine, Roman Emperor 10, 224, 243
convents, for visitors 46
Corno Grande 270
corruption 20–1
Cortona 154–5
credit cards 60
crime 19–20, 28–9
Crivelli, Carlo 193, 204–5

cultural organisations 57
currency 60

Dante Alighieri 81, 100, 115
Deruta 171
Dickens, Charles 128, 238, 250
documents 58
Domitian, Roman Emperor 229, 238, 159
Donatello 83, 89, 95, 103–4, 110, 112–13, 115, 127, 134, 135
drinking 52–3
drugs 29
Duccio di Buoninsegna 131, 134, 135

electrical current 58
'Ellipse', The 91
embassies 58
Empoli 96
entertainment 54
Etruscans 9, 81, 121, 140
    in Lazio 216–17, 254–5, 263–4
    in Tuscany 147, 148, 149, 154
    in Umbria 158, 163–4, 186
Eugene III, Pope 259

Fabriano 200–1
family, in Italian society 24–5, 30
Fano 77, 197–8
farm holidays 46–7
Ferentillo 182
Fermo 205
festivals 54–5, 131, 164, 171, 176, 197, 198, 259, 262
Ficonella 265
Fiesole 121–2
    arts festival in 55
    history of 82, 121
Firenze, Andrea di see Andrea di Firenze
Florence 72, 97–121
    artists from 103–4
    Boboli Gardens 114
    Cathedral 109–10
    churches

San Lorenzo 112
San Marco 116
Santa Croce 115–16
Santa Maria Novella 114–15
climate of 36, 97
festivals in 54, 55, 117
Galleria degli Uffizi 106–9
history of 82–3, 99–101
hotels in 119–20
Loggia dei Lanzi 105
Medici Chapels 111–12
Museo Nazionale del Bargello 112–13
nightlife in 117
Palatine Gallery 114
Palazzo Medici 117
Palazzo Pitti 113–14
Palazzo Vecchio 105
Ponte Vecchio 105
restaurants in 120–1
shopping in 117–18
transport to 97, 99
Foligno 170–1
Follonica 75
food 51–2, 84–5, 160, 192–3
Forte di Bibbona 75
Forte dei Marmi 75
Francesca, Piero della see Piero della Francesca
Francis, Saint 165, 166, 167, 168, 175, 203
Frasassi Caves 199–200
Frederick I (Barbarossa), Holy Roman Emperor 13, 172, 261
Frederick II, Holy Roman Emperor 13, 95, 159, 169, 182, 189, 199, 261, 268, 269
Fredi, Bartolo di see Bartolo di Fredi
Fregene 76

Gaddi, Agnolo 95, 116
Gaiole in Chianti 126
Galileo Galilei 88, 115, 179
Garibaldi, Giuseppe 15, 213
Gelli, Licio 27, 28

Genzano 260
Ghibellines v. Guelfs 13, 82, 138, 174
Ghiberti, Lorenzo 109–10. 113, 135
Ghirlandaio, Domenico 114, 177
Giambologna 122
Gigli, Beniamino 206, 207
Giotto 14, 81, 103, 123
    in Basilica of St Francis, Assisi 166
    frescoes of in Santa Croce, Florence 115–16
glossary 68–9
Gorge of Saggitarius 271
Gothic architecture
    in Tuscany 133
    in Umbria 161, 166, 169, 178
Goths 11
    in Lazio 229
    in the Marhces 192, 201, 202
    in Tuscany 82
    in Umbria 186
Gozzoli, Benozzo 117, 139, 170
Gran Sasso 270
Greeks 217, 264
Gregory VII, Pope 13, 151, 172
Greve in Chianti 126
Grosseto 149
Gualdo Tadino 176
Gubbio 174–6
    festival in 54
    history of 174
    hotels in 176
    Palazzo dei Consoli 175
    shopping in 175–6
Guido da Siena 135

Hadrian IV, Pope 147
Hadrian, Roman Emperor 237, 242, 256, 257–8
Hannibal 172, 188–9, 192
health care 58–9
hitch-hiking 41
homosexuality 34
horse riding 55, 75

hotels (see also under individual towns) 45–6

Il Bruco 76
Impruneta 127
insurances 59
Isernia 272

Jesi 199
John XXIII, Pope 26
John Paul I, Pope 26, 251
John Paul II, Pope 215, 219, 249, 251
Julius III, Pope 161

Keats, John 236
kidnapping 28–9

Ladispoli 76
Lake Trasimeno 188–9
L'Aquila 268–70
Larderello 136, 141
laundry 59
Lazio 71, 209–54
leather 118
Leo X, Pope 112, 219
Leonardo da Vinci 52, 96, 104
Leopardi, Giacomo 206–7
Lido di Tarquinia 76
Lippi, Filippo 95, 173, 242
Livorno (Leghorn) 90–1
Lodovica, Anna Maria 106
Lombards 82
Longobards 11, 91, 95
    in Lazio 261
    in the Marches 203
    in Umbria 158, 166
Lorenzetti, Ambrogio 132, 135
Lorenzetti, Pietro 132, 135, 154
Loreto 205–6
Lotto, Lorenzo 193, 199, 206, 207
Lucca 11, 82, 91–3
    Cathedral 92
    hotels in 93
    restaurants in 93

San Michele 92
  Tower 92–3
Lucignano d'Arbia 142
Lugnano 180

Macerata 55, 201–2
Machiavelli, Niccolò 127
Mafia 19, 28–9
Maitani, Lorenzo 186
Manfred, King of Sicily 13, 199, 269
Marches, The 71, 72, 191–207
  arts in 193
  food and wine of 192–3
  history of 192
  transport to 191
Marcus Aurelius, Roman Emperor 234
Maremma, The 148–51
Maremma Nature Reserve 76, 83–4, 148
Marina di Grosseto 76
Marina di Pisa 75
maritime power 86
Martini, Simone 89, 127, 131–2, 133, 135
Masaccio 117
Massa Marittima 72, 149–50
Mazzini, Giuseppi 15
Medici, family of 82, 100
Medici, Cosimo 130
Medici, Francesco 122
Medici, Lorenzo 100–1
Mercatale 127
Metaliferous Hils 141
Michelangelo 14, 101, 104, 108, 110–12, 115, 117, 151
  in Rome 214–15, 225–6, 232
  St Peter's 250
  Sistine Chapel 252–4
Michelozzi, Michelozzo 123, 127, 146
modern Italy 17–18
Molise 71, 267, 271–3
monasteries
  Abbadia di Fiastra 202
  Abbaia Isola 137
  Hermitage, Assisi 167–8
  Monte Oliveto Maggiore 142–3
  San Damiano, Assisi 168
  San Marco, Florence 116
  San Pietro in Valle 183
  Sant'Antimo 143–4
Montalcino 143
Monte Argentario 76
Monte Oliveto Maggiore 84, 142–3
Monte Vettore 191
Montecassiano 202
Montecatini Alto 93–4
Montecatini Terme 93
Montefalco 170
Montefeltro, Duke of 106–7, 152, 192, 194
Montefiridolfi 127
Montefollonico 146
Montefranco 182
Montemaggiore 198
Montepescali 149
Montepulciano 145–6
Monterchi 153
Monteriggioni 137
Monticchiello 145
Moro, Aldo 18
Morrea 271
motoring 38–9
Mount Cavo 259
Mount Eolo 179
Mount Erasmus 179–80
Mount Terminillo, 209
Mugello, The 83, 122–4
museums
  Chiusi
    Cathedral Museum 147
    Etruscan Museum 147
  Florence
    Cathedral Museum 110
    National Museum of Sculpture 112–13
  L'Aquila
    Abruzzo National Museum 270

Massa Marittima
  Mining Museum 150
opening hours of 62
Molise
  Samnite Museum 272
Perugia
  Archaeological Museum 164
Pesaro
  Ceramics Museum 196-7
Pisa
  Cathedral Museum 89
  National Museum of San
  Matteo 89
Rome
  Capitoline Museum 2233
  Etruscan Museum 240
  Roman National Museum
  243
San Miniato 96
Siena
  Cathedral Museum 134
  Civic Museum 132-3
Tarquinia
  Etruscan Museum 264
Mussolini, Benito 15-16

Narni 189
national characteristics 30-2, 71
  of Florentines 101
  of Romans 220-2
nature reserves
  Abruzzo National Park 271-2
  Villa Demidoff 122
Nemi 259
Nero, Roman Emperor 222-3,
  256
newspapers 60-1
Nocera Umbra 176
Norcia 184-5
Numana 79
Nuzi, Allegretto 201

opening hours 61-2
Orvieto 9, 186-8
  Cathedral 186-7
  fort 187

history of 186
hotels in 188
Osimo 201
Ostia 76
Ostia Antica 2255-7

Palombara 260-1
Panzano 126
Papacy 11-12, 158-9
  and the Vatican 249
paper making 200
party politics 22-3
passports 58
pasta 51
Paul II, Pope 206
Paul III, Pope 161, 162
pensioni 46
Perugia 9, 160-4
  Archaeological Museum 164
  Cathedral 161-2
  Etruscan Gate 163
  Fontana Maggiore 161
  history of 160-1
  hotels in 164
  jazz festival in 55
  National Gallery of Umbria
  162
  Palazzo dei Priori 162
  Piazzo Quattro Novembre 161
  San Pietro 162
  transport to 160
Perugrino 159, 163, 188, 198, 242
Pesaro 77, 196-7
Pescassaroli 271
Petrarch 153
Piano Grande 185
Pienza 144-5
Piero della Francesca 106-7, 151,
  152-3, 159, 162, 195
Pietrabbondante 273
pigs 184-5
Pinturicchio, Bernardino 134,
  159-60, 169, 233
Pippin, King of the Franks 11,
  158
Pisa 71, 85-90

Baptistry 88
Cathedral 86, 88
history of 82, 86
hotels in 89–90
Leaning Tower 87–8
museums in 89
regatta 54
restaurants in 90
transport to 85–6
Pisano, Andrea 89
Pisano, Giovanni 88, 89, 94, 133, 134, 161
Pistoia 94
Pitigliano 72, 84, 151
Pius II, Pope 134, 144, 145
Pius IX, Pope 199
Po, river 24
Poggibonsi 137
Poggio a Caiano 95
Poggio Sannita 272
police 34–5
Polino 182
politics 21–3
pollution 23–4
Ponte di Solestà 204
Ponte delle Torri 173
Porto Potenza Picena 79
Porto Recanati 79
Porto San Elpidio 79
Porto San Giorgio 79
post offices 62
pottery 171, 175, 187, 197
Prato 94–5
Pratolino 122
Preci 185
Principina a Mare 76
prosperity, of Central Italy 17–18
Puccini, Giacomo 92
Punta Ala 75

Quercia, Jacopo delle 92, 132, 135

Radda in Chianti 126
Radicofani 147–8
radio 61

Raphael 104, 108, 113–14, 159, 163, 195, 196, 215, 242, 251
Recanati 206–7
Red Brigade (Brigate Rosse) 18
Renaissance 14
in Florence 99, 102–3
in Lazio 263
in the Marches 194
Medicis and 100
in Rome 219
in Tuscany 82–3, 144–5
Renaissance architecture
in the Marches 194–5, 204
in Tuscany 95
in Umbria 178
restaurants (see also under individual towns) 50–2, 73
Ricasoli family 124, 126
Risorgimento 14–15
Riva del Sole 75–6
road network 40–1
Robbia, Andrea della 147
Robbia, Luca della 127
Roccatederighi 150
Roman Catholic Church 25–8, 232
Roman remains
Ancona 207
Ascoli Piceno 204
Assisi 167
Carsulae 179
Fano 198
Fermo 205
Fiesole 121–2
Ostia Antica 256–7
Rome 222–4, 26–31, 232–3, 237–9
Saepinum 272
Spello 169
Spoleto 171–2
Romanesque architecture
in Lazio 260
in Tuscany 87, 88, 92, 95, 96, 138, 143, 149
in Umbria 167, 169, 173, 180
Romans 10, 121, 158, 189, 199,

209, 216–18
Rome (*see also* Vatican, The)
  210–48
Appian Way 239
Ara Pacis 236–7
Arch of Constantine 224
artists of 214–15
Aurelian Walls 218
Capitol Square 231–3
Castei Sant'Angelo 242–3
Catacombs 238–9
churches
  San Luigi dei Francesi 242
  San Paolo fuori le Mura 243
  Santa Maria degli Angeli 241
  Santa Maria Maggiore 240–1
climate of 36
Colosseum 222–4
Column of Marcus
  Aurelius234
Etruscan Museum 240
Galleria Borghese 242
getting around in 211, 213, 220
history of 10, 216–19
hotels in 245–6
Imperial Forums 230–1
Jewish Quarter 239–40
main areas of 213–14
nightlife of 214, 243–4
Palatine Hill 229–30
Palazza Barberini 242
Palazza Doria-Pamphili 233–4
Pantheon 237–8
Piazza Navona 2238
Piazza del Popolo 236
Piazza di Spagna 235–6
restaurants in 246–8
Roman Forum 226–9
sack of 14, 219
Seven Hills of 214
shopping in 244
Temple of Jupiter 232
Theatre of Marcellus 239
Trajan's Column 231
transport to 211
Trevi Fountain 234–6

Roselle 149
Rosso Fiorentino 140
Rufina 124

Sabaudia 76
Saepinum 272
Saint Francis *see* Francis, Saint
Salimberi, Iacopo 196
Salimberi, Lorenzo 196
Samnites 217, 267–8, 270, 272,
  273
San Benedetto del Tronto 79
San casciano 127
San Gemini 180
San Gimignano 72, 138–9
  history of 82
  towers of 138
San Ginesio 202
San Miniato 95–6
San Piero a Sieve 122
San Pietro in Valle 183
San Sepolcro 152–3
Sanctuary of the Sacred House
  206
Sangallo, Antonio da 146
Sangallo, Giuliano 95
Sant'Andrea in Percussina 127
Sant'Antimo 84, 143–4
Santa Maria Macerata 127
Santi, Giovanni 196
Sarnano 202–3
Sarteano 147
Sassetta 132, 135
Sasso Tetto 202
Savonarolo, Girolamo 101, 116
Scanno 271
Scarperia 123
Scheggino 184
Schiavi d'Abruzzo 272
scirocco (wind) 36
Scolastica, Saint 184
self-catering accommodation 47
Senigallia 77, 79, 199
severus, Lucius Septimius,
  Roman Emperor 227, 230,
  242

Shelley, Percy Bysshe 90, 93
shopping 56
Siena 128–36
  Art Gallery 135
  artists of 131–2
  Campo 129
  Cathedral 133–4
  churches
    Baptistry 134–5
    San Domenico 135
    San Francesco 135
    Santa Maria dei Servi 135
  food and wine in 136
  getting around in 128–30
  history of 13, 82, 130–1
  hotels in 136
  Museo Civico 132–3
  nightlife in 135–6
  Palazzo Pubblico 129
  Palio 54, 131
  transport to 128
Siena, Guido da see Guido da
  Siena
siesta 62–3
Signorelli, Luca 140, 142, 152,
  154, 155, 177, 187, 206
Sinalunga 146
Sirolo 79
skiing 55, 191, 202
Socialist Party (PSI) 21, 23
Sodoma (Antonio Bazzi) 132,
  133, 135, 142, 146, 242
Sovana 84, 151
spa towns 93, 147, 179, 180
Spello 168–9
Sperlonga 77
Spoleto 11, 171–4
  arts festival in 55, 171
  Cathedral 172–3
  hotels in 173–4
  Roman bridge 171–2
  San Gregorio 172
  San Pietro 173
sport 55

Tacitus, Cornelius 179

Taddeo di Bartolo 135, 137, 139
Tarquinia 9, 263–4
taxis 43
telephone 63–4
television 22, 61
Terni 181
Tiber valley 158
time differences 64
Tintoretto 108
tipping 64
Titian 108, 114
Tivoli 257–8
Todi 177–8
  restaurants in 178–9
toilets 65
tombs, Etruscan 9, 147, 149, 164,
  263
  Cerveteri 254–5
  Tarquinia 263
Totila, King of the Goths 11,
  158, 160, 176
tourists 32–3, 102
train travel 42–3
trattoria 50
travel 38–44
Trevi 170
truffles 184–5
Tuscany 81–155
  food and wine in 84–5
  history of 81–3
  where to go 84–5

Uccello, Paolo 95, 107, 116, 196
Umbertide 176
Umbria 71, 156–89
  food and wine of 160
  history of 158–9
Urban IV, Pope 186
Urbino 193–6
  Ducal Palace 194–5
  National Gallery 195–6
Urbs Salvia 202

Val di Chiana 83
Val Tiberina 83, 151
valdarno 83

Valle Umbra 158
Valnerina, The 180–4
Vasari, Giorgio 104, 106, 115
Vatican, The 248–54
  St Peter's 249–51
  Sistine Chapel 252–4
Vecchietta (Lorenzo di Pietro)
  132, 133, 135, 144
Verrocchio, Andrea del 108, 159
Vespasian, Roman Emperor 222
Vespignano 123–4
Via Aurelia 10, 82, 255
Via Cassia 10, 82, 142, 147
Via Flaminia 10, 158, 172, 179,
  198
Via Salaria 10
Viareggio 75
Vicchio 123
Villa Demidoff 122

Villa Lante 263
villas 47
Vinci 96
Viterbo 261–3
  festival 54, 262
  history of 13, 261
  Palazzo Palace 261–2
Volterra 9, 82, 137, 140

watersports 55
wildlife 157, 271
wines 52–3
  of Lazio 209
  of the Marches 193
  of Tuscany 84–5, 143, 145, 151
  of Umbria 160, 170
women, travelling alone 33–4
World War I 15
World War II 16, 90, 174, 198